Social Media and Democracy

This book critically investigates the complex interaction between social media and contemporary democratic politics, and provides a grounded analysis of the emerging importance of social media in civic engagement.

Social media applications such as Facebook, Twitter, and YouTube, have increasingly been adopted by politicians, political activists, and social movements as a means to engage, organize, and communicate with citizens worldwide. Drawing on Obama's presidential campaign, opposition and protests in the Arab states, and the mobilization of support for campaigns in the UK against tuition fee increases and the UK Uncut demonstrations, this book presents evidence-based research and analysis. Renowned international scholars examine the salience of the network as a metaphor for understanding our social world, but also the centrality of the Internet in civic and political networks. Whilst acknowledging the power of social media, the contributors question the claim that it is a utopian tool of democracy, and suggest that a cautious approach to facilitate more participative democracy is necessary.

Providing the most up-to-date analysis of social media, citizenship, and democracy, *Social Media and Democracy* will be of strong interest to students and scholars of Political Science, Social Policy, Sociology, Communication Studies, Computing, and Information and Communications Technologies.

Brian D. Loader is Associate Director of the Science and Technology Studies Unit (SATSU) based at the University of York, UK.

Dan Mercea is Teaching Fellow in the Department of Sociology at the University of York, UK.

Routledge research in political communication

Social Media and Democracy

Innovations in participatory politics

Edited by Brian D. Loader and Dan Mercea

Routledge
Taylor & Francis Group

LONDON AND NEW YORK

First published 2012
by Routledge
2 Park Square, Milton Park, Abingdon, Oxon OX14 4RN

Simultaneously published in the USA and Canada
by Routledge
711 Third Avenue, New York, NY 10017

Routledge is an imprint of the Taylor & Francis Group, an informa business

British Library Cataloguing in Publication Data
A catalogue record for this book is available from the British Library

Library of Congress Cataloging in Publication Data
Social media and democracy : innovations in participatory politics / edited
by Brian D. Loader and Dan Mercea.
   p. cm. – (Routledge research in political communication ; 6)
   1. Political participation–Technological innovations. 2. Communication
in politics–Technological innovations. 3. Social media–Political
aspects. I. Loader, Brian, 1958– II. Mercea, Dan, 1980–
JF799.S62 2012
323'.04202854678–dc23   2011034945

ISBN: 978-0-415-68370-8 (hbk)
ISBN: 978-0-203-12697-4 (ebk)

Typeset in Times
by Wearset Ltd, Boldon, Tyne and Wear

Contents

Contributors

Lawrence Ampofo is a PhD candidate in the Department of Politics and International Relations at Royal Holloway, University of London.

Nick Anstead is a Lecturer in Media and Communications in the Department of Media and Communications at the London School of Economics.

Åsa Bengtsson is an Academy Research Fellow and Adjunct Professor of Political Science at Åbo Akademi University. She has published on economic voting, political participation, public opinion and minority politics.

W. Lance Bennett is Professor of Political Science and Ruddick C. Lawrence Professor of Communication at University of Washington Seattle, where he directs the Center for Communication and Civic Engagement.

Henrik Serup Christensen is a postdoctoral researcher in political science at Åbo Akademi University. His research interests include new forms of political participation and their status in representative democracy.

Jodi H. Cohen (PhD from Northeastern University in Sociology) is an Associate Professor at Bridgewater State University in Bridgewater, Massachusetts, USA. She primarily carries out research on issues of gender and sexuality, sport and heritage studies. A selection of published articles can be found in the *International Journal of Transgenderism* and *Women in Sport and Physical Activity Journal*.

Donatella della Porta is Professor of Sociology in the Department of Political and Social Sciences at the European University Institute, Florence. Among her recent publications are: (with M. Caiani), *Social Movements and Europeanization*, Oxford University Press, 2009; (ed.), *Another Europe*, Routledge, 2009; (ed.) *Democracy in Social Movements*, Palgrave, 2009; (with Michael Keating), *Approaches and Methodologies in the Social Sciences*, Cambridge University Press, 2008; (with Gianni Piazza), *Voices from the Valley; Voices from the Street*, Berghan, 2008; *The Global Justice Movement*, Paradigm, 2007; (with Massimiliano Andretta, Lorenzo Mosca and Herbert Reiter), *Globalization from Below*, University of Minnesota Press, 2006; (with Abby Peterson and Herbert Reiter), *The Policing of Transnational Protest*, Ashgate,

2006; (with Mario Diani), *Social Movements: An Introduction*, 2nd edition, Blackwell, 2006; (with Sidney Tarrow), *Transnational Protest and Global Activism*, Rowman and Littlefield, 2005.

Roman Gerodimos is a senior lecturer in global current affairs at Bournemouth University. He holds an MSc in European Politics and Policy (LSE) and a PhD in Political Communication (Bournemouth University). His doctoral thesis examined online youth civic engagement in the UK, focusing on young users' evaluations of NGO websites. His research interests include civic mobilisation, new media and international affairs, as well as British, European and Greek politics. He is currently researching the phenomenon of online citizen diplomacy and the role of emotions in the discourse of Greek terrorists and anarchists. Roman is the founder and convenor of the Greek Politics Specialist Group (www.gpsg.org.uk) of the Political Studies Association.

Brian D. Loader is Associate Director of the Science and Technology Studies Unit based in the Department of Sociology at the University of York, UK. He is the editor of the international journal *Information, Communication and Society* (published by Taylor & Francis) and has published widely and given presentations on social media and society.

Giovanna Mascheroni, holds a PhD in Sociology and Social Research and is Lecturer in Sociology of Communication and Culture at the Faculty of Political Science of the Università Cattolica del Sacro Cuore, Milan. She is the national contact of the EU Kids Online Project (www.eukidsonline.net), and cooperates with two research centres based at Università Cattolica: Modacult, and OssCom – a research centre on media and communication. She is interested in young people and new media, online participation, risks and opportunities of the Internet for children, and web 2.0 election campaigns.

Dan Mercea has recently received his PhD in Communication Studies from the University of York where he is currently a Teaching Fellow in Political Sociology. His thesis was an examination of the possible contribution of Internet-mediated communication to fostering greater participation in social movement protest events. He is currently in the process of publishing the main empirical results from his PhD research while he continues to pursue his interests in the application of digital media to political participation and engagement in extra-parliamentarian politics.

Ben O'Loughlin is a Professor of International Relations in the Department of Politics and International Relations and Co-Director of the New Political Communication Unit at Royal Holloway, University of London. He is Co-Editor of the Sage journal *Media, War & Conflict*. His latest book is *Radicalisation and Media: Connectivity and Terrorism in the New Media Ecology* (Routledge, 2011; with Akil Awan and Andrew Hoskins).

Jennifer M. Raymond (PhD from the University of Massachusetts, Boston, in Public Policy) is a faculty member in the PhD programme in Interdisciplinary

Studies at Union Institute and University and also serves as a visiting lecturer at Bridgewater State University, Massachusetts. Previously she was a senior researcher at the Center for Social Policy at the University of Massachusetts, Boston, where she conducted research and programme evaluation on homelessness and poverty-related issues. Jennifer's current research interests include the lesbian, gay, bisexual and transgender (LGBT) rights movement, and the impact of the legalization of same-sex marriage.

Joanna Redden is a PhD student in the Department of Media and Communications at Goldsmiths, University of London. Her work considers how media content and new media tools influence poverty debates and political responses in Canada and the UK. Other work has focused on online news and blog analysis. Joanna has worked in the field of politics as a researcher for a political party in Canada and in media as a reporter and researcher.

Alexandra Segerberg researches and teaches at the Department of Political Science, Stockholm University. Her research interests revolve around philosophical, political and empirical theories of collective action. She is currently working on a project on digital media and civil society networks funded by the Swedish Research Council.

Tamara A. Small (PhD, Queen's University, Ontario, Canada) is an Assistant Professor in the Department of Political Science at Mount Allison University, New Brunswick, Canada. Her research interests focus is digital politics: use and impact of the Internet by Canadian political actors. Her work has been published in the *Election Law Journal*, *Party Politics* and the *Canadian Journal of Political Science*.

Cristian Vaccari (PhD, Università IULM, Milan, 2006) is Assistant Professor in Political Communication at the Faculty of Political Science 'Roberto Ruffilli' of the University of Bologna. He studies political communication in comparative perspective, with a particular focus on the new media. He has authored and coauthored three books in Italian and his scholarship has been published in *Political Communication*, *Party Politics*, *New Media and Society*, *Journal of Information Technology and Politics*, *European Journal of Communication*, and *French Politics*, as well as in various international edited volumes. He has been a visiting scholar at the University of Oxford, Columbia University, Massachusetts Institute of Technology and American University, Washington, DC.

Ariadne Vromen is Associate Professor in the Department of Government and International Relations at the University of Sydney, Australia. She has ongoing research interests in political participation, including on young people, politics and the Internet.

Janelle Ward is Assistant Professor in the Department of Media and Communication at Erasmus University, Rotterdam, the Netherlands. She is interested in how new media are used to stimulate political engagement and participation.

Preface

This collection is the outcome of a small symposium that brought together leading authorities and commentators with scholarly interests in the potential innovative role of social media technologies for democratic politics. Whilst no longer 'new' as communication technologies, the World Wide Web and its concomitant array of social media platforms, such as Facebook, Wikipedia, YouTube and Twitter, continue to stimulate our collective imaginations for strengthening democracy and/or fears of oppression through surveillance. It was therefore perhaps apposite that our discussions of these latest prophesies should take place in one of the recently emerging democracies of Eastern Europe. For three days in July 2010, in the Romanian city of Cluj, participants presented research-based findings, exchanged theories, and argued over the respective merits of interpretative insights. Some of those debates and the findings to which they refer are outlined in the following chapters of this book.

The impetus for this forum arose from a perceptible assumption, increasingly to be found in the media, online and in a number of academic publications, that the widespread use of the Internet for social networking, blogging, video-sharing and tweeting has an elective affinity with participatory democracy. This emerging sense has been fuelled by the worldwide adoption of social media platforms by politicians, political activists and citizens as a means to engage, organise and communicate their views. Further support for the democratising capacity of this new generation of networked media technologies has been provided by its use for opposition and protests in the Middle East during the spring of 2011.

Such optimistic claims for the political benefits of social networking are in sharp contrast to much of the mainstream academic discourse surrounding the prospects for digital democratic governance. Here we find far more pessimistic accounts of the disengagement of citizens, particularly young ones, with democratic politics. Poor voter turnout, declining membership of political parties and negative opinion polls about representatives are trotted out with monotonous regularity as indicators of the poor health of the democratic body politic. Moreover, this is not the first time we have heard utopian claims for digital democracy that later had to be revised or even rejected. Perhaps imbued as we are with a view that democratic politics is sleazy, corrupt and self-serving, we should not be surprised if some commentators are apt to seek the perceived empowering functionality of social media as a means to facilitate stronger versions of democracy.

What then are we to make of this new version of networking democracy? Were the previous hopes for electronic democracy merely a false dawn awaiting the second generation of Internet technologies? Is there evidence that the inter-active, collaborative and user-generated content capacities of social media are essentially democratic features which could enhance participative and delibera-tive skills? Do the examples of the spontaneous and creative use of social net-working platforms to enable citizens to participate in a variety of transnational, regional and local campaigns, suggest political cognisance gained through expe-riential pathways? Does the focus for much online civic engagement that appears to be related to the kinds of identity and lifestyle politics associated with such concerns as environmentalism, sexuality, gender, global poverty or consumer activism, provide evidence for a new political culture that foregrounds the non-governmental domain? Or, by contrast, does analysis of online engagement with social media suggest a more cautious claim for its ability to change mainstream democratic politics? Much remains unclear and is of great interest to policy-makers and academics alike. In addressing these questions this collection attempts to make a modest contribution to the debate about the nature and extent of political engagement that is mediated by social media and what impact this may have upon our understanding and practices of democratic politics.

We would like to take this opportunity to thank all of the original participants in the symposium whose contributions made the event such a stimulating and insightful occasion. No such proceedings could take place at all, however, without the tireless efficiency of Sarah Shrive-Morrison from the University of York, UK, and Smaranda Moldovan from the Babeş-Bolyai University in Cluj to whom we are all most grateful. We would especially like to thank Mircea Maniu and Rodica Mocan for being such enthusiastic hosts and making our stay in the wonderful city of Cluj so memorable. Thanks are also due to the Romanian Cul-tural Institute and the British Council for their generous support for event. Finally, we would like to thank our partners Kim Loader and Suzi Guzu for their continued fellowship and to Dan's mother Ioana and Brian's children Will and Chris Loader.

Brian D. Loader
Ingleby Arncliffe, North Yorkshire, UK

Dan Mercea
York, UK

Chapters are reproduced with permission from the *Journal of Information, Com-munication and Society* and Taylor & Francis Group.

1 Networking democracy?

Social media innovations in participatory politics

Brian D. Loader and Dan Mercea

Introduction

The first wave of enthusiasm for Internet-based visions of digital democracy were largely predicated upon the desire to produce virtual public spheres (Loader 1997; Tsagarousianou *et al.* 1998; Blumler and Gurevitch 2001). Democratic governance, it was contended, could be significantly improved through the open and equal deliberation between citizens, representatives and policy-makers afforded by the new information and communications technologies. For cyber-libertarians this could even be achieved without the need for governments (Barlow 1996). For left-of-centre progressives it could enable stronger participatory democracy through the emergence of online agoras and Habermasian forums (Habermas 1962/1989; Hague and Loader 1999). The history of science and technology provides many instances of the fanfare of transformative rhetoric which accompanies the emergence of 'new' innovations which are then often followed by disappointment and more measured appraisal (Bijker *et al.* 1987). So perhaps it should have been little surprise that the utopian perspectives of the first generation of digital democracy were quickly replaced by findings that documented the myopia of such visions (Hill and Hughes 1998; Wilhelm 2000). Instead of transforming representative democracy the new media, as Hill and Hughes suggested, was more likely to be shaped by the existing entrenched social and economic interests of contemporary societies (ibid., p. 182). By the turn of the millennium a more accurate picture of the influence of the Internet upon democratic governance was emerging as the technologies were understood as part of the mundane activities of 'everyday life' (Wellman and Haythornthwaite 2002). Here was to be found the factionalism, prejudice and abuse which have all too often mired the aspirations of deliberative decision-making (Doctor and Dutton 1998). But perhaps more significantly, the very idea of a virtual Habermasian public sphere was subjected to extensive critiques from cultural studies scholars (McKee 2005) and feminist theorists (van Zoonen 2005). They have revealed how such models of deliberative democracy frequently privilege a particular style of 'rational' communication that largely favours white wealthy males to the exclusion of other identities (Pateman 1989; Fraser 1990).

Despite these setbacks to digital democracy, a fresh wave of technological optimism has more recently accompanied the advent of social media platforms such as Twitter, Facebook, YouTube, wikis and the blogosphere. The distinctiveness of this second generation of Internet democracy is the displacement of the public sphere model with that of a networked citizen-centred perspective providing opportunities to connect the private sphere of autonomous political identity to a multitude of chosen political spaces (Papacharissi 2010). It thus represents a significant departure from the earlier restricted and constrained formulations of rational deliberation with its concomitant requirement for dutiful citizens. In its place is a focus upon the role of the citizen-user as the driver of democratic innovation through the self-actualised networking of citizens engaged in lifestyle and identity politics (Bennett 2003a; Dahlgren 2009; Papacharissi 2010).

What then are we to make of these latest claims for digital democracy arising from the second generation of social media applications? Are they best interpreted as a further commercial incarnation of Internet mythology-making (Mosco 2005) destined to become absorbed through ubiquitous everyday incorporation? Or do they offer new opportunities for challenging dominant discourses and privileged positions of power? Is there evidence for the emergence of a more personalised politics being played out through social networks?

This edited collection is intended to provide an opportunity for a more grounded appraisal of the potential of social media for second-wave digital democracy. The chapters have all been selected for their critical insights and articulations with contemporary debates about citizenship and democratic culture(s). Our objective in this introductory chapter is to provide a wider context to these analyses by outlining some of the existing claims made for the democratic potential of social media and laying out a number of issues and questions informing our own thinking on the subject. In sum, it is our contention that with the more widespread use of social media and Internet technologies and their absorption into the mundane practices of lived experience their potential to shape social relations of power becomes all the greater. Yet such influence is likely to be in ways that are indeterminate and contingent upon a multitude of clashes between social agents, groups and institutions who have competing conceptions of networking democracy. Such contests are becoming very familiar such as, for example, the use of social media platforms for disclosing government secrets through Wikileaks (Leigh and Harding 2011), organising student protests in the UK, mobilizing opposition in Egypt, orchestrating election campaigns, challenging privacy laws through Twitter, lampooning politicians on YouTube and other manifestations. Such disruptive activity can play an important role in democratic politics but what is less clear is how social media is shaped by and in turn influences social relations of power.

Social media democracy

Much of the hyperbolic rhetoric heralding the catalytic prophesies of social media arise from its marketing origins (O'Reilly 2005). Yet this should not

obscure the enthusiastic assertions made by a number of prominent commentators (Benkler 2006; Jenkins 2006; Leadbeater 2008) that this latest generation
of communications technologies has inherent democratic capacities. These
writers share a common view that, in contrast to traditional mass media, networked media has the potential to reconfigure communicative power relations.
By making use of ever easier social networking and 'user-centred innovation'
(von Hippel 2005) citizens are able to challenge the monopoly control of media
production and dissemination by state and commercial institutions. Freed from
the necessities of professional media and journalist skills or the centralised
control and distribution of industrial mass media organisations, social media is
instead seen to be technologically, financially and (generally) legally accessible
to most citizens living in advanced societies. Equipped with social media, the
citizen no longer has to be a passive consumer of political party propaganda,
government spin or mass media news, but is instead actually enabled to challenge discourses, share alternative perspectives and publish their own opinions.

The openness of social media platforms facilitates the potential of what
Charles Leadbeater (2008) calls the 'mass-collaboration' of individuals and
groups who become the source of new innovations and ideas in democratic practices. This view has an affinity with the work of scholars in the field of science
and technology studies (STS) who have long argued for recognising the central
role played by 'social groups' in shaping the design and diffusion of new technologies (Winner 1986). The fluid and contingent nature of technological
innovation has been further exposed through the insights of feminist, actor
network and domestication approaches which have all in their respective ways
emphasised the importance of the 'user' in the co-construction of technologies
(Oudshoorn and Pinch 2005). Through such perspectives, the flexible and contested development and experimentation with social media technologies can
itself be seen as a democratic opportunity. But they also crucially dispel the
deterministic idea that social media are themselves inherently democratic and
that politics is dead. The acquisition of an iPhone or access to a social networking site does not in itself determine the engagement of citizens. As the first generation of digital democracy experiments demonstrated, the use of new media
for deliberation was strongly influenced by a complex range of socio-cultural
factors. In all likelihood, virtual public spheres and civic commons (Coleman
and Blumler 2009) met with limited success not because of the deficiencies of
the technologies but rather because the Habermasian model was incongruent
with the contemporary political and social culture of many societies. In evaluating the democratic influence of social media then, a more fruitful approach may
be to adopt the co-construction model with its more open, interpretive and contingent explanatory power, one that also recognises the influence of social diversity, inequality and cultural difference as important sources of power influencing
democratic innovation.

User-generated democracy?

A number of early indications suggest that we should be cautious in proclaiming the democratic potential of social media for significantly challenging the existing commercial and political dominance of many social groups. In the first place, if we consider social networks, in contrast to an even distribution of links representing a wide diversity of interests, we find instead that individual preferences reveal an unequal spread of social ties with a few giant nodes such as Google, Yahoo, Facebook and YouTube attracting the majority of users (Barabasi 2011). Such concentrations of hyperlinks to a few dominating spaces could be seen to grant a disproportionate authoritative influence over information sources for users. The potential for competition between political discourses may be restricted, for example, by such mechanisms as search engine ranking algorithms which privilege access to information (Halavias 2009). Richard Rogers, in his work with the Issue Crawler, has suggested that the strength of social ties and the density of their clusters can provide a visualisation of information politics as relational sources of power (2004). Whilst such analyses do not preclude the influence of citizen-users, we need more detailed and nuanced examinations of the actual use of social media before we can assess its democratic affordances.

What evidence we do have about social media platforms suggests that the most active political users are social movement activists, politicians, party workers and those who are already fully committed to political causes. Adopting the commercial model of social media as a means to target consumers, these users are attracted by its perceived cost-effective scalability to spread their ideas and attract recruits. Even the potential of citizen journalism appears to be restricted by the domination of a limited number of political bloggers (Rettberg 2008). Instead of facilitating an increasing host of active citizen-users, social media perhaps more typically facilitates online shopping, gossip and file-sharing between friends already known to each other.

Whilst clearly a cause for concern for those optimists wishing that more of their fellow citizens would join them in political discussions online, should we conclude that the everyday use of social media has limited potential for democratic innovation? In part the answer to the question depends upon what we regard as democratic activity. If we move beyond the traditional engagement with mainstream politics, such as voting, party membership, petitioning representatives and the like, and adopt a more fluid conception of democratic citizenship, a different focus and set of questions emerge that are more attuned to the potential changing perceptions of citizens who are less inclined to be dutiful and are open instead to a more personalised and self-actualising notion of citizenship. This is an approach which does not valorise the more rigid one-dimensional political identities of previous times but instead recognises the multiplicity of identity positions which citizens are required to grapple with in contemporary societies, where the spheres for democratic engagement reach into the private spaces to enable the personal to become political (Squires 1998). In this framework it may be possible to interpret the democratic potential of social media in a new light.

Papacharissi (2010), for example, points to how citizen-users can participate in campaigns whilst simultaneously enjoying television and/or chatting with family in the privacy of their own homes. Moreover, the very malleability of social media offers the prospect of innovative modes of political communication that may go beyond the constrictions of rational deliberative exchanges. It might facilitate Iris Young's exhortation that testimony, story-telling, greetings and rhetoric can all be employed as discursive forms of democratic engagement capable of enabling a more inclusive democracy (2000). Thus, we could look for the kinds of political self-expression more widely experienced and performed through a variety of text, visual, audio and graphic communication forms. The playful repertoires of innovative YouTube videos, mobile texting language, protest music and the celebration of trivia may all be regarded as aspects of the political.

Those sceptical of such broad definitions of politics are likely to reject the democratic potential of social media and instead point to its capacity to undermine serious rational deliberation. They will cite its use for negative campaigning and encouraging populist rhetoric and even extremism; a further means to sensationalise the public sphere and foster celebrity politics. Moreover, the very 'networked individualism' (Wellman *et al.* 2003) which characterises social media can be regarded as further evidence of the social fragmentation which is seen as corroding collective action and social responsibility (Putnam 2000).

To date perhaps the most obvious impact of social media upon democratic politics has been its disruptive capacity for traditional political practices and institutions. Distinctions have become blurred, for example, with mainstream news media increasingly reliant upon political blogs and citizen-user content, while the potential power of collaborative sharing has been demonstrated by the Wikileaks disclosure of US government foreign policy statements online. Different in style from earlier forms of civic participation, such disruption is effected by enabling citizens to critically monitor the actions of governments and corporate interests. It could potentially enable political lifestyle choices to be informed through shared recommendations from friends, networked discussions and tweets, and direct interaction with conventional and unconventional political organisations. What the more lasting effects of these disruptions might be remains to be seen and we have yet to know what the response will be from governments, corporations or judiciaries to such user-generated challenges.

Grounding the analysis

The foregoing debates and issues provide the context to the contributions that follow. They represent an attempt to investigate in detail how these competing claims may be playing out in concrete situations. In the opening chapter, Bennett and Segerberg propose that, in a political environment increasingly marked by the individualisation of choice (Giddens 1991; Bauman 2000), a dissipation of established solidarities and an entrepreneurial mode of engagement (Flanagin *et al.* 2006), collective action is growing new roots. At the heart of such renewal lie the social media of personalized, network-based communication (Hogan and Quan-Hasse 2010). Bennett and Segerberg's comparative analysis examined two contrasting protest networks that took shape in the run up to the 2009 G20 meeting in London. 'Put People First' was both ideologically and organisationally the more loosely articulated of the networks. By contrast, the 'G20 Meltdown' coalition united an ideologically consistent radical front of anti-capitalist and environmental organisations. Their deployment of social media stood in stark contrast. 'Put People First' placed an emphasis on the personalisation of both participation and collective goals. Its mobilisation strategy foregrounded the empowerment of prospective participants by harnessing the collaborative capacity of social media. 'Put People First' was able to both maintain its political focus and attain a level of cohesion that rivalled that of the more homogenous activist coalition. The latter, however, was not equally competent in its use of social media, relying on them principally for the distribution of calls for action. Most importantly, Bennett and Segerberg make a persuasive case that social media may contribute to the reconciliation of the competing pressures of achieving both personalisation and solidarity in collective action.

The inquiry into the G20 protests raised other crucial questions which cross over into deliberations of the relationship between social movements and media organisations as well as the power held by the media to represent a movement's public agenda. The allowances 'Put People First' made for personalised communication did not seem to dilute its core message nor hinder the dissemination of its appeals in the mass media. Their example may lend empirical support to the claim made in Chapter 3 by Donatella della Porta that social movements are beginning to stand on a more equal footing with media organisations in their capacity to depict their actions in their own desired light. This may be a recurring assertion made in relation to social movements' use of the Internet (Atton 2004; Castells 2007). However, della Porta locates its wider significance within the context of the power differential in the relations between social movements and more resourceful social actors such as the media or the state. Her theoretical exposition is an invitation to place social movements at the heart of the power dynamic which keeps democracy in an organic state of perpetual transformation. In this way, one is reminded that democratic institutions act not only as structural conditions for social movements. On the contrary, social movements have the agency to place democratic institutions at the centre of a normative debate which they can engender through networked communication. By so doing, social movements come to actively shape the structural conditions in which they operate, previously defined exclusively by the more powerful social actors.

Yet the media remain the main stage where public discourse is formed and, as Castells (2007, p. 241) contends, 'what does not exist in the media does not exist in the public mind'. In Chapter 4, Joanna Redden brings empirical evidence to bear on this assertion in her consideration of media representations of poverty in Canada and the UK. People's shared depictions of poverty are drawn from the media (Park et al. 2007). The media in the two countries, Redden argues, are systematically constructing representations of poverty which legitimate market-type evaluations of public policy interventions. Highlighting individual responsibility for material disadvantage and reifying statistical calculations which evidence public spending on poverty seem to leave little space for a reasoned assessment of its structural causes. Alternative discourses may, nonetheless, be bubbling up online where poverty activists are organising their contestation of the mainstream coverage of poverty. However, Redden reminds us that established media outlets have a much more prominent presence online. Activists are, therefore, faced with the uphill struggle to reset the debate and bring new democratic scrutiny over institutional responses to poverty. Ultimately, the networked communication that comprises tools for both interaction and dissemination may gradually enable resource-poor political actors not only to gain a foothold in the public realm but also perhaps to have a larger imprint on democratic politics.

In Chapter 5, Cristian Vaccari discusses the possibility that counter to entrenched notions of media organisations acting as the watchdog of democratic politics (Curran 1991), traditional media organisations may begin to deploy an arsenal of digital media to promote their own political agenda. In that way, media organisations may enter the political fray, mobilise their own support base and vie for political influence side by side with political parties and interest groups. Conceptualised as 'political parallelism' (Hallin and Mancini 2004), in the Italian context reviewed by Vaccari, this development seems guided by the self-interested aim of the media to enlist the support of citizen-users to a preset agenda rather than to empower citizens to add their own voices to the political debate. Yet, as Vaccari suggests, the networked circulation of the political content made available by the media organisations he observed[1] may concurrently be interpreted as a proactive move by the media to rekindle political participation.

In light of such evidence, one can only continue to question whether social media are at the forefront of a shift towards a more participatory political culture. That culture may be manifesting itself in the form of increasingly visible political vernaculars that challenge expert valuations of democratic processes. In Chapter 6, Anstead, O'Loughlin and Ampofo examine the conversation that erupted on Twitter in the wake of the leaders' debates in the UK 2010 general election. They followed the polemic that ensued on Twitter around the statistics for who won one of the three debates. Their analysis revealed that the purposeful deployment of social media to enhance the consumption of broadcast content can become hijacked by a 'viewertariat'. The 'viewertariat', according to these authors, is a growing constituency of citizen-users who actively engage in an often critical conversation about political content and its expert interpretation furnished to them by the media. Such engagement can produce the unintended consequence of generating competing expertise to that aired by media and political elites.

If such developments perhaps allude to another instance of political empowerment galvanized by social media, Twitter hashtags may bolster the position of traditional media outlets online. In Chapter 7, Tamara A. Small provides an insight into how hashtags – keywords attached to a posting designed to assign it to a running thread and expedite its retrieval – may link up the media to audiences previously outside their reach. #cdnpoli is the most prominent and perennial Canadian political hashtag which Small found to be a site of diverse interaction among elected representatives, journalists, individual bloggers and interest groups. Particularly notable were indications that the information flow generated through the #cdnpoli hashtag were at the forefront of a fast-paced transformation of political newsmaking. Thus, in spite of not advancing the democratic virtues of political deliberation (Dahlgren 2003), this political hashtag served the function of aggregating, distilling and directing political information. Last but not least, Small contends that contributions to the hashtag's flow of information may be regarded as another invigorating form of participation in democratic politics.

A persistent question in the research on political participation is whether it may be extended beyond a narrow constituency of politically active and informed citizens (Bimber 2003; Iyengar 2007). Henrik Serup Christensen and Åsa Bengtsson visit this on-going discussion which for some time now has had the Internet at its heart (Dahlgren 2009) in Chapter 8. Considering the case of Finland, which we are reminded stands out as a trailblazer of Internet penetration and computer literacy, Christensen and Bengtsson's rigorous empirical study raises a number of stimulating observations. On the one hand, their chapter supplies further confirmation that it is chiefly politically active and cognisant citizens that are utilizing the Internet as a vehicle for political participation. On the other hand, and more surprisingly, the Internet acts as an arena for political participation for people who are otherwise unengaged in politics. Thus, the Internet appears to contribute to a rise in political participation. At the same time, online political engagement may foster the deepening of people's overall political competence. Finally, the chapter also asserts that social groups that are politically marginalized, such as young people, are more likely to become politically active through the Internet. Given the mounting evidence (Loader 2007; Baron 2008; Bae Brandtzaeg and Heim 2009; Livingstone et al. 2011) that social media are especially popular among young people, we may expect that a significant part of their political actions will unfold on social media platforms.

In Chapter 9, having looked at youth organisations from the UK, Janelle Ward makes the case for a comparative analysis of the political engagement such organisations facilitate through websites or social media. Ward shows that in spite of aspirations to increase interactivity – particularly the co-productive type geared to co-opting young users in content creation – the vast majority of the 21 organisations in her sample did not attain that goal. Moreover, only one third of those organisations had established a presence on social media platforms. The social media users among the youth organisations were primarily employing them for top-down dissemination. Thus, organisational practices seemed slow to adapt in the face of changes in their online communication environment. Ultimately, Ward suggests that youth organisations may chiefly seek to inculcate a ready-made notion of citizenship through their online communication. In that logic, social media would tend to be used strategically to serve that or other predetermined purposes.

Such strategic thinking would seem to fly in the face of evidence discussed by Roman Gerodimos in Chapter 10 which pertains to deep-seated scepticism among young people about the level of civic empowerment purpose-built websites are actually able to deliver. Gerodimos employed a qualitative design based on focus group interviews with a purposive sample of undergraduate students who were invited to examine a number of pre-selected websites of organisations that espoused an apparent civic mission (e.g. Friends of the Earth). The ensuing analysis revealed a number of ideal characteristics in website designs that might foster both a meaningful and emotionally gratifying engagement of young constituencies with civic portals. High among them featured simplicity, the ease of use but also the higher attractiveness of video as opposed to textual content, the latter being regarded as more taxing on young people's attention. Most importantly, a friendly design along those lines appeared to offset even the most negative perceptions of civic organisations held by the research participants and led to consequential interaction with civic websites. More fundamentally, Gerodimos highlights that the design configuration of civic websites may benefit from an overhaul to more closely reflect the notions of civic participation held by young people. However, such a step might foreground a remote and individualized consumer experience that might be at the heart of young people's lived experience as well as intrinsic to commercial social media platforms such as Facebook, Twitter or YouTube. By so doing, civic websites could come to portray political action as chiefly the province of symbolic intervention and not civic agonistic interaction.

In Chapter 11, Ariadne Vromen inquires about the types of citizenship practices and ideals fostered by Australian civic websites tailored for young people. Resonating with other accounts in this collection, Vromen's longitudinal assessment of website content lends further support to the observation that civic organisations may be best suited for imparting a normative template for civic engagement that upholds the model of a dutiful young citizen. Such platforms may encourage civic participation within clearly defined bounds which will resonate with the policy guidelines of their patrons, governmental institutions. At the opposite end and in a minority, Vromen found websites that invited young citizen-users to contribute actively to the delineation of their online civic participation. Nonetheless, with some apprehension, civic websites had embraced social media.

In light of the central topic of this collection, perhaps one of the most poignant points to emerge from Vromen's analysis is that social media may be easily harnessed so as to add no more than a scripted and confined degree of bottom-up involvement in the construction of civic participation. One cannot thus fail to note that social media appear to be amenable to both appropriation and repurposing along established lines of power. From this perspective, their 'social' character may be double-edged: they can perhaps be instrumental to a horizontal organisation of political participation but are concurrently susceptible to reinforcing entrenched power dynamics in liberal democracies.

Worthy of notice in this context may be the proposition made by Giovanna Mascheroni in Chapter 12 that social network sites (SNS) such as Facebook may

be yet another scene where existing imbalances in political participation are replicated. Drawing on focus groups with Italian youths, her qualitative study
alludes to the political use of SNS by young people as being marginal to the
platforms' well-established deployment for social networking (Baron 2008) or
entertainment. Signs of innovation in participatory politics may come in the form
of SNS constituting a vehicle for the politically cognisant but perhaps socially
isolated to mobilise in support of single-issue causes and build solidarity
amongst themselves.

Returning to Christensen and Bengtsson's chapter, they posit that politically
marginalised groups may find a renewed impetus to become more active through
digital media. They further point out that Finnish women also seemed to be
heartily embracing the opportunity for digital participation. Examining a different national context, in Chapter 13 Cohen and Raymond focus on a social group
whose concerns they describe as often downplayed within the mainstream of the
US medical culture, pregnant women. The authors seek to map out digital networks of empathy and social learning for pregnant women that are articulated
through online discussion forums. They review evidence which suggests that
American women tend to be socialised into a deferential attitude towards
medical professionals which precludes them from voicing some of their anxie-
ties about the physical and mental experiences they associate with their pregnancy. Online forums may afford pregnant women the latitude to express the
entire gamut of questions and emotions they have about their condition and in
that way empower them to challenge entrenched medical practices. Cohen and
Raymond view online forums as one type of digital network among a myriad of
existing and emerging platforms for remote socialisation.

Conclusion

The chapters in this volume which document some instances of the influence of
social media upon democratic politics reveal a complex picture that should lead us
to be wary about celebratory accounts. It is clearly necessary to avoid the utopian
optimism of the earlier experiments in digital democracy. Yet they do also point to
the potential of disruptive moments and actions which open the possibilities for
some co-construction of networks and platforms where the formation, maintenance
and defence of political positions may be played out. Such relational sources of
power may be shaped through access to or exclusion from lifestyle choices, their
degree of inclusion to or exclusion from nodes of authoritative meaning, and the
opportunities they provide for competitive advantage over other groups and interests. Their mapping and analysis in future research could therefore provide important understandings of our contemporary political landscape.

Note

1 The Italian daily *La Repubblica* and Michele Santoro, the host of the most popular
Italian political talk show, *Annozero*.

Part I
Social movements

Pushing the boundaries of digital political participation

2 Digital media and the personalization of collective action

Social technology and the organization of protests against the global economic crisis

W. Lance Bennett and Alexandra Segerberg

Several broad trends are associated with the globalization of social and economic issues such as labour market inequities, trade practices, and climate change. First, government control over many issues has become both complex and dispersed, reflecting the need for social pressure to be applied to diverse national and transnational governing institutions as well as to corporations that have used global business models to gain autonomy from government regulation. Second, both within nations and transnationally, political issues are interrelated in ways that may cut across conventional social movement sectors: labour and human rights often occupy common agendas, and economic development initiatives may align with environmental causes. The resulting organizational incentives for greater flexibility in defining issues and protest strategies are magnified by a third factor involving the growing separation of individuals in late modern societies from traditional bases of social solidarity such as parties, churches, and other mass organizations.

One sign of this growing individualization is the tendency to engage with multiple causes by filtering the causes through individual lifestyles (Giddens 1991; Inglehart 1997; Bennett 1998; Touraine 2000; Beck and Beck-Gernsheim 2002; Micheletti 2003; della Porta 2005b). The organization of individual action in terms of meanings assigned to lifestyle elements (e.g. brands, leisure pursuits, and friend networks) results in the personalization of issues such as climate change (e.g. in relation to personal carbon footprints), labour standards (e.g. in relation to fashion choices), or consumption of food (e.g. associated with fair trade practices or the slow living movement). This may involve individuals resisting formal membership but joining in selected actions (Bimber *et al.* 2005; Flanagin *et al.* 2006). It may also include the desire to display such personalized action publicly, what McDonald (2002) describes as the pursuit of public experiences of the self rather than of collective solidarity.

There are, to be sure, several different forms of personalization and personalized politics. Some involve relatively autonomous action, while others entail a high degree of coordination. In addition, some personalized action repertoires involve merging of multiple issues and others involve intense engagement in a single cause. Our analysis addresses some of these differences by examining how different protest coalitions employ more and less personalized communication strategies with their publics by inviting different degrees of flexibility in affiliation, issue definition, and expression. These dimensions of personalization are observed both in terms of action framing and, perhaps more importantly, in the uses of various types of digital media.

The growing demand for personalized relations with causes and organizations makes digital technologies increasingly central to the organization and conduct of collective action. Communication technologies aimed at personalizing engagement with causes facilitate organizational communication and coordination at the same time as they enable flexibility in how, when, where, and with whom individuals may affiliate and act. Greater individual control over the terms of action creates the potential for more personalized identifications than may be characteristic of the collective framing commonly associated with the protests based on organization-centred and leader-driven collective action (della Porta 2005b). It also creates the potential for personal networks to play a more prominent role in a protest. Networks have long been recognized to be important in protest mobilization (McAdam 1988; Gould 1991, 1993; Diani 1995; Diani and McAdam 2003), but evidence from protests such as the 2003 global anti-war demonstrations indicates that digitally networked individuals with multiple affiliations, identities, and rich network connections are becoming increasingly central in the speed, scale, and organization of large protests (Bennett *et al.* 2008). The role of networks in individual mobilization, with the related capacity of 'bridging' organizational and personal level networks, can facilitate the diffusion of information and appeals between communities (Kavanaugh *et al.* 2005; della Porta and Mosca 2007). Indeed, the widespread adoption of digital media may be shifting the burden of mobilization from organizations to individuals, a point supported in a comparison of different domestic and transnational protests by Walgrave *et al.* (forthcoming).

All of these trends suggest that the personalization of political action presents protest organizations with a set of fundamental challenges, chief among which concerns negotiating the potential trade-off between flexibility and effectiveness. For organizations trying to mobilize participants who seek greater personalization in affiliation, definition, and expression, the associated demands of flexibility may challenge the standard models for achieving effective collective action (e.g. organizational coalitions based on shared political agendas expressed through ideological or solidarity-based collective action frames). Our first task in examining these developments in collective action is to understand how efforts to establish more flexible relations with followers may infuse an organization's or coalition's public communication and, in particular, its digital communication. We define 'personalized' communication on the part of an organization or coalition as involving the following: (a) the presence of cues and opportunities for customization of engagement with issues and actions; and (b) the relative absence of cues (including action frames) that signal ideological and definitional unanimity. The problem is that public communication of this kind would seem to be at odds with the emphasis on unity and alignment conventionally associated with the communication processes of effective collective action.

This chapter thus analyses three questions about digital communication in the organization of a protest, which all address the possibility that mobilizing individualized publics may come at the cost of the conventional political capacity of the resulting collective action networks. We analyse how different protest networks at the 2009 G20 London Summit used digital media to engage diverse individuals, and then we examine what such processes meant for the political capacity of the respective organizations and networked coalitions. In particular, we explore whether the coalition offering looser organizational affiliations with individuals displays any notable loss of public engagement, policy focus, or mass media impact. We also examine whether the networked coalition presenting more rigid framing of the protest and fewer personalized social media affordances displays any evident gain in network coherence, dominance, and stability according to the various measures introduced below.

Individualized technology and the organization of protest networks

This analysis is motivated by the combination of challenges associated with personalized communication and affiliation between organizations and their publics, which feed the concern that personalization ultimately undermines the political effectiveness of collective action. As noted, personalized communication in this context entails providing greater opportunities for individuals to define issues in their own terms and to network with others through social media, thus distributing the organizational burden among participants who may look to NGOs and social movement organizations more as facilitators than as active directors of actions. As also noted, this typically entails relaxing the requirement for more unified public communication processes often associated with efficacious collective action.

Concerns about trends towards personalized political action have been expressed by social movement scholars who theorize collective identity framing as crucial to the coherence of protest actions (Benford and Snow 2000; Tarrow 1998; Tilly 2004). Many observers also agree that protests in this era of relaxed individual affiliation have often been impressive in terms of speed of mobilization, scope of issues, and the ability to focus public attention on these issues in the short term. At the same time, the very features of a contemporary protest that are so impressive are also the ones that may undermine conventional political capacity such as maintaining agenda focus and strong coalition relationships (Bennett 2003a). Critics doubt that loose multi-issue networks that are easy to opt in and out of generate the commitment, coherence, and persistence of action required to produce political change (Tilly 2004). Variations in these concerns have been expressed by organizational communication scholars who question the capacity of organizations that impose strong membership requirements to mobilize publics that confer legitimacy on their causes or, conversely, whether the pursuit of more independent-minded publics reduces the integrity of organization identity and mission (Bimber 2003; Bimber *et al.* 2005).

Viewed from these perspectives, protest organizers face two potentially contradictory challenges. On the one hand, there is the task of engaging individualized citizens who spurn conventional membership for the pursuit of personalized political action. Since such citizens may be less receptive to unambiguous ideological or organization-centred collective action frames, the question becomes how to mobilize such citizens. On the other hand, organizations continue to face the challenge of achieving conventional political goals, which requires maintaining political capacity in areas such as mobilization and agenda control. In the language of political action that has developed in modern democracies, the effectiveness of collective action has hung on what Charles Tilly described as the ability to display 'WUNC': worthiness, unity, numbers, and commitment (Tilly 2004). It has also involved developing relations with the targets of claims and the ability to clearly communicate the claims being made. Mustering and maintaining such qualities, in turn, have depended on sustaining a certain level of formal and centralized organization (Tarrow 1998; McAdam *et al.* 2001).

The growing question for the organization of contentious collective action becomes how to achieve such capacity while sharing communicative control with individuals and other organizations. Communicating with publics through personalized (i.e. interactive and social networked) digital media seemingly compounds the tension between the two challenges. Various technologies may facilitate flexible communication as described above, but the interactivity of the digital and social media also threatens to compromise organizational control over communication and action (Foot and Schneider 2006; Gillan *et al.* 2008).

The struggle to balance flexibility and control is often reflected in the organization's most public of faces, its website. Many organizations use their website strategically to present information about themselves, their cause, and proposed actions (della Porta and Mosca 2009; Stein 2009). Aside from posting information, they may provide signals about themselves and their cause by linking to other organizations and inviting individual connections (e.g. the invitation to join a Facebook group). In a dynamic similar to 'friending' others on social networking sites, the extent to which other actors publicly respond – for example, by linking back, becoming fans, and contributing content – becomes part of the organization's public profile (boyd and Heer 2006; Donath 2008; Kavada 2009). Like the producers of fictional transmedia narratives (Jenkins 2006), protest organizers may choose to offer various points of entry into the protest space that speak to different publics. The organization's actions both enable and constrain action in the contemporaneous protest space (Foot and Schneider 2006) and potentially establish 'sedimentary' digital structures (Chadwick 2007) such as email lists that may be reactivated or redirected for future action (e.g. see the multiple uses of the follower lists from the Obama 2008 US election campaign). As with fictional 'fan edits', however, user contributions not only help constitute the organizational protest space but also expand it (e.g. through web links) and may end up diluting or contradicting the organization's messages about itself and its cause.

Three basic questions about the digital communication of organized protest thus emerge as central for assessing the general concern about whether looser organizational communication with publics undermines conventional political capacities associated with an organized protest:

- Does personalized communication undermine engagement strength (commitment and mobilization capacity)?
- Does personalized communication undermine agenda strength?
- Does personalized communication weaken organizational network strength?

The first question, about engagement strength, approaches the personalization of organizational communication from the perspective of participant mobilization in a protest. The ability to mobilize high numbers of co-present participants in an organized protest has evolved as a central means for organizations to signal the commitment of their supporters to both the targets of the protest and the general public (Tilly 2004). Early social movement framing theory underlined the importance for the mobilization process of communicating clear frames and alignment between the organization and the supporters' interpretative frames (Snow *et al.* 1986; cf. Polletta 1998). Subsequent studies explored how various kinds of heterogeneity reduce the effects of particular frames (Druckman and Kjersten 2003; Heaney and Rojas 2006). If organizations, by contrast, work to personalize communication about their proposed actions, does this then complicate protest coordination to the extent that it makes turnout weak and unpredictable and more difficult to convey as a unified act of commitment? The latter issue relates to the next point.

The second question centres on another conventional measure of political capacity, the ability to communicate clear collective claims to the targets of protest and the general public (agenda strength). While new media grant protest organizers crucial means of bypassing mass media (Bennett 2003a, 2005), the ability to disseminate claims through mass media is still assumed to be central (Gamson 2004). The important issues here are, first, whether personalizing communication with participants leads organizations to compromise their articulated goals (e.g. by underspecifying them) and, next, whether personalized protest messages result in incoherent noise which fails to travel well or at all in the mass media. Such problems were brilliantly illustrated in a segment in the popular US political comedy programme the *Daily Show*, which parodied the 2009 G20 Pittsburgh Summit protests as ineptly organized in terms of getting their message across. The mock reporter pointed to the success of the right-wing Tea Party movement and turned to a group of its activists to offer G20 protesters advice about 'staying on message', developing relationships with major news channels, and organizing more coherent events (*Daily Show* 2009).

Digital communication practices, finally, highlight a third area in which questions about political capacity in the context of personalized communication become relevant: the relations between protest organizations. The stakes involved in engaging individualized citizens are heightened when large coalitions must agree on messages, communication strategies, and social techno-logy affordances. The importance of considering relations between actors, issues, and events in complex and fluid contemporary protest ecologies (Diani 2003) is thus further underlined by the way public digital communication sheds light on organizational attempts to manage the collective action space. It invites attention to network strength, that is, the quality of the coalition's organizational network analysed in terms of relative prestige (coherence and dominance) in the digital protest space in relation to a single event and over time (dynamics). Network strength can be measured via linking patterns on organizational websites. Linking patterns are intentional decisions that signal the public affiliation prefer-ences of organizations. Since some organizations may link indiscriminately to others, we will adopt a tougher standard for assessing network inclusion, size, and coherence: co-link analysis, which admits an organization into a protest coa-lition only if it is linked to by at least two other organizations. Other measures of the strength and coherence of protest networks such as the relative equality of inlinking and outlinking among organizations will be introduced below.

Questions of relative prestige and mutual recognition in the protest space touch on the possibility that communicative flexibility with individuals may undermine the coherence of the organizational network, for example, dispersing the affiliation or linking patterns away from resource-rich and influential organi-zations, because organizations become more entrepreneurial in their shopping for followers. Contrary to expectations, Bennett et al. (2011) suggest that this is not always the case. Arguing that narratives and their distribution may constitute structuring elements of organizational solidarity networks, their study shows how conflict over competing (personalized consumer vs. collective economic justice) narratives was reflected in a fragmented network in the US Fair Trade movement, while tolerance for multiple narratives was reflected in a more cohe-sive network in the UK counterpart. The associated question in the present context is whether the communication of personalized narrative opportunities pertaining to the financial crisis affects a coalition's relative dominance of the collective action space in a protest event. Variations in these questions about communication and the organization of networks may also be posed with respect to the dynamics of the networks over time (Monge and Contractor 2003; Diani 2004): do similar network structures persist in protests over time; do they appear only in campaigns related to specific protest issues; and can they be traced in stable policy advocacy networks over time independent of protests and campaigns?

This chapter explores the tension lodged in the personalization of collective action from the perspective of these core questions about the organization and qualities of collective action. Our immediate case involves a related series of protests that attracted a diversity of organizations using very different mobiliza-tion communication strategies. The aim is to begin understanding whether the personalization of communicative relations with followers affected organiza-tional and coalition capacities in terms of engagement strength, agenda strength, and network strength. The protests in question occurred in London on the eve of the G20 Summit in late March and early April 2009, marking the first in a series of protests at various world power meetings in response to the global financial and economic crises.

The case of the G20 London Summit protests is interesting in several ways. The protests involved very different organizational networks seeking to mobilize publics to send messages to the G20 (and to larger publics) about how to address the world crisis. This case offers comparisons between collective action networks employing highly personalized communication and networks pressing more conventional collective action frames on their followers. The uses of digital media both in linking among organizations and in communication with publics allowed us to observe how relatively more and less personalized media affect both coalition structures and the general qualities of collective action strength.

Protesting the economic crisis

The world's 20 leading economic nations, the G20, met in London on 2 April 2009 amidst a global economic crisis. Their announced intention was to address the 'greatest challenge to the world economy in modern times' through common actions to 'restore confidence, growth, and jobs', 'repair the financial system', and 'build an inclusive, green and sustainable, recovery'.[1] The London Summit attracted a complex protest ecology involving multiple actors with different protest agendas and tactics. Several protests were planned. An earlier meeting in Paris of more than 150 civil society groups from all over Europe, including unions, student movements, faith-based, environment and development groups, had resulted in the agreement to divide the protests into two days: 28 March was to be the day of general mobilization, and 1 April (dubbed 'Financial Fool's Day') was to be the preferred day for direct action (Paris Declaration 2009). This division of the protest space into different days allocated to two large and different coalitions made a perfect natural laboratory for implementing our research designs.

The 28 March London mobilization was organized by Put People First (PPF), a UK civil society coalition of more than 160 development non-governmental organizations (NGOs), trade unions, and environmental groups (e.g. Oxfam, Catholic Overseas Development Agency, and Friends of the Earth). Their march for 'Jobs, Justice and Climate' in the central city drew an estimated 35,000 protesters (Put People First 2009). A coalition of other more militant groups planned a series of protests for 1 April. These included a Climate Camp encampment with some 2,000 participants in the heart of London; a smaller Stop the War coalition anti-war march; and an Alternative London Summit featuring a variety of academics, activists, and politicians. The largest of these events was organized by G20 Meltdown (Meltdown), an anti-capitalist umbrella group that led a 'Storm the Banks' carnival march protesting war, climate chaos, financial crimes, and land enclosures (e.g. the Anarchist Federation, The Anthill Social, and the Socialist Workers' Party). An estimated 5,000 protesters converged at the Bank of England from four different directions, each led by a differently coloured 'Horseman of the Apocalypse'. Protesters could join the Red Horse against war, the Green against climate chaos, Silver against financial crimes, or Black against land enclosures and borders (Wikipedia 2009). Our analysis focuses on two dominant protest coalitions, PPF and Meltdown, two networks that also pursued contrasting approaches to engaging individuals. We also include some measures from the Climate Camp website for comparison purposes, as Climate Camp represents a more radical network than PPF in terms of organizing more direct, confrontational actions, and yet it is unlike Meltdown in that it avoids collective action mandates and invites individuals with different ideas about the climate crisis to participate in these actions. Thus, its interactive media repertoire might be expected to fall somewhere between the other two networks.

Protest coalitions and personalized communication

Our first task involved investigating whether PPF and Meltdown displayed differences in the ways they communicated to individuals in the mobilization process. We analysed two ways in which the organizations could personalize communication on their websites: their framing of protest themes and the opportunities provided to site visitors to use technologies for interactive communication that often enabled personal content to enter the network. Analysis of each coalition's website and related social technologies indicates considerable differences between PPF and Meltdown: the PPF coalition presented a far more personalized thematic and technological interface, enabling individuals to send their own messages to the G20, while Meltdown issued a more rigid call to collective action, including encouragement to eat the bankers and end capitalism.

The differences in the communication approaches between PPF and Meltdown are instantly signalled in the images that animate their websites. As shown in Figure 2.1, the PPF site featured a banner of feet wearing rather everyday middle-class footwear walking together. By contrast, the Meltdown site featured a single black horse and rider storming over the Bank of England across ominous skies (Figure 2.2).

As suggested by the graphics, the PPF site places the average citizen at the centre of the proposed action and invites him or her to project his or her own interpretations on the activities. The phrase that characterizes the site is truly 'Put People First'. Not only is this the protest slogan, but a statistical content analysis shows this to be the most prominent distinguishing word cluster on the site.[2] PPF emphasizes the priority of 'people' while downplaying the specifics of the problem or solution. 'Crisis' is the second most prominent word cluster theme on the site, and yet details about causes and solutions are kept in the background.[3] PPF only requires that the reader recognize the economic crisis; it avoids problematizing or promoting one economic system over another. The site urges the reform of banking, finance, and trade systems, but it does not detail the direction of such reforms. The presentation instead emphasizes the detrimental consequences of the status quo for 'people', letting the reader identify the

Figure 2.1 Put People First Coalition homepage (April 2009). Used with permission.

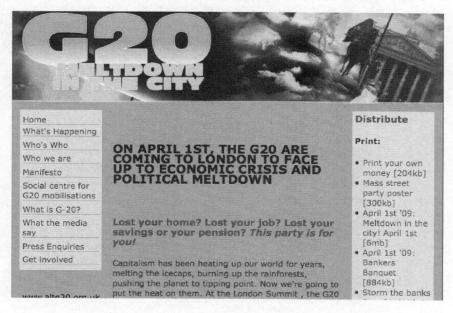

Figure 2.2 The G20 Meltdown homepage (April 2009). Used with permission.

message and action that he or she wishes to endorse as long as it amounts to 'putting people first'.

By contrast, Meltdown defined its concerns more narrowly and made it clear that these were not open to negotiation. Instead of associating the crisis and the summit with a plurality of problems and solutions, the reader is confronted with a dramatic larger-than-life narrative. The three primary word clusters tell the story that is underscored by the image in Figure 2.2. The first word cluster evokes the characters of the drama (personifying bankers as the source of the problem and Meltdown's horsemen as the agents of change),[4] the second cluster emphasises the crisis,[5] and the third cluster groups around a drastic solution: overthrowing capitalism.[6] The narrative is that a group of bankers has caused global economic catastrophe, and a group of 'horsemen' will come to the rescue by 'reclaim[ing] the City, thrusting into the very belly of the beast'. While PPF only required that the reader recognize the existence of an economic crisis, Meltdown insists that the reader recognize it as a *capitalist* crisis. The goal to 'overthrow capitalism' points both to the source of the crisis ('the dominance of finance capitalism is the problem') and a drastic solution. The four themes of the 'Storm the Banks' march provided some leeway for personalization (e.g. the encouragement to dress in costume), and yet the sub-themes are firmly ordered under the collective action framework of anti-capitalism. The aesthetic is often humorous, but the dramatization demands that participants either accept or reject the message as is.

In keeping with these differences in framing the protests, the coalition sites differed substantially in the extent to which individuals were offered interactive affordances that invited them to join on their own terms. In order to make these comparisons, we first conducted inventories of every interactive digital affordance used across a collection of seven related protests during 2009, beginning with the PPF, Meltdown, and Climate Camp sites in the London protests and continuing with the protests later in the autumn in Pittsburgh at G20 meetings (where two coalition sites were inventoried) and two additional UK coalitions mobilizing public demonstrations ahead of the Copenhagen Climate Summit in December. There were many bridges among these protests, including common organizational sponsorships, travelling Twitter streams, and general linking of the economic crisis with climate change issues (e.g. no economic solutions at the expense of climate action). The resulting inventory shown in Figure 2.3 gives us a broad spectrum of interactive affordances that enable individuals to make choices about how to participate (e.g. sign petitions, donate money, and come to demonstrations) and/or add content to the communication network (e.g. post videos, photos, blog comments, and calendar events). Each site was examined systematically by research assistants who were instructed to search each page within the top-level domains by clicking through all the links and recording the presence of any of the inventory items. Multiple instances of a technology on each site were recorded (e.g. multiple places to post photos relevant to different coalition activities), resulting in a total of 106 features identified across the seven sites. Figure 2.3 shows the inventory breakdown of interactive affordances found in all seven of the inventoried sites. Figure 2.4 shows the numbers of interactive

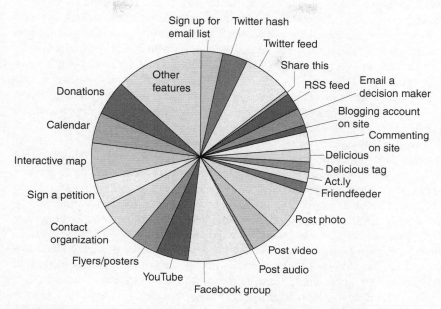

Figure 2.3 Relative occurrences of interactive technology features inventoried in seven related G20 and Climate Summit protest sites, 2009. Multiple instances of the site features were recorded. The number of total features was 106.

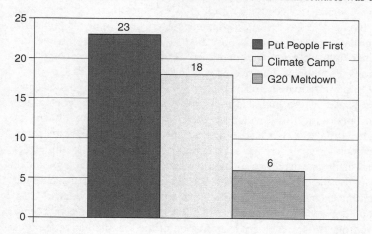

Figure 2.4 Technology inventory of three protest coalitions in 2009 London G20 protests.

technologies from the inventory list that were found in the three main coalition sites from the London March–April 2009 protests.

As can be seen in Figure 2.4, the PPF and Meltdown sites represent the two extremes, with PPF offering 23 personalized technological engagement mechanisms compared with Meltdown's six mechanisms. Climate Camp offers interesting comparison in between. For reference, the Meltdown site offered the fewest interactive technologies of any of the seven sites in the affordance inventory and PPF had the largest number. As noted above, Climate Camp is a radical organization that advocates direct actions but invites individuals with different ideas about the climate crisis to join these actions. Thus, Climate Camp is a network that is more radical than the PPF-centrist coalition, but less inclined to use collective action frames than Meltdown. It is worth noting that its personalized communication inventory is between the other two, but falls short of the PPF level of personalized engagement opportunities.

The PPF site offered many different opportunities for a visitor to enter the protest space. In keeping with the overall approach, the opportunity to 'send your own public message' to the G20 leaders appears at the centre of the first page under a photostream of happy and diverse protestors (see Figure 2.1). There were several means of eliciting information (signing up to receive email alerts, Twitter and RSS feeds, and a calendar) and invitations to publicize and organize this information (through ShareThis, Delicious, Twitter, and downloadable posters). Participants were also encouraged to contribute by using the #G20rally Twitter hashtag and by posting personal photos, videos, and audios relating to the protest. Bloggers could link to the featured Whiteband initiative 'G20 Voices', through which 50 international bloggers were brought in to cover the Summit onsite. Aside from the classic offer to buy T-shirts, the site offered PPF widgets for users to upload to their own blogs or Facebook pages and encouraged linking to the site by providing easy-to-follow instructions. A unique feature was the 'Obama-izer' widget, which allowed users to spread their own 'Obama-ized' likeness to his classic campaign poster (signalling his signature themes of 'hope' and 'change') and to post the PPF slogan of 'Jobs, Justice and Climate' on their own websites or social networking sites. Visitors could also join the coalition's Facebook group, which was linked off the main site.

By contrast, the Meltdown site offered only six technological points of entry into the protest space. These included a calendar, the invitation to contact the group, and the opportunity to download posters about the Meltdown event, to follow the organization's Twitter feed and (YouTube) videos, and to read or join the public Facebook group. There are several possible reasons for the limited set of technological affordances. These include the lack of financial, technological, and skill resources; the possibility that being under surveillance discouraged public information exchange; or the belief that over-use of the internet may impede developing grassroots resources (Diani 2001; Stein 2009). Despite these possible contributing factors, a closer examination of the six interactive features on the Meltdown site suggests an overall tone of limiting personalized participation. Indeed, the overall focus of the site was to present information unilaterally to the visitor. Few of the Meltdown affordances allowed users to customize their interaction with the mobilization. Even when information was attributed to people submitting posts, it was unclear who had submitted them or how this could be done. The exception to this one-way directionality was the Facebook group, where users could post not only comments but also photos and posters.

The PPF website meanwhile not only invited individual contributions in several different ways, but also tolerated postings straying far from its own organizational themes. For example, although official PPF statements did not focus on events aside from the G20 Summit and their own march, various participants using the site raised other issues, such as the death of a bystander at the hands of police at the Meltdown 'Storm the Banks' action on 1 April. Figure 2.5 shows a post to the PPF/Whiteband blog scroll, which linked to a blogger operating under the name of legofesto (http://legofesto.blogspot.com/), who recreated a Lego sculpture of the incident (posted on 15 May, www. whitebandaction.org/en/g20voice/blog?page=1).

It is also important to note that PPF offered points of engagement that were not easily filtered by the central organization. An example of this is the #g20rally Twitter hashtag. The organization encouraged supporters to use the hashtag to create a buzz around its march. While the hashtag was predictably used by the PPF organizers to show solidarity and report on the march, it was also used by others for very different purposes. Examples of the latter included critical comments, as in a picture of protesters eating at McDonald's that was retweeted with the following text:

> RT @(person's name) & @dothegreenthing Delicious irony of #g20rally anti-globalization protesters lunching @ McDonalds http://twitpic.com/2j2qb.

Other users updated followers with how the news was reporting the protests:

> Just heard – #G20rally not lead story. Spat with Argentina about Falklands is set to bump it.

Figure 2.5 Blogger legofesto recreates the death of a bystander. Copyright legofesto, used with permission.

Such examples suggest that the PPF protest space was open to individuals acting in ways showing little programmatic affiliation with the PPF coalition.

In summary, PPF went to great lengths to encourage personalized expression on its website. Meltdown explicitly endorsed the spirit of solidarity expressed in the Paris Declaration and consequently made efforts to highlight other London Summit protest events as well as provide contact information to the respective organizers (including PPF). Yet, their own communication stream was more one way and presented as an ideological narrative on the crisis that visitors could either take or leave. Seen in this light, it seems like Meltdown invited citizens to explore the diverse protest space around the London Summit but not to complicate the Meltdown message, while PPF encouraged personalized action within a PPF-defined protest context.

Personalized communication and protest capacity

Having established systematic communication differences between the two main protest groups, we now turn to examining whether there are any notable deficits in the political capacities of organizations and coalitions implementing more personalized communication strategies. We focus here primarily on PPF, as it was the coalition that presented the most personalized communication. In this analysis, we explore the areas of engagement strength, agenda strength, and network strength outlined earlier.

Engagement strength

Did PPF's more flexible terms of communication undermine their engagement strength – as measured in terms of direct mobilization of participants, indirect communication to general publics, and sustained future mobilization capacity? One of the clearest signals of engagement strength is participation in the protest march itself. As stated previously, an estimated 35,000 people attended the PPF march, compared with roughly 5,000 who turned out for the Meltdown demonstration a few days later (Wikipedia 2009). Were this the only difference between the two coalitions, we might say that a more moderate NGO coalition is more likely to mobilize a large turnout than a more ideologically extreme coalition proposing higher risk actions. However, the size of turnout is just one of the many measures that we used to compare the two coalitions.

Another measure of engagement capacity is the diversity of turnout. While we do not have precise indicators of diversity, the photos posted by participants and sponsoring organizations on various sites clearly show a broader range of people and messages in the PPF march compared with those posted from the 'Storm the Banks' march organized by the Meltdown coalition. Contrast, for example, the photos posted by Indymedia London (2009) with those posted on the CAFOD (2009) site.

As for engaging a broader public beyond the immediate demonstration, the mainstream media coverage was also far greater and more positive for the PPF activities. This is documented below as part of the analysis of agenda strength. What this means is that in terms of secondary engagement (i.e. people who were not there, but who heard about it in the press), the PPF activities reached a far wider audience with more positive messages.

Yet, another way of thinking about engagement strength is whether those mobilized in this particular protest were also kept in the communication network for future activities. One interesting indicator that the PPF network sustained its communication with participants was the continuing promotion by many of the same coalition organizations of future activities related to climate change and the forthcoming Copenhagen Climate Summit. We will discuss how these networks overlapped in more detail in the section on network strength, but at this point, it is worth noting that PPF continued to link to the topic of climate change and directed site visitors to the Stop Climate Chaos Coalition (SCCC). The SCCC, whose sponsoring membership overlapped considerably with that of PPF, was then coordinating 'The Wave' protest leading up to the UN Copenhagen Climate Summit. The Wave demonstrations, which took place on 5 December 2009, attracted an estimated 50,000 people.

A final indicator of the engagement strength of the PPF protest is the difference in what Chadwick (2007) refers to as sedimentary digital mechanisms that sustain histories of past events and leave behind communication links for people to organize future events. The PPF website was still up and functional at the time of this writing (a year and a half after the protests), with the 'put your message to the G20 here' box being replaced with a scroll of the messages left by people who had used that feature earlier. By contrast, the G20 Meltdown site was not updated after the summer of 2009 and was taken down shortly after that (although a Facebook group remained sporadically active at the time of this writing).

Agenda strength

The second question is whether personalized communication compromised the PPF coalition's conventional agenda strength. Our conclusion is that it did not. Despite the many invitations in the PPF environment for individuals to contribute to their digital protest space, the PPF policies and strategies were clearly presented and not up for discussion. The site presents a 12-point policy platform detailing the claims of the proposed march, which were directed at the UK government. Some of the points are more general, such as 'Compel tax havens to abide by strict international rules' and 'Work to ensure sufficient emergency funding to all countries that need it, without damaging conditionalities attached'. But other claims were more specific: for example, 'Deliver 0.7% of national income as aid by 2013, deliver aid more effectively and push for the cancellation of all illegitimate and unpayable developing country debts'. This suggests that PPF's flexibility did not unduly compromise the specificity and clarity of its public claims. In contrast, it is interesting that the Meltdown site, which signalled greater rigidity about its message, presented only broad goals directed at the system rather than a specific political target: '1. Participate in a carnival party at the Bank of England. 2. Support all events demonstrating against the G20 during the meltdown period (from 28 March onwards). 3. Overthrow capitalism.'

Another measure of agenda strength is the capacity of a protest coalition to communicate to broader publics through various media channels. A common concern about social movements and media is that news stories typically focus on violence or civil disobedience and not on the issue agendas of the protesters. Media coverage is even more problematic for transnational and global justice protesters who typically represent multiple issues, often leaving news organizations unable to summarize the point of the protest (Bennett 2005). Worse yet, particularly chaotic protests may even be subject to comedy treatments as in the example of the Pittsburgh events that were part of the series of protests as the G20 travelled to various locations. In our case, we investigated whether PPF's flexible and personalized communication compromised the diffusion of coalition claims and coverage in the mainstream media.

We analysed reporting of the protests in all English language print news media in the week of the summit protests (27 March–4 April 2009). Of 504 relevant items, 225 articles mentioned PPF and 165 mentioned Meltdown. Most mentions of PPF reflected the coalition's own emphasis on the 'unified' and 'unprecedented alliance' of 'mainstream' diversity behind the demand to 'Put People First'. Mentions of Meltdown meanwhile highlighted the radical profile of the associated groups and police anticipation of disruptive protests. The coalition's issue claims were seldom featured in the news. The valence of the reporting was more positive for PPF: 46 per cent of the total mentions of PPF were positive, 53 per cent neutral, and 1 per cent negative. For Meltdown, by contrast, only 3 per cent of the mentions were positive, 74 per cent neutral, and 23 per cent negative. This general pattern held irrespective of the political position of the news organization (e.g. the BBC, *Guardian*, and *The Times*).

Network strength

Our final question concerns whether more personalized communication through digital media necessarily undermines network strength. We analysed both the PPF and Meltdown coalitions from the perspective of their organizational network strength and the dynamics of their networks over time. The coherence and stability of protest networks can be thought of in terms of levels of mutual recognition and inclusion of coalition organizations in cross-linked networks. We measured recognition and inclusion in this case through various indicators based on hyperlink patterns among organization websites and campaigns. By these measures, networks that have less strength (i.e. stability and coherence) will display higher numbers of isolated organizations that receive few links from others.

In light of the differences in the protest narratives and frames found on the two main coalition sites, it is not surprising that two very different networks were formed by organizations listed as the members of the respective coalitions. As noted earlier, the Meltdown site mostly listed anarchist and anti-capitalist organizations (e.g. Rhythms of Resistance, The Laboratory of Insurrectionary Imagination, the Haringey Solidarity Group, and the Socialist Workers' Party). The PPF core members consisted mainly of large, well-established national NGOs working in the areas of development, trade justice, and environment (e.g. CAFOD, Oxfam, and Friends of the Earth). The interesting question that moves us beyond the lists of members of the two protest coalitions is how the solidarity networks of the two coalitions were organized. What were the observable patterns of giving and receiving recognition in the two large coalitions that shared and organized the London Summit protest space? What is perhaps surprising is that the PPF coalition, which advertised the most personalized affiliation opportunities, displayed by far the stronger network, suggesting that the personalization of the mobilization process, alone, does not necessarily undermine the resilience of the collective action structure.

Given our limited access to participants in these protests, we could not assess network relationships in a fine-grained ethnographic sense (e.g. who regularly calls whom to coordinate actions and what organization leaders or members attend meetings together). More importantly, a finer-grained ethnographic analysis would make it extremely challenging to piece together the extended solidarity networks of hundreds and even thousands of organizations that help communicate the messages of the core organizations and drive participants to their mobilizations. What we are seeking for the purposes of this analysis is a rough assessment of the qualities (e.g. size, organizational composition, and density of relationships) of the extended networks surrounding the core coalitions responsible for organizing the G20 protests. We can get a preliminary understanding of these network properties by assessing one of the most visible ways in which recognition is given or withheld in contemporary protest spaces: through the exchange of links on websites. For explanations of why intentional web-linking patterns constitute reliable indicators of network structure in cases like ours, see Rogers (2004) and Foot and Schneider (2006).

It is also important to recognize the limits of the methods that we employ here. Networks, do not, of course, reveal all of their dimensions through linking patterns. Neither al-Qaeda support organizations nor candidates in the US Congressional elections can be expected to link to their funding sources or to their covert strategy advisors, two important node clusters in their networks. However, web crawls of such disparate organizations may reveal insights into their support and resource networks (e.g. mosques or influential clerics involved in recruitment, in the case of al-Qaeda, or endorsements from respected public officials and organizations in the case of the Congressional candidates). More appropriate for our case is that social movement and NGO policy coalitions may signal who their close partners are or where people can go and what they can do to advance mutual goals. Just as importantly, organizations can choose not to link to others in public even though they may share some agenda overlap. For example, the Meltdown site linked to PPF, but that recognition was not returned, signalling that PPF wanted its public image to be cleanly associated with a financial reform programme and not linked to a blatantly anti-capitalist message.

More generally, then, the way organizations link (or do not link) to others signals various kinds of relationships in networks, such as influence (the degree to which an organization links out to others) and also prestige (the degree to which other organizations choose to link to an organization). Through this giving and receiving of links, we can detect things such as the numbers of isolated organizations in coalitions, the density of co-linking among organizations, and the relative equality in the distribution of links among organizations in a network. In order to find out how organizations in our main coalitions positioned themselves in relation to each other through intentional website linkages, we conducted web crawls to assess the co-linking patterns of the two protest networks using a set of starting points that each coalition site defined as core actors. The list of starting points for the Meltdown group was a large one (63 organizations), taken from the 'Who's Who' page on the site.[7] The PPF starting set was much smaller, taken from the list of the 14 organizations authorized to speak to the media on behalf of PPF.[8] Given the differences in the political nature of the two coalitions, there was no obvious way of finding comparable numbers of starting points. PPF clearly signalled its lead organizations, while Meltdown (perhaps reflecting its anarchist ethos) categorized all coalition members equally. More importantly, the relative number of starting points is not as critical as their representativeness. Since the network crawling method that we selected explores all the linking relationships from a set of starting points, network patterns will emerge as long as the starting points are broadly representative of the domain being investigated (in this case, two distinct protest coalitions).

The two respective sets of URLs were placed as starting points, or as a 'seed list', into Issue Crawler, a tool made available by Richard Rogers at the University of Amsterdam (for a detailed account of this tool, see www.govcom.org/scenarios_use.html, and Rogers 2004). The Issue Crawler identifies networks of URLs and locates them in a relational space (which we will refer to as a 'network map') on the basis of the co-link analysis. A co-link is simply a URL that receives links from at least two of the starting points for each iteration (or 'click') as the crawler moves out from the starting points. Thus, suppose we begin with Site A, Site B, and Site C, and crawls of the inlinks and outlinks for each turn up site D, which has links from sites A and C. Site D would be included in the network map as co-linking from two of the starting points. Suppose that on the second iteration or click of the crawl, the crawler finds that site D also links to site E, which, in turn, supplies an inlink to Site B from our list of starting points. However, site E receives no other links from the members of the expanding network. Under the chosen inclusion method, site E would not be included in the network map. The decision to use co-link analysis simply provides a test of whether networks are more constrained than, say, a snowball or single-link method, which would include more weakly tied organizations such as site E. As with most methodological choices, there are theoretical implications. Thus, we set a somewhat higher bar for network inclusion than other mapping methods would create. The rationale is that since we are interested in comparing networks in terms of density of linking and structural stability, the co-linking criterion puts the spotlight on organizations that emerge in more tightly connected networks.

We set the reach of the crawl at two iterations (or hyperlink clicks) from the starting points. This is the procedure that Rogers (2004) recommends for deriving a solidarity network that includes links among organizations extending beyond a particular issue focus and into support networks for larger categories of concern. For example, in this case, we wanted to capture the solidarity networks surrounding our two clusters of economic justice organizations. This opening to the solidarity network enabled the inclusion of more climate change organizations that advocate linking economic and climate justice causes, because they see global warming impacting already impoverished nations most severely. The question now becomes whether the coalition displaying more personalized engagement opportunities lost network strength in the bargain.

Despite its more personalized appeals to individuals, PPF turned out to have a much more coherent organizational network than Meltdown with its more rigid collective action frames. The crawler visited more than 2,000 URLs in each crawl and rendered a map and a co-link matrix (including directionality of links) consisting of the top sites sharing co-links in each network. The maps of the two networks are shown in Figures 2.6 and 2.7. The sizes of the nodes correspond to the relative numbers of the inlinks that a site received from other organizations. At initial inspection, both networks seem superficially similar, with the crawler returning the core networks of 97 organizations for PPF and 99 for Meltdown. Closer inspection, however, reveals that the networks are vastly different in terms of which of the coalition members ended up in them and the linking patterns among the core network members. The most dramatic observation is that many members of the Meltdown coalition dropped out of the network, because few of them were recognized by at least two other members. Even more interesting is that many of the organizations receiving greater recognition from the Meltdown members turned out to be the core players in the PPF network, suggesting that actors in the more centrist coalition represented some important levels of prestige (perhaps based on valuable information or other resources) for many of the Meltdown groups.

Inspection of the linking patterns shown in Figure 2.7 reveals that PPF centred on a tightly knit group of core organizations, including most of those listed in the media contact list. Indeed, most of these PPF starting points remained prominent in the core network, meaning that they received recognition from multiple other members of the network. By contrast, many of the organizations from which we launched the Meltdown crawl dropped out of the network, meaning that they did not receive widespread recognition from fellow members of the organizing coalition list. The contrast is dramatic. Only one of the 14 starting points dropped out of the PPF network, because it failed to receive links from two or more organizations in the crawled population. By contrast, fully 30 of the original 63 starting points dropped out of the Meltdown solidarity network

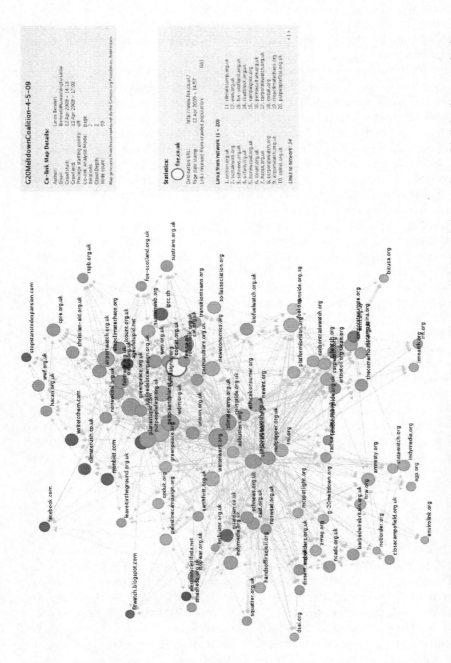

Figure 2.6 Core solidarity network of the G20 Meltdown coalition, with nodes sized by relative numbers of inlinks that organizations received from the network.

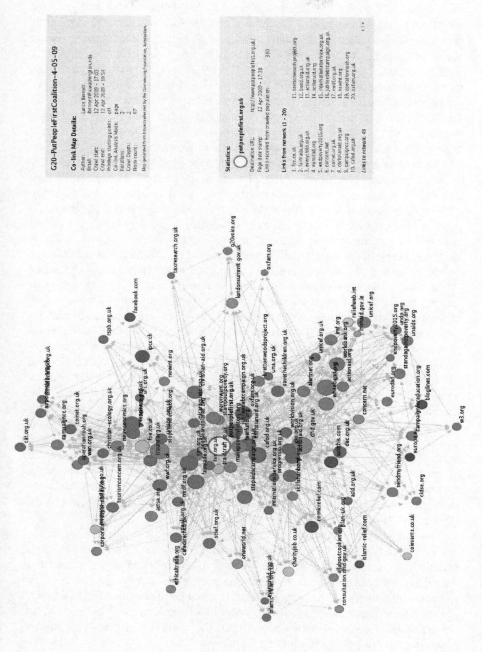

Figure 2.7 Core solidarity network of the Put People First coalition, with nodes sized by relative numbers of inlinks that organizations received from the network.

due to lack of recognition among other coalition members. This, of course, raises the question of who the organizations populating the Meltdown solidarity network are, if not primarily the original coalition members. As noted above, a number of prominent organizations associated with the PPF network emerge as a tightly linked group in the Meltdown network as well. In fact, a dominant cluster of most inlinked organizations in the upper half of Figure 2.6 turn out to be organizations that also appear prominently in the PPF network in Figure 2.7. In particular, six organizations appear near the centre of both networks: Oxfam, Friends of the Earth, People & Planet, World Development Movement, and SCCC. People & Planet and SCCC appear in both the PPF sponsor list and the Meltdown Who's Who list from which the crawls were launched. However, the other four were PPF sponsor organizations that did not appear in the Meltdown starting points.

The asymmetric inclusion of the PPF members in the Meltdown solidarity network does not mean that the two networks were the same. Although many PPF organizations appear in the Meltdown network, they do not dominate the network. Fully 14 of the top 20 most linked-to sites in each network were different. What accounts for this puzzling quality of the Meltdown network that it excludes many of its own coalition members, while affiliating in a solidarity neighbourhood that goes beyond PPF to include other organizations as well? Although environment organizations were a minority of the largely anti-capitalist starting points, they were disproportionately likely to associate with each other and with an extended string of environmental advocacy organizations to provide the core strength of the Meltdown network. Indeed, the top six most linked-to organizations in Figure 2.6 are environmental orgs: climatecamp.org.uk (receiving 33 links from the 99 other organizations in the core network); foe.co.uk (28); campaigncc.org (24); risingtide.org.uk (24); greenpeace.org.uk (23); and people-andplanet.org (23). Indeed, the top 20 most recognized organizations in the Meltdown network included 17 devoted entirely or importantly to climate change and environmental sustainability issues. Another member of the top 20 was an information network (Indymedia) that carried news and personal accounts from the protests and received 19 formal links from other members of the network. This means that only two core organizations in the Meltdown solidarity network ended up being focused mainly on the economic justice issues that were at the centre of the protests, and these were overlapping core members of PPF (Oxfam and World Development Movement).

This suggests that the formal Meltdown coalition focus on anti-capitalism quickly melted away if we consider the overall network strength of the coalition, which turns out to lie primarily with a subset of environment organizations and their extended network. Without this strong network built around the secondary environmental theme of the protests, there is a real possibility that the Meltdown coalition would have failed to reveal a coherent or stable network at all. In other words, when it comes to network strength, the economic justice wing of the Meltdown network suffered a bit of a meltdown.

Enough Meltdown member organizations pointed towards the PPF members and/or environmental organizations to morph the network in surprisingly different directions than one might have imagined just from examining the tone and membership of the coalition site or even from exploring all of the member websites. Perhaps, the most striking indicator of the low network strength of the original Meltdown coalition membership (in terms of observed relations among its economic justice organizations) is the fact that even the Meltdown coalition site sits outside the centre of its own network (appearing in the lower left of Figure 2.6). The Meltdown site ranked 27th out of 99 nodes in the network in terms of inlinks received from other organizations (13). By contrast, as shown in Figure 2.7, the PPF coalition site is the centre of its network, ranking first in recognition with inlinks from 38 other organizations.

The network strength pattern is clear: recognition clearly flows outward from the Meltdown coalition members towards a mix of environmental organizations and the dominant organizations in PPF. The reverse was most certainly not true, with the PPF members assiduously not linking to enough Meltdown organizations to include many of them in their network. Indeed, the Meltdown coalition site does not even appear in the network map of the PPF network.

This analysis seems to make it clear that conventional ideological or collective identity based action framing of public activities is not a prerequisite for network coherence (inclusion and density of relationships) among coalition members. One case surely does not establish a general law, and we expect to see a good deal more variation in terms of ranges of outcomes on the collective action framing side of the equation. That is, one suspects that there will be many scenarios under which collective action frames do produce more coherent networks than in the case of this largely anarchist and anti-capitalist Meltdown coalition that demonstrated relatively low network strength. However, the main point here is about the other case, PPF, where we have a fairly typical coalition of advocacy NGOs that shunned collective action frames and personalized their digital media engagement affordances without suffering evident loss of network strength.

Conclusion

The fact that the organizations in the Meltdown Who's Who list displayed relatively low levels of public recognition in their web links while a group of core PPF organizations appears prominently in the Meltdown network suggests the greater dominance of the PPF network in this protest space. This may reflect their resource advantage in terms of providing information, logistical coordination, and a better online communication infrastructure. In addition, the minority of the environmental organizations in the Meltdown coalition also turned out to dominate the network in ways that distinguished it from PPF, pointing, in particular, to the Climate Camp demonstration among the G20 activities and towards future protests leading up to the UN Climate Summit in Copenhagen at the end of the year. Thus, the Meltdown network was not without some distinctive structure, but it was a structure that notably did not include the majority of economic justice organizations in the coalition.

By contrast, the dominance of the PPF coalition was clear in terms of network inclusiveness, density of relationships, and prestige of the core organizations. There was a pronounced asymmetry in the levels and nature of recognition between the two networks. For example, the Meltdown coalition publicized (and encouraged participation in) the PPF march, but there was no discernible return publicity from PPF for the Meltdown event. Moreover, it was clear from the Indymedia feeds and photos that the Meltdown supporters joined the PPF march without disrupting the peaceful tone, which was a marked contrast to the more confrontational tactics employed by these groups in the later 'Storm the Banks' event. This asymmetrical capacity of the PPF network ended up serving well in terms of getting its message out, both across internal digital networks and in the mass media, which generally gave more and more positive coverage to the PPF activities.

In addition to these network dynamics that helped define the G20 protest space and the activities within it, there were also clearly many directly brokered arrangements and understandings that operated beyond the bounds of our observations. For example, the strategic mutual decision reached by the respective coalitions to divide the protest space into different activities and different days clearly enhanced the clarity of the PPF activities. Orchestrating separate protests and defining them clearly on the coalition sites and their associated social networks may have appealed to the greater propensity of people to turn out for peaceful demonstrations while contributing to favourable news coverage of a more clearly communicated message in the absence of disruptive noise from more anarchic demonstrators. At the same time, the asymmetry of the networking relationship structures also reinforces these divisions of the protest space and the communication structures that helped organize participants.

Perhaps, the most interesting finding in these data involves the clear evidence that the coalition that adopted more personalized communication strategies still maintained the strongest network. PPF was open to highly personalized affiliation, but it did not seem to have sacrificed much organizational control or political capacity in the bargain. The PPF coalition not only dominated the immediate protest space, but also provided clear pathways for people to join future actions (such as the later climate protests). While the Meltdown site soon disappeared, PPF left various sedimentary structures such as the coalition website as living memories of the G20 action, complete with the messages and photo galleries created by the participants themselves. Thus, the personalization of participation invited citizens into shared environments where they created important content and established interpersonal relationships both online and offline. At the same time, this individualized communication took place in the context of established messages and action opportunities defined by coalition members whose network relationships indicated strong levels of mutual recognition of action frames and agendas. In short, the PPF coalition opened the floor for varied individual perspectives (recall legofesto), but the overall effort remained managed and focused. This does not mean that traditional ideological vanguard coalitions have lost their place in collective action scenarios. The Meltdown coalition mobilized a substantial number of participants who engaged in a highly orchestrated action repertoire of confrontation and disruption of London public spaces. Moreover, the Meltdown plan clearly respected the PPF action, with many Meltdown activists participating in the PPF events without disrupting them. The ability of two such distinct coalitions to mobilize a broad spectrum of participants within the same protest ecology, yet to remain distinctive in terms of messages and actions, suggests a refinement of both strategy and communication.

These findings point towards a richer understanding of communication technologies in the organization of contentious collective action. Our analysis may help balance perspectives that have emphasized collective action framing, mass media, and more formal organizational memberships when thinking about conditions of effective mobilization. While other conditions surely produce weaker and less focused protests, it appears that organization networks can harmonize their agendas around message frames that are broad enough to invite diverse individual participation and coordinate this participation through fine-grained digital media applications that result in coherent collective action.

Acknowledgements

This chapter builds on the work supported by the Swedish Research Council grants Dnr 435–2007–1123 and Dnr 421–2010–2303. The authors wish to thank Nathan Johnson, Allison Rank, and Marianne Goldin for their research assistance. The chapter benefited from the comments received on the earlier versions presented at the ECPR General Conference 2009, the iCS Networking Democracy Symposium 2010, from Sidney Tarrow, and from the anonymous reviewers.

Notes

1 Available at: www.g20.org/Documents/final-communique. pdf (accessed 26 July 2009).
2 The keyword analysis was performed using Wordsmith, which identifies words that characterize a text by comparing a research text with a larger research corpus. By running Dunning's log-likelihood test, a cousin of the chi-square test, words are identified which appear more prominently in the research text. This test identifies not just frequency, but similarity of word ratios. If a word appears in a statistically significant higher proportion in the research text than in the research corpus, it is marked as a keyword. This provides word clusters that are significant to interpret. The complete cluster was 'Put, people, first, putting, we, public, essential'.
3 The keyword cluster included 'Crisis, economic, economies, financial, finance'.
4 'Bank, bankers, financial, executives, bankthink, shareholders, shares, horsemen, wave, public'.
5 'Meltdown, crises, crisis, crunch, anniversary'.
6 'Revolution, mobilization, rescue'.
7 The Labour Party (actually, the Alternative Labour Party), The Alternative G20 Summit, The Laboratory of Insurrectionary Imagination, Climate Rush, Climate Camp, Stop the War Coalition, Campaign for Nuclear Disarmament, Rising Tide, London Action Resource Centre, People & Planet, Earth First, Radical Anthropology Group,

Haringey Solidarity Group, Hackney Solidarity Network, London Coalition Against Poverty, Day-Mer, Aluna, Transition Towns, People's Global Action, Hands off Venezuela, Radical Activist, SchNEWS, noborder network, Network to End Migrant and Refugee Detention, Roadblock, AirportWatch, Climate Crisis Coalition, Plane Stupid, Transport 2000, Airport Pledge, Permaculture, Intergovernmental Panel on Climate Change, Post Carbon Institute, Campaign Against Climate Change, Greenpeace, Zero Carbon City, Corporate Watch, Corpwatch, The Heat is Online, The Centre for Alternative Technology, The World Alliance for Decentralized Energy, Biofuel Watch, Carbon Trade Watch, Platform, Simultaneous Policy, International Union of Sex Workers, IFIwatchnet, The Last Hours, Socialist Workers' Party, Government of the Dead, Rhythms of Resistance, Barking Bateria, Strangeworks, Whitechapel Anarchist Group, Stop Arming Israel, Anarchist Federation, Class War, The Anthill Social, Reclaiming Spaces, The Land is Ours Campaign, New Sovereignty, People in Common, Project 2012, The Student Occupation.

8 Available at: www.actionaid.org, www.cafod.org.uk, www.foe.co.uk, www.eweconomics. org, www. oxfam.org.uk, www.progressio.org.uk, www. savethechildren.org.uk, www. stopclimatechaos.org, http://www.tearfund.org, www.tuc.org.uk, www.waronwant.org, www.wdm.org.uk, www.whiteband.org, http://www.worldvision.org.uk

3 Communication in movement

Social movements as agents of participatory democracy[1]

Donatella della Porta

Introduction

Literature on social movements, mass media, and democracy has rarely inter-acted. Research on democracy has tended to focus on representative institutions, pragmatically using "minimalistic" operationalization of democracy as electoral accountability, and providing structural explanations of democratic develop-ments. Research on the mass media has also tended to isolate them as a separate power, reflecting on the technological constraints and opportunities for commu-nication. Social movement studies have mainly considered democratic character-istics as setting the structure of political opportunities that social movements have to address and – more rarely – looked at the constraints that mass media impose upon powerless actors. Structural, instrumental, and institutional biases, in various combination, have tended to characterize the three fields of studies.

More recently, in all three fields of knowledge, some opportunities for recipro-cal learning and interactions have developed, moved by some exogenous, societal changes as well as by disciplinary evolutions. In what follows, I would suggest that looking at the intersection of democracy, media, and social movements could be particularly useful within a relational and constructivist vision that takes the normative positions by the different actors into account. More broadly, this would mean paying attention to the permeability of the borders between the three con-cepts, as well as between the three fields they tend to separate.

I will do this by looking first at the debate on recent transformations of democracy, described by labels such as post-democracy or counter-democracy (Section 1). I will suggest here that the relegitimation of conceptualizations of democratic qualities such as participation and deliberation increases the rele-vance of social movements as democratic actors. I will then look at the debate on mass media and social movements (Section 2), with particular attention to the recent research on the potential of computer-mediated communication to improve democratic qualities by reducing power inequalities and improving access chances for weak actors. Finally, looking at recent research on the com-munication strategies of social movements, I will stress – together with the importance of recognizing their agency – the links between their communicative practices, and their conceptions of democracy (Section 3).

1 The democratic challenge

"The democratic ideal now reigns unchallenged, but regimes claiming to be democratic come in for vigorous criticism almost everywhere. ... In this paradox resides the major political problems of our time" (Rosanvallon 2008, p. 1). For a few years, it has been common for reflections on the "state of democracy" to start with statements very similar to the one with which Pierre Rosanvallon opens his *Counter-Democracy*. This concept – as also, for example, Colin Crouch's one of *Post-Democracy* (Crouch 2005) – points at the reduced capacity for intervention by elected politicians, as well as citizens' growing dissatisfaction with their performance. As confirmed over and over again by numerous empirical research, trust in real existing democracies (the REDs in Dahl's terms; Dahl 1998) as regimes based upon electoral accountability is limited by widespread phenomena such as the decline of electoral participation, and also the deep transformation in the political parties that has allowed electoral accountability to be weakened. The decline of party membership and, especially, activists (with the related spread of memberless and personalized parties) and the weakening of party loyalties (with the increase in electoral volatility and opinion voting) are tangible signs of these transformations (della Porta 2009c).

Even though not as common as the assessment of challenges to democracy, there is however a growing call for balancing the perceived crisis of the representative (electoral) conception of democracy with considerations for other ones that, even though not at all hegemonic, belong to deep-rooted traditions in both democratic thinking and democratic institutions that go beyond electoral accountability. Remaining with Rosanvallon, we can agree that

> the idea of popular sovereignty found historical expression in two different ways. The first was the right to vote, the right of citizens to choose their own leaders. This was the most direct expression of the democratic principle. But the power to vote periodically and thus bestow legitimacy to an elected government is almost always accompanied by a wish to exercise a more permanent form of control over the government thus elected.
>
> (Rosenvallon 2008, p. 12)

As he notes, in the historical evolution of democracy, alongside the growth of institutions of electoral accountability, a circuit of oversight anchored outside of state institutions became consolidated. In fact, the understanding of democratic experiences requires the consideration, at the same time, of the "functions and dysfunctions" of electoral representative institutions, and also of the organization of distrust. The different elements of what Rosanvallon defined as counter-democracy do not represent, in fact,

> the opposite of democracy, but rather a form of democracy that reinforces the usual electoral democracy, a democracy of indirect powers disseminated

through society – in other words, a durable democracy of distrust which complements the episodic democracy of the usual electoral representative system.

(Ibid., p. 8)

Thinking in terms of other conceptions of democracy paves the way for us to address contemporary transformations as not only challenges to, but also opportunities for, democracy. If mistrust is the disease, it might be part of the cure as well, since "a complex assortment of practical measures, checks and balances, and informal as well as institutional social counter-powers has evolved in order to *compensate for the erosion of confidence, and to do so by organizing distrust*" (ibid., p. 4, italics in original).

In the same vein as Rosanvallon, other scholars have stressed at the same time the crisis of the traditional, liberal (representative) conceptions of democracy and the revival of democratic qualities usually considered under the formula of a "democracy of the ancients." In particular, they put emphasis on the importance of a (free and committed) public. To take a few examples, Bernard Manin described the contemporary evolution from a "democracy of the parties," in which the public sphere was mainly occupied by the political parties, to a "democracy of the public" in which the channels of formation of public opinion are freed from the ideological control of the parties (1995, p. 295). This also means that the cleavages within public opinion no longer reflect electoral preferences, developing instead from individual preferences formed outside of the political parties.

In his *Post-democracy*, Colin Crouch (2005) observed that as politics and governments are losing ground or are conquered by privileged elites, the welfare state – as the product of the mid-century compromise between capital and workers – falls victim to a new, anti-egalitarian conception. Along with low levels of state intervention, the dominant neoliberal model is based upon an elitist conception of electoral participation for the mass of the citizens and free lobbying for stronger interests (ibid., p. 5). Growing mistrust however pushes the political elites to encourage "a maximal level of minimal participation" (ibid., p. 126). The continuous creation of new social identities, as well as their pressures to have their claims recognized, are dynamic challenges to the "world of official politics" (ibid., p. 131).

At a more normative level, the concepts of participatory and deliberative democracy have been used to stress, with growing success, the need to develop public spheres characterized by free and equal participation. Within participatory conceptions of democracy, to use Barber's (1984, p. 173) words, "at the heart of strong democracy is talk," and democratic talk requires listening as well as uttering (see also Downing 2001, pp. 47–48). With various emphasis, also, theorists of deliberative democracy stress the importance of communication, as in deliberative democracy people are convinced by the force of the better argument (Habermas 1996).

In the debate on transformations in democracy, social movements appear to play a potentially crucial role. Recognizing the democratic potential of mistrust means in fact pushing forward reflections on the democratic role played by non-institutional actors in the political system. Recent research on political participation noted that while some more conventional forms of participation (such as voting or party-linked activities) are declining, protest forms are instead increasingly used. Citizens vote less but are not less interested and knowledgeable about politics. And if some traditional types of associations are less and less popular, others (social movement organizations among them) are instead growing in resources, legitimacy, and members.

In several accounts of broad democratic transformations, social movements are presented as performing an important democratic function: not however of representation and negotiation, as in the labor movement, but as "watchdogs in their specific policy area" (Rosanvallon 2008, p. 63), calling attention to specific problems. Among others, Rosanvallon seems to conceive civil society and social movements as particularistic actors, able to voice protest but not to "understand the problems associated with a shared world." In his vision, the evolution toward a civic democracy "leads to fragmentation and dissemination where coherence and comprehensiveness are needed" (ibid., p. 23). At the root of this (feared) dissolution of the political "is a decline in global awareness of political action," with politics appearing "to be increasingly fragmented, deconstructed and opaque" (ibid., p. 254).

Similarly, Colin Crouch (2005) warns about the negative effects of those interest groups that, instead of pursuing a political program asking for institutional interventions, bypass the political institutions. Fragmentation is also singled out, with warnings about the unequal resources available for the different causes. In general, he notes that interest groups and social movements belong to the liberal political camp more than to the democratic one. One could read indeed, in Rosanvallon's counter-democracy as in Crouch's post-democracy, a sort of nostalgia for the global vision of (ideological) mass parties.

Summarizing:

a   Recent reflections on democracies point at the challenges to representative democracy.
b   But at the same time they also point to the opportunities for different democratic qualities.
c   These qualities include controls (oversights), participation and deliberation.
d   They are not new concepts in democratic theorizations and practices.
e   But they acquire emerging meaning in contemporary real existing democracies.
f   These democratic qualities point to the role of non-institutional actors in implementing democracy, with particular emphasis on the public spheres, from mass media to social movements.
g   However, this evolution implies a (feared) "depoliticization" and fragmentation, as social movements tend to be seen as particularist actors.

In what follows, I will discuss to which extent hopes and fears are supported by empirical research on social movements and their communication practices.

2 What media studies and social movement studies do (and do not) say on democracy

Notwithstanding the obvious and growing importance of mass media and social movements for democracy, the debate on their specific contributions to democratic quality has been selective in both fields. As I am going to argue, existing research tends to be structuralist and instrumental, paying limited attention to agents and their normative construction.

In media studies, conditions and limits of media contributions to democracy have not occupied a central place. When addressing the important role of an active and autonomous public sphere, research on political communication has tended rather to stigmatize the commercialization and/or lack of political autonomy of the mass media as a serious challenge to the performance of a "power of oversight" over the elected politicians. While various theorizations have mapped different types of public spheres (Gerhard and Neidhardt 1990), and traditionally research on political communication has stressed the role of different filters between the media-as-senders and the citizens-as-receivers (e.g., Deutsch 1964), research on political communication has mainly focused on the mass media as a separate power. The debate on democracy and the media has mainly been addressed by looking at the effects of the institutional settings on media freedom and pluralism (e.g., Gunther and Mughan 2000). Recent tendencies in the mass media – among them concentration, deregulation, digitalization, globalization, and the pluralization of publics – have ambivalent effects on democracy (Dahlgren 2009).

Some more attention to democracy has developed in studies around the new media. Research on the Internet has addressed the potential improvements, that digital communication could bring to democratic quality. So relevant are the expected effects of electronic communication considered to be that new concepts have been proposed, including e-participation (the possibility of expressing political opinion online), e-governance (the possibility of accessing information and public services online); e-voting (or e-referendum, with the possibility of voting online), or, even more broadly, e-democracy, defined as the increasing opportunities for participation online (Rose 2005).

As for *representative* democracy, the use of the Internet has been seen as improving communication between citizens and elected politicians, with increasing accessibility to information, occasions for feedbacks, and transparency. E-governance is supposed to reduce the discretionality of public administrators by improving public access. The Internet has been said to impact on democratic *participation* as well: as a horizontal, bi-directional, and interactive technology, it is expected to favor a multiplication of information producers (Bentivegna 1999; Warkentin 2001), as well as of information available for consumption (Ayers 1999; Myers 2001). As recently summarized by Dahlgren (2009, p. 190), "The open and accessible character of the net means that traditional centers of power have less informational and ideational control over their environment than previously." As for the *deliberative* quality of democracy, the Internet is said to increase the quality of communication by improving not only the number of sources of information but also their pluralism (Wilhelm 2000). The citizens' capacity for oversight grows as

> the powerful have been spying on their subjects since the beginning of history, but the subjects can now watch the powerful, at least to a greater extent than in the past. We have all become potential citizen journalists who, if equipped with a mobile phone, can record and instantly upload to the global networks any wrongdoing by anyone, anywhere.
>
> (Castells 2009, p. 413)

Multiplying the spaces for exchange of ideas, the Internet also improves mutual understanding by allowing for the development of multiple critical public spheres.

As for other technologies, opinions on the advantages and disadvantages of the Internet are split however (for a review, see della Porta and Mosca 2005). In research on its use in representative politics, concerns have been expressed especially about the uni-directional (top-down) use of new technologies by politicians and administrators alike (Zittel 2003, p. 3). The potential egalitarian effects are denied by scholars who stress instead the presence of a digital divide which increases rather than reduces inequalities, the lack of access to the web tending to go hand in hand with lack of access to other resources, both at individual and country level (Margolis and Resnick 2000; Rose 2005; Norris 2001). As for its deliberative quality, concerns have also been expressed with reference not only to the plurality of information, but also to the quality of communication online (Schosberg *et al.* 2005). The e-public spheres have been defined as "partial," elitist, and fragmented (Sunstein 2001; Curran 2003).

Additionally, increasing attention notwithstanding, the discussion on the improvement of democratic politics on the web tends to remain either highly normative or quite technical, with even some nuances of technological determinism. The debate on the Internet is, in fact, still perceived as the domain of techno-maniacs and utopian dreamers (Zittel 2004, p. 2).

These gaps in the reflections on communication and democracy have not been fully filled by social movement studies. Paradoxically, notwithstanding its obvious relevance for democracy (and vice versa), social movement research has been rarely concerned with democratic functions. Usually, democracies have been considered as the context of social movements, and some of the characteristics of representative institutions (especially territorial and functional divisions of power) have been seen as particularly important in favoring "healthy" (intense, but moderate) protest (della Porta and Diani 2006, chap. 8).

Research on social movements and communication is also a little frequented area. Media have been considered as important for social movements. As Gamson (2004, p. 243) observed, "the mass media arena is the major site of context over meaning because all of the players in the policy process assume its pervasive influence – either it is justified or not." Control of the media and of symbolic production therefore becomes both an essential premise for any attempt at political mobilization and an autonomous source of conflict. Even though it is debated to what extent protest events are first of all "newspaper demonstrations," i.e. oriented mainly at media coverage (Neveu 1999, pp. 28ff.), media are indeed the most obvious shaper of public sensitivity (Jasper 1997, p. 286). The success of protest action is influenced by the amount of media attention it receives, and this also affects the character of social movements (Gitlin 1980).

However, research has repeatedly confirmed the limited capacity of social movements to influence the mass media, which have selection but also descriptive biases when covering protest (Gamson and Modigliani 1989; Gamson 2004). A media bias against social movements endowed with little social capital (in terms of relations and reputation as reliable sources) to benefit journalists has been identified. Social movements have in fact been described as "weak" players in the mass-media sphere, and the relationships between activists and journalists as competitive (Neveu 1999). General tendencies (journalistic preference for the visible and dramatic, for example, or reliance on authoritative sources of information) and specific characteristics of the media system (a greater or lesser degree of neutrality on the part of journalists, the amount of competition between the different media) both influence social movements (see, for example, Kielbowicz and Scherer 1986). Recent evolutions towards depoliticization of the journalistic profession or increasing commercialization (Neveu 1999) have been said to further reduce activists' access. When social movement organizations and activists have been effective in producing newsworthy events, it has reputedly been at high cost, in terms of adaptation to the media logic. In his influential book *The Whole World Is Watching*, Gitlin (1980) described different steps in relations with the media, going from lack of interest to cooptation. Beyond the media, discursive opportunities in the broader public are quoted as determinants of movements' relative success in agenda setting.

This vision has some grains of truth but is also partial. As Charlotte Ryan observed long ago (1991), the focus on the inequality in the power of the different actors who intervene in the mass media has been useful in counterbalancing some naive assumptions of the (then dominant) gatekeeper organizational model that underestimated the barriers of access to the news by weak actors. At the same time, however, it risks underestimating the capacity for agency by social movement organizations as well as the active role of the audiences in making sense of media messages.

Summarizing:

a   Both media studies and social movement studies have paid limited and selective attention to democracy.

b   There has been a tendency to consider democratic institutions as the independent variable, that is the context that influence the qualities of media and social movements.

c   In media studies, the debate on the potential democratic functions of the Internet remained focused on its technological potential.

d   Social movement studies, on their side, have pointed at the selectivity of the mass media towards non-institutional actors.

As I am going to argue in the next section, research on alternative media has paid attention to social movements as agents of democratic communication, looking at their visions and norms but considering them in isolation from the most influential mass media. Given recent changes in the technological and cultural opportunities for protest, scholars in this field are now stressing more and more the blurring of the borders between the senders and receivers, producers and users, as well as the importance of normative visions in the choice of communication practices.

3 Social movements as agents of democratic participation and communication

Attention to agency is strong in research on the movement-near medias, variously defined as alternative, activist, citizens', radical, autonomous, etc. (for a review, see Mattoni 2009, pp. 26–29). In Downing's definition (2001, p. 3), "radical alternative media constitute the most active form of the active audience and express oppositional strands, overt and covert, within popular cultures." They are "media, generally small scale and in many different forms, that express an alternative vision to hegemonic policies, priorities and perspectives" (ibid., p. v). Studies on alternative media stress especially the differences in their content and rhetoric as well as in the ways in which they produce news. In general, they look, at a micro level, at the (decentralized) practices of news production. Radical, alternative media are considered as social movement organizations[2] of a special type, constructing a movement public sphere. Their *raison d'être* is the critique of the established media (Rucht 2004) and the promotion of the "democratization of information" (Cardon and Granjou 2003). In this way, they play an important role for democracy, by expanding the range of information and ideas, being more responsive to the excluded, and impacting on the participants' sense of the self (Downing 2001).

The analysis of alternative media has increasingly focused on the use of new technologies. The Internet has been said to multiply public spaces for deliberation thereby allowing for the creation of new collective identities (della Porta and Mosca 2005). In various campaigns and protest actions, online forums and mailing lists have hosted debates on various strategic choices as well as reflections on their effects. Most of the 266 websites that referred to the Global Justice Movement analyzed during the Demos project (della Porta 2009a and 2009b; della Porta and Mosca 2005) provide a significant amount of information, improving opportunities for political education through articles, papers, and dossiers (90 percent of the cases), and also provide conferences and seminar materials for interested users (78 percent). Websites served broadly as means for self-presentation to the outside, being used as sort of "electronic business cards" that well represent the organization's identity, through information on its past history and current activities. A large majority (about 80 percent) of our social movement organizations also provide information on their website on the physical existence and reachability of the organization (80 percent) and publish the statute (or an equivalent document) of their organization, so improving the transparency about their internal life. The potential for mobilization through the web is also widely exploited, especially for offline protest, with the publication of their own calendar (60 percent) and also of initiatives of other organizations as well as providing concrete information (through handbooks or links to useful resources) on offline forms of action (36 percent). About two thirds of websites advertise the participation of their organization in a protest campaign. About one third of the sampled websites provide instruments for online protest, such as e-petitions, netstrikes, and mailbombings. Also about one third of the websites provide open spaces for discussion through specific applications like forums, mailing lists, blogs, or chat lines, that allow for multilateral interactivity. The Demos survey of participants in the Athens European Social Forum (ESF) in May 2006 confirms that the Internet represents a fundamental means of communication among activists of the Global Justice Movement (Mosca and della Porta 2009, see also della Porta and Mosca 2005, p. 171, on the first ESF in Florence in 2002). In particular, a very high percentage of respondents (between 75 and 85 percent) use the web to perform moderate forms of online protest (less than one third employ more radical ones such as netstrikes), to exchange information with their own group, and to express political opinions online. Virtual communities have been shown to be capable of developing a sense of community (Freschi 2002; Fuster 2010).

Doubts are expressed, however, about the capacity of alternative media (online and offline) to go beyond those who are already sympathetic to their cause, and to reach the general public. Social movements do indeed develop different movement strategies to address the mass media (from abstention to attack and adaptation, Rucht 2004). Meso-media, circulating information between the activists, have however to meet the uneasy task of reaching the mass media, if they want their message to circulate outside movement-sympathetic circles (Bennett 2005; Peretti 2004).The digital divide, the scarce effects of "virtual" protest, the limited use of the participatory and deliberative potentials have been mentioned as shortcoming of computer-mediated communication (e.g. Curran 2003; Rucht 2004; della Porta and Mosca 2005; Fuster 2010).

Some recent reflection on social movements and their communication practices have however started to challenge a vision of alternative media as separated from the broader media field, also stressing the importance of the activists' normative visions in shaping communication strategies. Research on alternative media stress the agency of social movements and their communicative practices, as well as the integration of (or at least overlapping between) different actors and fields of action in media (Gamson 2004). Characteristics of these media are their critical, counter-hegemonic content and their capacity to involve not only (or mainly) professional journalists, but also citizens in news production, given their horizontal links with their audience (Atkinson 2010). Participatory activists are said to overcome the distinction between audience and producers, readers and writers through co-performance (ibid., p. 41).

An important recent innovation in research on social movements and the media has been the conceptualization of a media environment (similar to Bourdieu's field) in which not only different spokepersons intervene, but also different types of medias interact. In Mattoni's definition (2009, p. 33), a media environment is an "open, unpredictable and controversial space of mediatization and communication, made up of different layers which continuously combine with one another due to the information flows circulating within the media environment itself." As she observed (ibid., p. 34), "in complex and multilayered media environments individuals simultaneously play different roles, especially in particular situations of protest, mobilization and claims making." A continuous flow of communication between what Bennett (2005) conceptualized as micro, meso, and macro media also makes the boundaries between news production and news consumption more flexible.

In recent reflections, the focus of attention is not so much (or no longer) on the abstract "power of the media," but more on the relations between media and publics: the ways in which "people exercize their agency in relation to media flows" (Couldry 2006b, p. 27). Media practices become therefore central, not only as the practices of the media actors, but more broadly on what various actors do in relations with the media, including activist media practices. Not only is "reading media imagery ... an active process in which context, social location, and prior experience can lead to quite different decoding" (Gamson *et al.* 1992 p. 375), but people participate more and more in the production of messages.

Some recent trends appear to have facilitated this blurring of the borders between news reception and news production. Not only are citizens active processors of media messages but, as Lance Bennett observed, "people who have long been on the receiving end of one-way mass-communication are now increasingly likely to become producers and transmitters" (2003c, p. 34). The increased capacity of normal citizens and activists to produce information has been seen as a consequence of post-modern individualization, with an increasing fluidity and mobility of political identities (ibid.), but also to specific changes in the media field, such as

> 1. New ways of consuming media, which explicitly contest the social legitimacy of media power; 2. New infrastructures of production, which have an effect on who can produce news and in which circumstances; 3. New infrastructures of distribution, which change the scale and terms in which symbolic production in one place can reach other places.
>
> (Couldry 2003, p. 44)

In fact, looking at new trends in "communication power," Manuel Castells has noted that "the production of the message is self-generated, the definition of the potential receiver(s) is self-directed, and the retrieval of specific messages or content from the World Wide Web and electronic communication networks is self-selected" (2009, p. 55). In this way, "The media audience is transformed into a communicative subject increasingly able to redefine the process by which societal communication frames the culture of society" (ibid., p. 116).

Recent research has looked not only at the permeability of the borders between media producers and media consumers, but also at the important effects of the symbolic and normative construction of the relations between media and social movements, journalists and activists.

Attention to agency and normative (and social) construction has been growing in research on social movements and the Internet that has stressed its potential for social movement communication. New media have transformed the ambitions and capacity for communication of social movements. In particular, the Internet is exploited for online mobilization and the performance of acts of dissent: the term "electronic advocacy" refers to "the use of high technology to influence the decision-making process, or to the use of technology in an effort to support policy-change efforts" (Hick and McNutt 2002, p. 8). Also, in part thanks to the Internet, transnational campaigns grew to be longer, less centrally controlled, more difficult to turn on and off, and forever changing in terms of networks and goals (Bennett 2003a). Given their larger flexibility, social movement organizations have emerged as more open to experimentation and permeable to technological changes, with a more innovative and dynamic use of the Internet. Given the low costs of computer-mediated communication, the new technologies offer cheap means for communication beyond borders. Moreover, the Internet has facilitated the development of epistemic communities and advocacy networks (Keck and Sikkink 1998) that produce and spread alternative information on various issues (Olesen 2005). This has been particularly important for the mobilization of transnational campaigns (Reitan 2007).

Beyond their instrumental use, the new technologies have been said to resonate with social movements' vision of democracy at the normative level. Fast and inexpensive communication allows for flexible organization and more participatory structures (Smith 1997; Bennett 2003a). More generally, the Internet

> fits with the basic features of the kind of social movements emerging in the Information Age... To build an historical analogy, the constitution of the labor movement in the industrial era cannot be separated from the industrial factory as its organizational setting... the Internet is not simply a technology: it is a communication media, and it is the material infrastructure of a given organizational form: the network.
>
> (Castells 2001, pp. 135–136)

The use of the Internet is "shaping the movement on its own web-like image," with hubs at the center of activities and spokes "that link to other centers, which are autonomous but interconnected" (Klein 2002, p. 16).

Research on contemporary movements has in fact confirmed the importance of normative visions in determining the use of new technologies. Differences, and even tensions, in the use of new technologies by various social movement organizations and activists reflect different conceptions of democracy and communication.

If communication is becoming more and more relevant for some contemporary movements, this is not only because of its instrumental value. Social movements have traditionally criticized representative conceptions of democracy, which are based on the principles of delegation and majority votes. They have since long being considered as the carriers of participatory visions and practices of democracy, with criticism of delegation, horizontal conceptions of internal organizations (often with refusal of a structured leadership), and positive emphasis on the importance of direct involvement of citizens in decision-making. In some contemporary social movements, such as those active on issues of global justice, the development of arenas – such as the social forums – of reflection and exchange of ideas among a plurality of different social and political actors testifies to the growing democratic importance of the construction of free public spheres. Their visions and practices resonate in fact more and more with what normative theory has defined as deliberative democracy, referring to decisional processes in which, under conditions of equality, inclusiveness, and transparency, a communicative process based on reason (the strength of a good argument) and able to transform individual preferences leads to decisions oriented to the public good (della Porta 2005a).

Within participatory and deliberative visions, research on democracy inside the Global Justice Movement pointed to the growing attention to values related to communication in an open space, respect for diversity, equal participation, and inclusiveness (della Porta 2009a). The importance of conceiving social movements as spaces for networking, with a positive emphasis on diversity, is present in particular in the World Social Forum, as well as in the macro-regional and local social forums. In their normative self-conception as an inclusive public sphere, their main organizational challenge is seen in their capacity to address the tension between the need for coordination and respect for the autonomy of the various organizations and activists that participate in various networks, forums, and coalitions. Networking involves in fact different and diverse actors, particularly at the transnational level.

In several contemporary social movements, this has been nurtured under the conception of an "open space method" of internal democracy that should produce strength from diversity. A positive understanding of diversity, including each organization's own internal diversity, is shared, based on recognition of the history of the different organizations that converge. The networking logic reflects, and at the same time contributes to, the spreading of embedded sets of values oriented towards the building of horizontal ties and decentralized coordination of autonomous units (Juris 2008) as well as reciprocal identification.

In social movement networks, different democratic qualities are discussed and practiced with shifting emphases. Research on the European Social Forums has observed in fact the presence of different democratic forms of internal decision-making, with various balances between participation versus delegation of power and deliberation versus majority voting in internal decision-making (della Porta 2009a and 2009b). The balance between these (and other) democratic qualities is experimented with, criticized, adapted. These normative visions tend to shape the actual communication practices that are themselves far from being evaluated only or mainly in terms of their instrumental values.

Conceptions of democracy inside and outside the groups tend to filter the potentials of technological innovations (Pickerill 2003, p. 23), so pointing at different genres (Vedres *et al.* 2005) or styles (della Porta and Mosca 2005) in the politics on the web. In various studies, the relationship between communication strategies and conceptions of democracy emerges as relevant. According to a survey with the representatives of social movement organizations present at the ESF, while most of them tended indeed to frame new media as crucial (della Porta 2009b), a more limited number stressed the peculiar capacity of the Internet to promote participation and deliberation, highlighting that new technologies can facilitate the spreading and sharing of power and considering Internet tools such as mailing lists as (potentially at least) "permanent assemblies." Open publishing and open management systems are employed only by a few groups in order to widen participation in organizational life and to democratize the organization, avoiding the concentration of power in the hands of few technology-skilled individuals.

Contextual and organizational characteristics contributed to explain the strategic choices made by social movement organizations. As a reflection of national culture, in our research we found that organizations in Germany, Great Britain and Switzerland tended to privilege transparency and provision of information, while those in France, Italy and Spain privileged identity building and mobilization, reflecting the broader mobilization strategies of the Global Justice Movements in these countries. But also different SMOs tend to exploit different technological opportunities, producing websites endowed with different qualities that apparently reflect different organizational models. In particular, SMOs oriented towards more formal and hierarchical organizations, and therefore more traditional representative visions of democracy, seem to prefer also a more traditional (and instrumental) use of the Internet, while less formalized groups, privileging participation and deliberation as consensus building, tend to use more interactive tools online, as well as various forms of computer-mediated protest. Less resourceful, informal, and newer SMOs tend to develop a more innovative use of the Internet, while more resourceful, formal, and older groups tend to use it as a more conventional medium of communication (Mosca and della Porta 2009). Comparing Wikipedia, social forums, Flickr, and wikiHow as examples of online creative communities, Mayo Fuster (2010) has noted that the different types of governance of interactions between platform providers and creative communities are related to different conceptions of democratic decision-making. In her analysis of how activists use old and new technologies in an emancipatory way, Stefania Milan (2009) compared community radio and radical Internet projects, linking the repertoires of action, networking strategies, and organizational forms to the activists' motivations and ideological/cultural backgrounds, with particular attention to the normative meanings of internal democracy as well as relations with the users.

Similarly, research at the individual level also confirms the importance of political commitment in influencing the use (and type of use) of the Internet. Surveys of activists of the Global Justice Movement have in fact indicated that, while gender and education have no relation to the frequency and form of Internet use, the level of activism of the interviewees is, as the more mobilized population uses the Internet more intensively and in more innovative ways. The various uses of the Internet all increase with identification with the movement, multiple organizational memberships, participation in protest events, and the use of multiple forms of political participation (della Porta and Mosca 2005).

Summarizing: research on social movements with a focus on the mass media has developed some important observations on:

a   social movements' capacity for networking diversity
b   experimenting with different conceptions of democracy
c   intervening in various ways in politics
d   participating in various ways in media arenas
e   protest campaigns' ability to affect activists' perceptions of the media (Couldry 2000)
f   the normative rather than instrumental constraints that influence different social movements' uses of the media.

Conclusion

Democracy, media, and social movement studies have developed with relatively few links with each other. Recent challenges to representative conceptions of democracy create opportunities for reflecting on the role that social movements and their communication play in participatory and deliberative visions of democracy.

This may be done in two ways which build upon two different streams in research on social movements and communication practices. First, as far as research on the power of the media and their exclusionary practices toward social movements is concerned, we have to invest more in the conceptualization of a media field, in which different actors converge and contribute to news production. Second, as far as research on alternative media is concerned, we should systematically address social movements' visions of democracy and their effects on communicative practices.

Building upon some recent contributions in all three fields of study allows us to develop a view which is capable of:

a   taking into account the agency power of social movements in the construction of democracy and communications, rather than considering political and media institutions only as structural constraints
b   looking at the relations within the different fields of democracy, media and social movements that are strictly interwoven with each other

c　considering the way in which norms and visions affect the use of social
movements' (as well as other actors') strategies towards democratic institutions as well as communication fields.

Notes

1　This is the revised version of a keynote speech presented at the conference on *Networking Democracy? New Media Innovations in Participatory Politics*, Babeş-Bolyai University, Cluj, Romania, June 25–27, 2010. I'm grateful to the conference organizers
and participants for useful observations.
2　A social movement organization is traditionally defined as an organization that gathers
resources from the surrounding environment and allocates them in order to achieve the
social movement goals.

Part II
Participation dynamics
Intersections between social and
traditional media

4 Poverty in the news

A framing analysis of coverage in Canada and the United Kingdom

Joanna Redden

The United Kingdom and Canada have some of the highest rates of poverty and inequality among developed nations (Pasma 2010; Brewer *et al.* 2008; Yalnizyan 2007; Unicef 2007; Morissette and Zhang 2006; Babb 2005). These high levels have persisted throughout the periods of economic growth experienced in both nations over the last three decades and it is likely they will now increase as a result of the present economic climate (MacInnes *et al.* 2009; Oxfam 2009; Yalnizyan 2010, 2009). History demonstrates that definitions and political responses to poverty are bound up with the dominant social, political and economic ideas and practices of a time as evidenced by just a few examples: the incarceration of those with little or no money in workhouses in the nineteenth century in the United Kingdom and Canada, the expansion of supports for the unemployed after World War II, or the introduction of workfare in the 1990s in some provinces in Canada. How poverty is understood and is defined affects how pressing the issue is perceived to be, and what people choose to do or not do about it (Lister 2004; Jørgenson and Phillips 2002; Edelman 1977). As Lister argues, 'poverty' must be recognized as an always contested political concept because how it is understood influences the extent to which social action, through the redistribution of resources is necessary (2004). This chapter aims to provide some insight into contemporary definitions of poverty by identifying the frames that dominate mainstream news coverage in Canada and the United Kingdom and discussing their significance.

It has long been argued that the mass media 'limit the frames within which public issues are debated' (Gamson and Wolfsfeld 1993; Iyengar 1994; Gamson 2004; Snow and Benford 1992; Benford and Snow 2000; Ferree *et al.* 2002), and so 'narrow the available political alternatives' (Tuchman 1978, p. 156). Identifying the frames that dominate poverty coverage and thereby direct what poverty means is significant because many people, particularly when they have no direct experience with poverty, learn about it through the media (Park *et al.* 2007; Reutter *et al.* 2005, 2006). How the issue is framed affects whether or not responsibility is assigned to the individual or to wider social practices and circumstances (Iyengar 1994). Moreover, policy, political action and advocacy are often developed with the media in mind or as a response to media demands (Davis 2007a, 2007b, 2010b; Fenton 2010; Kuhn 2002; Golding and Middleton 1982).

Previous theorists (Bauman 1998; Gans 1995; Katz 1990) argue that in part Western societies do not do enough to address poverty because the issue is not presented in the mainstream media as a social problem with social solutions. They argue that those living on low income are most often stereotypically portrayed and blamed for their poverty. These concerns have been supported by a variety of analyses of poverty coverage in the United Kingdom, the United States and Canada (Golding and Middleton 1982; Kensicki 2004; Sotirovic 2001; Misra *et al.* 2003; Iyengar 1994; Bullock *et al.* 2001; Gilens 1999; de Goede 1996; McKendrick *et al.* 2008; Hackett *et al.* 1999). This chapter contributes to this previous research by identifying significant similarities in the frames that dominate mainstream news coverage (print and online) of poverty in Canada and the United Kingdom, and also by comparing mainstream news coverage to content on alternative news sites.

A framing approach is valuable when investigating poverty coverage because embedded in the approach is the recognition that the issue can be covered in multiple ways (Van Gorp 2007). Identifying dominant idea packages or frames in coverage provides an efficient way to quantify patterns and to quickly identify similarities and differences. As Kitzinger argues, the notion of framing is useful when investigating news content because it goes beyond the idea of bias and accounts for the fact that all representations are 'shaped in some way or other' (2007, p. 137). Frames, as Van Gorp argues (2007, p. 63) are part of a culture, they draw on shared codes or norms and invite people to read articles in a particular way. Of course individual interpretations will vary depending on the individual and his or her background.[1]

There have been no cross-national comparisons of poverty coverage. However, Canada and the UK are uniquely poised for comparison given their similar political and media models and the similar paths taken: in both nations post-World War II movements toward greater equality were largely halted with the advent of neoliberal policies and rhetoric (Walker and Walker 1997; Brandolini and Smeeding 2007; Cornia *et al.* 2004).

Poverty and constructions of a 'deserving' and 'undeserving poor'

Constructions of a 'deserving' and 'undeserving poor' have influenced what poverty means and approaches to the issue for centuries (see Lister 2004; Piven and Cloward 1997; Fraser and Gordon 1994; Katz 1990; Golding and Middleton 1982). It was decided at the outset that any attempt to investigate poverty coverage and its implications would need to capture coverage of groups typically represented as 'deserving' and 'undeserving'. In contemporary politics, news coverage and activism, children are often constructed into a group identified as the 'deserving poor'. In the 1980s many anti-poverty activists in Canada decided to focus on child poverty to strategically counter the dominant and pervasive neoliberal emphasis on individual responsibility (Wiegers 2007). In the UK the Child Poverty Action Group was established in 1965 to campaign to eliminate child poverty. In 1999 Tony Blair committed the then New Labour government to 'eradicate' child poverty by 2020. The target was enshrined in the Child Poverty Act of 2010. Although the Canadian Government has not set any poverty reduction targets, a New Democratic Party motion in 1989 to eliminate child poverty by 2000 was passed in the House of Commons with all-party support. Further, nearly every province and the territories have introduced poverty reduction strategies that at minimum address, if not outright target, child poverty. In Canada and Britain children are widely identified across the political spectrum as not being responsible for their plight. Seniors may be the only other group in both societies to be represented as frequently as the 'deserving poor'.

Choosing which type of group construction to analyse as representative of constructions of the 'undeserving poor' proved more challenging. In the end, the decision to focus on immigrants[2] as an example of 'undeserving poor' discourse was based on two factors. The first was the increasing focus and negative stereotyping of immigrants as a group to be blamed for the rising insecurities due to stagnating of wages, unemployment and cuts to social services as a result of global neoliberal restructuring (Sales 2007; Greenslade 2005; van Dijk 1989; Redden 2007). Throughout the 1990s and into the 2000s both Canadian and British governments have been changing their immigration legislation and policy, moving toward more 'selective admission' with an emphasis on attracting 'skilled immigrants' (Robinson 2010; Brown and Tannock 2009; Tannock 2009; Kofman *et al.* 2009; Bauder 2008; Arat-Koc 1999). The sometimes explicit but always implicit message underlying these changes has been that some immigrants (namely those identified as highly skilled) provide an economic benefit to their new country while others pose a 'burden' (Kofman *et al.* 2009; Bauder 2008; Tannock 2009). Two recent examples of this focus are the UK's 2008 implementation of the points-based system of immigration and the refinement of Canada's system in order to fast-track the entry of immigrants in select occupations. Both countries have also tightened and restricted the rights of those entering under 'lower' skill categories or temporary work categories; these individuals are not provided with the same rights to settle, gain citizenship or bring their families (Tannock 2009; Nakache and Kinoshita 2010). These policy changes codify deserving and undeserving categories of migrants, the highly skilled as deserving and the 'lower' skilled as undeserving. It was speculated at the outset of this investigation that focusing on news coverage when policy changes were implemented would provide a means to investigate if immigrants are being explicitly or implicitly constructed into an 'undeserving poor' group.

Second, immigrants, particularly recent immigrants, are one of the groups most affected by poverty in Canada and the UK (Hatfield 2004; Picot *et al.* 2008; Platt 2007). In the UK the child poverty rate for the majority is 14.6 per cent, while it is 23.3 per cent for children in minority and immigrant families (Smeeding *et al.* 2009). In Canada the child poverty rate for the majority is 13.7 per cent and 21.7 per cent for minority and immigrant families (ibid.). Immigrants who arrived in Canada after 1990 were more likely to live in poverty than those who arrived in the 1970s and 1980s (Picot and Sweetman 2005). This is despite both the fact that they were more educated than most Canadians and the economic upturn of the late 1990s that saw the overall unemployment rate drop from 9.4 per cent in 1995 to 6.8 per cent in 2000 (Fleury 2007). It is also despite changes in the immigration selection process in the 1990s to attract more skilled immigrants due to the perception that they were more likely to succeed in a knowledge-based economy. Research indicates that those entering under the skill-based category in recent years are more likely to suffer persistent poverty than those entering via the family stream category (Picot *et al.* 2008). Fleury concludes that 'recent immigrants to Canada face more employment barriers than other working-age Canadians' (2007, p. 43). The difficulties that new immigrants encounter have gotten worse more recently (Fleury 2007; Picot *et al.* 2008). The factors contributing to persistent poverty among skilled immigrants include a failure to recognize foreign credentials, demands for Canadian work experience and discrimination (Galabuzi 2006; Danso 2009).

In the UK there are large polarities in income between those from different countries of origin (Platt 2007). There has been a dramatic increase in the percentage of immigrants possessing 'high skills' and increased levels of education over the last 20 years but employment and wage outcomes differ (Dustan and Fabbri 2005). Kofman *et al.* (2009) note that many high-skilled migrants work in low-skilled and low-wage jobs. Dustmann and Fabbri (2005, p. 460) note that white immigrants have similar employment prospects and in fact higher wages than British-born whites with the same characteristics, non-white immigrants 'have, on average, lower employment probabilities' and lower wages. A range of factors, including discrimination, play a significant role (Platt 2007). Migrant men typically earn 30 per cent less and women typically earn 15 per cent less than their British-born counterparts. For migrant men it takes about 20 years to close the gap, while it takes women six years. Different nationalities experience different rates of catch-up with Europeans closing the gap quickest and Asian men not catching up at all (Dickens and McKnight 2008).

This chapter provides a framing analysis of the news content surrounding two similar events in Canada and the United Kingdom that were selected in order to capture coverage of child poverty and the 2008 immigration system changes mentioned above. The events selected are as similar as possible to enable a comparison of coverage: (1) Child poverty campaigns: Campaign 2000's release of its annual report on 21 November 2008 (Canada) and the Campaign to End Child Poverty protest held on 4 October 2008 (UK); (2) Immigration policy changes: the Canadian Conservative government's implementation on 28 November 2008 of policy changes designed to 'fast-track' skilled immigrants and the roll out of the UK government's new points-based system for immigration beginning 29 February 2008. News texts are selected for the two weeks before and after each event.

The research questions guiding the analysis are: What frames dominate poverty and immigration mainstream news coverage in Canada and the United Kingdom (online and offline)? Does a framing analysis of alternative news content provide insight into the ways in which mainstream news content is limited? The final section of the chapter discusses the results of this analysis and considers the implications of the findings.

Although the main objective is to provide an analysis of poverty and immigration coverage, the analysis of mainstream and alternative online news enables an assessment of the extent to which this coverage differs from print coverage. An appraisal of online news is both timely and relevant. While most people in Canada and the UK still rely on television as their main news source, more and more people are going online to supplement their news consumption (Statistics Canada 2010; Office of National Statistics 2009; Ofcom 2007; Zamaria and Fletcher 2008). Much of the hope that the Internet would revitalize democracy was in some way related to the fact that it provided seemingly endless space for content, thereby enabling mainstream news providers to deliver more in-depth, detailed pieces and more varied content (Bruns 2005; Pavlik 2001; Gunter 2003). This analysis indicates that any hoped-for revitalization of news is not, for the most part, happening within most mainstream news spaces.

Method

To ensure a representative sample, broadsheet press, tabloid and mid-range (present in UK only) sources were selected based on circulation, narrative type and readership. The broadsheet sources analysed for the UK include: *The Times* (centre-right) and *Guardian* (centre-left) (McNair 2009; Jones *et al.* 2007). The tabloid sources include those with the widest circulation: the *Sun* and the *Daily Mail* (Bednarek 2006).[3] Canadian sources include the only national papers: the *Globe and Mail* (centre-right) and the *National Post* (right-leaning) (Soderlund and Hildebrandt 2005). The *Toronto Sun* and the *Toronto Star* (left-leaning) were also selected as they represent the provincial broadsheet and tabloid with the widest circulations (Canadian Newspaper Association 2010). Articles from both print and online editions were analysed. In both nations, the public broadcasting websites for the CBC and the BBC are the most popular online nationally based news sites[4] and these are also analysed. The alternative news sites analysed include Rabble.ca[5] and Mostly Water[6] (Canada) and Indymedia[7] and Red Pepper[8] (UK). Rabble.ca and Red Pepper operate as online magazines. Mostly Water and Indymedia operate as continually updated news sites.

For mainstream print articles, the LexisNexis database was used to collect articles for the UK sample, and the Factiva database was used to collect articles for the Canadian sample. Mainstream news site search engines and alternative news search engines were also used to collect the online news sample.[9] The search term for the child poverty sample was 'poverty', and the search terms for the immigration sample were 'immigration' and then 'immigrant'. Only articles relating in some way to the Canadian or UK national context were selected for analysis.

Issues did arise in relying on databases and search engines to collect the sample. Collecting articles through databases like Factiva and LexisNexis means that analysis is limited to text, excluding any visuals. Relying on website search engines proved problematic for the *Globe and Mail*. The *Globe and Mail* site search engine provided access to stories that were published online, but any material that might have accompanied the story on the web page when originally posted was removed so it was impossible to determine what supplementary material might have been present when the stories were originally posted.

In total 1,561 mainstream news articles were analysed in my contemporary sample (Table 4.1).

Following Gamson and Modigliani's (1989) model, an initial survey of roughly half the articles was conducted to identify the frames appearing to dominate coverage, and to then count the presence or absence of these frames in the overall sample. The two most significant are individualizing and rationalizing frames. These are summarized below:

Individualizing Frame

Discourses of individual responsibility dominate coverage, and it can be argued are tapping into a master frame of liberal individualism which dominates all news coverage (König 2004). Coverage in the poverty sample is identified as being individualizing if poverty is presented as an individual's responsibility. As little mainstream immigration coverage focuses directly on poverty, coverage in the immigration sample is coded as individualizing if the article focuses on an individual as responsible for problems or solutions.

Rationalization Frame

Poverty is often discussed in reference to statistics and the cost of various programmes. In these cases poverty is presented as an issue to be evaluated based on quantification, calculation and cost-versus-benefit analysis. In immigration coverage, immigrants are often presented as a 'cost' or a 'benefit' to society in economic terms.

Table 4.1 Number of articles in mainstream news sample by organization

News organization	Poverty	Immigration
Canada		
Globe and Mail	57	72
Toronto Star	132	138
National Post	17	49
Toronto Sun	17	28
CBC News online	11	18
United Kingdom		
The Times	92	120
Guardian	176	218
Daily Mail	72	154
Sun	30	57
BBC News Online	41	62
Total	645	916

As previously mentioned, print content is compared to its online news counterpart to identify similarities or differences.

Although the number of articles sampled from alternative news sites is small, the content is strikingly different from mainstream news content and illustrative. The alternative news sample is comprised of UK content: Red Pepper 6 articles, Indymedia 10 articles. Canadian content comprises: Rabble.ca 29 articles, Mostly Water 11 articles. Coverage on these sites differs significantly in that rationalizing and individualizing frames do not dominate. An analysis of this content reveals the strong presence of social justice frames as summarized below:

Social Justice Frame
Poverty is framed in relation to quality of life and as a matter of rights in relation to equality of distribution or recognition (Fraser 1999). The need for collective action or response is often implicit or explicit.

All material was coded for the presence or absence of these three main frames. Further articles were qualitatively assessed to better understand how these frames are constructed, and to consider the implications of their presence or absence.

Findings: analysing contemporary news coverage

Rationalizing and individualizing frames dominate contemporary mainstream news coverage offline and online. In Canada and the UK online content most often mirrors offline content, and therefore there is little expansion of poverty discourses on mainstream news sites. These findings echo previous research that mainstream online news content differs little from offline print content (Tewksbury and Rittenberg 2009; Barnhurst 2002; Sparks *et al.* 2006; Hoffman 2006; Li 1998).

Rationalization

The dominance of rationalizing frames is evident in Table 4.2. Poverty is most often in the UK and very often in Canada presented as an issue to be evaluated and understood based on quantification, calculation and cost–benefit analysis (rationalizing frame). It is common for statistical breakdowns or quantifications, particularly in the case of child poverty, to be presented without any detailed discussion of the causes of poverty or arguments for its elimination. The measurement of poverty in much news coverage is thus presented in and of itself.

In Canada much coverage of child poverty focuses on government action or plans for action (during my sample period the Ontario Liberal Government released its poverty reduction strategy). In these stories the costs of proposals dominate, as the *Globe and Mail* article 'Liberals promise to lift 90,000 Ontario

Table 4.2 Percentage of articles in mainstream news coverage with rationalizing frames

News organization	Rationalizing frames
Canada	
Globe and Mail	47
Toronto Star	37
National Post	50
Toronto Sun	29
CBC News online	52
United Kingdom	
The Times	80
Guardian	58
Daily Mail	78
Sun	72
BBC News Online	84

children out of poverty' (4 December 2008) illustrates. The article begins by summarizing what the new strategy promises:

> $300 million in new initiatives, and commits the government to reducing the number of children living in poverty by 25 per cent over five years. It includes a $230 million annual increase in the provincial child benefit by the end of the five-year plan, which will provide up to $1,310 for each child in a low-income family. Another $10 million will fund an after-school program for children in high needs neighbourhoods.

The focus of this coverage, as in other articles, is not the proposals themselves, but the money being spent on them. The emphasis on cost is seldom followed with any discussion or rationale explaining the reasons behind the introduction of particular policies. The emphasis on cost provides an immediate indication that government is doing something, but little opportunity to consider why these actions are deemed necessary and if in fact they are adequate. An emphasis on cost also implicitly sets up a comparison: are the services worth the money? Relieving poverty then is associated with monetary value and not social value. Further, the numbers are presented without any historical context. Contextual information and discussion of the social value of action add urgency and build mass public support. The a-historicity and compressed style of news formats is often at the expense of context. This becomes a particular problem when governments step away from proposals, or say they are unaffordable, as the Ontario Liberal government at the time of writing (2011) has done in relation to aspects of its poverty reduction strategy.

As indicated, rationalizing frames are even more common in UK coverage. The BBC provides the most coverage of the End Child Poverty Campaign in my sample, but their article 'Child Poverty Ranked High in City' (30 September 2008) demonstrates the limitations of coverage when the focus is on numbers:

The Campaign to End Child Poverty report said 75 per cent of children in the Bradford West constituency were living in or close to poverty. It ranked eighth out of 174 constituencies, with the Ladywood area of Birmingham coming top at 81 per cent.... Arshad Hussain, Conservative councillor for Toller in Bradford West, said the figures were shocking. 'It is very disappointing to hear so many families in this area are struggling and certainly this issue needs to be looked at', he said.

This article places emphasis on the new numbers, the poverty statistics by constituency released by the End Child Poverty Campaign. These numbers meet news demands for something new and for easily reproducible facts. The numbers also adhere to news demands to present information in a compressed format.

The presentation of statistics in relation to poverty is in and of itself not a problem. Statistics can be used very effectively to detail just how pervasive poverty is. Activist organizations have been successful both in Canada and in the UK in getting media and political attention by quantifying the extent of the problem. The sheer size of the problem makes it an issue that is difficult for the media and politicians to ignore. New numbers also help make the issue 'new' and thus newsworthy. However, the extent to which child poverty numbers are reported without mention or limited discussion of the causes identified or the solutions activists are proposing presents a problem: without such discussion it is difficult to draw attention to and connect widespread problems with potential solutions.

In the UK there has been a relatively continuous process of measuring poverty since the beginning of the twentieth century with the work of Rowntree in 1901 and Booth in 1903 (Platt 2005). However, as history demonstrates, measurements do not dictate in any uniform way how poverty is addressed. For example, in 1834 measurements of poverty were used to justify the punishment and incarceration of those who were poor in workhouses through the Poor Law Amendment Act (ibid.). Yet, conversely, a number of social surveys quantifying poverty span the pre- and post-Second World War period, a period that saw the publication of the 1942 Beveridge Report. Although as some argue the report was not radically progressive, it demonstrates an assumption of social solidarity and collective action (Harris 1999), and did advocate full employment, universal family allowances, a free national health service and a unified flat-rate social insurance system for all classes (Abel-Smith 1992). By contrast, the doubling of poverty between 1979 and 1991 (Stewart 2005) did not lead Margaret Thatcher to view poverty and inequality as problems or change her embrace of neoliberalism (Platt 2005). The point these examples raise is that calculation and quantification of poverty alone do not influence policy, but rather the frames and ideological packages accompanying or attached to such forms of measurement influence how the meaning of poverty is constructed and what is done about it. The problem, to be discussed in greater detail, is that news reporting and its emphasis on 'facts', which really means an emphasis on numbers, lend themselves to market-based processes of evaluation.

In relation to immigration coverage, rationalizing frames are also consistently present but are of a different character. First, there is very little direct connection between immigration and poverty in the media content. In this the *Guardian* and the *Toronto Star* are exceptions, connected to their more detailed coverage on poverty discussed below. However, poverty does form the subtext of coverage that instrumentalizes migrants in relation to costs versus benefits. In Canada, immigration coverage focuses on how immigrants can benefit Canada's economy. In the UK immigration coverage focuses on the cost of migration/immigration.

The *National Post* article titled 'Immigration Levels to be Maintained' (29 November 2008) provides an illustrative and representative example of how the issue is presented in terms of both quantification and calculation, but also in relation to the economy. The article begins:

> Despite uncertain economic times, Ottawa announced plans yesterday for Canada to take in up to 265,000 new permanent residents in 2009 and to speed up the processing of applications for potential new Canadians in dozens of high-demand occupations.

In the opening four lines the writer of this article establishes on what terms these immigration changes should be viewed. Despite the various social justice and human rights-based arguments put forward by critics at this time, the argument against the new rules given most weight in the *Post* is an economic one, that current immigration levels are not advisable given the present economic downturn. Immigration is discussed solely in relation to jobs and the economic climate. It is very common in Canadian coverage, particularly in the *Globe* and the *Post*, for immigrants to be discussed in relation to business and business management. As immigrants are increasingly portrayed as valuable only on economic and labour grounds it becomes easy to present this group of people as a homogenous group, and once this is done it becomes even easier to attach defining characteristics to the created group. It must be noted that *Toronto Star* coverage of immigration is different in that in my sample there were a number of stories that focused on family experiences.[10] News coverage in relation to immigration is far more negative in the UK than it is in Canada, as considered in greater detail below. Migrants are often discussed in terms of their 'cost' to UK society particularly in the *Sun* and the *Daily Mail*.

Individualization

The extent to which poverty is presented as a matter of individual responsibility differs by news organization.

As evident in Table 4.3, poverty is presented as an individual responsibility in much mainstream news coverage. These frames often enter broadsheet coverage through the quotes of others, and in the case of the *Guardian* run counter to comment or opinion pieces published. There is far less coverage depicting individual responsibility in news content on the two public broadcasting sites and in

Table 4.3 Percentage of articles presenting poverty as an individual's responsibility

News organization	Individual responsibility
Canada	
Globe and Mail	54
Toronto Star	18
National Post	59
Toronto Sun	41
CBC News online	6
United Kingdom	
The Times	30
Guardian	26
Daily Mail	40
Sun	30
BBC News Online	17

the *Toronto Star*. Individualizing frames do a great deal of affective work through drawing on longstanding stereotypes,[11] and particularly when linked to underclass depictions of those on low income, or those who are migrants.

In the Canadian poverty sample there are more depictions of the poor as an 'underclass' than in the UK sample as indicated in Table 4.4. In Canada, 'underclass' depictions are referenced through portrayals of the poor in relation to crime, addiction and laziness, or descriptions of where the poor live as undesirable and unsafe.

It is much more common for underclass depictions to be present in relation to migrants in the UK than in Canada as indicated in Table 4.5.

The discursive construction of migrants as an 'underclass' is different from the construction Katz (1990) identifies in American poverty coverage in the 1980s. While migrants can also be depicted as lazy, criminal or morally corrupt, most often in UK tabloid coverage they are constructed as an underclass through

Table 4.4 Percentage of articles presenting 'underclass' depictions of the poor

News organization	Underclass depictions
Canada	
Globe and Mail	33
Toronto Star	11
National Post	29
Toronto Sun	29
CBC News online	18
United Kingdom	
The Times	19
Guardian	12
Daily Mail	15
Sun	33
BBC News Online	7

Table 4.5 Percentage of articles presenting underclass depictions of migrants

News organization	Underclass depictions
Canada	
Globe and Mail	8
Toronto Star	6
National Post	8
Toronto Sun	32
CBC News online	5
United Kingdom	
The Times	37
Guardian	18
Daily Mail	61
Sun	67
BBC News Online	21

suggestions that they refuse to integrate or are linked to extremism, and through being identified as 'illegal'. There are clear links being made in coverage between class and immigration. These depictions are not making reference to white-collar workers nor are they the immigrants both Canadian and UK governments are referring to when they speak of 'skilled immigrants', the doctors, nurses, and entrepreneurs both countries are trying to recruit. Rather, they link depictions of an 'undeserving poor' to migrants in a slightly altered form as people who are depicted as costing the UK money and taking advantage of social services. The fact that research demonstrates the opposite is the case (Dustmann *et al.* 2009) seems to have little influence on this type of coverage.

Underclass depictions often enter coverage through the quotes or arguments of others, particularly politicians. In this way UK immigration coverage is unique in that much negative coverage of the issue is related to a political comment or event. To illustrate, in the *Guardian* article titled 'National: Cultural Sensitivity Putting Rights at Risk, Warns Cameron' (27 February 2008), negative portrayals come via Cameron's statements. This article quotes Cameron's speech, in which he argues that a 'cultural cloak of sensitivity' is preventing figures in authority from protecting basic human rights for fear of upsetting ethnic minority communities. The article reads:

> Cameron said: 'For too long we've caved in to more extreme elements by hiding under the cloak of cultural sensitivity. For too long we've given in to the loudest voices from each community, without listening to what the majority want. And for too long, we've come to ignore differences – even if they fly in the face of human rights, notions of equality and child protection – with a hapless shrug of the shoulders, saying, "It's their culture isn't it? Let them do what they want".'

In this article Cameron portrays all immigrants negatively through his very broad generalizations. He uses the term 'extreme', which connotes ideas of terrorism.

He turns to two specific cases in his speech as examples that in effect stand in for all immigrant families and generate images of these families as behaving violently. In this way an 'us' and 'them' divide is generated. The divide is further generated by the opposition created through Cameron's implication of conflict through the phrase 'we've caved in'. In effect, immigrants in Cameron's language are presented here as threatening human rights, notions of equality and child protection in the UK.

Throughout much UK tabloid coverage immigrants and migrants are presented as the source of Britain's problems, as in the *Daily Mail* article 'What's the Point of Citizenship Classes When We've Already Surrendered Our National Identity' (10 March 2008). Immigrants in this article, particularly Muslim women and men, are 'othered' through their presentation as polygamous and as a threat to British identity and to social services.

> Unlike America, many immigrants come to Britain not to make money but because they are attracted by the welfare state upon which they become instantly dependent.
>
> Indeed, the welfare state has itself eroded the bonds of duty that underpin true citizenship...
>
> Things like mass immigration which must be stopped; multiculturalism which must be abandoned; human rights law which must be abolished; the welfare state which must be remodelled; and membership of the EU which must be renegotiated.
>
> There are growing signs that David Cameron recognises at least some of this.
>
> If he can summon up the courage to take this agenda and run with it, he will find not only that he speaks for the nation he may save it.

In this article we see the isolation of immigrants as the source of Britain's problems. Muslim women and men are particularly targeted as a threat and a drain on the system. The solution to the 'problems' identified as facing Britain is presented in the guise of David Cameron who is presented as a hero figure able to 'fix' everything.

Online news potentials

While rationalizing and individualizing frames dominate online and offline content, there is some noteworthy online content that speaks to web potentials. The *Toronto Star*, the *Guardian*, the BBC and the CBC all provide valuable supplementary material in some cases in my sample. It is significant that three of these are not private business enterprises: the BBC and CBC are public broadcasters and the *Guardian* must operate commercially but is owned by a foundation and funded by the Scott Trust. The *Toronto Star*'s coverage is tied to the paper's anti-poverty advocacy during my period of analysis through its 'War on Poverty' series and accompanying web page which now no longer exists. All of these sites would often supplement stories with video, audio, backgrounders, factsheets or links to external groups and reports. The addition of this material did at times demonstrate how space could be used to add density to coverage. The significance of this content is that it is static, still available (with the exception of the *Star* page), and therefore can be used as a resource in ways that newsprint publications or broadcasts cannot, given the ease of Internet access.

Social justice

Content on alternative news sites counters and challenges much mainstream news coverage. As indicated in Table 4.6, almost all alternative news content presents information in reference to social justice and rights-based discourse. Among mainstream news sites, the *Guardian*, the *Toronto Star*, the CBC and the BBC are unique in providing larger percentages of content with social justice frames. Roughly a quarter of articles in the *Guardian* and the *Toronto Star* present social justice frames. This is linked to the structural commitments of both news organizations to cover poverty; both had far more poverty content in my sample than any other news sites and interviews with staff at both organizations reveal they dedicate reporters specifically to covering poverty and inequality.

How social justice is presented across alternative media does differ but overall the idea presented is that everyone should be treated fairly and equally and should share in the benefits of society. Social justice frames are often bound together with critiques of capitalism.

Missing from most mainstream news coverage of poverty is capitalism critique and the role of the present economic system in generating poverty.[12] Such

Table 4.6 Percentage of articles in mainstream and alternative coverage with social justice frames

News organization	Social justice frames
Canada	
Rabble.ca	72
Mostly Water	100
Globe and Mail	11
Toronto Star	23
National Post	14
Toronto Sun	13
CBC News online	21
United Kingdom	
Red Pepper	67
IndyMedia	90
The Times	9
Guardian	26
Daily Mail	1
Sun	1
BBC News Online	15

critiques are strongly present in the alternative news content analyzed. In the Red Pepper article 'The Irresponsibility of the Rich' (August/September 2008) Lister calls for a need to change contemporary approaches to the issue and the terms of debate.

> One reason for New Labour's timidity is that even those who subscribe to a more egalitarian agenda fear that it will alienate the electorate.... If even a Labour government is not prepared to make the case for redistribution, then perhaps the public comes to believe the case is a weak one and that government does not have a legitimate role to play in narrowing the gap.
> If that is what has happened, then one of our main challenges is how to change the terms of the public debate and make the case for tackling inequality.

In this article Lister identifies the terms of debate as a key battleground in any attempt to reduce poverty. The article also explicitly connects inequality and poverty. Critiques of the levels of poverty and inequality in the UK are tied to a critique of government and how it has approached the problem. Poverty and inequality are put into social, political, economic and historical context. Further, through identifying government economic policies as fuelling inequality a specific causal factor is identified.

The Rabble article 'Free Markets Fail' provides a direct critique of the present economic system. The limited mainstream news coverage linking poverty to the economic crisis in my sample would often present the crisis as limiting the potential and resources of governments to address poverty. This article provides a different perspective and argues that the economic crisis demonstrates the danger in relying solely on markets:

> For proponents of market economics, rooting out market imperfections such as trade unions, unemployment insurance and welfare payments, and relying on flexible wages instead was thought not only to cure unemployment, but in its wildest expression, say in the *National Post*, to provide a living wage as well. Except that falling rates of industrial unionism, and a weakened social safety net, increased inequalities, not to speak of re-introduced begging on the streets and widespread homelessness.
> ...The market does not abolish power relationships: it facilitates the accumulation of market power in fewer and fewer corporate hands.
>
> (Cameron 2008)

Cameron echoes the argument put forward by many critics of neoliberalism, namely that attacks on trade unionism in addition to cuts to employment insurance and other social services have resulted in higher rates of poverty and inequality (Harvey 2007; Bashevkin 2002; Finkel 2006). In very few words Cameron provides some historical context and identifies specific policy changes as being causal factors in poverty.

Unique in Indymedia coverage in my sample is its attention to companies that are profiting from the UK government's practice of detaining asylum seekers. In portraying asylum seekers as being exploited by a profiteering system of detention and deportation, this coverage counters *Daily Mail* and *Sun* coverage in particular.

This brief analysis provides ample indication of how poverty and immigration on these sites are discussed largely with reference to social justice and rights. Issues and events are also very often contextualized, with critiques of capitalism common. Alternative news in this way can be viewed as critical media which in effect present, as argued by Fuchs (2010), suppressed possibilities. However, the ability to communicate does not necessarily lead to political influence (Dean 2009). While alternative news sites and advocacy sites do provide significant tools and resources for activists and others to organize and share information (Bennett 2003; Fenton 2008), the news sites in particular are not easily accessed unless individuals know where to find them or are not already viewing alternative publications that provide links to these sites. Further, these sites do not often show up on the first or second pages of Google results, limiting their potential reach. Neither Rabble, Mostly Water, Red Pepper or Indymedia turn up in the first ten pages of Google.ca or Google.co.uk searches using the keyword 'poverty'.[13] This is significant given the dominance of Google in Canada and the UK, and previous research in the United States and in Europe indicating that most Internet users do not venture beyond the first page of search results (Jansen and Spink 2005, 2006).

Discussion of findings

Mainstream Canadian and UK coverage of child poverty and immigration are dominated by rationalizing and individualizing frames. In contemporary news coverage frames that rationalize package discussions in terms of quantification, calculation, cost–benefit analysis and instrumental reason. Frames that individualize package issues in relation to discussions that isolate specific individuals and groups, avoid thematic discussions, while also employing depictions that blame or place responsibility for poverty on the individual. The latter is unsurprising and supports previous analysis of poverty coverage in the United States (Iyengar 1994; Gilens 1999; Misra *et al.* 2003) and the UK (Golding and Middleton 1982; McKendrick *et al.* 2008). The former has not been discussed in this poverty research. Rationalizing frames are most common in coverage where 'the poor' being discussed are portrayed as deserving, or in immigration coverage where immigrants are discussed in terms of economic cost or benefit. Individualizing frames are most common in coverage where blame or responsibility is being ascribed, or where the focus is on politics. The dominance of these frames can in part be explained by their congruence with news norms, in particular, news demands for facticity – largely numbers which give the appearance of being scientistic, precise and accurate; the journalistic emphasis on immediacy; the fact that the news must be new; the compressed style of information, which, when combined with the requirement of 'newness', lends itself to a-historicity; and the tendency to personalize stories as a method of engagement and narrative tool (Tuchman 1978; Bell 1991; Hall 1993; Knight 1998; Schudson 2003).

But what is the political significance of the dominance of these frames? I would like to suggest that both facilitate and reinforce market-based processes of evaluation and representation, that these frames privilege neoliberal rationalization and approaches to these issues (Foucault 2008; Lemke 2001; Brown 2005; Couldry 2010). My suggestion is *not* that each article fully presents or for that matter embraces neoliberal ideology. Instead, news articles bit by bit reinforce market values by reinforcing market-based processes of evaluation and schema of thought by privileging individualizing and rationalizing frames in the representations of poverty and immigration. In this way neoliberal rationality becomes a part of culture and gets embedded in daily life, to draw on Couldry's idea (2010), as market-based approaches to issues become 'normal' and 'rational'.

Poverty, particularly child poverty, may remain an object of attention and continual discussion, but when viewed through market-based criteria the issue is transformed into one that revolves around targets, the cost versus benefits of government action in economic terms and not in terms of social or human value or rights. Ongoing presentations of poverty in the news in terms of market criteria facilitate viewing the issue in terms of individuals and individual responsibility, a view that is easily shifted to blame, as evidenced by the fact that the only poverty seeming to warrant collective response now is child poverty. There is a 'surface of transfer' (Senellart 2008, p. 330): while people may continually talk about poverty in market terms they are not actually engaging in discussions that pinpoint the causes of such high levels of poverty and inequality in Canada and the UK. For example, the identification of and responses to poverty reduction targets suggest that poverty is being dealt with, while the actual causes of poverty such as the continual drive for lower wages and increasing job insecurity (MacInnes *et al.* 2009; Ferrie *et al.* 1999; Raphael 2007) remain unaddressed. In relation to immigration there is a valuing of humans purely in terms of economics, the economic value migrants bring to their new country. An ongoing practice of viewing humans in this manner implicitly renders undeserving and potentially a threat all those perceived not to possess the skills needed to meet economic expectations, such as asylum seekers and 'unskilled' migrants. Market-based thinking in these ways presents a short-cut with economic cost versus justice, for example, becoming the first principle and practice of evaluation when determining issue meaning, significance, whether or not to act, and how to act.

Conclusion

These findings support the view that changing problematic representations and approaches to poverty and immigration which blame the individual and marginalize the structural causes of poverty require much more than trying to ensure the media provide more positive images of poverty (Mooney 2010). Analysis of alternative news content demonstrates the extent to which social justice frames are missing from much mainstream poverty and immigration coverage. When social justice frames are combined with an emphasis on context and social and political critique the focus shifts to systems and structures leading to inequality, and not to individuals as objects for blame. Anti-poverty activists and advocacy organizations such as the Joseph Rowntree Foundation and Campaign 2000 are advancing these arguments in their work. Increasing and expanding the presentation of these arguments and social justice frames within mainstream news coverage would present a challenge to market-based approaches to the issues.

More historical, social, political and economic context is needed in poverty coverage. This argument is put forward with full awareness that such coverage requires structural changes and investment at a time when there are *fewer* journalists in Canada and the UK doing *more* given ongoing cuts to newsrooms in both countries and increased new media demands (Lee-Wright 2010, Phillips 2010, Curran 2010, Waddell 2009). However, my results show that a news organization's structural commitments, and the space and time devoted to poverty coverage influence content. For example the *Toronto Star* and the *Guardian*, devote significant resources to poverty coverage. The BBC and the CBC, as mentioned above, take added steps to enhance online coverage. All are less likely to publish articles that place responsibility for dealing with poverty on the individual, and more likely to present coverage within social justice frames. One way of addressing the shortcomings in poverty reporting in the UK and Canada would be to designate reporters to a poverty beat, though this would require widespread public interest in the issue, and so would be likely to follow and not precede the success of an anti-poverty campaign, and market-driven news organizations are unlikely to see such a move as attracting advertisers. Nevertheless there is some precedent. Following the release of statistics indicating that millions of Canadians were living in poverty in 1968, and the establishment of a Royal Commission to investigate the issue, a number of newspapers across the country established poverty beats and devoted reporters specifically to cover poverty. The result, argues the National Council of Welfare in its 1973 report, was enhanced coverage that focused on the issues and not 'the myths'. This precedent reflects the benefit of structural change. If you devote a journalist to an issue and provide the needed resources, namely the time to generate specialist knowledge on the issue, this will reflect how often the issue is covered and most crucially how it is covered. Given the extent to which media coverage influences political action (Davis 2010a, 2010b; Meyer 2002; Soroka 2002a, 2002b), it is also highly likely that having reporters regularly generating well-informed coverage will lead to more political action on the issue.

History also demonstrates the influence a more radicalized mass media institution can have. The *Toronto Star*'s 'War on Poverty' series (2007–2008) did succeed in drawing political attention to the issue. Although the series has ended, it points to the significant role a news organization can play when it takes on a sustained advocacy position. More directly, the radical press of the nineteenth century did lead to 'cultural reorganization and political mobilization of the working class during the first half of the nineteenth century' (Curran 1998, p. 225; 2003b). Key are Curran's observations that the radical press aided in the institutional development of the working-class movement by publicizing meetings and activities, conferring status on movement organizers by reporting them and their actions, and by giving a national direction to 'working-class agitation' (Curran 1998, p. 225). Activists are using alternative media and new technologies to inform each other about events and activities; the challenge is that, unlike the radical press of this earlier period, they do not have a mass audience. Without a mass audience it is impossible to 'disrupt' ongoing problematic representations and direct agitation in a national direction, which effectively means targeting and changing institutions, policies and practices.

Notes

1 Individual interpretation depends on a range of factors including degree of attention, interests, beliefs, experiences, desires and attitudes (Van Gorp 2007, p. 63).
2 While the focus of this study is on news coverage of immigrants, given the political and media mixing of discussions of immigrants, migrant workers, asylum seekers and refugees, it is impossible to discuss news coverage of immigrants in isolation from these other groups. As noted by Gabrielatos and Baker (2008), who analysed UK press coverage from 1996 and 2005, in media coverage there is often confusion and conflation of the four terms.
3 Bednarek (2006) notes that given the change in formats of broadsheet papers to be more similar to tabloid formats it may be more useful to categorize the two groups as popular press and quality press. She also outlines some significant differences in readership demographics: the tabloids vastly outsell the broadsheets, the broadsheets draw most readers from the middle classes. Jones *et al.* (2007) note that the tabloids have a majority working-class readership.
4 Based on Alexa.com search, 25 January 2011.
5 Rabble.ca ranks 5,620 on Alexa.com, and has 1,165 sites linking in (Alexa.com, September 2010). It averages 130,000 unique visitors per month.
6 MostlyWater has been online since 2004 and grew out of the resist.ca newsfeed. In Canada the site is ranked 71,193 and 292 sites link to Mostly Water (Alexa.com).
7 Of the sites analysed Indymedia is the most studied (just several examples: Hoofd 2009; Pickard 2006; Platon and Deuze 2003; Kidd 2002). The first Indymedia Center and site were started in 1999 in Seattle to cover protests against the World Trade Organization. There were more than 150 Independent Media Centers around the world when last counted (Indymedia 2007). Recent figures indicate that the indymedia.org site gets about 100,000 page views a day, with the Indymedia sites as a whole estimated to get between 500,000 to two million page views a day worldwide (Indymedia 2007).
8 Red Pepper has been online since 1995 and is ranked 121,585 in the UK (Alexa.com, September 2010). There are 588 sites that link to Red Pepper.
9 The exception is Red Pepper, which publishes bi-monthly, and so for the immigration analysis content it was analysed from the December/January 2008 and February/ March 2008 issues in order to have a sample of at least three articles. The poverty content was sampled from the August/September 2008 issue.
10 The *Toronto Star* often presented stories from the perspective of immigrant families, in relation to immigrants and refugees seeking political or policy changes. For example, 'The Trauma of Raising Kids an Ocean Away' (15 November 2008), 'A Mother's Tale Seen Through Eyes of Adversity' (24 November 2008), 'Immigrants

Saving for Education Study Finds' (24 November 2008), and 'Joblessness a Double Blow for Immigrant Family' (1 December 2008) all focus on family challenges and so broaden depictions of immigrants beyond notions of workers/labour.

11 For an historical overview of the roots of contemporary poverty discourses see Lister 2004, pp. 99–123; Golding and Middleton 1982, pp. 6–56; Fraser and Gordon 1994; Katz 1990; Piven and Cloward 1997.

12 It must be noted that Polly Toynbee's coverage of the End Child Poverty Campaign report and march entitled 'In the Face of the Apocalypse, Heed not Horsemen's Advice' (Toynbee 2008) was unique in my sample and indicates that coverage could be different. In this 'Comment Is Free' piece Toynbee connects the campaign to a critique of the economic crisis and political responses to it as not heavy-handed enough. She urges Brown and New Labour in the time left before the election to restore fairness by readjusting tax rates to ensure the rich pay more and the poor pay less. The article is an important one to raise as an example because it serves as a reminder that discourses do not operate within sealed environments. Instead, as Atton (2002) observes, there is a complexity of relations between radical and mainstream media and overlap is apparent when ideological perspectives are shared.

13 Search conducted 6 May 2009 and 5 July 2010.

5 The news media as networked political actors

How Italian media are reclaiming political ground by harnessing online participation

Cristian Vaccari

Introduction

The impact of information and communication technologies (ICTs) on Italian politics has followed a peculiar route by comparison with other Western democracies. The combination of a mass media system historically intertwined with politics (Hallin and Mancini 2004, pp. 89–142; Marletti and Roncarolo 2000; Roncarolo 2002) and the supremacy on television of the centre-right leader and current Prime Minister Silvio Berlusconi (Grandi and Vaccari 2009) creates opportunities for oppositional movements and political entrepreneurs to take advantage of online tools for engaging citizens. As the right dominates on television, which is the medium through which most Italians acquire political information (Legnante 2007), the left has an incentive to create alternative competitive advantages in digital media and interpersonal communication (Campus *et al.* 2008).

Italian parties, however, have generally been slow and cautious in harnessing the participatory potential of the Internet (Vaccari 2008), particularly because party bureaucracies have been reluctant to cede control over message production and distribution. Moreover, low Internet penetration has provided little encouragement to prospective innovators: according to Eurostat, in 2009 just 52 per cent of Italian households had Internet access, significantly fewer than the 65 per cent European Union average; only 42 per cent of the Italian population went online at least once a week, as opposed to 60 per cent in the EU; finally, whereas 29 per cent of European citizens had interacted with public authorities online in the previous three months, only 17 per cent of Italians had (Eurostat 2010). On the other hand. non-institutional actors such as social movements (Mosca 2010) and the popular comedian-turned-anti-politician Beppe Grillo (Vaccari 2009) have been more innovative and successful in fostering online engagement.

Recently, however, a new wave of participatory efforts has been sparked by a different type of institutional actors – mainstream mass media and, specifically, politically oriented newspapers and television personalities. In particular, *La Repubblica*, Italy's second largest newspaper (whose circulation amounted to slightly less than 500,000 in 2009)[1] and most popular news website (with over

1.3 million unique daily visitors as of March 2010),[2] began in 2009 to collect signatures for online petitions to protest against initiatives by the Berlusconi government, a strategy soon imitated by right-leaning newspapers. Online petitions have become important components in the repertoires of collective action of civil society actors, social movements, political institutions and campaign organizations (for an overview, see Mosca and Santucci 2009), but their use by news organizations to pursue political causes constitutes a significant innovation.

On television, the most popular progressive talk-show host, Michele Santoro, took advantage of media convergence to publicize and broadcast a protest rally against parliamentary regulations that had prompted public broadcasting company RAI to temporarily cancel Santoro's programme, *Annozero*, the most followed political talk show in Italy, in the month before the regional elections of 28–29 March 2010. Digital media were harnessed to organize the rally, to spread the word about it, to raise funds for it and to allow citizens to watch the event live. Thus, a prominent member of the media elite relied on digital media to bypass television's filter, a practice that is common among social movements and fringe parties but quite unusual for journalists.

In this chapter, we will provide an in-depth analysis of these two cases in order to show that digital media have allowed an expansion in the repertoires of collective action (Tilly 1978) not only of political parties, social movements and interest groups, as noted by Chadwick (2007), but also of news media organizations and personalities *to the extent that they are characterized by political parallelism*. Originally developed with respect to the press by Seymour-Ure (1974), media political parallelism has been defined by Hallin and Mancini as 'the degree to which the structure of the media system parallel[s] that of the party system' (2004, p. 27). Although the strongest manifestation of parallelism occurs 'when each news organization is aligned with a particular party', contemporary news organizations more commonly side 'with general political tendencies' rather than specific parties (ibid.). Media–politics parallelism can be observed in media content, organizational connections between media and parties or other political entities, partisanship of media audiences and journalistic role orientations and practices (p. 28). The argument that we will develop through our case studies of Italy is that if news organizations or personalities engage in political parallelism, then they can be expected to take advantage of online participation by their supportive audiences to achieve political goals, similarly to political actors.

The case of Italy is a particularly good example of parallelism between media and politics. A study based on 1999 data ranked Italy first among 15 European countries in terms of television–party parallelism, fourth in press–party parallelism and second in the combined index of media–party parallelism (Van Kempen 2007, p. 310). Thus, studying Italy allows us to observe how political parallelism affects the mainstream media's online endeavours in a context where such parallelism is particularly strong. That said, our case studies are also valuable in comparative perspective because political parallelism is by no means a unique characteristic of the Italian media system. On the contrary, it can be found in other Mediterranean and polarized pluralist countries (Hallin and Mancini 2004, pp. 90–124) and is not uncommon in other types of media systems: for instance, in the press of northern European or democratic corporatist countries (ibid., pp. 178–183) and among some key players in North Atlantic or liberal countries, such as the British press (ibid., pp. 210–213) and American cable news channels, blogs and talk radio (Davis and Owen 1998; Baum and Groeling 2008). Thus, because media political parallelism is widespread among Western democracies, the dynamics that we will identify in our Italian case studies can be generalized to other Western democracies to the extent that parts of their media systems exhibit a certain degree of political parallelism.

Our argument will be developed as follows: in the next section, we will summarize the transformations of political organizations fostered by digital media and the main characteristics of the Italian media system. In the two following sections, we will then analyse our cases – *La Repubblica*'s online petitions and Santoro's assemblage of a convergent network to broadcast his rally – in order to provide an in-depth description and interpretation of how two prominent politically engaged media actors employed digital media to mobilize their supporters in pursuit of their political battles. In the concluding section, we will summarize our findings, present a critical discussion of these phenomena, and suggest some implications for future research.

Literature review: changing forms of political organization in a polarized pluralist media system

Research on Internet politics has recently begun to address the changes brought about by ICTs in the distribution of power, resources and opportunities for collective action among various types of political organizations. In particular, Chadwick has highlighted that 'the Internet, by creating an environment where rapid institutional adaptation and experimentation is almost routine, encourages "organizational hybridity"' (2007, p. 284). Digital media increasingly enable political actors to integrate and move flexibly among various types of organizational repertoires, so that entities as different as parties, movements and interest groups now share similar online mobilization practices. To account for these organizational varieties, Flanagin *et al.* (2006) have proposed the concept of a 'collective action space' organized around two axes: one contrasts personal modes of interaction (i.e. with direct contact and development of relationships) with impersonal ones (i.e. with no interaction among participants); the other distinguishes between entrepreneurial modes of engagement (i.e. spontaneously activated) and institutional ones (i.e. bureaucratically controlled). Digital networks help organizations accommodate both personal and impersonal interactions among their members and promote both institutional and entrepreneurial endeavours. The US-based movement MoveOn.org is probably the most successful example of this new type of hybrid political organization, as it can quickly switch between different operational modes depending on context, opportunities and resources (Karpf 2009). Such hybrid organizations have peculiar features and potentially significant political implications: according to Chadwick (2007), they create appealing forms of participation that integrate online and offline endeavours, foster horizontal trust among citizens and groups, fuse subcultural and political discourses, and create and expand lasting relational networks. These developments might result in an opening up of hierarchical political organizations towards what Bimber (2003) has called 'post-bureaucratic' forms of engagement, or they might be confined to peripheral facets of organizations, so that power-holders remain sealed off from bottom-up pressures (Chadwick 2007, p. 297).

Whereas most of the literature on the organizational implications of digital network repertoires of collective actions has focused on parties, candidates, interest groups and social movements, little consideration has been given to the possibility that the mainstream news media may also take advantage of digital repertoires of engagement in a way that resembles that of other political actors.

This situation might be especially likely in countries such as Italy, where the relationship between politics and the media has historically been characterized by a strong degree of media–party parallelism and journalism has been more oriented towards commentary than factual reporting, resulting in external rather than internal pluralism, weak professionalism and exploitation of the news media by political elites (Hallin and Mancini 2004). Both print and broadcast media in Italy have been characterized by subordination to parties and interest groups seeking to wield political influence. When, between the 1970s and the 1980s, the parties' grip on Italian society declined and the public broadcasting monopoly on television was broken, spurring a process of commercialization that also involved the press, a new style of adversarial journalism was pioneered by the newspaper *La Repubblica*. Founded in 1976, it explicitly aimed at achieving political goals independently from parties, as its founder Eugenio Scalfari stated in the first issue: 'This newspaper ... doesn't pretend to follow an illusory political neutrality, but declares explicitly that it has taken a side in the political battle. It is made by men who belong to the vast arc of the Italian left' (quoted in Hallin and Mancini 2004, p. 101). *La Repubblica* initially aimed at breaking down the fault lines that kept Italian politics polarized between Communists and Christian-Democrats, thus hoping to dismantle the polarized pluralist party system that made alternation in government impossible (Sartori 1976, pp. 116–128). After realizing that this goal was unattainable, the newspaper changed its mission and 'became an important channel of communication within the established system, enhancing the ability of the political elite to interact and communicate with one another' (Marletti and Roncarolo 2000, p. 216). To achieve this objective, *La Repubblica* pioneered a particular type of interpretive journalism that focused on 'backstage' reporting and openly suggested political and electoral strategies to be adopted by the parties on the left. Soon this activist stance was imitated by many other news organizations and journalists, as this style allowed them to assert their autonomy by fighting political battles directly and independently rather than as party mouthpieces. Following *La Repubblica*'s lead, Italian journalists thus affirmed a peculiar form of professional independence, expressed as 'the right – but also the duty – to hold a position in the political debate, openly siding with one side (not necessarily a party), one way of thinking, one mood' (Roncarolo 2002, p. 75).

A similar pattern can be observed in television journalism. Italy's broadcasting policy has historically been characterized by 'the heavy use of television as a political battleground' (Mazzoleni 2000, p. 161). Parties and broadcasters, both public and private, have been entangled in a web of mutual relationships and commitments. In the 1970s, the breakup of public monopoly and the birth of commercial television had the potential to depoliticize the system, but the emergence of Silvio Berlusconi's three-channel national conglomerate as the only private competitor to the three-channel public broadcasting corporation created the conditions for further politicization. In the 1980s, Berlusconi's channels openly supported the Italian Socialist Party, whose leader Bettino Craxi crucially helped legalize the enterprise; subsequently, the media tycoon's decision to found a political party in 1994 and his ascent as leader of the centre-right coalition magnified the political role of television, as he heavily employed it to build and sustain consensus. Moreover, television journalists also embraced the new politicized style that part of the press underwent, especially in talk shows, which 'typically have clear orientations and offer journalists the opportunity to engage in active commentary that is usually not possible on news broadcasts' (Hallin and Mancini 2004, p. 109). These programmes have become quite successful and their presenters have achieved high popularity, which has elevated them to the status of authoritative political spokespersons. In the last decade, the best-known political talk-show host has been Michele Santoro, who is the subject of our second case study.

The peculiar degree of political parallelism of the Italian mainstream news media creates incentives for them to take advantage of the enlarged repertoires of collective political action fostered by digital media. In the past, Italian news media had only indirect, although by no means ineffective, ways to influence parties and institutions, such as voicing some viewpoints more than others, setting the agenda and attempting to lead public opinion on particular issues. By contrast, the web now allows the news media to directly engage their publics in collective action to exert pressure on parties and institutions. Our hypothesis, thus, is that the new political communication environment, and in particular the possibility to promote participation through Internet-based hybrid repertoires, has enabled those news organizations and personalities that engage in political parallelism to adopt mobilization techniques and organizational arrangements similar to those employed by political parties, interest groups and social movements. The case studies that we will discuss will help develop and specify this hypothesis.

La Repubblica's e-petition campaigns

On 28 April 2009, in the run-up to the European Parliament elections of 6–7 June, *La Repubblica* wrote that Prime Minister Berlusconi had attended a party in Casoria (near Naples) for the eighteenth birthday of a girl named Noemi Letizia. On the day the scoop was published, Berlusconi's wife, Veronica Lario, claimed in an interview that she was surprised to hear that his husband had attended the party, as he had failed to do so for all of his own children. Mrs Lario also claimed that Berlusconi's rumoured plan to select some attractive young women to prop up his party electoral lists was 'shameless rubbish'; ultimately, less than a week after the scandal erupted, she filed for divorce. The controversy was one of the dominant issues in the media during the campaign and was further ignited by Berlusconi's choice to go on a popular television talk show, *Porta a Porta*, to defend himself from accusations of misconduct. As not all aspects of the relationship between Berlusconi and Miss Letizia had been clarified, on 14 May 2009 *La Repubblica* published ten unanswered questions for Berlusconi, which probed his relationship with Letizia and also his criteria for selecting female candidates and the state of his mental health, as his wife had hinted he was suffering from compulsive sex addiction. As Berlusconi failed to answer the questions in a way that *La Repubblica* found satisfactory, the newspaper reprinted them every day. Subsequently, a new scandal erupted on 17 June, when *Il Corriere della Sera*, Italy's most circulated newspaper, wrote that Patrizia D'Addario, a woman who had been selected as a local candidate by a Berlusconi lieutenant in 2009, claimed that a businessman had paid her to attend some parties at the Prime Minister's private residence and that she had had sex with him once. In order to increase the pressure on Berlusconi, on 25 June *La Repubblica* published 'ten new questions' that demanded clarification on both the Letizia and D'Addario scandals. Once again, the questions delved into Berlusconi's health conditions and were republished every day. Whereas the Prime Minister had not directly reacted to the previous questions, on 28 August he filed a civil lawsuit for defamation against *La Repubblica*, claiming that the questions were meant not to elicit answers, but to spread innuendo on his private conduct.

The lawsuit was a threat to *La Repubblica* both economically and symbolically and it had to respond with matching strength and resonance. The newspaper rebutted Berlusconi's accusations in editorials and news reports and attracted the attention of the international press by publishing English translations of both sets of questions and other relevant articles on its website. However, *La Repubblica* also took the unusual step of promoting an online petition to directly mobilize supporters in defending the newspaper and challenging the Prime Minister. Authored by three jurists (who were also columnists for the newspaper), the petition denounced the lawsuit as part of a ploy to silence the free press, manipulate public opinion and weaken Italian democracy. The petition featured prominently in both *La Repubblica*'s print and online editions and ended up collecting 462,262 signatures, about the same number as the newspaper's daily circulation.[3]

This was not the first time that *La Repubblica* had collected signatures for an online petition. In July 2008, while the centre-right majority in Parliament was passing the so-called 'lodo Alfano', a law (subsequently repealed by the Constitutional Court) which suspended criminal trials for the Prime Minister and the

Presidents of the Republic, House and Senate until completion of their terms, *La Repubblica* launched an online petition that denounced the law as a threat to the Constitution and demanded its withdrawal. The initiative garnered 150,000 signatures before the law was passed.[4] In October 2008, 250,000 people supported an online petition hosted by *La Repubblica* in support of novelist Roberto Saviano who had been threatened by the Camorra, which he had acutely described in his best-selling book *Gomorra*.[5] In March 2009, as the Berlusconi government was considering a 'housing plan' that would deregulate the construction business, *La Repubblica* hosted an online petition authored by three architects who denounced the provision claiming that it would damage the environment and the urban landscape in Italian cities; about 60,000 signatures were collected.[6] In June 2009, right before the petition on press freedom, more than 200,000 signatures were garnered for a petition that called for the withdrawal of a government draft law that would have restricted telephone wiretappings for criminal investigations.[7] In October 2009, more than 100,000 signatures were collected for an online petition that criticized Berlusconi for not respecting the dignity of women after he had mocked Rosy Bindi, a prominent opposition female figure.[8] Finally, in November 2009, Saviano was the first signatory of an online petition that asked the government to withdraw a draft law that would terminate criminal trials that had lasted longer than six years, which could result in the closing of thousands of cases without any sentence. This petition has been *La Repubblica*'s most successful so far, with over 500,000 signatures.[9] In all these instances, the newspaper heavily publicized the petitions in its print edition and especially on its website by periodically recapping the number of signatures that had been collected, emphasizing support by popular figures and restating the reasons why the petitions had been started.

These episodes illustrate that organizing online petitions has become a habitual endeavour for *La Repubblica* and it has enabled the newspaper to support its editorial campaigns by mobilizing large numbers of its readers online. As a result of *La Repubblica*'s successful efforts, its two main right-wing counterparts – *Il Giornale*, owned by Berlusconi's brother, and *Libero* – quickly began to promote their own online petitions. First, in the autumn of 2008 *Libero* launched various e-petitions to support different initiatives of the Berlusconi government, such as its university reform.[10] Then, in September 2009, *Il Giornale* partnered with Daniela Santanchè, a conservative politician and advertising executive, for a petition campaign to abolish the television licence fee after the public broadcasting company aired a special issue of Santoro's talk show about Berlusconi's sex scandals.[11] Unlike *La Repubblica*'s, *Il Giornale* did not devise a web interface for supportive readers to sign the petition, but asked them to send an email to a dedicated address instead. The initiative reportedly elicited 'an avalanche' of emails, as many as 6,500 on the first three days,[12] but because of the way the petition had been implemented, a final count of signatories comparable to those of *La Repubblica*'s petitions is not publicly available. Finally, in August 2010 *Il Giornale* launched a petition campaign against Gianfranco Fini, President of the House of Deputies and cofounder of the Berlusconi-led People of Freedom party, who had become increasingly critical of the Prime Minister. The petition asked Fini to resign from office and could be signed by email, mail, fax, or text message.[13] In just a few days, *Il Giornale* claimed to have received more than 35,000 signatures.[14] Subsequently, it periodically printed the names of the most recent signatories in alphabetical order, although it once again failed to provide a public running tally and final count of signatures.

In sum, this analysis illustrates that Italian partisan newspapers increasingly employ online petitions to engage supportive readers in their editorial campaigns. The petitions, however, are not implemented as a genuine opportunity for citizens to make their voices heard; rather, they are devised as tools through which the newspapers can show tangible signs of support for their editorial campaigns. From this perspective, the online petitions promoted by these newspapers turn out to be mostly an instrumental, top-down endeavour in which professionals who work in or gravitate around the newsroom (editors, journalists, columnists or affiliated intellectuals) author the appeal and citizens respond by signing it. It may be out of sensitivity for these issues that in 2010 *La Repubblica* began to cover online petitions organized by civil society groups rather than initiating its own. Thus, it publicized a 200,000-member Facebook group protesting against the editor of the main public television news programme for inaccurately reporting on a judicial verdict that indirectly involved Berlusconi,[15] as well as covering a civil society e-petition against the wiretapping overhaul, which collected over 240,000 signatures.[16] However, on 21 September 2010 the newspaper itself started a new petition, written by one of its columnists, to demand an end to Berlusconi's attempts at securing judicial immunity.[17] The petition garnered more than 150,000 signatures.

In sum, newspapers involve their readers as petition *signers*, but not *authors*. This is because, as we have seen in the second section, Italian partisan newspapers see their mission as influencing the strategies of the political elites and the views of the public, not as serving their readers' need for information, responding to their preferences and voicing their demands.

Michele Santoro's protest rally as an experiment in media convergence

One of the distinguishing features of polarized pluralist media systems is that 'the news agenda is not considered to be governed purely by journalistic judgments of "newsworthiness", but is a question of public policy' (Hallin and Mancini 2004, p. 109). Political coverage is thus highly regulated and subject to decisions made by parties or politicized authorities (see Mazzoleni 2000). One key institution in the governance of public service broadcasting (RAI) is a parliamentary oversight commission, one of whose tasks is to regulate the conduct of RAI during election campaigns. In the run-up to the 2010 regional elections, the commission passed new regulations that mandated that all programmes of political information, including talk shows, had to guarantee equal access to all candidates from all regions, as in formal candidate debates. According to most

judicial interpretations, the overhaul implied that, if a talk show invited one candidate for the presidency of one region, it also had to invite all other presidential
candidates in that same region; moreover, if a programme focused on the elections in one region, it also had to discuss the elections in all other regions that
were about to vote. The combination of these requirements compelled talk shows
that wanted to cover the regional elections to invite a total of 53 presidential candidates from 13 regions throughout the month-long campaign, an obviously
impractical task. The rule was opposed by RAI journalists who claimed it would
make their job impossible, but it was duly implemented by RAI's board of
administrators, which cancelled all political talk shows in the four weeks prior to
the vote. Subsequently, the Authority for Communications, an independent body
tasked with overseeing compliance with media laws by both public and private
broadcasters, extended the rule to private television as well, but the decision was
subsequently overturned by an Administrative Court. The result was paradoxical
and politically consequential, as public television could not broadcast talk shows
about the campaign, whereas Berlusconi-owned private channels could and did.

The opposition denounced the overhaul as a manoeuvre to tighten Berlusconi's
control on television: among the four RAI talk shows that were cancelled because
of the new rule, two, *Ballarò* and, especially, Santoro's *Annozero*, were hosted by
progressive journalists and were constant targets of criticism by the Prime Minister. As we have seen, Santoro had heavily covered the scandals that had affected
Berlusconi in the previous year; moreover, in 2004 he had been elected Member of
the European Parliament with a centre-left list, although he had resigned from
office one year later. After RAI's decision, Santoro claimed that he would not
accept being silenced and asked the National Italian Press Federation (FNSI), the
main journalists' union, to help him organize a public rally in Bologna on 25
March 2010. The event, named *Raiperunanotte*, was officially a union protest, but
it was staged as a special edition of Santoro's talk show, where the host and his
guests denounced the 'gag rule' imposed by the parliamentary commission and
dramatized some recent news that Berlusconi had pressured various RAI executives and members of the Authority for Communications to silence *Annozero*. As
RAI refused to broadcast the protest event, Santoro and his staff set out to take
advantage of media convergence and assembled a heterogeneous media network
to cover the event that comprised local broadcast channels, national satellite channels, radio, streaming on various websites (including *La Repubblica*'s) and satellite links to public screenings in many Italian cities. Recorded video footage of the
event was also posted on YouTube and on various news websites.

The event was unquestionably a success and by far the greatest online happening in Italian history. Research by an independent company based on a web
survey of 1,382 citizens, representative of the Italian population of Internet
users, found that 70 per cent of respondents were aware of Santoro's event, 4.1
million had followed it live, and five million had watched recorded excerpts,
combining for a total 6.3 million individuals who had engaged with the rally at
some point.[18] This compares to an average audience of 4.9 million for *Annozero*
on RAI, of which 3.7 million are Internet users. Among those who watched the

event live, 35.9 per cent followed it via web streaming, 35.5 per cent on local broadcast or digital terrestrial television and 20.8 per cent on satellite television (Human Highway 2010). The market-research nature of the survey and its reliance on an online sample, although representative of the Internet population, obviously warrant caution, but the size of the audience that watched the rally is surely remarkable given the still limited Internet penetration in Italy and the one-off nature of the event. Another significant achievement was reached in fundraising, as almost €58,000 net were collected through online donations and more than €82,000 through bank transfers (for which the Internet was in all likelihood quite important, as the event's dedicated website was one of the few outlets where fundraising information was available). Thanks to these resources, which constituted more than half the overall budget, the event was fully funded and even generated a surplus that was donated to charity.[19]

Raiperunanotte showed that digital media convergence can be effectively employed to bypass politically motivated limitations on broadcast television. Santoro realized that the audience of his television programme would be eager to watch it online and through various other narrowcast channels. He also understood that outrage at the cancellation of the show would galvanize his followers to spread the word about the rally. By assembling a convergent network of various small- and medium-scale outlets, Santoro harnessed digital media to garner an audience whose size was comparable to that of his television programme. As far as distribution is concerned, *Raiperunanotte* was a success story that may encourage the development of Internet politics in Italy by showing that creating a successful media event is now possible even without broadcast television and that the Italian Internet audience is now eager to engage in 'rich media' experiences that involve audiovisual content as well as text. However, on the production side, the contents, tone, style and structure of the event closely resembled those of *Annozero* and no attempt was made to take into account the fact that the conditions under which the audience would experience the show would be significantly different from those of the RAI programme. This lack of flexibility was probably due to Santoro's natural instincts as a television character, which make him a broadcasting star, but poorly equip him to fully harness digital media environments to enable audience engagement.

Thus, similarly to what we have found for newspapers' online petitions, no attempt was made in *Raiperunanotte* to take advantage of the participatory potential of the Internet, as no opportunity for users to engage directly with the show was explored or promoted. Whereas in the run-up to the rally Santoro's supporters were encouraged to spread the word about the event (for example by embedding a widget on their websites, blogs and social network profiles) and to help fund it, during and after the event little was asked of them besides redistributing content related to the show. The whole effort can thus be characterized as a significantly innovative public-relations and television-production endeavour, which adopted a top-down approach to the organization and production of the show's content, while relying on decentralized supporter engagement to enhance promotion and distribution.

Discussion and conclusions

While the cases that we have analysed involved only a partial subset of the Italian news media during a contentious timeframe, they can be considered representative of the strategies and behaviours of the larger realm of Italian news media that are characterized by political parallelism, among which *La Repubblica* is the most circulated left-leaning newspaper and most visited news website and Santoro is the most popular progressive television journalist. Because the experiments in online engagement that we have studied involved high-profile mainstream figures, they can be expected to constitute a model for other political subjects among parties, civil society actors, interest groups, social movements and news media engaging in political parallelism. Santoro's successful experiment in media convergence and networked broadcasting is particularly likely to set an example that others will try to emulate, while, as we have seen, *La Repubblica*'s e-petition campaigns have already been imitated by conservative competitors. Thus, not only are these endeavours significant per se, but they are also likely to spur emulation and adaptation by other political actors.

Our analysis has shown that participatory uses of digital media now constitute a valuable political resource for news organizations and professionals that have historically been involved in the political battlefield rather than practising neutrality. It is precisely because most of the Italian media aim at influencing their audiences and steering the political debate that the Internet's engagement potential has become valuable for them in ways that are not different from those of movements, interest groups and parties. Thus, combining evidence from the literature on collective action, particularly the hybridization of organizational repertoires enabled by digital networks, with comparative analysis of the relationships between institutional mass media and politics, has enabled us to develop insights that may enrich and expand research on both topics.

With respect to organizational hybridity, we have fruitfully extended the logic of the theory to a peculiar type of political actor that has often been overlooked – politically engaged news media – by showing that online petitions offer them an opportunity to demonstrate their influence through the displaying of tangible and widespread reader support for their editorial stances. Reliance on this type of online engagement tools should be conceptually distinguished from other web-based participatory efforts promoted by the news media, such as experiments in citizen journalism. While the former are employed by the media to achieve political goals, the latter are resources to improve the media's information-gathering capacities and relationships with their audiences. While the two facets can coexist in the same news organization, they pertain to different functions, which in turn generate different outcomes on public opinion and the political system.

With respect to the political communication environment, we have shown that the structure of the institutional media system has profound consequences on how different types of players adopt Internet tools for political action. The availability of digital network repertoires of collective action provides new avenues for the media to manifest their political parallelism. Given that a tendency toward politicization of part of the news has recently been observed in countries such as the United States and has been a stable feature of the press in liberal media systems such as Great Britain, in democratic corporatist media systems such as Germany and Scandinavian countries, and in polarized pluralist media systems such as France and Spain, the phenomena that we have uncovered are by no means limited to the Italian context but can be expected to develop to some extent in most Western democracies.

The cases that we have analysed in this chapter are instances of instrumental, top-down management of digital media to foster citizen participation defined rather narrowly as adhesion to media elites' self-interested and self-defined political objectives, rather than promoting expressive, bottom-up efforts driven by grassroots influence and aiming at goals identified by an active subset of the public. In other words, the role of online engagement promoted by news organizations is best understood as an extension of *the media's own political leverage* vis-à-vis institutions and other elites rather than an expansion of *citizens' influence* on, let alone ownership of, news and politics. As with the online activities of most institutional actors (Ward and Vedel 2006), promoting spontaneous citizen participation and empowering the periphery against the centre is usually not among the priorities of the organizations that engage their supporters online. In the mainstream media's harnessing of digital network repertoires of collective action, therefore, we see the opening of a conduit for audience participation that is not likely to significantly empower the public, as it is limited to the acceptance and distribution of messages produced by institutional sources. The chain of command is still sealed off from outside influence, which is only mobilized to promote and deliver messages devised by the media elite. This approach by newsmakers also affects the degree of novelty of the contents that are produced and circulated through digital networks, which we have found to be generally lacking. Particularly in Santoro's case, the televised show that was displayed via digital media was produced in the same way as on broadcast television and no effort was made to turn the active audience of the event into a productive, 'read-write' public (Hartley 2009).

These findings have ambiguous implications. On the one hand, the provision of limited and targeted channels of online citizen engagement by strategic media actors can be seen as a specimen of Howard's (2006) notion of 'managed citizenship', that is, the instrumental use of digital media to channel participation to empower the elites rather than making them accountable to their followers. On the other hand, Norris claims that democratic theory implies a shared responsibility between parties and journalists for 'stimulating interest in public affairs and encouraging the different dimensions of civic engagement' (2000b, p. 32). From this perspective, the cases analysed here could be seen as instances in which the media not only encourage political interest and participation, but create opportunities for engagement, thus taking their democratic obligations one step forward.

Online petitions and distributed broadcasting are only a limited subset of the possibilities for collective action enabled by digital media. Future research should further delve into other online participation efforts promoted by politically collateral news media and extend the logic employed in the design of this study by looking at how other types of actors and organizations may take advantage of digital network repertoires of collective action to engage citizens in political activities. As the context and players of networked democracy maintain a fluid and developing character, devising case studies can help generate insights on emerging political communication phenomena, which can then be specified and tested through comparative and quantitative research. Moreover, this study has shown that variables related to the 'old' media have a significant impact on the 'new' media. Therefore, greater efforts should be devoted to understanding how each historical layer of media development affects the adoption and integration of new technologies, paradigms and platforms.[20] Investigating the influence of the mainstream media, both as contextual factors and as active players, on the development of digital media may help us better understand both realms.

In conclusion, this study has shed light on the role of the news media as relevant political actors that are now capable of advancing their goals through digital repertoires of collective action, such as online petitions and convergent broadcasting networks, that were previously thought to be the exclusive purview of parties, interest groups and social movements. The democratic potential of such efforts, however, has been found to be rather limited, as the promotion of online political engagement by the news media implies more a reviving of their own political clout than an opportunity for citizens to voice their demands to both the media and the political system. Greater involvement by their readers and viewers may increase the political influence of the media, but not necessarily of the public.

Notes

1 See www.primaonline.it/2010/03/25/79419/quotidiani-novembre-2008–2 (accessed 17 May 2010).
2 See www.primaonline.it/2010/05/04/80296/audience-online-a-marzo-2010 (accessed 17 May 2010).
3 See www.repubblica.it/2009/08/sezioni/politica/berlusconi-divorzio-23/appello-repub blica-sabato/appello-repubblica-sabato.html and http://temi.repubblica.it/repubblica-a ppello/?action=vediappello&idappello=391107 (accessed 14 May 2010).
4 See www.repubblica.it/2008/07/sezioni/politica/giustizia-7/firme-appello-chiuso/firme-appello-chiuso.html (accessed 14 May 2010).
5 See www.repubblica.it/2008/10/sezioni/cronaca/camorra-4/saviano-adesioni/saviano-adesioni.html (accessed 14 May 2010).
6 See www.repubblica.it/2009/03/sezioni/economia/crisi-21/cdm-rinvia/cdm-rinvia.html (accessed 14 May 2010).
7 See www.repubblica.it/2009/06/sezioni/politica/ddl-sicurezza-6/duecentomila-firme/duecentomila-firme.html (accessed 14 May 2010).
8 See www.repubblica.it/2009/10/sezioni/politica/berlusconi-donne-2/firme-22ottobre/firme-22ottobre.html (accessed 14 May 2010).
9 See www.repubblica.it/2009/11/sezioni/politica/giustizia-16/appello-16-novembre/

appello-16-novembre.html and http://temi.repubblica.it/repubblica-appello/?action=v
ediappello&idappello=391117 (accessed 14 May 2010).

10 See www.libero-news.it/news/4219/Le_firme_per_la_Gelmini.html (accessed 14 May
    2010).

11 See www.ilgiornale.it/interni/rai_perche_pagare_santoro_firmate_noi_abolire_canone/
    27–09–2009/articolo-id=386139-page=0-comments=1 (accessed 14 May 2010).

12 See www.ilgiornale.it/interni/cresce_popolo_no_canone_piovono_migliaia_adesioni/
    canone_rai/29–09–2009/articolo-id=386400-page=0-comments=1 (accessed 14 May
    2010).

13 See   www.ilgiornale.it/interni/raccogliamo_firme_mandare_casa_fini/09–08–2010/
    articolo-id=466220-page=0-comments=1 (accessed 30 September 2010).

14 See   www.ilgiornale.it/interni/mandiamo_casa_fini_gia_raccolte_35mila_firme/11–
    08–2010/articolo-id=466434-page=0-comments=1 (accessed 30 September 2010).

15 See   www.repubblica.it/politica/2010/02/28/news/appello_tg1–2460213/index.html
    (accessed 17 May 2010).

16 See www.repubblica.it/rubriche/la-legge-bavaglio/2010/05/16/news/sit-in_alla_rai_e_
    stati_generali_85_mila_firme_contro_il_decreto-4102149 (accessed 17 May 2010).

17 See www.repubblica.it/politica/2010/09/21/news/cavaliere_ci_dica_se_la_legge_uguale_
    per_tutti-7266376/ (accessed 30 September 2010).

18 The total audience estimate is smaller than the sum of the two audience figures
    because many viewers watched both the live streaming and recorded excerpts.

19 See www.facebook.com/notes/rai-per-una-notte/il-bilancio-di-raiperunanotte/3855010
    66325 (accessed 14 May 2010).

20 See Anstead and Chadwick (2008, pp. 69–70) regarding the impact of the old cam-
    paign communication environment on the adoption of Internet electioneering in the
    United States and United Kingdom.

6 Trust, confidence, credibility

Citizen responses on Twitter to opinion polls during the 2010 UK General Election

Lawrence Ampofo, Nick Anstead and Ben O'Loughlin

Introduction: mediatized democracy and the 2010 UK General Election

> I wish the media would stop over-analysing, bombarding us with stats and polls and trying to manipulate our opinions! @MissLeeLeeeeeee[1]

> this polls are crazy Does appear we're heading 4 a hung parliament I have a bad feeling Libs will go with Tories... @teessidedazza

> Being told to turn phone off by @crossy but can't stop reading stuff about #leadersdebate surely the polls are wrong... @ajcross

In the months that preceded it, the 2010 UK General Election was widely discussed as being the country's first Internet political contest. However, as it transpired, the centrepiece of the election was to be on television, not online, in the form of the three televised debates staged in the weeks before polling day. In part, this was because these were the first televised leaders' debates in a UK election. It was also because of the impact they had on the polls, seeming to boost the support of the third-placed Liberal Democrats and undermine the position of the incumbent Labour leadership and the Conservatives, who had previously led comfortably. The ultimate electoral outcome of this process is up for discussion (despite their post-debate surge, the Liberal Democrats went on to lose seats, but it might still be contested that this surge cost the Conservative Party an outright majority) but what is beyond dispute is that the debates certainly played a major role in shaping the campaign (Kavanagh and Cowley 2010).

However, it is inappropriate, we would contend, to understand the relative significance of the television debates vis-à-vis the Internet. Rather, we share Chadwick's view that news media is now made up of 'assemblages in which the personnel, practices, genres and temporalities of supposedly "new" online media are increasingly integrated with those of supposedly "old" broadcast and press media' and that old and new media 'simultaneously engage in competitive and cooperative interactions' (Chadwick 2011a, pp. 25, 32). Hence, as Hoskins and O'Loughlin (2007, pp. 13–17) had earlier written, the integration of social media into broadcast practices creates 'renewed' mainstream media. Indeed, Chadwick documents in detail the manner in which major news organizations in the UK used real-time reaction worms, live blogs and Twitter trackers to present viewers of the 2010 leaders' debates with a form of augmented liveness where viewers were not just confronted with a live broadcast but a live broadcast with live responses (and responses to live responses) embedded within it. Consequently, we reject the idea that the 2010 election was a zero-sum game, wherein the contest can be defined through reference to one media type, such as an *Internet election* or a *television election*. Instead, the interaction between uses of different media could create and reveal new forms of information, discussion and relationships.

This should not be surprising. In the past, shifts in the technology of communication have brought about changes in the way news was constructed and who was commenting on it. For example, the demands of 24-hour rolling television news led to a class of frequently appearing talking heads known from the early 1990s as the commentariat (Hobsbawm and Lloyd 2008; Stevenson 2010). In turn, the development of the Internet, and especially very simple social publishing services, lends itself to a new phenomenon wherein individual viewers are able to share their thoughts on the media they are consuming in real time as they watch, perhaps with thousands or even millions of people. We term this emergence of large numbers of citizen-users as the viewertariat (Anstead and O'Loughlin 2011). We employ the term citizen-users to define those who are performing roles defined as public-political through the use media technologies.

This development, while at its very early stages, and still the preserve of a relatively small minority of the population, has huge potential to shift the way both individual audience members and audiences collectively respond to and understand broadcast information, and relate to those producing it. While we do not accept the idea that audiences have ever passively absorbed information as it is presented to them, we would contend that the growing ability to discuss, seek additional information and publicly express doubt will change the way news is consumed. This chapter is an early attempt to understand this process, using the second leaders' debate in the 2010 UK election as a case study. In particular, we are interested in examining how people relate to information they are given about the outcome of the debate – especially, who they are told the winner is.

In common with practice in much of the world, media organizations announced a winner minutes after the debate finished. They did so by referring to opinion polls taken during or seconds after the debate's duration. However, our examination of comments on the social media site Twitter found that this information was treated in a number of distinct ways, and certainly not accepted at face value or seen as a definitive truth. This conclusion speaks to broad issues within the study of politics and media.

First, it allows us to address a core concern within modern politics, namely how citizens relate to political elites. It particularly speaks to issues of trust, and how the wider population assesses the credibility of statements made by politicians, journalists and pollsters. Second, it allows us to consider and problematize the idea of mediatization, one of the dominant paradigms for contemporary discussion of the relationship between the media and other elements of society. So far, studies of mediatized politics have addressed how media logics penetrate and drive the decisions and practices of political actors. If, as Deuze writes (Deuze 2011, p. 138, emphasis in original), 'Our life is lived *in*, rather than *with*, media', then we must explore not only how political elites adapt their behaviour but also how ordinary citizens question, interact with, and even contribute to elite politics and its mainstream mediation. As Chadwick (2011b) documents, we are witnessing 'hybrid' media systems through which political elites and non-elites together assemble or constitute political events. This chapter moves this research trajectory forward through analysis of the views expressed, positions taken and roles performed by members of the viewertariat around a single political event. We find, for instance, that alongside the expected partisanship, cynicism and humour, some viewertariat performed a lay tutelage function, informing others about how procedures work, historical precedents and the nature of opinion poll methodologies, which suggests a commitment to informed democratic participation and reflection. Are there ways, then, that democracy is enhanced with 140-character communications?

Mediatization, the viewertariat and opinion polling

In the broadest sense, mediatization can be thought of as a process wherein the logic of the media comes to dominate the decision-making and behaviour of other institutions in society (for various definitions of the term see Strömbäck 2008, p. 231; see also Livingstone 2009b). This process has been noted in various social contexts, including religion (Hjavard 2008), war (Cottle 2006), memory (Hoskins 2009) and electoral politics (Strömbäck and Dimitrova 2011). Certainly, in this last case study, the evidence for mediatization seems particularly clear. Spin doctors are now central to political organizations, while politicians speak in broadcast-friendly sound bites, crafted and tested for rapid consumption (Esser *et al.* 2001; Schier 2000). This would seem to be strong confirmation of media norms and expertise entering into other spheres.

Any discussion of the ramifications of mediatization has to include two related elements. First, mediatization leads to the increasing dominance of so-called media logics, defined as the increased ubiquity of formats favoured by media when 'format consists, in part, of how material is organized, the style in which it is presented, the focus or emphasis on particular characteristics of behavior, and the grammar of media communication' (Altheide and Snow 1979, p. 10). Crucially, the dominance of these formats expands beyond the boundaries of the traditionally defined institutions of 'the' media, and colonizes other systems within society. Thus media logics usurp the role played by other rationales for decision-making, notably political logics (Strömbäck 2008). In other words, politicians and their advisers start to adopt the same norms and evaluative criteria as media actors when making decisions. However, it must be noted that is by no means a deterministic process; Strömbäck and Dimitrova (2011) observe how the cultures of some institutions may mitigate against the diffusion of such norms.

Judged on these terms, the innovation of leaders' debates in the UK general election would seem like prima facie evidence of mediatization, and a victory for media logics over political logics. After all, broadcasters had been lobbying for such an event during a number of previous election cycles, always to have them vetoed by one or more of the political parties. In the run-up to 2010 though, a group of news journalists and producers, led by Sky News's Political Correspondent Adam Boulton, were successful in persuading all three of the major parties to enter into negotiations for a televised debate, and eventually finding a format that all could agree on (BBC News Online 2009).

Second, the concept of mediatization raises important ontological issues. Rather than politics being an independent sphere of practice that media report on, political actors adapt their behaviour to the imperatives of the media environment as a whole and each medium on a tactical basis, refining the form and content of their public address to fit whatever values are particular to that medium based on presumptions about how they and the broadcast will be understood and evaluated by the audiences they seek to appeal to *as well as* how content may be remediated across other formats. For example, in his historical account of US presidential TV debates, Alan Schroeder writes that live debating and the outcomes they generate can only be understood through the prism of television, writing that 'presidential debates are best apprehended as television shows, governed not by the rules of rhetoric or politics but by the demands of their host medium. The values of debate are the values of television: celebrity, visuals, conflict, and hype' (Schroeder 2000, p. 9). Thus the logic and grammar of televised debates is very similar the world over – an excitable build-up with much discussion of the possible outcomes and how the event relates to the current state of the race; the actual broadcast itself; and then minutiae-level post-debate analysis. Political actors conform to this media logic too by placing partisan spokespeople in the so-called 'spin room', able to receive questions and advocate for their side in the post-debate analysis. It is through these processes that the event comes to exist for the audience.

In common with other areas of modern electoral coverage, opinion polls have also taken a central role in post-debate coverage. Certainly, in the 2010 UK case, it was opinion polls taken in the immediate aftermath of the first debate, showing Nick Clegg as the clear winner, that kickstarted the surge in support for the Liberal Democrats that did so much to shape the overall election campaign. Ultimately then, more than anything else, it is post-debate polls that shape coverage and define the winner, shaping the mediatized reality.

This creates a problem, however, since opinion polls are hardly objective measures of fact, for several reasons. While some have argued for the utility of polls as a method to empower the public (most famously Gallup 1939), the role they play in contemporary election campaigns raises a number of questions. For example, it has been claimed that they undermine discussion of policy issues, in favour of a focus on the competitive aspects of electioneering (Rokeach 1968,

p. 547) and sampling techniques under-represent certain parts of the population (Althaus 1996). Perhaps most importantly though, opinion polls are not just simply mirrors that can be held up to reflect public opinion. Instead, they involve the use of imperfect methods to construct an object for discussion, 'public opinion', giving the news media great scope to interpret and project meaning (Broh 1980, p. 516). This ability is especially significant when it becomes clear that polls can shape opinion, rather than just reflect it, with citizens moving their support behind a candidate who seems to have momentum (Mutz 1995). Broadcasters and newspapers are likely to be driven by particular motivations in their analysis. In the UK case, newspapers are partisan, endorsing parties in the election. In addition, news outlets are often driven by a market imperative (Strömbäck and Dimitrova 2011), and seek to relate the story in a manner that is attractive to people, to maximize their audience share. It is this tendency which has fuelled the rise of infotainment news coverage (Brants and Neijens 1998) and leads news providers to offer compelling narratives to frame their stories, even if it leads to over-simplification (Strömbäck 2008). Great emphasis is placed on the speed with which information is bought into the public domain relative to competitors, even if this leads to decreased accuracy (Gowing 2009).

In televised debate coverage then, we find a contradiction: opinion polls are a flawed measure (or rather a construction) yet they retain great authority, often taken as factual, and play a significant role in creating a mediatized reality in the immediate aftermath of televised debates. There is some evidence, however, to suggest that audiences do not take mediatized presentation at face value and are capable of navigating this tension. These processes have been noted in large-scale mixed-methodology studies of news consumption in the UK (Coleman *et al.* 2009; Couldry 2008). These studies indicate a variety of understandings held by citizens about the credibility of news reporting and whether they trust the information they are being presented with. For instance, Coleman *et al.*, examining working-class audiences in Leeds, UK, found that people noticed the disjuncture between their everyday lived experience and the way in which their communities were covered in the news reporting. This discrepancy led these news consumers to critically reflect on how news is produced, and what 'news' even was. In particular, interviewees began to express the view that national news reporters belong to an elite cohort along with politicians who have no personal connection to working-class life in the UK, and who produce moralizing statements and reports about lifestyle choices of working-class citizens. Interviewees lacked confidence in the ability of such elites to represent life from the perspective of working-class citizens, and hence working-class interviewees did not trust the news reports journalists produced. For these citizens, information posted on the Internet by *people like them* had more credibility than news from elite journalists (Coleman *et al.* 2009, p. 39). The study is significant to this paper because it demonstrates how particular engagements with media can catalyse reflection and re-evaluations of people's own understanding of media, news and their relation to them.

Exposure to different media menus also affects what news people find credible. In a three-year audience ethnography of 245 news consumers across 12 UK cities, Gillespie and O'Loughlin (forthcoming) found that multilingual, diasporic or migrant communities were used to comparing news media coverage from the UK, news from a homeland (for example, Pakistan), and often also news in a particular language (such as Spanish or Arabic) or oriented towards a certain religion (what they loosely termed 'Muslim news'). This habitual practice led to greater reflexivity about how journalism operates, and an expectation that no single news source will deliver 'the' truth of an event, but that audiences must piece together a range of sources and perspectives to build up a credible picture for themselves. In contrast, many English-speaking 'white majority' news consumers expected mainstream news to transmit a factual account, such that if they followed this news ('the news') they could consider themselves to be informed citizens. Consequently, they expressed a sense of unease and unsettledness when news reports on mainstream channels were later proven to be inaccurate. What these studies make clear is that, despite the growing mediatization of the news and internalization of media logic in wider society, the various practices and expectations of news consumers indicate how a lack of confidence or even mistrust towards news and news organizations remains.

Mediatized elections in which poll data is used to shape coverage and potentially voter behaviour, alongside longstanding questions of how trust and confidence in elites and news are generated, sustained or undermined, together provide the backdrop to this chapter. In the past, while doubts might have existed in the minds of some viewers and readers, there was only very limited space to articulate and develop them publicly. Now, with the emergence of services such as Twitter, and the on-going convergence of media experience – whereby it is becoming increasingly common to comment online while watching a broadcast event – citizens have a new and readily accessible space in which to express their doubts and thoughts on the information they are being given. Mediatization changes the potential capacities of citizen-users. We present now what they did with those capacities in this leaders' debate.

Research questions and data

This paper focuses on Twitter reactions to polling around the second debate, held in Bristol on 22 April 2010. In all, five companies produced post-debate polls, the details of which are shown in Table 6.1. As can be seen, these drew on a range of data-gathering methodologies and sample sizes. Furthermore, they were commissioned by a number of different broadcasters and newspapers. The exception to this is Angus Reid, a Canadian pollster, which was a new entry to the UK political scene, and was seeking to raise its profile by conducting surveys during the election campaign.

This figure demonstrates the sharp divergence in methods and sample sizes employed by pollsters to conduct their surveys. In part this is a product of the conditions they are working under. Since televised debates had never occurred

Table 6.1 Post-debate polls conducted on 22 April 2010

Pollster	Commissioner	Sample size	Notes on method
Angus Reid	N/A	935	Online survey of British adults who had watched the televised debate. Weighted according to current age, gender and region information.
ComRes	ITV	2,691	Telephone survey based on panel of 15,000 people planning to watch the debate and who had agreed to be called afterwards. Automated calls were used to find out their views.
ICM	*Guardian*	504	Telephone survey of previous poll participants who said they would watch the debate. Sample weighted to reflect those who said they would be watching the debates.
Populus	*The Times*	904	Online interviews. Participants contacted before the debate and asked whether they intended to watch.
YouGov	*Sun*	1,110	Internet survey, taken immediately after the debate. Results weighted to reflect viewer base of the debate.

Source: Information from Angus Reid 2010; ComRes 2010; ICM 2010; Populus 2010; YouGov 2010.

before in the UK, the methods were obviously experimental in this national context, with pollsters trying to apply their techniques to a new format of event. Speed was also a priority, with many television companies reporting poll findings within 15 minutes of the end of the debate. It is open to question whether the unprecedented nature of the event and rapidity of the process damaged the integrity of the poll data being gathered. Certainly, concerns have been raised that Liberal Democrats were over-represented in post-debate polling, and that this may be one reason why Nick Clegg performed so well (Chadwick 2011a, p. 33). The commissioning of polls by individual media organizations also created certain tensions. Particular broadcasters and publishers tended to focus on the survey data that they had organized, to the exclusion of other findings. For example, at the end of the debate, Sky News immediately broadcast the YouGov/*Sun* poll, while ignoring the others (*Sun* and Sky News are both part of the Murdoch-owned News International, along with *The Times*).

The second debate was chosen as the case study because of the interesting and ambiguous findings from the polls that were published in the immediate aftermath, with no one clear winner emerging. This contrasted with the first debate, where every poll showed Nick Clegg as the winner. The lack of clarity in the outcome is shown in Figure 6.1, which illustrates the discrepancy of findings: three polls put Clegg ahead (ComRes/ITV, ICM/*Guardian*, and Angus Reid) while two put Cameron ahead (Populus/*The Times* and YouGov/*Sun*).

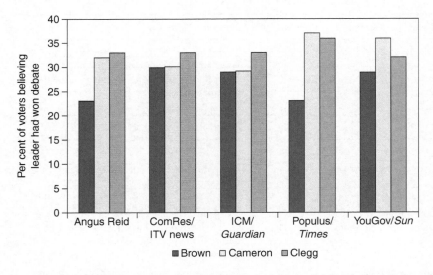

Figure 6.1 Results of post-debate polls conducted on 22 April 2010 (source: Information
from Angus Reid 2010; ComRes 2010; ICM 2010; Populus 2010; YouGov
2010).

Our central interest is how this data was received and responded to by users
of Twitter. Twitter was studied because of its profile and high use during the
debate period – more than half a million debate-related tweets were sent during
the election campaign (O'Loughlin and Linguamatics 2010). The service is also
relatively open (other social media services, such as Facebook, exist on much
more private platforms, meaning that accessing information posted by users
poses considerably larger challenges, as well as raising more ethical issues).

To further understand these processes, we want to consider the following
research questions:

• How does the viewertariat discuss and reconcile ambiguity in polling data?
• What particular arguments are employed to justify the views of tweeters?
• To what extent do questions of trust or confidence enter into this debate?
• Do exchanges of information educate and inform about opinion polling?

The analysis was based on a dataset of more than 60,000 tweets gathered during
and immediately after the second televised leaders' debate by the Cambridge-
based text-mining company Linguamatics. This was a two-stage process. First,
information was harvested using a web crawler that was developed to gather
content from Twitter's streaming application programming interface (API). This
was set to search for a number of terms related to the televised debates. Second,
this broad corpus was sifted using a natural language processing (NLP) technology, which had been especially created to automatically analyse the semantic

construction of tweets. In this particular case, we were looking for tweets that offered negative criticism and comments on opinion polling within the broad sample (O'Loughlin and Linguamatics 2010).

As a result of this process, a sub-dataset of some 496 tweets was created. This may appear to be a relatively small proportion of the total number, but we propose its significance for two reasons. First, the original sampling technique was very broad, so would have picked up a great many tweets just tangentially referencing the existence of the debate. Thus the proportion of polling-related tweets relative to other politically focused comments is far higher than it appears when compared to the total dataset. Second, the value of tweets extends far beyond the individuals commenting, and includes those who read them (Chadwick 2011a). As a result, a small number of posts can quickly be seen by a very large audience.

Another issue that should be addressed is the user base of sites like Twitter. It is true that social networking sites are used by a group of people which is unrepresentative of the population as a whole. Certainly, during the 2010 election, the evidence would seem to suggest that these technologies were far more likely to be used by younger citizens to talk about politics (Painter 2010). This is in itself interesting, given the much vaunted decline in youth participation. Furthermore, we would argue that tweets have a qualitative as well as a quantitative significance. Even through a skewed user base, they have the potential to offer us insights into how citizens relate to contemporary media and political elites.

Responses to polling on Twitter

Explaining perceived discrepancies: elite manipulation or stupid citizens?

As noted above, the defining characteristic of polling conducted in the immediate aftermath of the second leadership debate – in contrast to the first – was the lack of clarity in the results. Unlike media organizations though, which tended to focus heavily on their own particular poll findings, Twitter users were able to note the discrepancies that were emerging. At the simplest level, comments expressed confusion at this turn of events:

> Con 42 per cent Lib 42 per cent Lab 14 per cent on @SkyNews but other polls are all over the place so sod knows ... @Booooothman

> how is it YouGov instant poll has polar opposite results to @channel4news #leadersdebate – were they watching the same debate? ... @E11ie5

> So three different polls give three entirely different results ... @hoxtonhandmade

We find two distinct ways in which Twitter users overcome this ambiguity. First, the space was rapidly filled by suspicions that polls were politicized and intentionally manipulated to affect public opinion rather than just represent it. Hence, the debate triggered reflections about the relationship between public opinion, media and parties, and, in the process, questions about credibility and trust were raised, and in particular the power held by political elites. The first set of actors frequently blamed was mainstream media. A common figure in this discourse was Rupert Murdoch. Interestingly, members of the viewertariat frequently referenced Murdoch or his relatives personally:

> Lib Dems ahead in every single poll except the one Rupert Murdoch made up #leadersdebate #iagreewithnick #goNick ... @aldridgesarah

> What percentage of the Murdoch family made up that poll?... @bengluke

This is perhaps unsurprising, given the prominent role played by Murdoch in British politics for a number of decades. Certainly, British politicians have regarded him as a significant figure, going to great lengths to court his support (for evidence of this, see Blair 2010, pp. 95–96; Campbell 2007, pp. 214–216). Related to this was a belief that News International as a whole was engaged in a direct attempt to manipulate results:

> RT @SusanCalman: In a poll made up by Murdoch media the leaders debate results Clegg 1 per cent Brown 1 per cent and Cameron 134 per cent and a gold star.... @ByRICHaRD

> This appears to be hard evidence of right wing press manipulating polls to favour David Cameron htt ... @C_M_Carter

> Sun censors poll and other media manipulations to stop Clegg http://bit.ly/coJoMo ... @scottsherrard

> Sky handling of #LeadersDebate was a disgrace, Boulton sniped at Clegg, Kay B fighting with Labour and LD, poll a joke #... @badjerry

These suspicions, while short on evidence, were grounded in recent British political history, notably the perceived power of the *Sun* newspaper to shift the electoral landscape. While the extent to which newspapers can genuinely change voters' political preferences is a subject of academic debate (McCombs and Bell 1996; McCombs and Shaw 1972), the *Sun* has deliberately built its own mythology, most infamously through the 'It's the *Sun* Wot Won It' front page, published the day after the Conservative Party's narrow 1992 election victory (for a Labour perspective on the *Sun*'s role in the 1992 election, see Linton 1996). Indeed, the *Sun*'s hold over the popular imagination is clearly illustrated in our data corpus by the fact that no tweets accuse *The Times* of manipulating data, even though it is also owned by Rupert Murdoch and its opinion poll, conducted by Populus, offered very similar findings.

The second group blamed for manipulating polling evidence were pollsters themselves. YouGov came in for particularly strong criticism here. There is no reason to believe that such suggestions have any grounding in what actually happened, not least because all major UK pollsters are regulated by the code of conduct issued by the British Polling Council (2011). Nonetheless, rumours of malpractice circulated:

> YouGov completely discredited as a polling organisation – just calling up Sun readers ... @paulprentice

> YouGov discredited as an anti-#LibDems push poll? ... @CaroUnLimited

Push-polling occurs when a fake opinion poll is conducted simply to impart negative messages about a political opponent to members of the public (Elving 1996, p. 444). The origins of this particular rumour seem to come from one individual's recollection of a poll conducted by YouGov. An account of this process was then published on the weblog of Craig Murray, the former British Ambassador to Uzbekistan, and now a human rights activist. In it, Murray claimed that the first questions asked in the survey were both highly leading and very negative about the Liberal Democrats (Murray 2010). The reality of the situation seems to be that the polling call in question was not for a public survey, but was instead commissioned by an opposition party – during the election YouGov had contracts with the Conservative, Labour and Scottish National Parties – to test various messages they might use against the surging Liberal Democrats (Curtis 2010). Here we find evidence of one of the central abilities of socially diffuse groups seeking to attribute meaning to media content – namely, the capacity to draw on different pieces of information in order to support their worldview and use it to challenge what is presented to them by mainstream media. Through the blogosphere and then on Twitter, the common process of message-testing changes into the far more sinister practice of push-polling. This 'evidence' was then, in turn, used to discredit post-debate polls.

Media actors and pollsters were both seen as capable of manipulating the outcomes of polls in isolation. However, others suggested a more complex and multi-headed conspiracy, involving a variety of actors:

> @campbellclaret poll panel made up of Murdoch, wade, coulson and tebbit #leadersdebate ... @blackburnvotes[2]

> Just said the *Sun* newspaper aka YouGov manipulates polls to it's own advantage #LeadersDebate ... @marjieN

> Sky News using discredited polls (YouGov owned by Tory candidate) to influence election ... @mdtauk

> simple tory party crap supporters force media to fake poll/news reports to favour the party ... @salmanj10

These comments point to a belief in a more complex process of manipulation, undertaken by different elements of a political–media complex. In so doing, they echo previous findings about public distrust of the broader and conflated political elite (Coleman *et al.* 2009). One tweet above all others encapsulated this feeling, taking the view to its logical conclusion, referring to an unidentifiable agency manipulating the outcome of post-debate polls:

> They are trying to influence outcome of #leadersdebate by fake polling ...
> @frugaljoystick

While theories of manipulation towards the Conservative Party were frequently advanced by the viewertariat on Twitter, there was room for other arguments to emerge, some offering diametrically opposing interpretations. Presumably referring to the ComRes/ITV and ICM/*Guardian* polls, a few suspected the Liberal Democrats manipulated the polls in their favour:

> #ge2010 Rogue poll, wishful thinking for the Lib Dumbs – did Von Clogg create the thing himself I wonder?... @DJPNZ

> The LibDems astonishingly good at manipulating statistical collection – online polls etc. Wonder who their 'Minister of Deception' is?... @SarahPortsmth

There were also a couple of counterintuitive tweets. One commentator attacked ITV for downplaying the success of the Liberal Democrats, even though their poll did make Clegg the winner of the debate, presumably because they did not feel the tone of the coverage reflected either the data or the actual contents of the debate:

> It feels like ITV are manipulating the 'live polls' to get rid of what was a resounding lead for Clegg ... @mikebull

Another member of the viewertariat looked to pre-empt all these debates by speculating on how polls would be attacked (though at the same time commenting only on one poll which offered a single interpretation of events):

> YouGov poll: David Cameron performed best in Sky News Debate (36 per cent), Nick Clegg (32 per cent), Gordon Brown third (29 per cent) > LAB will call it a joke!... @barmyarmyuk

A second broad response to poll discrepancy was to question the perceptions of fellow citizens (that is the people who had been polled), and to argue that they had judged content of the debate incorrectly. A number of tweets criticized the polls based on the tweeter's impression of which candidate won the debate:

> I'm sorry but the instant polls are wrong, Brown wiped arse with horrid Dave ... @BritishRT

These polls are ridiculous, what on earth were the people watching who said Cameron was best in that debate?... @Mrs_Penguin

GB clearly the only leader in the debate, why do the polls say opposite? ... @VickiCB

RT @CidValkyrie: wants to know if polling people made up the debate polls or if the sample were watching another debate?... @NatRaybould

The polls tonight are wrong, anyone who thinks Cameron was best wasn't watching the right channel ... @robstroudUK

This mode of evaluation is attacked by some, however, who admit their judgements are predefined; in other words, they undermine the notion of a 'blank slate' electorate whose minds will only be made up when assessing the persuasiveness of the leaders' arguments that night:

Yer actually all polls say different, i find gordon brown annoying so will always think he's worst his smile freaks me out ... @joeytip

RT @woodo79: CLEARLY WHOEVER I SUPPORT WON THE DEBATE, ALL THESE OTHER SO-CALLED POLLS ARE WRONG! ... @Matt_WDWR

As discussed earlier, to feel informed, citizens need to be able to have confidence that news media will deliver what they expect, and studies indicate that UK citizens expect a certain reliability and validity to information provided by mainstream news sources such as the BBC, ITV or Sky News. A 'rogue poll' ruptures confidence since it lays bare the potentially politicized or even corrupt relationship between polls and media who report upon them. Opinion polling is part of the electoral infrastructure, a regular 'scientific' statistical measure which enables individual citizens to gauge how their own positions fall within the broader population, and how opinions in that broader population might be shifting. Polls allow citizens to reflect on what might cause such broader public opinion shifts, and whether such causes should have a bearing on their own positions. A lack of confidence in the instant opinion polls opened a space to reflect about why polls were inaccurate or discrepant. Based on their tweets, this led some viewertariat members to lose trust in media and political elites, or in other citizens.

Interaction among the viewertariat: lay tutelage and engaging the elite

The theories offered by the viewertariat to explain the discrepancies in polling results tend to be very partisan in nature. However, there are other things occurring during the debates that have equal significance. In particular, we note two forms of interaction that point to distinct types of political engagement. First, patterns of public discourse emerge with genuine enquiries being made as to the conduct of post-debate polling and responses being offered. While not always accurate, this lay tutelage annotates the debate coverage offered by the traditional media and frequently does add significant caveats.

Again, a common source of questions was the discrepancy between polls. Occasionally though, questions related to issues such as sampling would be included in the comment:

> How can poll of polls say two completely different things? ... @largeburrito

> Is Sky's rogue poll because it's disproportionately watched by Tories? ... @ Paul0Evans1

As well as these open questions, there were also some comments that indicated fundamental confusion about the process of opinion polling:

> The Yougov panel is clearly not made up of LBC listeners based on our latest poll on the debate last night http://bit.ly/doczVD ... @ robinpembrooke

> According to the @channel4news instant poll, Clegg was winning throughout, but Brown made up the points to be level-pegging by the end #fb ... @ JTAN

These comments are both referencing open-access straw polls being carried out on websites while the debates were ongoing. The fundamental weakness of such data-gathering techniques has long been known (Squire 1988), but with the advent of the Internet, open-access polls have become far easier to organize. Sir Robert Worcester, the founder of pollster MORI, has termed such Internet surveys as 'voodoo polls', and criticized a number of media organizations, including the London radio station LBC, for citing them without necessary caveats (Worcester 1999). The comparison between an open-access poll and research based on a representative sample is clearly spurious, but it seems that the large variety of polls and surveys taking place online around the televised debates greatly confused the issue.

Some interventions in the discussion offer far more useful comments though, drawing on historical examples or even criticizing mainstream media for the way poll results are being reported:

> rogue polls are possible without a conspiracy ... @benc4

> #leadersdebate these polls are ridiculous: nothing on sample sizes etc. ... @ YourButler

1992 the polls were wrong by a factor of 8 per cent points due partly 2 'shy' Tory voters not responding ... @JonSHarvey

The three arguments above all offer helpful insights for those following post-debate discussions – namely, that the statistics of polling will not guarantee identical outcomes from multiple polls; that in their rush to report the headline figures, journalists were not giving much information on method; and that, in the past, British polls have suffered from particular methodological difficulties that undermined their overall accuracy. Here then we find assertive and accurate statements relating to polling method, adding extra information to that being provided by broadcasters.

Others went further in their critique. Instead of drawing attention to the problematic nature of particular polls, these offered a broader argument against the great emphasis being placed on polling as such during the coverage:

Will people stop reading too much into polls, swing is never uniform and polls can be wrong #ge10 #vote4change ... @Dillan1986

#ge2010 calm down people from all parties the polls were always going to be crazy after the debate ... @MartinHeneghan

Such statements attack the very foundations of modern media election coverage, which looks to create a dramatic narrative and focuses on the 'horse race' aspect of the contest. In these tweets we find arguments against core aspects of mediatized elections, rejecting the principles of speed and instant reflection that govern its communication.

A second form of interaction was very evident in the sample. In contrast to the lay tutelage, this was more confrontational and relied on using the structural architecture of Twitter, especially the @username convention. This is used to facilitate a direct conversation between users. What is especially evident from our sample is that this ability was frequently used to challenge the interpretations offered by politicians or those closely linked with them:

@ericpickles Oh Mr P. You would say that, the Twitter stream and the polls say different #leadersdebate ... @grahamjones

RT @iaindale I bet the instant polls won't say this but I score this Cameron, Brown with Clegg in third > They say exactly the opposite!... @OliverCollinge

@BevaniteEllie How can you say he won when every single poll shows the opposite?... @Roberts

These tweets contain a couple of interesting elements. First, they are addressed to a range of political actors, drawn from both traditional party power structures and the new media environment. Eric Pickles was Conservative Party Chairman during the campaign, while Iain Dale was a prominent Tory blogger. Ellie Gellard (known as BevaniteEllie) used Twitter and YouTube to launch pro-Labour campaigns. Her success on these platforms led to her being invited to speak at the launch of the Labour Party manifesto, on the same bill as then Prime Minister Gordon Brown (Taylor 2010). Second, the Tweeters all use polling data to attack the prominent figure's interpretation of the debate. In some cases (notably the comment directed at Eric Pickles), they are selective in the information they choose to draw upon in making their argument.

This would suggest that the interactions happening on Twitter around the televised debates represented a distinct model of communication, wherein citizen-users have near real-time access – admittedly to greater or lesser degrees, depending on the willingness of the elite actor to participate in a conversation – to individuals who they would have been unable to contact and engage with in a more traditional media environment. This creates an interesting tension, as it is the same elite actors who many members of the viewertariat argued were responsible for warping the poll results or the way in which the debates were reported.

Conclusion

The 2010 leaders' debates in the UK exemplified the mediatization of politics. It is not simply that mainstream media coverage was augmented by digital enhancements – worms, liveblogs and Twitter trackers – but that media logics defined the parameters of action for political leaders, journalists and, we might have thought, citizens. Nevertheless, the very ways in which the event was mediatized opened space for criticism and confusion; when a practice appears dysfunctional in some way, its mechanisms are laid bare, and in this case the most notable mechanisms were opinion polls. Citizens frequently compared their own experience – their own reactions to the debates or their conversations with their own social circles offline and online – with what opinion polls (reported by journalists) seemed to show, and noted the discrepancy. Catalysed by the divergent numbers and narratives emerging from different news organizations in the immediate aftermath of the second election debate, members of the viewertariat expressed their concern at the failure of these democratic devices to live up to expectations of accuracy, transparency and being free of political interference. This shortfall indicated both what procedures these citizens *would* have confidence in and the bases of their mistrust in political and media elites.

What was less predictable was the development of networks of lay tutelage, where users annotated poll findings with additional information, precedents and explanations. While some of these comments were factually misplaced, others were genuinely insightful and provided a corrective to the haste offered by mainstream television in their post-debate analyses. Perhaps most interestingly, other commentators rejected the very idea of forming judgements from opinion polls at all, denigrating the polls' importance. In doing this, they are not just rejecting the poll data and its presentation from a specific evening. They are also questioning the paradigmatic representation of the very 'public opinion' which political leaders were presumably courting – a paradigm that has done so much to construct contemporary election coverage.

Studies of mediatization have explored how media logics become integrated into institutions, practices and the habits and calculus of actors. However, the use of Twitter during the second leaders' debate seems to point us to something different. We earlier cited Deuze's notion of 'media life', the idea that "Our life is lived *in*, rather than *with*, media" (Deuze 2011, p. 138, emphasis in original). For Deuze this represents a new condition both ontologically and normatively, since it is by identifying and theorizing the new ways people use media that we can conceive new ways of acting and, in the case of this chapter, doing democracy. It is clear that we now need to start thinking and attempting to theorize a form of mediatization that is driven not by elite production (and thus an elite monopoly on the production of meaning) but by ways in which elite media practices interact with socially diffuse media practices. Earlier, we noted Chadwick's recent studies that show how old and new media and their users 'simultaneously engage in competitive and cooperative interactions' through which non-elite users augment and in some cases drive mainstream news stories by publishing information through social media. The case of the viewertariat and the UK leaders' debate extends this insight. A diversity of meanings is constructed at the interstices of elite and non-elite media content in real time (Castells 2007). Additionally, the ways in which some citizen-users respond to this environment indicate something about their understanding of how democracy should be working. In particular, commitment to the continued importance of an informed public is suggested by the emergence of a lay tutelage function performed by a viewertariat who provide information and explanations about polling and elections to fellow citizens who express confusion or frustration. The effect on mainstream media, polling or politicians is not straightforward. If confusion is reduced, this could enable citizens to reconnect with the mainstream election coverage. Equally, however, such lay tutelage could make citizens more aware of the problems of polling, election journalism and pollster–party–media links and either disconnect from mainstream electoral politics or urge procedural reform.

This is not just a debate for democratic theorists. Broadcasters must acknowledge that previous measures of good practice – such as the speed of their reporting and analysis – will be challenged by alternative metrics such as transparency or demonstrable impartiality. Through email, SMS and social media, news organizations have the opportunity for more and richer audience feedback and participation, which should enable them to have greater understanding of audience expectations and confidence about how audiences will respond. However, such feedback and participation open space for audiences to challenge news agendas, framing of coverage and other aspects that professionals had previously regarded as their prerogative. Already, parties, news organizations and citizens themselves are beginning to adapt and establish new institutional practices and relationships. The minor breaches, misunderstandings and conflicts that arise in such a transitional period, such as the controversy around opinion polling documented in our analysis, allow us to continue to address longstanding questions of trust, confidence and credibility in political communication.

Notes

1 In this article we have included the public name of the user posting the tweet cited, so that readers can search back through that user's profile to access the same tweets discussed here.
2 Rebekah Wade was Chief Executive of News International and former Editor of the *Sun*. Andy Coulson was Editor of the *News of the World* (the *Sun*'s sister Sunday paper) until 2007 and during the 2010 UK general election was Conservative Party Communications Director. Norman Tebbit was a prominent Conservative MP, Cabinet Member and Chair of the party during the Thatcher administration.

7 What the hashtag?

A content analysis of Canadian politics on Twitter

Tamara A. Small

The controversial presidential election in Iran was the number one news topic on Twitter in 2009 (Twitter 2009). People tagged information on the protest with the hashtag #iranelection. Twitter was considered by many to be crucial for the reporting of events on the ground. *Time* magazine reported that

> when protests started to escalate, and the Iranian government moved to suppress dissent both on- and off-line, the Twitterverse exploded with tweets from people who weren't having it, both in English and in Farsi. While the front pages of Iranian newspapers were full of blank space where censors had whited-out news stories, Twitter was delivering information from street level, in real time.
>
> (Grossman 2009)

This event and others like it have led to a debate in the popular literature that Twitter is a new source of journalism (see Ingram 2008). Proponents argue that Twitter has been central to breaking news by providing real-time updates. Other examples include the 2008 Chinese earthquake, where it is claimed that tweets of the earthquake bested major news organizations like CNN and BBC (Siegler 2008) and the 2008 terrorist attacks in Mumbai, where "moments after the first shots were fired, Twitter users in India, and especially in Mumbai, were providing instant eyewitness accounts of the unfolding drama" (Beaumont 2008). Twitter can be a source of breaking news because it is "a real time global communications platform" (Jewitt 2009, p. 2345). It allows anyone with access to the web, via computer or even cellphone, to immediately share eyewitness accounts with others all around the world. There is some evidence that Twitter is changing newsgathering practices. An online survey of print and web journalists in 2009 found that 52 percent used Twitter for online research (George Washington University and Cision 2009). Thus Twitter is a democratic media because it allows for democratic activism. Others are less convinced of Twitter as a form and/or source of journalism. These critics point to the vast amount of inaccuracies and unsubstantiated rumour tweeted. For instance, during the Mumbai attacks, a tweet (allegedly) from the Indian government asked twitterers to stop posting messages about police and military operations. It was retweeted numerous times and was even included in a BBC web story. After the tweet could not be verified, the online editor of BBC News issued a *mea culpa*. Misinformation was very prevalent in tweets on the Iran election. Twitspam, which tracks Twitter spammers, posted a list of possible fake accounts, some of which were thought to have connections with the Iranian security apparatus (Twitspam 2009). The site warned people to block fake accounts and avoid retweeting information. Critics contend that there is no way to know if information posted on Twitter is credible. James (2009) points out "One function of mainstream media journalism is to disseminate information we've determined to be reliable. … But the reliance on Twitter and Facebook is essentially throwing the doors open to everything and anything."

Whether or not Twitter contributes to quality information about current events, there should be little doubt that Twitter is changing how people and news organizations exchange and consume information. With 50 million tweets per day (Twitter 2010a), hashtags are central to organizing information on Twitter. A hashtag is what Twitter calls a tag. Designated by a "hash" symbol (#), a hashtag is a keyword assigned to information that describes a tweet and aids in searching. Hashtags are not native to the Twitter platform. Rather they are a community-driven convention, popularized during the San Diego forest fires in 2007. Hashtags "organize discussion around specific topics or events" (Fitton *et al.* 2009, p. 127). Moreover, hashtags allow for community by organizing people by interests or events. By using hashtags, tweets can be sent to a larger audience than one's followers. Indeed, one does not have to be a Twitter user to follow the conversation because hashtags are visible to anyone. Hashtags are searchable through Twitter, Google, and trending sites such as What the Hashtag?! or hashtag.org. In May 2010, What the Hashtag?! was trending more than 13,000 hashtags.

This exploratory research is designed to answer three questions:

1   Who uses political hashtags?
2   What is the nature of tagged tweets?
3   To what extent does Twitter allow for political conversation and participation?

Despite the aforementioned debate about Twitter as a forum for breaking news, this analysis shows that informing is the primary function of a political hashtag such as #cdnpoli. The value of a political hashtag, or Twitter more broadly, derives from the real-time nature of the information shared. The remainder of the paper is organized as follows. The first section focuses on Twitter – what it is and who uses it. This chapter will draw on the literature on political blogging to help understand the role Twitter might play in politics. This literature is explored in the second section. The final section outlines the methodology and the selection of data. Each research question is answered in turn.

Twitter: what is it and who uses it?

Twitter is a microblogging site established in 2006. Microblogging is a form of blogging, but smaller. "Microblogging applications share a set of similar characteristics: (1) short text messages (2) instantaneous message delivery, and (3) subscriptions to receive updates" (Jansen *et al.* 2009, p. 3861). There are several microblogging sites online like Jaiku and Qaiku; however, worldwide, Twitter is the premier microblogging site. Twitter allows subscribers to write a 140-character status update called a "tweet" to the question: "What's happening?" Tweets can be posted by instant or text message, cell phone, and third-party applications including Facebook, email, or the web.

Twitter has experienced explosive growth. In February 2008, Nielsen News reported that Twitter had almost 500,000 users; within a year that number had increased 1,382 percent (McGiboney 2009). Sysomos Inc reports that 72.5 percent of Twitter users signed up in the first half of 2009; the report suggests that the star power of Ashton Kutcher and Oprah Winfrey contributed to this growth (Cheng *et al.* 2009). Only a very small proportion of Twitter users are Canadian. An Ipsos Reid (2009) survey reported, "26 per cent of online Canadians are aware of Twitter. Of those, 6 per cent reported using the social networking tool." Sysomos Inc research concurs. Their data suggest that 62 percent of all Twitter users are from the United States whereas only 5.69 percent are from Canada. This said, Canada has the third largest Twitter population according to this study.

Why do people use Twitter? One of the first studies on Twitter focused on this very question. According to Java and colleagues (2007, p. 2) there are four main uses of Twitter: "daily chatter, conversations, sharing information and reporting news." Zhao and Rosson's (2009) study of Twitter and work also identifies three motivations for microblogging. First, similar to the concept of daily chatter, people twitter to provide personal updates about their life. Users see microblogging as a "quick and easy way to share interesting and fun things happening in daily life activities; it lets users keep in touch with friends and colleagues, especially who are outside our life cycles" (Zhao and Rosson 2009, p. 246). Second, Twitter allows users to post real-time information. The final motivation for using Twitter is to gather "information interesting and useful for their work and other personal interests" (ibid., p. 247). Zhao and Rosson call this use a "people-based RSS feed." By following the tweets of others, whether they are friends, family, or interests, a user can instantly receive timely updates with minimal effort. This study seeks to contribute to the small but growing literature on Twitter by focusing on the political aspects of the microblog.

Literature review: what the blogosphere can tell us about the Twitterverse

As noted, there is very little scholarly published work on microblogging and politics. There is an extensive academic literature on traditional blogging and political communication. This chapter will draw on this literature to contextualize the role that Twitter might play in politics. A blog is a website featuring a frequently updated personal journal or diary accessible to the public. Several features typify blogs: self-expression, editorial control, hyperlinking, and interactivity (Small 2008). To be sure, blogs and microblogs are different applications.

> Compared to regular blogging, microblogging fulfills a need for an even faster mode of communication. By encouraging shorter posts, it lowers users' requirement of time and thought investment for content generation. This is also one of its main differentiating factors from blogging in general. The second important difference is the frequency of update. On average, a prolific bloger [*sic*] may update her blog once every few days; on the other hand a microblogger may post several updates in a single day.
>
> (Java *et al.* 2007, p. 57)

This said, microblogging *is* a form of blogging. Moreover, both are part of a broader technology trend called web 2.0. Compared to its predecessor, web 2.0 changes the nature of participation online to "read/write," "where the online audience moves beyond passive viewing of web content to actually contributing to the content" (Sweetser and Weaver Lariscy 2008, p. 179). Web 2.0 is thought to contribute to e-democracy. Breindl and Francq (2008, p. 21) argue that web 2.0 and e-democracy

> Both stress the importance of enhancing the role of Internet users. As e-democracy wishes to involve increasingly cyber-citizens in the political process, new web 2.0 applications may contribute to augment the impact of Internet users in the democratic system.

This connection between web 2.0 and e-democracy makes microblogs like Twitter of concern for political scientists. Since blogs and microblogs are similar, the academic literature on blogging can provide researchers with ways of conceptualizing Twitter and politics in lieu of any direct literature. As in the popular literature on Twitter, there is much debate about how blogs affect politics. Two key themes are prominent in the literature: (1) the relationship between the blogosphere and the mediasphere and (2) the potential of blogs to stimulate greater political participation. The research questions and the methodology of this study were informed by these two key themes.

The blogosphere and the mediasphere

According to prominent Internet politics scholar Stephen Coleman (2005, p. 274):

> The most transformative impact of blogging is upon journalism. Journalists are increasingly setting up their own blogs in order tell the stories that are filed but not used, collect information from their readers and audiences, and promote activism around issues that concern them. Not only professional

journalists, but a new breed of citizen-reporters, utilising mobile-phone cameras and discrete networks of intelligence, are breaking down the old dichotomy between message-sender and message-receiver.

Blogging, it is argued, involves ordinary citizens as active producers of news. Whether it is called alternative journalism or participatory journalism, through blogging individuals can play "an active role in the process of collecting, reporting, sorting, analyzing and disseminating news and information – a task once reserved almost exclusively to the news media" (Lasica 2003, p. 71). The scandals involving Trent Lott and Dan Rather are oft-cited examples of the ability of the blogosphere to have a tangible impact on politics.[1] In both cases, it was the blogosphere not the mainstream media that set the agenda. Moreover, first-hand reporting from events like September 11 and the 2004 tsunami occurred on blogs. In 2003, Mitchell noted, "when big news breaks, it's tough to beat a weblog." Bloggers also challenge the mainstream by performing a watchdog role. According to this argument, "bloggers are not merely linkers and followers of traditional media sources. Instead, bloggers challenge traditional news sources, which they believe is biased, arrogant, elitist, and corrupt" (McKenna and Pole 2008, p. 98). Bloggers saw the traditional media as derelict in their duty as a watchdog in the Rathergate and Lott scandals.

Not everyone supports the notion that blogging is journalism. The main argument against is that journalism is a profession. "Bloggers, in general, know little about independent verification of information and data. They lack the tools and experience for in-depth research. They don't know how to fact-check" (Andrews 2003). Research tends to show that blogs are more akin to punditry than journalism. Pointing to the personalized and narrative style of war blogs, Wall (2005, p. 165) concludes, "While absorbing some traditional news values – timeliness, for example – this new news genre at least in part embodies characteristics that challenge our notions of what constitutes traditional news." Scott's (2007) analysis of four American A-list blogs shows that bloggers rarely perform the task associated with news making. Rather blogging is merely commenting on political events and media stories. Davis (2009 p. 64) concurs; "bloggers are rarely news gatherers; they are aggregators and disseminators of information. They collect information and then pass it on to their readers."

On Coleman's first point, there has been a conflation of the blogosphere and the mediasphere in recent years. Media organizations created blogs on their websites, while some journalists also set up their own blogs outside of their media organizations (called j-blogs). Mainstream media blogs and j-blogs developed in reaction to the growth of influential independent bloggers. Such blogs are an "attempt to recapture journalism authority" (Robinson 2006, p. 65).

Impressionistically, there is a connection between the Twitterverse and the mediasphere. As we saw in the first section of this chapter, similar comments have been made about Twitter and journalism as in the case of blogging. Moreover, journalists and media organizations in Canada are twittering. The *Globe and Mail* and CBC News and prominent Canadian columnists all tweet.

Blogs and political participation

Richard Davis (2009, pp. 34–35) aptly sums up the interconnection between blogs and political participation when he writes:

> A recurring theme of news coverage of the newly emergent political blogo-sphere was the medium's potential for enhancing political participation. The political blogosphere was termed the "netroots," that is, the home of online activists who are using their newfound power to revolutionize politics. The term also suggests that the blogosphere was a highly democratic and inclusive medium that reflected the public's opinion rather than that of elites.

The interactivity of Internet is central here. Interactivity "concerns the relationship of the user with the communication supply and the relationships among the users themselves" (Bentivegna 2002, p. 54). Blogs, by definition, are interactive by nature. Most blogs allow site visitors to respond to the commentary of the blogger. As Coleman (2005, p. 274) puts it "Blogs are fast becoming sophisticated listening posts of modern democracy."

There is some evidence of blogs contributing to political expression in Canadian politics. Koop and Jansen's (2009, p. 172) study of Canadian blogs found "that Weblogs (at least those that enroll in a blogroll) are not simply soapboxes for people to spout off. People's ideas are read, debated, and discussed. In this respect, bloggers are engaging in democratic dialogue with one another." Moreover, Small's (2008) case study of the parliamentary blog, Garth Turner Unedited, concluded that the blog created a virtual community of a small but committed group of participants and a substantial number of readers. Garth Turner Unedited had a "conversational character. The blog comments are not soliloquies. Rather posters read, reflect and react to both the blogger's entries and also to the comments of fellow posters" (ibid., p. 116).

Twitter, too, has the potential to contribute to political conversation. First, followers are able to respond to others. This process is known as @replies. Java *et al.* (2007, p. 62) found that about one eighth of all tweets in their analysis contained a conversation. Honeycutt and Herring (2009) found that around 30 percent of tweets were @replies. They conclude that Twitter is a "noisy environment" (p. 1) where "successful exchanges can and do take place" (p. 9). Another aspect of Twitter that is considered interactive is retweeting. Retweets are the reposting of the tweets of another twitterer, similar to email forwarding. Boyd and colleagues (2010, p. 1) argue that a retweet is a type of conversation.

> While retweeting can simply be seen as the act of copying and rebroadcast-ing, the practice contributes to a conversational ecology in which conversations are composed of a public interplay of voices that give rise to an emotional sense of shared conversational context.

The final research question focuses on the issue of political participation. Through @replies and retweets, we can assess the interactive capabilities of Twitter, thereby, determining if it creates a space for political conversation.

Data and methods

Like blogging, a lot of what is tweeted is unrelated to politics. Hashtags, therefore, are central to understanding the political aspects of Twitter, as they help to organize tweets around a single topic. A "hashtag that catches on forms an instant community around it. Most of these are short-lived. Others become ongoing conversations, recurring real-time events, or entire movements" (Fitton *et al.* 2009, p. 127). There is some evidence that political hashtags have a place in Canadian politics. Another study by this author, on how Canadian politicians use Twitter (Small 2010), found that hashtags were used on 70 percent of the Twitter accounts examined. Moreover, the study determined that there were different categories of hashtags being used. Some hashtags could be categorized as "partisan." That is, the hashtag was related to a specific political party or view (#pcpo = Progressive Conservative Party of Ontario). Conservative think tank the Manning Centre encouraged right-wing Canadians to use #roft (Manning Centre for Democracy n.d.) in all tweets in order to create a right-wing online community. The second category was "political" tags. For instance, #ableg (Alberta Legislature) was a common tag for Albertan politicians of all party stripes. Finally, politicians occasionally tagged tweets with "non-political" hashtags (i.e. #Canucks for Vancouver Canucks). This previous research suggests that the use of hashtags allowed parties and leaders to communicate well beyond their followers and extend their message into other aspects of Twitter. An impressionistic examination of these hashtags demonstrated that it was not just political parties and party leaders using political tags. Individuals, journalists, bloggers, and interest groups were also found. This study seeks to move beyond that impressionistic understanding of political hashtags by conducting a more systematic analysis of Twitter.

The method of this paper is content analysis. Content analysis is "a technique for examining information and content, in written or symbolic materials" (Neuman 1997, p. 31). Anderson and Kanuka (2003, p. 174) point out that content analysis is an appropriate method for e-research, though it is "often associated with the analysis of text documents and in e-research documents are often e-mail, chats or computer conferencing transcripts." This methodology generates research that is valid, rigorous, reliable and replicable (Sampert and Trimble 2010). The coding scheme, developed and tested in March 2009, is found in Table 7.1.

There are three related units of analysis in this study. The first is the hashtag #cdnpoli. #cdnpoli is the hashtag for tweets about Canadian politics, particularly federal politics. It is selected because it is the highest ranked hashtag on Canadian federal politics according to the website politwitter.ca. Almost 30,000 tweets were tagged with #cdnpoli between January and April 2010; an average of 7,491 per month.[2] A non-random sample of tweets from #cdnpoli during the week of

Table 7.1 Coding scheme

Part 1 Contributors
Categorize each profile as one of the following. The categories are mutually exclusive.

- politician
- news organization
- journalist
- individual
- blogger (self-identified by providing URL to blog)
- interest group
- think tank
- other organization (i.e. polling firms)
- other (list)
- cannot tell

Part 2 Categories of tweets
Categorize each tweet as one of the following. The categories are mutually exclusive.

Category	Definition	Example[1]
Comment	A tweet includes a comment about politics; does not include any links to other information or news.	LeDeenoe Here come an attack against Guergis from Liberal! #cdnpoli #hoc #qp
Comment on news	A tweet that includes a comment about a news story; must include a link to a news website.	ReDa_ (Reda) I'm afraid the Harper government has made it the last bout of Bush-ism on the continent. (about Canada) http://is.gd/bIeuu #cdnpoli
Comment on online information	A tweet that include a comment on online information; must include a link.	tony_tracy NFB Film showcases the growing gap in #Canada, shows human side of the #economic #crisis: http://j.mp/9KfxZc | #cdnpoli #economy #canpoli
Comment on a tweet	A tweets that includes a comment about another tweet; must include a retweet.	PSchammy Of course she does – RT @wicary Afghan detainees: Blatchford bemoans lack of attention paid to Colvin's critics. http://tgam.ca/MvX #cdnpoli
Conversations	A tweet that is a public message sent from one person to another; distinguished from normal updates by the @ username prefix.	RamaraMan @stanton_brucemp @brownbarrie #LPC had sponsorship #CPC has #EAP advertising. Both pissed away tax $$ foolishly! http://is.gd/bN4i8 #cdnpoli
News	A tweet that contains a link to a news website; not by a journalist or news organization that tweets its own content. Includes the headline or a version of it.	jimbobbysez Lt. Gen Andrew Leslie ordered to plan top-down reorganization of entire military http://ow.ly/1Fkrm #cdnpoli

Table 7.1 Continued

Category	Definition	Example[1]
Online information	A tweet that contains a link to online information (i.e. blogs, websites, social networking sites) that is not from a news website.	democracyreform #cdnpoli #demreform Why there will not be an election over the privilege issue http://ow.ly/17dGaX
Retweet	The reposting of someone else's tweet. Must include RT.	RT @impolitical: Guergis should have answered that question #QP A minister of state shld be able to answer her file's own questions #cdnpoli
Not relevant	A tweet that is unrelated to the hashtag	

Part 3 Other
Categorize each tweet. These are not exclusive to each other or to above categories.

Mentions	A tweet that mentions or acknowledges another twitterer in a tweet; distinguished by the @username in the message.	twiternair I am putting my body weight behind @M_Ignatieff regarding GG support #cdnpoli #cpc #lpc #ndp @vijaysappani
Other hashtag	The inclusion of one or more other hashtags.	RT @a_picazo: Did I miss something? Is Iggy the PM? – Tories pounce as Ignatieff prorogues himself http://tgam.ca/JwQ #cdnpoli #fail #lpc

Note
1 All tweets are verbatim. Underlines indicate a hyperlink.

26–30 April was examined. This was a very active period in Canadian federal politics.[3] The second unit of analysis is the individual tweet. A tweet is a post on Twitter. It has a 140-character limit. The tweet must include the hashtag #cdnpoli. Third, the profile associated with each tweet was also analyzed. This information is used to answer the first research question (Part 1 in Table 7.1). Twitter profiles can include a photo, name, location, website and bio (160-character limit). The type of information and the amount of detail can vary from profile to profile. To be sure, there are limitations to this approach. As boyd and Ellison (2007) point out "While most sites encourage users to construct accurate representations of themselves, participants do this to varying degrees." Overall, 1,617 tweets and related content from #cdnpoli were read and coded, representing 21.5 percent of tweets of the monthly average in 2010 of tweets on #cdnpoli.

Who uses #cdnpoli?

The community of contributors to #cdnpoli is wide-ranging including individual, bloggers, media organizations, journalists and interest groups. Table 7.2. depicts

Table 7.2 Contributors to #cdnpoli (*N* = 1,600)

Contributor	Percentage
Other	31.2
Individuals	30.8
Bloggers	23.3
Media	9.6
Don't know	2.7
Politicians	1.4
Interest group	0.9
Other organization	0.3
Think tank	0.0
Total	100

contributors to #cdnpoli. Two-thirds of tweets came from two categories: Individuals and Other. The category of Other warrants some explanation. Most of the tweets in this category come from just two accounts: Blogging Tories (23.8 percent) and Progressive Blogger (59.8 percent). These are two of the most prominent political blog aggregators in Canada. Aggregators are sites that gather information from multiple websites. Blogging Tories aggregates from blogs from the right of the political spectrum, while Progressive Blogger aggregates from left and centre-left blogs. These sites then tweet the titles and the URLs of the blog posts aggregated. This appears to be automated. Progressive Blogger, for instance, uses a service called dlvr.it, which posts content on social networking sites for subscribers of the service. Given the popularity of Twitter, the goal is to expand the reach of the bloggers they represent, in hopes that bloggers may attract new readers. Individual bloggers are also prominent contributors to #cdnpoli. Twenty-three percent of contributors to #cdnpoli are bloggers.[4] Not all bloggers were political bloggers however. Food blogs and personal interest blogs were also found. This supports a previous finding that the "use of Twitter is highly intertwined with the use of other social media" including blogging (Lenhart and Fox 2009, p. 5).

As suspected, there is a connection with the mediasphere and Twitterverse. Media organizations and journalists contributed about 10 percent of #cdnpoli tweets. Every major news organization in Canada was represented. Emmett (2008) points out "news organizations increasingly are turning to social networking tools in their efforts to compete in a challenging and fast-changing media landscape." This study provides evidence that this is the case for political reporting in Canada.

These data are interesting not only for who is using #cdnpoli, but for who is not. And politicians are not. Not even 2 percent of tweets on #cdnpoli were from a Canadian politician. Only five current Members of Parliament tagged their tweets. The others include a couple of federal candidates, a provincial politician, and a few municipal politicians. Like blog aggregators, it would seem that a political hashtag would be an excellent place for a Canadian politician to extend his or her message. What explains this finding? Despite the popularity of Twitter, only a minority of Canadian politicians are using the microblog. Blevis's (2010) examination found that only 37 percent of MPs had Twitter accounts (in January and February 2010). Only 20 percent of them were considered active. Small (2010) examined the use of Twitter by provincial and federal party leaders in 2009. She found that only 36 percent of their tweets included a hashtag. More-over, she determined that party leader tweets were most likely to be status updates (54 percent). The "tweets focus on what the leader did or was going to do, where the leader had been or was going to be" (Small, forthcoming). Status updates, in general, are extremely uncommon on this particular hashtag (Table 7.3). As will be demonstrated, #cdnpoli focuses mainly on informing. Adding the #cdnpoli to a politician status update would be inappropriate given the mores of this online community. Given that #cdnpoli is the premier political Twitter destination in Canada, it can be suggested that Canadian politicians are missing an opportunity to share information with a willing and interested audience.

What the hashtag? Categories of tweets on #cdnpoli

Contributors do not tag tweets with #cdnpoli indiscriminately. Only 17 tweets (1.1 percent) were coded as Not Relevant to Canadian politics. Some were about other political topics; others were spam. According to Twitter, 1 percent of the total volume of tweets per day is spam (Twitter 2010b). It is evident that con-tributors to this hashtag are thoughtful about what they tag. Contributors do, however, use multiple hashtags. The hashtags of the major Canadian political parties are frequently used as are political tags like #roft. People-related tags such as #pmharper occurred occasionally. Some of the tweets on #cdnpoli were even tagged with #bustyhookers or #douchebags. Only 40 percent of tweets were tagged solely with #cdnpoli. Contributors seek to get their message out to as many people as possible.

It was seen in the introduction of this chapter that the popular literature has framed Twitter as a forum for original and breaking news. However, this inter-pretation of political hashtags is incomplete. Original reporting on #cdnpoli was minimal. Not even 1 percent of tweets analyzed were coded as reporting (Table 7.3). It is not that original reporting is not a function of the political Twitterverse,

Table 7.3 Categories of tweets on #cdnpoli

Category	Percentage
Informing	71.1
Commentary	18.9
Conversations	7.4
Not relevant	1.1
Reporting	0.9
Status updates	0.7
Total	100

but people are clearly using Twitter in a different way than the breaking news frame suggests. This section addresses the second research question and assesses how people use political hashtags by examining what contributors tag. Table 7.3. reports the findings from the content analysis. The primary function of #cdnpoli is informing. In this sense, #cdnpoli is an aggregator – contributors scour the Internet for relevant information on Canadian politics and use #cdnpoli as a dissemination feed. Although informing is the main function, contributors do occasionally talk on #cdnpoli. There is a moderate level of commentary on the political hashtag. Contributors opine about the issues of the day. Commentary, in many cases, is still very closely related to informing.

Informing

Perhaps the mantra of a contributor to #cdnpoli is: "I found this, and you should check it out." The majority of tweets were informative, that is, they disseminated online information through the hashtag. Informing accounts for 71 percent of the tweets examined. Twitterers glean political information from the Internet to pass on to their followers and followers of the hashtag. Contributors share various types of information on the #cdnpoli (Table 7.4).

Forty-seven percent of informing tweets disseminated online information like links to blogs, YouTube videos, Facebook and other websites.[5] The reason for this has already been touched on – blog aggregators. Every tweet by Blogging Tories and Progressive Blogger were coded as sharing information. As noted, these two aggregators simply tweet the titles and the URLs of posts from their member blogs. For instance,

> **Prog_Blog** #cdnleft #cdnprog In praise of virtual communities (The Woodshed): A lot of stuff has been written about the. ... Available at: http://dlvr. it/dqb7 #cdnpoli

Blogging Tories and Progressive Blogger skew the data towards sharing information as the largest informing category, as these accounts contribute 76 percent of tweets in this category. Bloggers, media, individuals, and organizations occasionally share information, but are more likely to tweet news stories.

Earlier we saw that like j-bloggers, media organizations and journalists contributed to Twitter. Another connection between the Twitterverse and the

Table 7.4 Information disseminated on #cdnpoli

Type of information	Percentage of informing
Online information	47.0
Retweets	36.6
News	16.3
Total	100

mediasphere is evident from the results of the content analysis. Sixteen percent of informing tweets disseminated news reports. Contributors simply tweet the headline (or a version of it) and a link. Compressing sites, such as tinyurl.com, are used to shorten URLs to ensure that links can fit into the 140 characters. A random selection of tweets from the sharing news category provides an accurate snapshot of the type of content posted.

> **a_picazo** Omar Khadr considered for release months after capture, hearing told Available at: http://bit.ly/anBAex #cdnpoli #canpoli

> **wicary** Toward a unified comprehension of Speaker's ruling: @aaronwherry calls out Margaret Wente and @nationalpost. Available at: http://bit.ly/9bOih0 #cdnpoli

The first example, from a blogger, demonstrates the typical format of headline and URL. Occasionally, a twitterer may provide a bit more detail about the story as in the final example from the *Globe and Mail* online editor Stephen Wicary. Sharing news was the main task of media organizations and journalists on the hashtag. Whereas Wicary tweeted a story from another news organization, the media usually tweet their own news stories. For instance,

> **CdnPress_Ott** Lobbyists irked by Jaffer #cdnpoli #jaffer Available at: http://ow.ly/1Do1G

Almost 50 percent of the tweets by media organizations and journalists posted links to their own news. This is a promotional use of Twitter. As John Dickerson (2008), chief political correspondent for Slate, notes in his article in Harvard's *Nieman Reports*, "Twitter entries build a community of readers who find their way to longer articles." Most news organizations make it extremely easy for people to tweet content, often including a "tweet this" button on stories.

In addition to disseminating news and other online information, contributors to #cdnpoli also share the tweets of others, better known as retweeting. It was noted in the section on political participation that boyd and colleagues (2010) saw retweeting as conversational. This analysis concurs only somewhat with their perspective. There were different types of retweets on #cdnpoli, some of which are conversational and some of which are not. Thirty percent of tweets examined in the entire sample were retweets. The majority of these are informing retweets that forwarded information and are not conversational.

For example,

> **smithjoanna** RT @TorontoStarNews: Auditor battling Ottawa's culture of hidden receipts Available at: http://bit.ly/bWkbIc #cdnpoli

> **jimbobbysez** RT @PaulDewar: We've ceded leadership in fighting crimes agnst humanity; Cda has responsibility 2 act in Congo Available at: http://bit.ly/9sNtr6 #cdnpoli

The first example from smithjoanna is a retweet of a *Toronto Star* news story. The next example is a retweet of a tweet link to a news story posted by New Democrat MP Paul Dewer. With the exception of the RT+username, these tweets look precisely like the ones examined previously. The difference is that the contributors likely found this information, not by scouring the Internet, but on their own feeds. These are tweets of people the contributors follow. What is interesting about these examples is that none of the tweets were originally posted to #cdnpoli. Rather a user reads the tweet from their own timeline or another hashtag, deems it relevant to Canadian politics and shares it with others on #cdnpoli. boyd and colleagues (2010, p. 6) suggest that one motivation of retweeting is "To amplify or spread tweets to new audiences." Informing retweets rebroadcast information. Rather than contributors saying "I found this, and you should check it out," they are saying "a person I follow found this, and you should check it out." Disseminating information remains central.

The difference between this chapter and the work by boyd and colleagues (2010) on the conversationality of retweets is really about differing definitions of interactivity. In an oft-cited article, McMillan (2002, p. 163) writes "interactivity means different things to different people in different contexts." For instance, interaction can be user-to-user, user-to-document, and user-to-system. If we are concerned with the democratic potential of the Internet then we are more concerned with usertouser interaction. Chadwick's (2006, p. 84) definition of e-democracy is illustrative: he defines it as "efforts to broaden political participation by enabling citizens to connect with one another and with their representatives via new information and communication technologies." The retweets quoted above cannot be considered conversational if one employs a user-to-user definition of interactivity.

Commentary

Close to one-fifth of tweets on #cdnpoli include commentary from the contributor. These tweets can be divided into two types of commentary: opinion and informing (Table 7.5). Opinion commentary, like an op-ed article in a newspaper, expresses the viewpoint of the author. The following examples are illustrative.

E_Kess Ok seriously, Bev Oda needs to get her story straight. Agreement with Clinton or not? How hard is that? #cdnpoli

Table 7.5 Types of commentary on #cdnpoli

Types of commentary	Percentage of commentary
Opinion commentary	61.0
Informing commentary	39.0
Total	100

flanaganagan I can't wait for the following to play out in Ottawa: "I'm sorry, Mr. Speaker, but those documents are BURIED AT SEA!!! MWA-HAHAHA!" #cdnpoli

The contributor uses the entire 140 characters to opine. Though opinion commentary is the more prominent type of commentary, it only makes up 11.5 percent of tweets in the sample.

The second type, informing commentary, as the name implies is closely related to the category of informing. Indeed, these tweets look extremely similar to the ones discussed in the previous section, except contributors go beyond the mere dissemination function by adding a pre- or post-comment. Given the 140-character limitation, the commentary tends to be extremely brief. As with informing tweets, contributors comment on and share a variety of information including media reports, blogs and other tweets. For instance,

> **MatSiscoe** Yeah, sure, why NOT let the Bloc look at sensitive Nat'l Security docs? Available at: http://bit.ly/96nMF5 #cdnpoli #roft #whatabadidea

> **CanadianArts** Interesting speech by Ignatieff to AFPTQ: Culture: A Liberal Party of Canada priority Available at: http://bit.ly/ctG9hm #cdnpoli #lpc #hoc #quebec #arts

In the first example, the contributor comments on a new story from the *National Post.* Commenting on news was the most common type of informing commentary. The second is an example of commenting on online information; the Canadian Conference of the Arts (an interest group) comments on a speech by the leader of the Liberal Party posted on the party's website. The comment tells followers the contributor's opinion on the information and/or provides cues to what followers should look for in that material. Despite the commentary, the contributor is still sharing online information. The "check it out" nature of informing tweets that we saw in the previous section is still evident.

#cdnpoli and political conversation?

As discussed, one key question in the blogging literature relates to whether blogs provide a forum for political engagement and conversation. If blogs contribute to political expression and e-democracy, can the same be said of a microblog? Table 7.3 shows that only 7.4 percent of tweets are conversational. To engage in a conversation, contributors used either the reply or the retweet button. The following examples of each:

> **stribe39** @natnewswatch er, you're presuming he wouldn't be taking 45 mins to reject the opposition parties motion? #cdnpoli

> **YukonGale** Cuz Harper's done so much 4 women here RT @kathlee-nogrady Cda "deplores" Irans appt 2 UN womens rights panel Available at: http://bit.ly/aLVv5P #cdnpoli

The first example is @reply where blogger stribe39 responds to a news story tweeted by the news aggregator National News Watch. @replies account for only 50 tweets (3.1 percent). To comment on another's tweet by retweeting can often begin a conversation (boyd *et al.* 2010), as in the second example, YukonGale's responds to Kathleen O'Grady's tweet (sharing news). Comments on a tweet account for 68 tweets (4.2 percent). The following example is an exchange found on #cdnpoli between two contributors using both conversational features of Twitter:

> **dominionpundit** Cdn Parliament refuses to disclose expenses of MPs.Politicians self-police LOL Available at: http://is.gd/bQzYD #roft #tcot #cdnpoli

> **joey88lee** We pay, they spend; they spend, we pay. RT @dominionpundit: Parliament refuses to disclose expenses of MPs.Politicians self-police? #cdnpoli

> **dominionpundit** @joey88lee give kudos to #LPC MP @MichelleSimson for posting expenses online. Hope she leads again this yr.Other MPs shd be shamed. #cdnpoli

Like many contributors, dominionpundit tweets a news story with a comment. joey88lee retweets it adding his own comment. dominionpundit responds using an @reply.

With less than 10 percent of tweets on #cdnpoli considered conversational, it is difficult to suggest that this hashtag is, to use Honeycutt and Herring's (2009) phrase, a "noisy environment." Indeed, that study of @replies found about 30 percent of tweets were conversational. What might account for the difference? First, the units of analysis differ in the two studies. Honeycutt and Herring examined Twitter's public timeline, which is a real-time list of all tweets posted by most users. The public timeline is very different from a hashtag, which is organized around a particular topic. Second, if one of the interactants does not include the hashtag in a reply, a conversation may take place, but not on #cdnpoli. It is possible that #cdnpoli encourages more conversation between contributors than is apparent on the tag. The architecture of Twitter makes it difficult for researchers to assess the conversationality on a hashtag. Third, O'Reilly and Milstein (2009, p. 121) note that one problem with replying on Twitter is that it "gives recipients no way of knowing which message an individual is responding." This is unlike a blog where comments are typically located directly below the blog post. Some @replies can lack context. Recall the first example in this section by stribe39. It is not especially clear what stribe39 is talking about. If National News Watch tweets frequently, any possibility for conversation may be lost. Moreover, Twitter is asynchronous. This means that the sender and receiver do not need to be present at the same time for a conversational exchange to occur.

An arbitrarily long time can exist between exchanges. Hashtags may not be conducive for interactive exchanges.

Blogs, microblogs, and politics

This chapter drew on the literature about the political blogosphere as a way of helping to understand the potentials of the political Twitterverse. Two key debates from that literature were examined: the potential of blogs to stimulate greater political participation and the relationship between the blogosphere and the mediasphere. Given the similarities between blogs and microblogs, these debates were explicitly and implicitly examined in this paper. What conclusions can be drawn? At first glance, this analysis may appear to demonstrate the limited ability for political participation on Twitter. As seen in the previous section, @replies and commenting on retweets were extremely rare on #cdnpoli. This hashtag is not a forum for political conversation. This makes the Twitterverse different from the political blogosphere, where commenting is central. However, participation can take many forms. For instance, the Canadian Election Study team (Gidengil *et al.* 2004) includes activities such as signing a petition, writing a letter to the editor, writing to a political official, and/or talking with others about politics as participatory. Hundreds of individuals and bloggers contributed to #cdnpoli. Indeed, more than 50 percent of tweets came from these two groups. Posting on a political hashtag can be seen as a participatory act. Contributors to #cdnpoli are political junkies. Given the information they share, it is evident that contributors are heavy consumers of political information – they read news articles and blogs and follow other political twitterers and hashtags. Moreover, they disseminate this information to others. Given that information is central to citizenship, this function should not be understated. Though #cdnpoli may not provide a forum for political discussion, it is still a forum for political expression.

On the second debate, this chapter has shown a connection between the political aspects of the mediasphere and the Twitterverse. First, we saw the existence of j-twitters as contributors to #cdnpoli. Second, a considerable amount of media content is shared on #cdnpoli. Though most scholars would not suggest that political blogs have displaced the mainstream media, many do see blogs as changing the media environment (Davis 2009). This case study suggests that mainstream media has less to fear from the Twitterverse than the blogosphere. Contributors amplify the scope of news stories beyond the media's audience reach. Unlike blogs, commentary, original reporting, and the watchdog functions are second to informing. In this way, media organizations may be an important beneficiary of political hashtags like #cdnpoli. The "check it out" nature of #cdnpoli may actually push traffic to the websites of media organizations. Despite similarities between blogs and microblogs, they each appear to interact in different ways with politics and political communication.

#cdnpoli – a people-based RSS feed

Even though Twitter has been around since 2006, academic literature on the intersection between politics and microblogging is scant. This chapter has sought to recertify this, through an exploratory examination of political hashtags. Since hashtags organize tweets around particular themes and topics, they provide us with a way of examining the political aspects of Twitter. Zhao and Rosson's term "people-based RSS feed" is apt in the case of this hashtag;

> Micro-blogging is useful for gathering valuable information for people's personal work and other interests. From an information provider's perspective, this is because users often share a piece of information when they find it very interesting and useful. From a reader's perspective, information posted by a person the reader has deliberately selected to follow is perceived as useful and trustworthy.
>
> (2009, p. 247)

Though Zhao and Rosson's study relates to Twitter and work-related practices, #cdnpoli is definitely a people-based RSS feed. Informing is the primary goal of contributors to #cdnpoli. Collectively, contributors to #cdnpoli amass, compile, and extend political information. If one wants to get a sense of the most relevant and current information on Canadian politics, then #cdnpoli serves as an excellent resource. The value of a political hashtag, or Twitter more broadly, derives from the real-time nature of the information shared on it.

Acknowledgments

My thanks to the anonymous reviewers for their thoughtful comments, and Hannah Saunders for her assistance in the data collection and coding.

Notes

1 In 2002, at Strom Thurmond's birthday, Republican Senate Majority Leader Trent Lott lamented that if Thurmond had become president, the United States "wouldn't have had all these problems." Thurmond ran on a segregationist platform in 1948. Though journalists were in attendance, the comment was not initially reported. Bloggers, conversely, were instantly critical. The praising of Thurmond's campaign was likened to praising of segregation. The intense focus of the blogosphere on Lott renewed the media's attention and "converted Lott's gaffe into a full-blown scandal" (Drezner and Farrell 2004, p. 33). Lott eventually resigned. As in the Lott case, the sustained negative attention by bloggers led to the resignation of prominent journalist Dan Rather in a scandal known as "Rathergate." In September 2004, Rather questioned George W. Bush's National Guard service in a *60 Minutes* report. Shortly after airing, the authenticity of the so-called "Killian documents" was challenged in the blogosphere, by providing evidence that the documents were bogus. The mainstream press later took up these concerns. Though CBS initially defended the veracity of the documents, the network eventually capitulated. Rather was forced into early retirement.
2 Based on statistics from politwitter.ca.

3 First, the International Co-operation Minister announced that the government would not include abortion funding in its G8 child and maternal health-care policy on April 26. Second, the Speaker of the House delivered a historic ruling on privilege in the House of Commons. Finally, one of the individuals at the center of a current political scandal testified before the House of Common's government operations committee on April 28.

4 A blogger was distinguished from an individual if a link to their blog was provided in the profile.

5 33.5 percent of the entire sample.

Part III

Digital political participation in stasis or flux?

8 The political competence of Internet participants

Evidence from Finland

Åsa Bengtsson and Henrik Serup Christensen

Introduction

The state of democracy has been a concern in the established democracies in recent decades, as levels of electoral turnout and party membership have been dwindling and citizens growing increasingly disenchanted with the dated political systems (Norris 1999; Pharr and Putnam 2000; Putnam 2000). The role of the Internet in all of this has become a debated topic (Norris 2001; Jennings and Zeitner 2003; Xenos and Bennett 2007a; Mossberger *et al.* 2008; Bennett *et al.* 2008). Initially, optimists claimed the Internet would help revitalize the disaffected citizenries (Ayres 1999; Scheufele and Nisbet 2002; Bennett *et al.* 2008). However, sceptics have started to doubt the capabilities of the Internet to foster civic mobilization, fearing a digital divide (Norris 2001) or the depoliticizing effects of the Internet (Jennings and Zeitner 2003, p. 312). The implications of the Internet for the state of democracy are still a matter of debate.

A central issue in the debate about the potential effects of political activity on the Internet concerns what is here termed political competence, although slightly different labels are used in the literature for similar concepts (Delli Carpini and Keeter 1996; Milner 2002; Dalrymple and Scheufele 2007; Grönlund 2007). Behind the different terminologies is the common idea that to fulfil the role of a democratic citizen, it is necessary to be not only willing but also able to participate in political affairs. Whereas the willingness to participate concerns the extent of citizen engagement in public affairs as a purely quantitative measure, the ability to do so refers to the competence of citizens to further their interests in a purposeful manner (Milner 2002, p. 1). It thus calls attention to the qualitative aspect of participation. It is not enough that citizens are active; they should also be able to act effectively. Accordingly, if the Internet is to provide a genuine cure for democratic ills, Internet activists also need to possess the necessary civic skills to further their interests successfully. If the Internet mobilizes civic-minded and capable citizens, it becomes untenable to dismiss these activities as inconsequential or even harmful for democracy.

This suggests that the relationship between the Internet, political competence and political participation can manifest itself in different ways. It may be that the Internet does not mobilize any new activists, and at best only provides new tools for those already active. In this sense, the Internet may make participation easier for the already active, but it does little to help activate previously passive segments. A different portrait is that the Internet does indeed mobilize new segments. However, the mobilized segments constitute 'virtually active' citizens with little clue about how to further their interests effectively, and the Internet therefore becomes a political playground for those incapable of participating in traditional political arenas. Finally, a more positive scenario expects the Internet to mobilize previously passive segments who, vitalized by the technological possibilities, bloom into both active and capable citizens who just happen to prefer other ways to voice their political preferences.

This chapter examines which scenario most adequately describes the situation in a Finnish context. Research on this has so far been scant in a European context, mainly due to lack of suitable data. The Finnish Election Study 2007 provides a rare opportunity to examine the relationships, as it not only contains the 'standard indicators' on participation, socio-economic characteristics and political involvement, but also includes indicators on political participation on the Internet and factual political knowledge.

Political participation on the Internet

A growing disenchantment with political affairs has been a cause for concern in the established democracies. This finds its expression in critical citizens with lower levels of confidence in the key democratic institutions (Norris 1999; Pharr and Putnam 2000). Additionally, citizens are less inclined to participate in national elections (Franklin 2004) and traditional political organizations such as political parties (Putnam 2000; Morales 2009).

The decline in participation has been a particular concern. Whereas critical citizens can have positive effects from a democratic perspective (Inglehart 1997; Norris 1999), some extent of citizen involvement is indispensable in a democratic system. Although elitist theories of democracies have maintained that citizen involvement need not go beyond electoral participation (Schumpeter 1942), this attitude has been challenged from several perspectives (Pateman 1970; Barber 1984; Delli Carpini and Keeter 1996, pp. 49–61). Irrespective of the potential explanations for the decline in political involvement, it clearly poses a challenge to contemporary democracies where participation is generally considered a democratic good. Although a rise in more issue-specific and sporadic forms of political mobilization may offset the drop in traditional participation (Dalton 2006, p. 73), this development is still the cause of some concern.

The Internet has been hailed as a potential remedy for these democratic ails (Ayres 1999; Norris 2001; Scheufele and Nisbet 2002; Bennett *et al.* 2008). Different perspectives exist for understanding the impact of the Internet on democracy and the structures that enable and constrain actors in their online activities (Parvez and Ahmed 2006). Participation on the Internet can involve electronic versions of traditional forms of participation – e-voting or online petition signing – but also completely new forms of cyber involvement such as politically motivated hackings (Jordan and Taylor 2004). The Internet can also enhance traditional participation by easing the dissemination of information on activities and events to a broader public and making coordination easier for activists (Ayres 1999; Bimber 2001; Scheufele and Nisbet 2002).

Most empirical studies of the Internet and political participation have examined its capacity to enhance involvement in traditional forms of participation (Ayres 1999; Bimber 2001; Dimaggio *et al.* 2001; Scheufele and Nisbet 2002; Jennings and Zeitner 2003; Bennett *et al.* 2008), whereas studies of participation on the Internet as such are more uncommon, although certainly not unheard of (Best and Krueger 2005; Bengtsson and Christensen 2009). Although the status of participation via the Internet is contested, it has nonetheless been argued that the Internet may have a profound impact on how and why citizens become active (Coleman and Blumler 2009). Other studies have raised doubts about the purported effects of the Internet on civic engagement, and have at best found a limited effect on the propensity to be actively involved in political affairs (Bimber 2001; Scheufele and Nisbet 2002; Dimaggio *et al.* 2001). Even if Internet users are found to be active in political matters, any independent effect disappears when controlling for other factors such as socio-economic status and psychological involvement in politics (Bimber 2001, p. 61). However, other studies have suggested that even if online participants in many respects are similar to traditional participants, there are some differences (Best and Krueger 2005).

Additionally, most of these contributions have not examined Internet activists as a specific group of activists, not to be confounded with activists who mix online and traditional participation. If the Internet is expected to mobilize new segments of the population not otherwise politically active, the characteristics of these may be diluted when grouping them with activists who are active both online and offline. It may therefore be appropriate to examine the characteristics of pure Internet participants as against traditional activists and those who utilize both online and offline participation. This suggests there is good reason to re-examine the relationship between the Internet and the willingness and ability of citizens to participate politically.

Participation and political competence

The state of political competence has also been a cause for concern in contemporary democracies. The well-known connection between high socio-economic status and the propensity to be active has led some to worry that the decision-makers receive a distorted message since the opinions of privileged activists do not reflect those of the general population (Delli Carpini and Keeter 1996; Verba 2003, pp. 671–672). Somewhat contrary to this, others contend that not only are the resource-rich more active, they are better citizens (Verba 2003). In this perspective, greater equality in participation may constitute a deskilling of activists, leading to participation that is largely incapable of influencing decisions (Topf 1995, p. 71). However, a general lack of civic competence among the population constitutes a more serious democratic problem than inequality in the distribution of these, as citizens need skills to fulfil their obligations as democratic citizens (Delli Carpini and Keeter 1996, pp. 55–61). Although large inequalities in civic skills may also constitute a democratic problem as it advantages the privileged few over the majority, any notion of equality of civic skills ought to aim at the highest possible level.

Involvement as a purely quantitative measure does not make it possible to determine whether the participants are also effectively furthering their interests. To be able to function effectively, citizens need to be able to comprehend the political system and evaluate the consequences of alternative actions. The concept of political competence is somewhat vague, and an array of terms such as 'civic skills', 'political knowledge', 'political information', 'civic literacy' and 'civic competence' have been used to refer to related aspects of this (Grönlund 2007). What these different approaches have in common is the notion that in order to function effectively as a citizen, it is necessary to understand how the political system functions and how to navigate effectively as citizens (Verba *et al.* 1995, pp. 304–305; Grönlund 2007, pp. 399–401; Dalrymple and Scheufele 2007, pp. 97–99). Milner (2002, p. 3) includes both the willingness and the ability to participate in his concept of civic literacy, thus confounding the two elements. A more apt conceptualization treats the two elements as two distinct aspects of political participation. Political participation as a quantitative measure of the level of mobilization relates to the willingness to participate, whereas the qualitative aspect of political competences concerns the ability to participate effectively.

Differences also persist over what skills are necessary and how to determine that participants possess them. One approach uses individual characteristics such as socio-demographic resources (Verba *et al.* 1995) or associational involvement (Best and Krueger 2005) as proxies for political competence. A different approach gauges the capabilities of citizens more directly through differences in factual knowledge about the political system and the actors that inhabit it (Delli Carpini and Keeter 1996; Milner 2002). This factual knowledge has been argued to be the best available indicator for how well citizens grasp the functioning of political matters (Delli Carpini and Keeter 1993, p. 1180). Informed citizens hold more stable and consistent opinions and are less susceptible to propaganda, more receptive to relevant information and more likely to tie objective group conditions to their policy views and connect their policy views to evaluations of public officials in instrumentally rational ways (Delli Carpini and Keeter 1996, p. 265; Galston 2001, pp. 223–226). Nonetheless, others argue that factual bits and pieces are poor indicators of the ability of citizens to comprehend political matters, and it is therefore advisable to use additional indicators to gauge political competence (Dalrymple and Scheufele 2007, p. 97).

The literature is somewhat ambiguous when it comes to the role of the Internet and political competence. Some fear that the Internet may perpetuate the existing differences in participation, granting the politically proficient a further advantage by creating a digital divide in participation (Norris 2001). Others argue that Internet proficiency may help improve the political competences of citizens (Milner 2002, p. 131; Dalrymple and Scheufele 2007). A final interpretation sees a risk that the Internet mobilizes a sort of second-rate activists who are incapable of furthering their demands through the traditional political venues (Schulman 2004). This latter criticism is especially important for the present purposes, since it suggests that although the Internet may help mobilize citizens, the consequences for the quality of democracy may still be negative due to the deskilling of the virtual activists.

As the discussion above has made clear, in order to assess the implications of the Internet for political participation, it is necessary to consider both the quantitative and qualitative aspects; i.e. the willingness to participate and the ability to do so effectively. It is not only important to learn more about the extent to which the Internet has the potential to activate new groups of citizens. The political competence of the Internet participants is just as important when evaluating what implications the advent of the Internet has had for political participation.

Research design

The overall aim of this study is to explore relationships between the Internet and the quantitative and qualitative aspects of political participation and through this to examine which of the scenarios outlined in the introduction best describes the situation. The scholarly debate revolves around the potential of the Internet when it comes to mobilizing new groups of citizens to become politically active. Another related theme involves the question of whether citizens politically active on the Internet can be described as politically competent or if the Internet merely is a playground for 'virtually active' citizens with little clue about how to further their interests effectively. Accordingly, the empirical part of this paper sets out to answer two research questions that address what we here label the *quantitative aspect* and the *qualitative aspects* of participation:

1   Does the Internet mobilize citizens not previously active in political matters?
2   Are participants who engage in political matters via the Internet competent democratic citizens?

Finland provides a good opportunity to study these questions, as it has been one of the forerunners of the Internet revolution in Europe. In the late 1990s, Finland was recognized as Europe's Information Society and had high levels of Internet literacy and Internet subscriptions (Milner 2002, pp. 131–132). Even if these differences may have evened out in recent years, there is little doubt that Internet use is particularly well integrated within Finnish society. For this reason, it may well provide a preview of things to come in other countries. In addition, the Finnish Election Study (FNES) 2007 (FSD2269) provides a rare opportunity to examine these questions since it not only contains a wide set of indicators of political participation in traditional and more recent forms of political engagement on the

Internet, but also high-quality indicators of political competence, such as objective political knowledge.

The Finnish National Election Study (FNES) 2007 is a post-election survey conducted after the parliamentary elections in March 2007.[1] The data were collected in two stages. The first stage involved face-to-face interviews with 1,422 respondents based on quota sampling.[2] The second part was collected via a self-administered questionnaire, to be returned by mail, answered by 1,033 of the respondents interviewed in the first stage. The questions used here were located in the first part of the study. The survey includes an oversample of Swedish-speaking respondents, which is controlled for by using appropriate weights.

The dependent variable

The dependent variable of the study is political participation. To examine differences between participants in traditional offline participation and the participants in activities over the Internet, we operationalize this into an online and an offline dimension. For traditional offline participation, the indicators include eight activities, rating from highly conventional activity in political parties to the use of violence and civil disobedience.[3]

Although it is common praxis to differentiate between different modes of political participation (Bengtsson and Christensen 2009; Verba *et al.* 1971; Teorell *et al.* 2007), participation offline is in this study treated as a one-dimensional phenomenon. This approach makes it possible compare participants in online and offline activities, and is also used by, for example, Best and Krueger (2005) and Jennings and Zeitner (2003). The second dimension includes activities related to political participation on the Internet and involves three actions: contacting, signing petitions and political discussion. For more information on the activities included in the scales, see Tables 8.1 and 8.2.

Based on the two indexes of participation, a variable consisting of four categories of citizens is created, which forms the dependent variable in the subsequent analyses. The first category consists of totally passive citizens, the second contains those who only engage in offline participation, the third cat-

Table 8.1 Political participation offline

	Percentage	*Number*
Signing a petition	45	638
Contacting	18	260
Writing a letter to a newspaper	12	172
Party activity	10	146
Demonstration (peaceful)	7	92
Civil disobedience	1	14
Demonstration (violent)	0	5
Used violence for political purposes	0	6

Note
The question covers activity during the last four years.

Table 8.2 Political participation on the Internet

	Percentage	*Number*
Signed a petition	28	397
Discussed political matters	15	211
Contacted political decision-makers	11	160

Note
The question covers activity during the last four years.

egory consists of those who act politically solely on the Internet, and the fourth and final one contain citizens who engage in political matters both online and offline. The dependent variable of the study is thus a nominal categorical variable with four values grasping passivity, offline activity, online activity, and mixed activity. For a descriptive presentation of the dependent variable, see Table 8.3.

A dilemma in creating this variable involves the questions on activities that can be performed both online and offline, i.e. contacting and signing a petition. The phrasings of the questions on traditional activities do not explicitly clarify that they concern offline activities, but are more general (as is common for this kind of indicator). Due to the absence of specifications, it seems likely that respondents who have performed the activities on the Internet indicate having performed the activity here as well.[4] Accordingly, it is not possible to determine whether these activities were performed online or offline. Unfortunately, no ideal solution to this problem exists. To exclude activities that risk overlapping online and offline would substantially underestimate the share of citizens who are politically active. To treat the respondents who answer yes to both questions as participants in both off- and online activities would overestimate the mixed group. The third possible solution to resolve this predicament is to treat respondents who answer yes to performing these two activities both online and offline as online activists. Although this risks overestimating the number of online participants, as respondents who have indeed performed the activity in question both online and offline will be coded as only having performed it online, it seems a more intuitive solution, not least since the study has a specific interest in citizens active on the Internet. In addition, further analysis of the values on the key explanatory variables confirms that these respondents resemble the online

Table 8.3 Political participation off- and online

	%	N
Passive	35	504
Offline participation	29	414
Online participation	16	234
Double participation	19	269
Total	100	1,421

participants more, which suggests this to be the most apt solution (details not presented). The analyses were carried out with both alternative codings with no substantial change in the results. We therefore do not believe that this biases the inferences to be drawn.[5]

Independent variables

The main independent variables revolve around the concept of political competence. As explained, exactly what this complex concept involves is a disputed topic (Grönlund 2007; Dalrymple and Scheufele 2007). For this reason, our models include several indicators for the skills necessary to act as politically competent citizens. The most direct measure is factual political knowledge. How to best measure factual knowledge has also been debated in the literature (Mondak 2001; Delli Carpini and Keeter 1993, 1996). Here, the factual knowledge of the respondents is measured by an index based on answers to five questions concerning actors and institutions in the Finnish political system.

Three other indicators of how well respondents comprehend political matters are of more indirect nature. The first is internal political efficacy, defined as the subjective feeling of being able to affect political matters, which has been used in a number of studies to measure political knowledge (Asbjørnsen and Vogt 1992). This does not probe the actual degree of political competences, and a cynic may even argue that political incompetence is conducive for the subjective feeling of political efficacy. Nonetheless, previous research suggests that this aspect is related to higher levels of political involvement and educational attainment (Niemi *et al.* 1991, p. 1411), both of which are important for the political competence of citizens as well. Another indicator used is the level of education of the respondent, which serves as a proxy for the general knowledge level of citizens, as well as the ability to process and make sense of the information they are provided with (Verba *et al.* 1995, p. 305). The final indicator concerns media exposure during the election campaign. This is an index that measures the extent to which citizens followed the political campaign via different sources of media (11 different sources) and serves as an indicator of how much political information citizens acquire and of how politically aware they are (Norris 2000a, p. 246).

In order to avoid spurious effects we also introduce a set of control variables in the model. In the first model we control for age and gender and in the second we include a control variable for Internet use. For detailed information about the coding of all variables used, see the appendix.

We begin the empirical part with addressing the first research question by outlining the object of study. Descriptive data on citizens' political activity on the Internet and offline in traditional political activists clarify the extent to which the Internet helps mobilize citizens. We then continue with a presentation of the bivariate relationships between aspects of political competence and political participation. This serves as a first step in finding out whether citizens who are politically active on the Internet can be considered politically competent.

Following this, we analyse the behaviour of citizens using multinomial logistic regression analysis in order to ascertain differences in the effects of political competence for the three groups of participants. Multinomial logistic regression is used to analyse the relationships of the dependent variables with more than two unordered categories. To use this method makes it possible to compare offline activists, online activists and the mixed group to the passive part of the population, and to discern whether the indicators of political competence explain who participates in what activity. A pessimistic scenario expects Internet activists to be less politically competent than traditional activists, whereas a positive appraisal expects the Internet activists to be as or even more politically competent.

Empirical analysis

The quantitative aspect: the Internet as an activating media

The pattern of political participation in Finland largely resembles what is found in other mature democracies. Turnout in parliamentary elections has decreased considerably since the 1980s, but other forms of engagement such as contacting, signing petitions and demonstrations have gained in popularity (Bengtsson and Christensen 2009; Bengtsson and Grönlund 2005; Norris 2002). As can be seen in Table 8.1, the most popular activity by far is signing a petition. This is non-demanding in terms of both time and effort needed, and has been used by as many as 45 per cent of the Finnish population during the four years preceding the election in 2007. The second most popular way to be politically active is to contact political decision-makers. This activity, which can be considered far more demanding than signing a petition, has been used by almost 20 per cent. Less common, but still used by more than 10 per cent of the Finnish citizens during the period is to write a letter to the editor of a newspaper and to be active in a political party. Only 7 per cent of the Finnish citizens engaged in demonstrations, and participation in more confrontational and illegal activities was almost non-existent. According to this, the Finnish citizenry is relatively active in traditional activities performed offline.

Our knowledge about the extent to which citizens are politically active on the Internet is far less developed. Table 8.2 displays information on the extent to which the Finnish citizenry has used the Internet for three political activities during the last four years. To sign a petition is also the most common activity among those using the Internet as a medium for political participation. Almost 30 per cent of the respondents state that they have done this at least once during the four years prior to the 2007 parliamentary election. The second most common political activity is to use the Internet to discuss political matters, which 15 per cent have done. To use the Internet in order to contact political decision-makers can be considered as the most demanding of the three, since it involves the articulation of specific demands in order to achieve a political outcome. We still find that this activity has been performed by more than 10 per cent during the last four years. The results presented in Table 8.2 suggest that the Internet is used for political purposes to a relatively large extent by Finnish citizens.

The descriptive presentations above portray the Finnish citizens as relatively active in political activities, offline as well as online. However, the question about the activating effect of the Internet is still left unanswered. In order to assess this quantitative aspect, a combined index is presented in Table 8.3. The index makes a distinction between citizens who are politically passive, citizens who are active offline or online-only and citizens active both on the Internet and in more traditional ways. This makes it possible to examine whether it is the same citizens who are active on the Internet and in more traditional ways, or if the Internet helps promote activity among new segments.

The group of politically passive during the preceding four years amounts to 35 per cent of the Finnish population. According to this, about a third of the population refrained from any kind of political activity, although it should be kept in mind that this excludes turnout in elections as well as acts of political consumerism. About 30 per cent of the population participated in at least one of the traditional forms of participation outside the Internet, the percentage of people who only engage in political activities via the Internet is 16 per cent, and the share of the population active in both online and offline activities amounts to almost 20 per cent. These figures clearly suggest that the Internet has a substantial activating effect, since 16 per cent of all respondents indicate that they would not be active without the possibilities for participation offered by the Internet. Although most citizens active on the Internet are also active in offline activities this certainly suggests that the Internet is not only a tool for political engagement among the already active, but involves new groups of citizens in political matters. Even if it possible that these citizens would be active in more traditional ways if the Internet had not offered virtual possibilities, it seems fair to conclude that the Internet has helped keep citizens active in political affairs. They mixed group only constitutes slightly more than half of the ones who choose to use the Internet as a tool for political engagement. As was discussed in the section on research design, it is problematic to distinguish between activity offline and online when it comes to signing petitions and contacting political decision-makers, as these can be performed both online and offline. The strategy used here to mitigate this problem was to treat all who answered yes to these activities both offline and online as online activists. This runs the risk of exaggerating the share of pure online activists and underestimating the share that is active in both ways. With the opposite strategy, that is likely to underestimate the share of online activists, the share of citizens active solely on the Internet decreases to 9 per cent. Accordingly, the conclusion that the Internet activates new citizens holds with this strategy as well.

Hence, the Internet appears to contribute positively to mobilizing citizens in Finland. It may be, however, that the citizens mobilized in this manner, being incapable of political navigation, have gone astray in the maze of politics. To examine this line of questioning, we turn to the qualitative aspect of participation understood as the political competence of citizens.

The qualitative aspect: participation on the Internet and political competence

The following section is devoted to the question of the political competence of the Internet activists compared to participants in more traditional activities outside the virtual world. Since political competence is an important qualitative ingredient of political participation, it is of interest to see whether the virtual participants are capable of acting politically in a skilful and competent manner. The first step involves comparing the mean scores on the four indicators of competence among the four groups of citizens: passive, offline participants, online participants, and the mixed group. The results are presented in Table 8.4.

The table displays the mean scores for the four indicators of political competence – political knowledge, internal efficacy, education and media exposure. The most obvious, and maybe least surprising observation that can be made is that the least politically competent citizens on all counts are those who are politically passive. The mean scores are significantly lower in this group compared to the active citizens, whether offline, online or in both ways. This finding calls attention to the inherent link between the quantitative and qualitative aspects of political participation, as being active leads to higher levels of political competences, creating mutually reinforcing relationship between the two (Milner 2002). The second but slightly less consistent finding is that the most politically competent citizens appear to be the group which is active both online and offline. This group of citizens displays the highest mean level of political knowledge and the highest level of internal efficacy, and follows the election campaign in the media more than other citizens do. Independent t-tests reveal that the difference in mean scores between the groups with citizens active both offline and online and the other politically active citizens are not statistically significant in all cases. Nonetheless, this suggests that the most competent citizens are likely to pursue their goals both online and offline. When it comes to the level of education, the pattern is broken as the highest mean level of education is found among citizens who are only politically active on the Internet. A comparison of online and offline activists shows that the citizens active on the Internet display the highest competence level on average, although only the result for education is statistically significant. Even if the differences are marginal on all other counts except education, the mean levels are generally higher among online participants.

Accordingly, the results suggest that the Internet participants are competent activists. If anything, the ones who are only active offline are slightly disadvantaged compared to other activists, although they are certainly more competent than the passive part of the population. Based on these bivariate analyses of political competence and political participation, the conclusion is that there is no cause for pessimism concerning the relationship between Internet participation and political competence. On the contrary, it seems as if citizens who use the Internet as a tool for political participation are more politically competent than other activists are.

Table 8.4 Political participation off- and online and political competence (mean values)

	Political knowledge (mean)	Internal efficacy (mean)	Education (mean)	Media exposure (mean)
Passive	0.61	0.26	0.39	0.27
Offline participation	0.66	0.36	0.49	0.30
Online participation	0.68	0.37	0.57	0.31
Double participation	0.72	0.46	0.52	0.36
Total	0.66	0.34	0.48	0.30
Anova (between groups)	$F_{(2.02)} = 12.99***$	$F_{(7.55)} = 29.17***$	$F_{(6.15)} = 2.05***$	$F_{(1.41)} = 26.39***$

Note
*** $p < 0.001$

To examine this claim further, Table 8.5 presents the results of a multinomial regression, where the three active groups are compared to the passive segment of the population. This makes it possible to examine the characteristic of the three groups of participants while controlling for other potential influences. Two models are presented in Table 8.5. The first model is the 'base model', which includes indicators for political competence together with control variables for age and gender as central socio-demographic characteristics. The second model, the 'control model', introduces a variable that grasps the extent to which citizens use Internet regularly in order to control for potential spurious relationships between political competence and political activity.

The base model largely corroborates the previous findings and shows that the indicators for competence are positively related to being included in all three groups of activists. The only exception is political knowledge for offline participants, where the effect turns out to be statistically insignificant. Offline participants are thus not on average more knowledgeable about political matters than the share of the population who are politically passive when controlling for the effect of other factors. The effects of the other competence variables are also generally weaker for these traditional participants, whereas the online and mixed group tend to deviate more strongly from the passive citizens. The only exception to this concerns internal efficacy, or the personal feeling of political competence, where the effect is slightly stronger for traditional activists compared to the online activists. Nonetheless, traditional activists may feel more competent, but this subjective sense is not supported by the more objective measures. Overall, there is again little to suggest that Internet activists are any less competent citizens than other activists. Although the mixed group of people who are politically active both online and offline tends to consist of the most competent citizens, the pure Internet activists are not far behind on most counts, and they even tend to be better educated than the mixed group. The least competent group is the traditional activists who restrict themselves to participation offline, although even they tend to be more competent than altogether passive citizens.

Even if it is not of primary concern for this chapter to examine whether the Internet only promotes participation among groups of citizens who traditionally have been active, it is of interest to note that the control variables age and gender suggest this is not necessarily the case. As could be expected, Internet participants are predominantly younger citizens. The younger cohorts still primarily use these relatively new technological advances, even if the differences may be expected to even out over time, as the younger generations can be expected to continue to take advantage of these possibilities as they grow older. Slightly more surprising is the tendency for the Internet activist to be predominantly female. It is often thought that Internet users tend to be predominantly male, but these results suggest that women are over-represented among users of the Internet for political purposes. This indicates that the Internet may help even out the gender gap in political participation that has been a persistent finding in most studies of political participation (Verba *et al.* 1995; Norris 2002). Both of these results suggest that the advent of the Internet may help mobilize groups who are

Table 8.5 Multinomial regression analysis for political participation on- and offline, with passive citizens as reference category. Non-standardized regression coefficients (*b*) with standard error in parenthesis

		Base model			Control model		
		Offline	Online	Both	Offline	Online	Both
Political competence	Political knowledge	0.50 (0.33)	1.66*** (0.42)	1.83*** (0.41)	0.37 (0.33)	1.24** (0.43)	1.33** (0.42)
	Internal efficacy	0.83*** (0.25)	0.72* (0.32)	1.69*** (0.29)	0.74** (0.25)	0.40 (0.33)	1.35*** (0.30)
	Education	1.02*** (0.28)	1.90*** (0.34)	0.97*** (0.33)	0.89*** (0.29)	1.39*** (0.35)	0.43 (0.34)
	Media exposure	1.85** (0.56)	3.59*** (0.71)	5.25*** (0.66)	1.79*** (0.56)	3.36*** (0.72)	5.02*** (0.68)
Control variables	Gender (male)	−0.10 (0.14)	−0.77*** (0.18)	−0.57** (0.18)	−0.09 (0.15)	−0.76*** (0.19)	−0.55** (0.18)
	Age/100	−1.50*** (0.43)	−6.61*** (0.58)	−5.05*** (0.53)	−0.70 (0.52)	−4.02*** (0.68)	−2.26*** (0.63)
	Internet usage				0.49* (0.20)	2.11*** (0.33)	2.24*** (0.30)
	Intercept	−0.90*** (0.30)	−0.54 (0.35)	−1.71*** (0.36)	−1.39*** (0.36)	−2.57*** (0.48)	−3.86*** (0.47)
Model statistics	−2 Log likelihood	3,323.37***			3,232.35***		
	Cox and Snell R^2	0.26			0.30		
	Nagelkerke R^2	0.27			0.32		
	McFadden R^2	0.11			0.13		
	N	1,392			1,392		

Notes
***$p<0.001$ **$p<0.01$ *$p<0.05$ (*)$p<0.10$. Dependent variable: a variable with four values: passive citizens, citizens politically engaged offline, i.e. not on the Internet, citizens politically engaged on the Internet and citizens politically engaged off- as well as online. Entries are non-standardized regression coefficients. Group of comparison is the passive citizens. All variables are measured on a scale between 0 and 1. For more information about the variables see appendix. Multicollinearity diagnostic statistics show that there is no cause for concern.

less active in offline activities. However, more research is necessary to settle conclusively whether this is actually the case.

There is a risk that the relationship between political competence and political activity on the Internet is affected by the overall propensity to use the Internet. If politically competent citizens in general have a higher tendency to use the Internet, the positive relationship between political competence and activity on the Internet might be a spurious finding created by the fact that citizens who use the Internet for all kinds of purposes would also use it for political ones. If this were the case, we would expect the effect of the political competence variables to lose their significance in this control model. As can be seen in the results for the control model, the introduction of this additional control variable indeed does weaken the effects of most competence variables and even causes some findings to lose significance. The latter is the case for education, where the group of mixed activists can no longer be shown to be better educated than the passive citizens, and for internal efficacy, which is no longer a significant trademark for the Internet activists. The offline activists still differ from the passive citizens in these two regards, but do not differ when it comes to factual political knowledge.

Nonetheless, although the effects on the political competence variables on most counts are weaker, the overall conclusions essentially remain unchanged. That Internet activists tend to be politically competent cannot just be attributed to a general predisposition for using the Internet for all purposes. It would seem that Internet activists in no respect emerge as a form of second-class activists. Indeed, they are more politically competent than passive citizens, and as competent as or even more competent than citizens engaging in traditional political participation offline.

Conclusion

In recent years, it has become a pressing concern to revitalize the somewhat dated established democracies, where citizen apathy and indifference towards political matters are mounting problems. If the situation in Finland portrays a road for others to follow, the Internet offers possibilities for remedying some of these democratic ills.

The impact of the Internet on both quantitative and qualitative aspects of political participation – the willingness and ability to participate – has been debated in the literature. Following an initial exhilaration over the potential benefits of the technological advances presented by the Internet, sceptics have increasingly passed more cautious judgements over the impact of the Internet on the state of democracy, as it may increase existing disparities and even depoliticize participation.

Nonetheless, and although uncertainties certainly persist, the results presented here suggest that the Internet as an arena for political participation is occupied by citizens who both are active and possess a high degree of political competence. In fact, judged by the impact of the Internet on political participation in

Finland, it may be that the best is yet to come. First, the results of the analyses presented here suggest that the Internet helps mobilize a sizeable segment of the population not engaged in political affairs in any ways outside the virtual world. Although it may be that without the lure of the Internet, these people would be engaged in traditional activities, a more reasonable interpretation seems to be that the Internet has actually mobilized this segment. Although the data material used here made it difficult to pinpoint the exact magnitude, the results certainly suggested that the Internet has a positive impact on the quantitative aspect of citizenship, helping increase the level of participation.

Second, and just as importantly, the results suggest that the citizens participating via the Internet are not mere playground activists, as they are generally as politically competent or even more so as activists in offline forms of participation. The results corroborated the ruling orthodoxy from previous research that active citizens are more capable than passive citizens. However, most results even suggest that the most competent ones are the one who utilize the Internet for participation. The most capable citizens tend to be the ones who participate both online and offline, which is hardly surprising given the mutually reinforcing link between participation and political competence. The results even suggest that citizens who only participate over the Internet tend to be as capable as or even more so than active citizens who only engage in more traditional offline activities. There is nothing to suggest that Internet activists constitute a sort of second-class activists led astray by the virtual world. Instead, they appear to be able to comprehend political matters as well as anyone.

The results even suggest that the Internet offers possibilities for participation to frequently marginalized groups in society. That young people are more likely to participate via the Internet is well documented. More surprising is the suggestion that the Internet also furthers the political participation of women.

Although it is necessary with more research to determine whether similar trends may be found elsewhere, all of this certainly suggests that it is too early to dismiss the positive impact of the Internet on democratic participation.

Appendix

Dependent variable

Political participation offline

Respondents were asked:

> *During the past four years have you done any of the following or do you feel you might in the future:*
>
> • *write a letter to the editor?*
> • *contact political decision-makers on some issue?*
> • *sign a petition?*

- *involve yourself in the activity of a political party?*
- *participate in peaceful demonstrations?*
- *demonstrate civil disobedience by participating in illegal, non-violent activities?*
- *participate in the kind of demonstrations that have previously involved violence?*
- *use violence to reach political goals?*

Score: 1 = Have done over the past four years; 2 = Have not done but might do; 3 = Would not do under any circumstances; 4 = Can't say.

Respondents replying 'Have done over the past four years' are coded 1. Others are coded 0.

An index based on the eight activities are created so that all respondents who state they have participated in one activity (or more) are coded 1 and the inactive are coded 0.

Political participation online

Respondents were asked:

During the past four years have you done any of the following on the Internet, or do you feel you might in the future:

- *sign a petition?*
- *contact decision-makers?*
- *discuss politics?*

For categories as well as coding see above.

Political participation in combination

A nominal categorical variable with four values based on activity offline and online: 0 = passive citizens; 1 = only offline activity; 2 = only online activity; 3 = mixed activity.

Independent variables

All independent variables are coded on a scale from 0 to 1.

Political competence

Political knowledge: Five questions about political matters which were combined in an index counting the number of correct answers, divided by five. The questions are as follows:

- *'Who* [of the following] *was the Finnish Minister of Foreign Affairs during 2006?'*

- *'What party* [of the following] *is the second largest party in the new parliament measured in terms of mandates?'*
- *'What country* [of the following] *is a permanent member of the United Nation's Security Council?'*
- *'Who is entitled to vote in Finnish parliamentary elections?'* [Four choices were offered]
- *'What is meant by a parliamentary form of government?'* [Four choices were offered].

1 = high political knowledge; 0 = low political knowledge

Education: 1 = lower and higher academic degree; 0.8 = polytechnic degree; 0.6 = unfinished polytechnic or academic degree; 0.4 = lowest level tertiary education; 0.2 = upper secondary level education; 0 = lower secondary level education.

Internal efficacy: A statement: *'Sometimes it feels like politics is so complicated that I don't understand what is going on.'*
1 = strongly agree; 0.67 = partly agree; 0.33 = partly disagree; 0 = strongly disagree.

Media exposure: An index was created from 11 options about media usage during the election campaign.
How much attention did you pay to media coverage of the parliamentary elections from:

- *television debates and party leader interviews?*
- *television news and current affairs programmes?*
- *television entertainment programmes featuring politicians?*
- *radio programmes?*
- *newspaper articles?*
- *news concerning the election on the Internet?*
- *websites of the candidates and political parties?*
- *Internet blogs?*
- *candidate selectors on the Internet?*
- *television advertisements?*
- *newspaper advertisements?*

Four choices were offered: A great deal; A fair amount; Only a little; No attention at all. Answers to all choices were added and divided by 11.
1 = high media exposure, 0 = no media exposure

Control variables

Gender: 1 = man, 0 = woman
Age: Age in years divided by 100
Internet usage: *'How often do you use the Internet?'*
                   1 = daily, 0.75 = a few times a week, 0.5 = about once a week,
                   0.25 = occasionally, 0 = not at all.

Notes

1 The primary investigator of the Finnish National Election Study 2007 was Professor Heikki Paloheimo, University of Tampere. The data base can be ordered from the Finnish Social Science Data Archive (www.fsd.uta.fi).
2 The quotas were based on age, gender and province of residence of the respondents.
3 As the interest lies in examining how Internet participants compare to more traditional participants, the analysis disregards more ambiguous forms of political participation such as political consumerism (Micheletti 2003).
4 This assumption seems plausible since these questions were asked before the ones concerning activities on the Internet.
5 For more information about the impact of this choice, see the discussion on page 140.

9   Reaching citizens online

How youth organizations are evolving their web presence

Janelle Ward

Introduction

The aim of this chapter is to examine how UK-based youth organizations draw on a theoretical conception of citizenship (their 'offline' philosophy) when making choices about web presence (their 'online' structure). Web presence, in this case, consists of both the official website and social networking sites. There is little research that directly addresses the perceptions of web producers, particularly of civic-geared organizations like non-profits (Kenix 2008) and even fewer that compare these views to content. The research question is: How do youth organizations view young people as citizens, and how is this view communicated via their websites and on their Facebook and Twitter profiles?

The United Kingdom is the contextual reference point in this research. It provides an interesting country case as it has a rich heritage of theoretical work as well as a focus in recent years on coming to terms with a 'crisis' of citizenship, particularly among youth (e.g. Henn *et al.* 2002). This has resulted in much academic and press attention to this issue, a recent introduction of citizenship education into school curricula, and numerous government-sponsored initiatives as well as a thriving alternative sphere where single-issue campaigns and pressure groups are growing in influence. The UK is also a technologically advanced society with high Internet penetration rates, and scholars and practitioners in this context have demonstrated interest in reviving relations between government and the people, for example with an enthusiasm for applying e-democracy to this challenge (Coleman and Gøtze 2002).

Contemporary citizenship

An apt beginning is with a description of the theoretical landscape in which youth organizations operate. Though by no means mutually exclusive, there are two predominant views of youth citizenship in contemporary society: For the purposes of this chapter these are termed conventional and non-conventional citizenship (Ward 2008). Both operate in an environment of 'apathetic' youth who do not vote, are not concerned with their elected officials and forgo involvement in traditional political matters (Delli Carpini 2000), but this development is viewed differently by each. Conventional citizenship often draws on the notion that youth are demonstrating disengagement from the political process. Some see the health of a representative democracy as resting on the extent and nature of citizen engagement (Almond and Verba 1963; Pattie *et al.* 2003). Therefore disengagement is grounds for apprehension, particularly within the youth cohort: 'young people are at the point in their lives where they are most motivated to construct identities, to forge new social groupings, and to negotiate alternatives to given cultural meanings' (Livingstone 2002, p. 4). The end goal is to reconnect youth with traditional institutions and thus allow those institutions to regain their legitimacy. Coleman (2008) sees these types of citizens as 'managed' citizens, who need socialization to learn the skills to properly function in a democracy; their perceived apathy must be managed in order to create good citizens. In a similar vein, Bennett (2008) refers to them as 'dutiful citizens', those who are obliged to participate in pre-existing democratic processes, such as voting.

Perhaps youth are apathetic when it comes to traditional political behaviour. But for those embracing non-conventional citizenship, this apathy stops at the ballot box. Non-conventional citizenship sees young people as dynamic and empowered. Coleman (2008) calls for recognition of this 'autonomous' citizenship, a view that encourages youth to create their own democratic agenda. Likewise, Bennett (2008) identifies 'actualizing' citizens, where each citizen finds meaning in individual purpose rather than government structure, and focuses on issues like consumerism rather than voting to perform an active role in democracy. For example, 'elite-challenging forms of participation are becoming more widespread' (Inglehart 1997, p. 236). Giddens (1990) looks to 'lifestyle' politics: When local and global issues collide, lifestyle choices become increasingly important. Further, for those engaging in non-conventional citizenship, 'Many of the participants ... do not appear to see a contradiction between their national political apathy (not voting in elections) and their transnational engagement' (Chadwick 2006, p. 30).

Although research into evolving citizenship has often been conducted in the United States, there is also evidence for both of these views in the British context. Alderman (1999, p. 128) sees the UK as having

> become two nations politically: on the one hand, that of two parties which continue to monopolize power at the parliamentary and governmental level and, on the other, that of the single issue groups and protest movements, whose membership has long since outstripped the active grassroots support the parties can call upon.

Communicating to young citizens online

In this setting, youth are active online and Internet-based activities are a frequent part of their lives. Today's youth grew up in a computer-mediated environment, and are sometimes referred to as 'digital natives' (Prensky 2001). Because of this, youth organizations that want to promote civic or political engagement and encourage various types of political participation should ensure that they have a successful online presence. The organization's website should, at minimum, have a better chance of speaking to this age group, and at most may be able to assist in reversing the problem of political disengagement (for conventional organizations) or help youth to embrace a new look at political life (non-conventional organizations).

Indeed, scholars have examined how the Internet can reach citizens in order to improve their civic or political participation. The claim follows that online technology may be able to capture the interest of particularly youth, who are already active online and knowledgeable about high-tech communication (Ward *et al.* 2003). This online interest will then transfer to increased rates of traditional participation. A great deal of research has examined the content of such political websites, both in general (Carlson and Strandberg 2007; Gibson *et al.* 2003; van Selm *et al.* 2001) and focused on youth (Bennett and Xenos 2005; Montgomery *et al.* 2004; Ward 2008).

But how, precisely, are these websites addressing youth? More broadly, what possibilities does online communication offer youth organizations to reach their young audience? Advances in technology provide a restructuring so that political actors can now supply an original, unmediated message to the public. With its combination of textual, auditory and visual components, the Internet provides an increased opportunity to present civic and political material to citizens, but also allows those citizens to interact with each other and the organization. Here, a website is seen as an online structure of communication (Schneider and Foot 2002) that provides an official window to the world.

Here, online structure is envisaged as having the potential to communicate a particular stance on citizenship. Recent research has attempted to connect similar views of citizenship to how content is presented online by youth organizations. For example, Wells (2010) puts forth a similar argument. He examines comparable models of citizenship (along with Bennett 2008, dutiful and self-actualizing models of citizenship) with, following Coleman (2008), managed versus autonomous styles of communication. In a comparable vein, this chapter argues that it is possible to visualize web presence as a space for providing information and achieving various aims of the producer (one-way communication) but also as a direct link to the user, providing a means for citizens to respond to the organization (interactive communication). What remains to be seen is whether these types of communication are inherently different on conventional versus non-conventional organizations' websites.

One-way communication is generally based on the notion of sender to receiver, and is primarily informative in nature. It utilizes a broadcast model and does not request or receive feedback from audience members or users. Traditionally academics have noted that political websites hold an administrative or information function and a networking or campaigning function (Ward *et al.* 2003; see also Schneider and Foot 2002). Key to these functions is the unmediated message conveyed to citizens; little emphasis is placed on interaction with citizens. Websites operate as an official online representation of the organization and typically focus on information provision. For example, organization biographies or text about campaigns can be considered one-way communication. Bennett (2008) notes that conventional, 'dutiful' citizens most often participate in organizations that employ one-way methods of communication.

Further, and despite an historical focus on information functions, academics generally agree that websites hold the potential (and perhaps, normatively, should provide) for spaces of interactivity and discussion (Gibson *et al.* 2003). So websites can also be participatory, which implies their function extends beyond an official 'about us' space and attempts to engage interested parties in a variety of ways, most notably through interactive communication. These spaces can facilitate 'interactive linkages between citizens and parties' (Norris 2003, p. 23) but also provide a means for oppositional voices to be heard. Initially meant to describe face-to-face communication (Rafaeli 1988), interactive communication has evolved as technologies have become more complex in their possibilities for interaction. Downes and McMillan (2000) see interactive communication as at a minimum, two-way, and as having a flexible outlook on the concept of time, such as when messages are received.

More recently, and the focus here, Xenos and Foot's (2008) transactional interactivity is accomplished through 'carefully managed forms of exchange … a preference for features that return strategic goods for the campaign while involving a relatively small investment of resources' (p. 63). This may include features that allow organizations to gather information from visitors, such as email addresses or demographic particulars. Websites can also endorse co-productive interactivity, which embraces 'the notion of interactivity as user-control … by clicking, typing, accessing, and surfing a site the user provides input that generates noticeable changes in output' (pp. 64–65). Co-productive interactivity works by enabling comments on news stories or blog postings online, or allowing users to rate features or leave feedback in transparent ways, where users have a higher level of content control. It also includes opportunities to influence the content of the site, for example through direct interaction with web producers. Xenos and Foot (2008) argue that young Internet users favour co-productive interactivity. At the same time, web producers are found to be the least likely to adopt this type of interactivity, as it gives more power and control to the user. For example, an analysis of youth parliament websites in the UK demonstrates that while they provided comprehensive coverage of political issues relevant to youth, there was actually very limited online interaction available (Gerodimos 2005a).

Given these possibilities, technology clearly provides room for youth to express themselves in new ways within more traditional structures. Youth are apt at forming online networks around current issues (Smith *et al.* 2005). Content creation takes place when individuals are able to produce their own blogs, vlogs (video blogs) and podcasts. Coleman and Rowe (2005) focused on young people's practice of sampling and remixing content and argued that this helps create new and individual meaning to media texts. However in the context of organizational websites, in order to thrive such practices must be made available to users. Co-production as such is argued to be particularly characteristic of web 2.0 (Chadwick 2009), pointing to the importance of examining this new arena of online communication.

Online communication in a web 2.0 environment

As this chapter additionally focuses on adaptation to 'new' online spaces in the form of social networking sites, it is important to place these sites (under the larger umbrella of web 2.0) in the context of the earlier discussion. There are not many differences between utopian claims of web 2.0 and the original e-democracy proponents, who argued that technology could reconnect citizens with governments and open up new civic spaces online (e.g., Trippi 2004). Web 2.0 can be seen a loose collection of 'second-generation' web-based technologies and services designed to facilitate collaboration and sharing between users (Ward 2009). O'Reilly (2005) highlights the value of capturing the collective intelligence of many individuals: web 2.0 is not about centralized control and static web pages. Rather, it sees users as co-developers and co-creators. Chadwick characterizes web 2.0 as 'the mashing together of different data in pursuit of goals that differ from those originally intended by the producers of those data' (2009, p. 23). All of this results in web producers having less control over their online messages, and creates a fascinating environment in which to study how organizations have adapted. Particularly relevant here is how organizations are using web 2.0 applications for interactive communication purposes, though the use of these applications for one-way communication is also a possibility for exploration.

Web 2.0 applications include blogs and wikis as well as social networking sites that encourage user-generated content such as YouTube and Facebook. Though other web 2.0 applications have been adopted by relevant organizations, this chapter will focus on two of the best-known social networking sites: Facebook and Twitter. Founded by Mark Zuckerberg, Facebook began in 2004 as a Harvard college application and rapidly expanded. It is now one of the most popular online social applications with over 400 million users worldwide. Twitter was created by Jack Dorsey in 2006. It can best be described as 'a store and forward best effort delivery system for text messages' (Krishnamurthy *et al.* 2008). Twitter currently has 100 million users worldwide. Scholars have noted that social networking sites are popular among young people (boyd and Ellison 2007). Research has examined use of such networks in terms of civic behaviour. For example, Zhang *et al.* (2010) find that use of social networking sites is significantly related to increased civic participation, but not political participation. They also note that interpersonal discussion on these sites fosters both civic participation and political activity.

Therefore it is interesting to examine more traditional content (on websites) with newer adaptations (on Facebook and Twitter). Keeping in mind a theoretical link to citizenship (i.e. how these online spaces are being used to reach young citizens), the analysis will focus on three particular types of online communication possible via online content: one-way communication (e.g. informational content), transactional interactivity (e.g. ways of gathering information from web users) and co-productive interactivity (e.g. allowing users to contribute to the content of the website/social networking site).

Methodology

Empirically, this chapter presents two primary focal points. First, it reviews the aims and strategies of youth organizations via interview findings with web producers, and illustrates these findings with a look at websites. Second, it provides a preliminary look at the organizations' more recent move to web 2.0. Originally, the research selected a group of 21 youth organizations where relevant individuals were interviewed and web content was examined in mid-2007 (see Ward 2008 for a more detailed methodological discussion). For the current chapter, and to facilitate a comparative approach to web analysis, seven of these organizations were selected based on whether they demonstrated adaptation to web 2.0. In April 2010, all websites were revisited to determine whether a social networking presence was communicated from the homepage.[1]

Because of its emphasis on the organizational perspective and an analysis of corresponding content, this chapter is able to provide a close look at the possible connection between citizenship philosophy and strategies of presenting online content. However, it leaves out a crucial piece of the puzzle in how to reach young people online: the perspective of youth themselves. Though this can be seen as a weakness, the approach can also be viewed as a valuable resource for future research that queries youth directly. Its value lies in providing a more insightful understanding of how youth organizations communicate to youth online.

Some youth organizations selected for this analysis are more intricately connected with UK governmental politics and usually encouraged cooperation with government through official channels, thus could potentially be considered as having a more conventional view of citizenship. These four, all registered charities or private companies limited by guarantee, are the UN Youth and Student Association of the UK (UNYSA, the youth wing of UNA-UK, or the United Nations Association); Youth Information (part of the National Youth Agency); Young Scot (a Scottish registered charity); and the UK Youth Parliament (run by Democracy for Young People Ltd). The three remaining organizations may be seen as more unconventional, in that they profess more of a distance from governmental politics and instead concentrate on issue campaigns or lifestyle politics. They include one UK-registered charity: the SPEAK Network (a network connecting together young adults and students to campaign and pray about issues of global injustice), and two campaigning organizations (their eligibility to be registered as a charity is restricted due to campaigning activities): Viva! (Vegetarians International Voice for Animals, legal name Viva! Campaigns Ltd, which promotes vegetarianism or veganism as the best way of saving animals) and Greenpeace UK, which is legally known as Greenpeace Ltd.

Organizations were contacted and asked for the most appropriate individual to participate in a Skype interview. This individual would need to answer questions about website strategy and maintenance. Respondents ranged from a campaigns manager to a web editor (see Table 9.1 for a full list, including relevant URLs). The interviews sought to comprehend how each organization perceived its online presence, to explore concepts and expectations of youth and how they communicate with this target group, and to probe for a deeper understanding of the interviewee's views towards democratic citizenship and how these views have influenced the website's content.

The current research also provides a descriptive analysis of website content (both on the website and the move to social networking sites) to better understand the actual online practice of the chosen organizations. Drawing on a combination of interview analysis and analysis of web presence, the research sought to answer the question:

> How do youth organizations view young people as citizens, and how is this view communicated via their websites and on their Facebook and Twitter profiles?

Interview analysis was inspired by a method introduced by Mayring (2000). Transcripts were read in their entirety, and from this initial impression were coded for emerging categories. Next, condensed transcripts were sorted into relevant dimensions and, through a process of rereading and continuous modification (Mayring terms this feedback loops), issues were focused on based on recurring patterns of response, theoretical relevance or noteworthy variations. Websites were examined before the interview to help make the interview process more fluid. Specific aspects of the site such as information and engagement features, campaigns or details about the organization were then used to better structure the responses of interviewees. A post-interview website examination helped to highlight consistencies and inconsistencies between producer views and content. The results also include a preliminary examination of how these organizations have adapted their web presence to web 2.0. Though primarily descriptive at this stage, it provides a good starting point for examining evolving online content.

Results: the web producer view and website content

Though all youth-focused, some organizations function as information providers and others identify primarily as campaign organizations. Some, through mission statements, declare an outright affiliation with external democratic values and goals, while others hold a more internal focus. For example, Youth Information sees their web presence as aiming to 'be one that they use for good, reliable information'. In contrast, Viva! mainly aims to change people's attitudes and behaviours about animal consumption: 'The best way to stop the destruction and the cruelty is to stop eating animals now – go vegetarian, or better still, vegan.'

Table 9.1 Interviewees/organizations selected for analysis

Name of organization	URL	Role of interviewee	Web 2.0 adaptation (as advertised on homepage as of April 2010)
Conventional:			
Youth Information	www.youthinformation.com/	Web coordinator	Facebook, Twitter
Young Scot	www.youngscot.org/	Communications Manager	Bebo, Facebook, Flickr, MySpace, Twitter
UNYSA (UN Youth and Student Association)	www.una.org.uk/youth/	Campaigns and Education Officer	Facebook, Flickr, Twitter, YouTube
UK Youth Parliament	www.ukyouthparliament.org.uk/	Central Services Coordinator	Facebook, Twitter
Non-conventional:			
Viva!	www.viva.org.uk/	Campaigns Manager	Facebook, MySpace, Twitter
Greenpeace UK	www.greenpeace.org.uk/	Web Editor	Bebo, Facebook, Flickr, MySpace, Twitter, YouTube
SPEAK Network	www.speak.org.uk/	Support team	Facebook

What they all have in common is that they address young citizens in various ways.

The results section begins by illustrating interviewees' views towards youth and how these views relate to online content. Next, it turns to more general organizational objectives and strategies, looking particularly at one-way and interactive communication on the websites. Then it examines these types of communication on the social networking sites Facebook and Twitter. The chapter ends with a conclusion and discussion of the insights uncovered throughout the research process.

Views towards youth as citizens

Young people were targeted online in a number of ways. The most obvious indicator is through a statement of age range, for example a wide focus like Young Scot (targeting 12- to 26-year-olds). Viva! had established a network of speakers who went into schools around the country to discuss animal rights and vegetarianism. Inclusion of these organizations in citizenship education makes sense considering the curriculum requirement to inform students about political structures and process but also about politically significant current events (Coleman 2008). Others focused on those over 18 and enrolled in universities. UNA-UK oversees the United Nations Youth and Student Association (UNYSA) which is active on university campuses.

Beyond an age range, interviewees often expressed a clear opinion about why youth should be targeted. Youth Information, whose website was first launched in 1997 at the Labour Party Conference, said that they realized 'young people were slipping through the net, there was this gap between childhood and adulthood where a lot of people were losing focus or losing their way'. As for an online focus, organizations saw youth as technologically savvy, and realized that if they wanted to reach this group, they should do it online.

Underlying this is the issue of how young people are viewed as citizens. Most acknowledged that youth are apathetic or agreed that young people are portrayed this way. However when it came to solving this apathy, differences emerged between organizations. Both conventional and non-conventional organizations agreed that focusing on issues (whether through information or campaigns) is a successful way to reach youth, but used this strategy in different ways. This is because their goals as organizations differed in either aiming to connect back to traditional politics or simply wanting to raise awareness of (and encourage action towards) an issue.

To illustrate, the more conventional organizations that hoped to unite youth with official political channels recognized the disparity of interest between (perceived) youth indifference and their goals, but also highlighted the importance of fighting it. When asked explicitly about what role they saw their websites playing in democracy, the Youth Information interviewee pointed me to a web page called Countering Political Apathy. They wanted young people to know their vote counts:

there is interest in topics so young people have been out protesting but actually they don't transfer interest in that political issue to national government or even local government ... we've given it a focus about getting young people to understand at the very highest level that their vote counts.

As for the more non-conventional organizations, on the surface this view was the same but was enacted quite differently. When comparing issue-based politics to party politics, the Greenpeace interviewee argued that most young people were much more interested in participating in issue-based campaigns: 'One thing we can do online is broaden that out and to involve people in very simple actions like sending an email to a company about their policies.'

In essence, both conventional and non-conventional organizations saw young people as citizens who need socialization in order to learn to fully participate in democracy. There was a desire to connect with youth and use these methods of socialization to encourage participation that continues throughout the lifespan. This is revealed in views towards apathy: Those connected to government (more conventional organizations) cautiously acknowledged this but felt they could draw youth in by first enticing them with issues and later showing them the importance of government. Non-conventional organizations instead were free to dismiss the importance of any eventual enthusiasm for traditional politics.

The results now turn to look at organizational objectives in order to understand why and how organizations communicate to youth in the ways that they have chosen. Differences presented themselves in citizen philosophy. But do organizations differ in their presentation online? The next section will explore these issues.

Organizational objectives and one-way communication

Interviewees expressed a number of convictions about their organizational objectives, both theoretically and more practically in terms of their websites. At a basic level, all selected organizations used their websites as an information provision tool in order to educate young people. Interviewees were generally very positive about the increased reach and ease of turning to online sources. Also frequently noted was cost-effectiveness, increased access to resources and, for member-based organizations, their use as a tool to attract new members and put them in touch with existing members.

Beyond an informative approach, organizations wanted to see young visitors engaged and participating in various goals and campaigns. A similarity among the organizations was this 'inform then involve' approach. Basically they believed that if users digested the educative element of the organization, then young people would follow by participating in political matters:

> if you understand the issues and become passionate about them, then you will automatically understand the fact that playing your part in the

democratic process can have a really big impact … the democratic engagement aspect flows from that.

(UNYSA)

In general, all organizations usually encouraged engagement from their target
audience, though most strived for a balance between the two. Young Scot noted:

> We're not a campaigning organization we're here to gather information and
> then step back and say 'you make up your own minds about this'. We don't
> tell people how to vote, I mean we don't even necessarily, we don't even
> tell people to vote we just get them the information that we hope will
> encourage them to vote.

Notably, even when using an 'inform then involve' approach, content was
mainly in the form of one-way information provision. Conventional organizations often claimed to be presenting a value-free position; for example, the
Young Scot interviewee made it clear that it was up to young people to decide
how they felt about issues. This view is somewhat reflected in the content of the
website, which was divided into an impressive number of issue-based sections
for example on law, sport and leisure, money, and other general areas of interest.
Opportunities for action in this case were directed at the government; this was
further illustrated with a number of corresponding links that provided more
information about the political system. Youth are encouraged to use their voice,
but only in pre-approved directions.

Informing young citizens about issues (via one-way communication) was a
mainstay on all websites. Thus far a number of patterns have emerged from the
analysis. Though they share important functions, such as the importance of
addressing young people and a positive view of the Internet as a communication
tool, organizations demonstrate different views on citizenship as well as practical ways of establishing these views online. Conventional organizations want
to create government-friendly citizens and often pursue this aim with issue-based
strategies. Non-conventional organizations also use their websites for youth outreach, but provide more stand-alone opportunities for issue-based protest and
activism. I now turn to a closer look at opportunities for interaction online.

Transactional and co-productive interactivity: evidence from interviews and website content

In essence, interactive communication opens up the content of a website to outsiders. Interview results showed that interactivity, no matter what the stated
purpose of the website, was seen as a positive development. Interviewees verbal-
ized a similar distinction between transactional and co-productive interactivity,
following Xenos and Foot (2008). To review, transactional interactivity is
enacted by collecting personal information from users and also facilitating means
for users to donate to the organization. The ability to contact the organization

(and in the process, for the organization to collect information from users) was present on all websites. More common on non-conventional websites was the ability to join the organization, as they often rely on membership fees and donations for support. Viva!, for example, allowed potential members to join various supporter categories (e.g. Viva! Friend, Activist, Life Supporter) that varied in their financial obligations.

Yet, previously and almost exclusively confident in their message and outlets, when the issue of co-productive interactivity arose all interviewees spoke of a lack of development on their websites and how they 'should' be more interactive online. Co-productive interactivity allows users to comment and candidly interact with the producers on the site (e.g. allowing youth to upload their own podcasts or comment on an embedded blog). Generally speaking, few had already introduced some interactive elements on their websites. Greenpeace was an exception; the interviewee told me that 'We've recently opened up commenting on our website and we have people saying you know I think what you're doing is completely wrong but we can then come back and justify what we're doing'.

Websites often included polls where users could make a selection from a pre-approved list of options. These were usually related to a contemporary topic and aimed to facilitate feedback on the website. Blogs and other means of co-production were scarce. What was particularly interesting was that interviewees often reported to be interacting with users via email and sometimes through more structured focus groups, and did claim to incorporate such feedback on the website, though this was not particularly apparent in the content.

Finally, results turn to a preliminary look at how organizations have adapted to web 2.0. Does such a move increase possibilities for young citizens to interact online? Or do organizations continue their preference for one-way communication in the world of social networking?

Results: preliminary analysis of web 2.0 adaptation

As noted in the interviews, in 2007 a number of organizations were already contemplating a move to social networking sites.[2] For example, several mentioned MySpace and Facebook profiles. But alongside praising their reach, an interviewee also admitted: 'I mean, getting onto these sites was actually just to establish our presence again. We were just very aware that if we didn't do it, someone else would.' Therefore it seemed important to utilize social networking both to protect their image and to increase their reach. Others saw social networking as another way to strengthen the bond with their target audience: 'We have a Viva! MySpace as well so we're trying to keep up with the trends ... it's obviously a very good networking tool that young people are using now.'

Online communication on Facebook

Facebook is used primarily as a means to keep in contact with friends and acquaintances (boyd and Ellison 2007) but commercial and non-profit organizations also benefit from reaching out to potential supporters. Facebook pages can keep individuals up to date on organizations they are interested in following but its format also allows users to interact with the producers of these pages (and each other). Despite these opportunities for interaction, the conventional organizations analysed here seemed to mainly use Facebook for one-way communication with their supporters, primarily in the form of information provision. By setting all content as 'public', Young Scot allowed postings on the wall and also had space for discussions, though this space was not often utilized. The non-conventional organizations, on the other hand, demonstrated more interaction with their supporters via Facebook. Viva! seemed to generate more interest from outsiders through comments on posts, and even engaged with dissenters on the public wall. For example, a young man wrote with some remarks about the direction a campaign on 'pig prisons' took (18 June 2010) and the Viva spokesperson wrote back one hour later with a thoughtful reply:

> We are a vegan campaigning organisation. We do not want any animal killed for meat. However, there is a sliding scale of suffering in a farming. Factory farms tend to be the most cruel. Making kinder dietary choices comes from being informed.

Greenpeace UK has taken a similar path, and boasts many 'likes' and comments from supporters on almost every post. The SPEAK Network reminded visitors that 'Posts on the wall do not necessarily reflect SPEAK's views'. Though used infrequently, the discussions section on SPEAK's Facebook page showed an interesting example of co-productive interactivity. On 8 June 2010 an individual started a discussion about the lack of meat at SPEAK events (uppercase in original):

> I WOULD LOVE TO GO AND SUPPORT SPEAK EVENTS LIKE VOCAL TRAINING … FROM WHAT I HAVE HEARD THE FOOD IS LIKELY TO BE VEGETARIAN OVER THIS WEEKEND. AS SOMEONE WHO IS INTERESTED IN SUPPORTING YOU IN YOUR WORK I FEEL STRONGLY THAT IF THAT'S THE CASE I WOULD NOT GO TO VOCAL TRAINING.

A SPEAK representative replied the next day, listing seven substantial reasons why SPEAK had chosen to offer vegetarian food at its events.

Online communication on Twitter

Twitter allows users to post 'tweets' that can vary from communicating informational content to providing a way of interacting directly with one's followers (via an @ reply). Twitter users can also show support for those they follow by 'retweeting' a particularly interesting message (RT). Generally the organizations seemed keen – as with Facebook – to provide information for members. That is, Twitter is mainly being used as a broadcasting medium – providing relevant information followed by a link. When looking specifically at conventional organizations, @ replies were generally reserved for communicating with other organizations, rather than young people themselves. Youth Information aims specifically at providing information for youth, so perhaps a focus on other experts in this area makes strategic sense. Generally the same pattern can be seen on the Young Scot Twitter feed, which is primarily geared at information provision and encouraging followers to participate in various activities. Some interaction was seen, for example, on 15 June 2010: '@RetrooJellyBean hey, sorry for the delay, for new young scot cards the best thing to do is ring infoline free on 0808 801 0338, thanks!' This demonstrates that the administrator of Young Scot's Twitter account is at least occasionally engaging in direct conversation with followers. The non-conventional organizations also used Twitter for broadcasting purposes, with a few minor exceptions (Viva!: '@ceilioe thanks for following!!' on 17 February 2010). The exception was Greenpeace UK, which seems to have embraced Twitter for the interactive potential it offers.

All interviewees agreed that the importance of online presence would increase over time. But with evidence of an apparent hesitation to embrace online interactivity, what does this say about producers' willingness to ease control of the message? For most organizations, co-productive interactivity is still hypothetical. If realized, what are the consequences for the philosophy – and even the legitimacy – of the organization? These questions, along with a concluding look at the results found in this chapter, are discussed in the next section.

Conclusion and discussion

Drawing on a theoretical framework that highlights evolving views towards citizenship, the first aim of this paper was to examine potential differences between conventional and non-conventional approaches to citizenship.

Communicating citizenship online

In line with their stated focus, all organizations see youth as an important group, but conventional organizations attempt to bring youth back to government though various forms of education and action while non-conventional organizations challenge this standard by focusing exclusively on particular issues. Both types of organization find themselves operating within a climate of political change where traditional approaches are arguably losing credibility. Given this, both types express concern about maintaining their legitimacy. For example, the 'have your say' focus of conventional organizations works on a larger scale to legitimize democracy by demonstrating connections to government bodies and officials. Non-conventional organizations express more of an issue with legitimizing their campaign goals and work to create a community of like-minded supporters to strengthen the possibilities for campaign success.

In sum, the primary difference in perspective between the organizations is that conventional organizations work to shape government-friendly citizens, while non-conventional organizations perhaps encourage the construction of more government-challenging citizens while emphasizing their own campaign goals. However, particularly in reference to youth, the socialization element is in place for both types of organizations. Young people are seen as technologically savvy, but still need guidance in issues of citizenship. This philosophy extends across the board, and shows an urgency to reach youth while they are still open-minded: 'Get'em while they're young.' Therefore both organizations seem to hold to a more conventional view of citizenship that invites socialization and management of youth behaviour.

Tying citizenship to online communication strategies

Do these variations in views of youth citizenship relate to online content? More generally, how is organizational strategy manifest via the Internet? Online content does seem to demonstrate a strategy on the part of organizations: in terms of online communication, strategically youth organizations operate by attracting their target audience and building numbers and participation through both information and opportunities for engagement. But content remains mainly one-way, perhaps again providing an indication of a belief in socialization. For example, conventional organizations agree that they provide issue-based information and engagement opportunities on their websites in order to grab attention with a hope of ultimately growing interest in more traditional arenas.

On social networking sites, this trend shifts somewhat,at least in the small sample observed here. Non-conventional organizations seem more open to inter-acting in co-productive ways with their supporters via Facebook and Twitter. This finding raises the question: does such use of co-productive interactivity thus support a new, more non-conventional type of citizenship? It has been argued that less traditional political organizations (social movements, for example) with a looser structure thrive on the many-to-many variety of communication that is found online (Bennett 2003c). Or perhaps such a response is just a symptom of non-conventional organizations' supporter bases, which may be inherently more passionate about the issues that these organizations focus on, like animal rights or the environment.

Yet, at the same time, web presence is never a finished product. It can always be improved, thus failure is built into the logic of the website. So far, web presence seems to be a means of providing information. Perhaps, then, interactivity may not be necessary. Then why do organizations report wanting more from their online presence? Is it simply an aspiration to keep up with the trends? Or is it a reflection of their desire to re-evaluate their views towards youth as citizens?

This presents a conundrum, where organizations seem set in their views of youth as citizens yet also express a desire to broaden their online presence. Allowing opportunities for co-production particularly on social networking sites like Facebook and Twitter shows that organizations are open to the perspectives of their audience, at least to some degree. However given the overall lack of this interactivity, a struggle is illuminated between how they think they should appear and how open they are willing to be. Further, when organizations mention interactivity they seem to be focusing more on strategic aims (i.e. how it can contribute to prescribed goals) than being ultimately concerned with audience input.

This chapter contributes to an understanding of how online spaces reflect views towards citizenship. With the current political climate of changing notions of citizenship and new uses of communication technologies, the analysis conducted here reveals theoretical underpinnings of youth organizational websites and gains insight into what type of citizen youth organizations are trying to shape. At the same time, much has changed in recent years: The first part of the analysis was conducted in 2007, and the world of online communication has evolved in many ways since then. This chapter does provide a preliminary look at a move to web 2.0, but more rigorous analysis is needed in future research. A particularly interesting angle is one that compares old content to new, in order to examine whether organizations are indeed evolving their online communication style. Research should examine how these organizations are adapting to the web 2.0 landscape and determine whether such participation is indeed opening up communication between youth organizations and their young audiences.

Communication was examined here primarily in terms of communication from political elites (in this case, youth organizations) to citizens. To further this research it would be relevant to update the interviews with the organizations to see what they have to say about web 2.0 content. For example, almost all of the 21 organizations originally interviewed said they wanted to increase interactivity in the future (Ward 2008) and many pointed to social networking as a way to do this. However, only seven of the organizations had made this move as of April 2010. Further, despite their potential for interactivity, it is important to remember that a presence on social networking sites is no guarantee of interactive content. As results here have shown, Facebook can still be used primarily as a broadcast medium. The same holds true with Twitter. It is also vital to ensure that youth have a voice in future research and users are queried about their perspectives of online content. For example, other recent research finds that rather than demanding more interaction, youth are often passive online (Chu 2010), potentially providing support for a more information-based strategy on social networking sites.

Notes

1 Though this method leaves room for criticism (a presence on social networking sites may exist that is not linked to the organization's homepage), focusing on this link demonstrates organizations' understanding of clearly communicating a comprehensive web presence. It also provides an easier avenue for future researchers to find the social networking profiles and ensure a connection to the proper organization.
2 Some, like Viva! and Greenpeace had already done so, though analysis of this content was not included in the research conducted in 2007.

10 Online youth civic attitudes and the limits of civic consumerism

The emerging challenge to the Internet's democratic potential

Roman Gerodimos

A narrative of civic apathy and political disengagement has become increasingly prevalent in the UK, amongst other liberal democracies. Phenomena such as low electoral turnout, declining party membership, mistrust in government and contempt for politicians, have been cited as indicators of a crisis of participation, particularly marked amongst younger people who appear sceptical towards the formal institutions and processes of politics (Stoker 2006; Pattie *et al.* 2004). A sense of disconnection between political leaders and younger citizens is a particular symptom of this crisis.

However, given the role of the media in the process of political communication and the increasingly embedded presence of the web in youth everyday life, the potential of the Internet as a facilitator of youth engagement has been the subject of a growing body of scholarship (e.g. Loader 2007). The Internet's unique properties for symmetrical and interactive communication, but also as a means of actual participation (through donations, petitions, etc.) make it a potentially ideal tool for youth empowerment. Coupled with a broader conceptualisation of civic action – to embrace activities as diverse as ethical consumption and charity concerts – two broad questions have emerged: whether the Internet has become the driver of a different paradigm of political communication and participation, one which is more fluid, flexible and inclusive; and whether the medium is facilitating the participation of citizens, especially young people, who would not normally consider engaging with offline or traditional politics (e.g. Livingstone *et al.* 2007).

The field of online youth civic engagement has recently incorporated a number of important contributions across the spectrum of production, content and use. The European-wide project CivicWeb produced valuable evidence regarding the production and content of civic websites (e.g. Banaji 2008), as well as a survey of young people's Internet uses. Partly based on that data, as well as on a comprehensive web content analysis, Ward (2008) explored the narratives of producers, websites and young people in electoral and non-electoral contexts with particular reference to the emergence of a consumerist approach to citizenship. A series of studies has looked at how young people use the Internet focusing especially on whether politically active users constitute a distinct demographic or whether the Internet has a genuinely important role in facilitating engagement (e.g. Mesch and Coleman 2007; de Vreese 2007). Another set of studies examined the content of political (Xenos and Bennett 2007b) and non-governmental organisations' websites (Gerodimos 2008; Burt and Taylor 2008, Kenix 2007).

However, there is still a lack of research directly linking young people's civic needs and motivations not only to their Internet uses in general, but also to specific civic websites. In particular, there are no known studies featuring qualitative civic site evaluations by young users. Coleman *et al.* (2008) linked youth engagement to Internet uses and gratifications and subsequently applied that framework to an examination of civic websites' usability, although their research employed an experimental design within the context of US case studies. The aim of this chapter is to address this gap by bringing together the study of youth civic motivations along with young peoples' experience of civic websites and consider the implications of the emerging mode of civic consumerism for the democratising potential of the Internet.

Objectives and research design

In order to link young people's civic motivations to their evaluations of civic websites the following objectives were set:

RO1 To explore the factors that would motivate young people to become (or would demotivate them from becoming) more active citizens.

RO2 To establish how these motivating factors translate into specific website features that might facilitate awareness and engagement.

RO3 To examine users' evaluations of four civic websites and compare those to their prior expectations.

Data for this study were derived from four user evaluation sessions, each lasting one and a half hours, in which a total of 46 young people took part. A purposive sampling strategy was chosen for this research with the aim of exploring how highly Internet-literate but politically disengaged young people evaluate online material on emerging civic issues, the hypothesis being that such a community would offer a considerable margin for the Internet to constitute a potentially effective means for civic empowerment (as opposed to demographic groups that are both Internet literate and already engaged, or those who are neither mobilised, nor digitally literate). Hence, following a preliminary survey of media students' civic attitudes and online habits within a vocationally oriented university which confirmed the suitability of this community (Gerodimos 2005b), a cohort of second-year undergraduate students were invited to participate. While the collection of a range of views and backgrounds is important, the aim of the sampling strategy was not to gather a representative sample of a population but to explore the narratives and interactions of a specific target group.

The process followed in each of the four sessions was identical. Participants initially completed a series of questions on demographic data, civic motivations

(RO1) and expectations from civic websites (RO2); they were then offered the chance to rate three current issues (fairtrade products, organic food and farming, climate change) according to their interest in these causes. Each user was then allocated one of three identical evaluation briefs for the websites of the Fairtrade Foundation, the Soil Association and the Friends of the Earth (FoE). The allocation of the briefs was based on two criteria, namely the participants' pre-stated preferences and the need to distribute the briefs as evenly as possible, although no notable differences in evaluations were observed based on the level of pre-existing interest. The choice of these three sites was based on a number of factors, including their central role in the UK's online public sphere (as established through a preliminary hyperlink network analysis), as well as their high profile and presence in British civil society at large.[1]

Having completed the review of the first site, users were shown a short animation clip that featured on the homepage of The Meatrix – the fourth website sampled in this study. This short film is the focal point of the website and introduces the visitor to its agenda. The inclusion of The Meatrix in the sample of websites was deemed useful as the web content analysis preceding this study had shown that its online presence and mobilisation approach are markedly different from that of established civic organisations' websites (Gerodimos 2005b). After the screening, participants were asked to review the site using an evaluation sheet. Having completed their individual written responses, all users then took part in a group discussion, the purpose of which was to complement the questionnaires and further explore questions of motivation and Internet use with the added advantage of group dynamics and interaction.

Focus group discussions are particularly useful for triangulation purposes when employed in conjunction with other data-gathering techniques, such as the individual written evaluations. Such group sessions are used for the 'study of audience interpretations of cultural and media texts' (Bryman 2001, p. 348) and are especially appropriate for research questions relating to consumers' own uses and gratifications. Central to the utility of focus groups are the patterns of interaction among participants and the joint construction of meaning via disagreement and argumentation. Jansky and Huang (2009) highlight the benefits of employing a multifaceted approach to soliciting end-user input, which includes the use of focus groups.

Hence, this study combines elements of group usability testing (GUT), task based focus groups (TBFG) and multiple-user simultaneous testing (MUST) (Downey 2007; Nielsen 2007): it involved many participants individually while also simultaneously evaluating the chosen sites. The structure of the sessions was similar to the protocol followed by Downey (2007), that is, initial user profile survey, followed by the basic task of individuals reviewing the site, followed by a usability issues (group) discussion. This approach alleviates the danger of co-discovery which is common to usability focus groups (Nielsen 2007) as users convened to groups after having experienced websites on an individual basis. The actual evaluation was largely unprompted and near natural (Nielsen 2008) with only a couple of minor tasks being given towards the end of the evaluation of The Meatrix, so as to test certain navigation problems that had been identified during the original content analysis. Furthermore, Macefield (2007) notes that qualitative techniques (such as the post-evaluation semi-structured group discussions) can provide indications of causation mechanisms (i.e. of the mental models users have of the interface and how that affected their response to it).

The structured (close-ended) variables from the four sheets were entered into SPSS (Statistical Package for the Social Sciences). The data were analysed using frequencies, cross-tabulations, composite variables and the visual comparison of small groups or sets of variables. The qualitative data (i.e. the open-ended responses that the participants handwrote on the sheets totalling more than 26,000 words) were typed manually into Word for each participant separately. They were treated both as self-sufficient narratives highlighting common themes, patterns, outliers and questions, and as supplements to the group discussion transcripts. These responses were also matched to individual participants' close-ended answers and discussion contributions so as to create profiles for each participant.

The four group discussions were transcribed into Word and went through a process of distilling, which included repeated readings, notes in the margin and the development of codes (themes), which were revised throughout the analysis (Creswell 1998, pp. 140–141), thus combining the flexibility of an open-minded approach with the pre-existing research agenda in order to create a process of reflexive analysis (Croghan *et al.* 2006). The transcripts were then colour-coded based on ten themes: site content and empowerment tools; site design, navigation and page layout; site interactivity and community-building; efficacy and encouragement/positive framing of issue; use of fear or threats/negative framing; donations; 'getting there' and 'going back'; trust, reliability and branding; expectations v. perceptions; clear purpose or overall point of the site.

'Rules of engagement': youth civic motivators and demotivators

For the first part of the study, participants were asked to reflect on the things that motivate them to become, and demotivate them from becoming, more active citizens. One of the aims of this open-ended approach was to establish how young people themselves conceptualised active citizenship. The written responses were then reduced to nine motivators (Table 10.1) and nine matching demotivators (Table 10.2), which can broadly be classified under three categories: efficacy and relevance; accessibility and appeal; system and society.

Despite the richness of the data, clear patterns emerged. The single most important factor (both motivating and demotivating) is the availability (or lack) of accessible, appealing and constructive communication that acknowledges young people's needs, abilities and cultures (codes 4, 5, 6). However, it is vital to stress that when we refer to communication, we do not simply refer to the messages, campaigns and arguments that political leaders or organisations

Table 10.1 Civic motivators (codes)

Group	Code no.	Code	Occurrences	Category tally
A Efficacy and relevance	1	Feeling I could make a difference or that my voice counts	11	26
	2	Getting more out of it or being able to see the benefits	3	
	3	Explanation of how the issue directly affects my self/family/community	12	
B Accessibility and appeal	4	Being more informed/inspired	8	35
	5	Being more encouraged to express myself; being listened to	6	
	6	More accessible, appealing, youth-oriented, less patronising material	14	
	7	Resources (more free time/money/ energy)	7	
C Systemic/ social	8	Knowing others care or have same beliefs	5	9
	9	Better politicians; less negativity	4	

Table 10.2 Civic demotivators (codes)

Group	Code no.	Code	Occurrences	Category tally
A Participation does not produce positive results	1	Feeling I could not make a difference/my participation has no effect	10	16
	2	If things got worse; views or policies I strongly disagree with	5	
	3	Not relevant to me	1	
B Participation is forced, difficult or resource-intensive	4	Threats and feeling forced to act	2	24
	5	Not being encouraged or not having enough opportunities to express my opinion or participate	4	
	6	Inadequate, inaccessible, complicated, confusing information	11	
	7	Too demanding (too expensive/takes too much time)	7	
C Systemic/ social	8	No one cares; less concern by others	2	9
	9	Scandals; disliking politics	7	

produce in a top-down way; many of our participants expressed frustration at the lack of accessible channels for the expression of their own voice:

> Making things more accessible to young people would motivate me to be more active. Perhaps to feel that when we discuss public affairs online we will be listened to – otherwise it's all complaining and nothing being done.
>
> (Participant no. 3.22)

Furthermore, many thought of political discourse as patronising, inaccessible and, often, even intimidating:

> I feel debates in class/groups would make me more inspired in taking a stance within society. At the moment I am too lazy because I don't know enough and therefore don't care enough. I would like more interaction with people [of] my own age on political matters because I would not feel so intimidated to speak out.
>
> (Participant no. 1.03)

The appearance of information/communication at the top of the list of (de)motivating factors seems paradoxical given that we are witnessing an abundance of political messages almost to the point of over-saturation, yet at the same time many citizens find it difficult to follow the public debate. This gap between production and reception could partly be attributed to different agendas: Coleman and Rowe (2005) argue that the agenda set by political parties and the media has been too remote from the interests of ordinary voters; young citizens' lack of interest should not be conflated with a disengagement from politics altogether.

Furthermore, our study concurs with the view that young people today are facing a considerable lack of efficacy which is linked to their scepticism about the ability of the individual citizen to make a difference. Efficacy, in its various articulations and expressions, is the keyword that recurred most often throughout the various parts of this study. Many young people reported feeling simply powerless:

> [Would demotivate:] The current feeling that whatever I do will have no effect on the world, just a tiny demographic powerless to change anything.
>
> (Participant no. 1.02)

Directly linked to efficacy, is the relevance (or irrelevance) of political discourses and messages to these citizens' everyday life; according to one participant's quite typical response:

> By seeing how events and issues would affect me personally or area am in. If it's an issue that does not necessarily impact upon my life directly it tends not to be a direct concern of mine.
>
> (Participant no. 2.17)

Hence, the onus lies with the political communicators who have to 'sell' not just their cause or issue but also – and perhaps this is a relatively recent development – appropriate tools for action which have capacity for change. These young people do not reject democratic politics, public affairs or civic participation as such; there was very little evidence of apathy or systemic rejection in the data, although frustration and scepticism were quite common. Kirshner *et al.* (2003) argue that young people are 'critically aware of their social and political environments' and keen to engage when presented with the opportunity to influence positive change. However, critical awareness is not enough on its own and can, in fact, act as a double-edged sword. If such opportunities for meaningful participation are lacking, awareness can lead to withdrawal and apathy rather than empowerment.

If there is one major contrast between the participants' civic narratives and the established norms of democratic participation, that would be the absolute lack of any reference to collective action. Collective identity, membership of organisations of collective action or simply references to collective mechanisms for participation are nowhere to be found in their responses. Coupled with the afore-mentioned deficit of efficacy, it almost appears as if these young people have diagnosed that, as individuals on their own, they are unable to change the world, yet that frustration does not lead them to take the initiative, integrate with others, join groups or participate in collective efforts, but to withdraw to the realm of their own lifeworld and express what can only be described as civic loneliness. Several participants wished they could see other young people caring about similar issues (Code 8, Table 10.1); knowing that others have similar beliefs or face common issues would act as a motivator:

> If other people my age/interest were doing similar activities I would also join in.
>
> (Participant no. 2.13)

> Being shown that other people care about issues would motivate me more.
>
> (Participant no. 3.21)

Seminal models of persuasion and behavioural intentions (such as Ajzen and Fishbein's Theory of Reasoned Action (1980) and Ajzen's updated model of Theory of Planned Behavior (1991)) have highlighted the role of subjective norms as catalysts for action: individuals take seriously into account what others – especially those in their immediate social environment – expect them to do or not do. However, it is fascinating that in the case of civic action there was no reference to peer pressure or established social norms about participation and, in fact, the reverse was true as participants called for the establishment of such norms.

In summary, this section has singled out four key factors that emerge from young people's own civic narratives, factors that ought to be taken into account in any effort to develop user-aware civic material on the web:

- lack of meaningful communication between young citizens and the political system, including the lack of accessible and appealing material
- lack of efficacy
- emphasis on the individual lifeworld
- ambivalence towards the collective.

It is obvious that these factors are not independent of each other. Rather, it could be argued that they all constitute symptoms of the same phenomenon: the distancing of the citizen from the public sphere, and the economic and socio-cultural shift towards the private realm inhabited by segmented individuals who are increasingly treated and act as consumers. The implications of this theme are further explored below with reference to specific examples of youth attitudes towards online material.

Applying civic motivations to the web: young people's needs from civic websites

Having reflected on key motivators and demotivators, the participants were then asked to apply those factors to specific features that they would ideally expect to find on an issue-oriented civic website. Further probes were given to the participants by asking for specific examples of online facilities or other materials that would motivate them to support that cause, by changing their consumer behaviour or political attitude or by contributing their time, money and effort to it. The question was split into three sections covering website content, design and interactivity in order to further facilitate the analysis. The data was distilled using a variety of analytical tools, looking at parameters such as the interpretation of the question, the variety and depth of responses, the originality or conventionality of features mentioned as well as the specific applications listed, the adjectives and words used to describe their needs and expectations, and the descriptive qualities sought by participants.

The first theme emerging from the data is young people's need for practical information that provides them with a compelling justification of *why* a given issue or civic cause is important, and a demonstration of *how* they can make a real difference. Almost half of the participants cited information as a key factor, with more than a third referring specifically to pieces of information that would make them feel that they can make a difference, such as evidence of how past action has brought tangible benefits. Transparency seems to be a key issue and questions such as 'Who is affected and how?', 'Where does my money go?' and 'Who benefits from my actions?' recurred in a variety of forms:

> Facts about the issue, i.e. why it's important. Real info/statistics etc. that are relevant to me – how will issue affect me, my country, Europe, the world? Needs to be tangible/real.

> (Participant no. 4.46)

How we can help. What the problem/issues are and how they affect me. High level of information about the issue. Who we will be helping.

(Participant no. 2.13)

The quest for a persuasive rationale and effective set of tools also includes the question of how others have already contributed to that cause, which could be linked to the afore-mentioned need to see that other people are already participating.

The second major theme was the clear preference for direct, emotive and personal communication coupled with an emphasis on easy, convenient and cost-effective ways of helping. 'Easy' was by far the commonest adjective used by participants, while one out of five respondents specifically mentioned images that promote empathy:

NSPCC website – there are moving photos and stories which make the reader feel guilty, and want to support them. They could put how any small donation can make a big difference, making the viewer feel they'll have an effect.

(Participant no. 3.27)

This respondent clearly articulated what is a major issue for many citizens – the need to be able to see the benefits of one's actions, which has a direct effect on that individual's sense of efficacy and can lead to a virtuous cycle of political participation (Bowler and Donovan 2002). Indeed, the website of the National Society for the Prevention of Cruelty to Children (NSPCC) is a good example of an organisation that is addressing some of the questions raised by these young people by featuring pages that are entitled 'What we will do with your money' and using interactive donation boxes that allow the user to see the benefits of each possible donation amount (Figures 10.1 and 10.2). By using emotive language and giving users simple choices about their participation, the NSPCC website seems to facilitate both awareness through direct communication and convenience through practical tools.

However, this pattern of responses could also be interpreted in a more critical way, as it essentially denotes a *consumerist* approach to citizenship, which sees civic participation as a choice that has to be marketed in appealing and beneficial terms to the consumer (citizen), rather than as a duty or ritual within a broader democratic community:

Clear good background information = giving me examples on how I can easily/non-time-consuming make an impact already, without spending too much money.

(Participant no. 4.45)

Furthermore, these users' preference for emotive pictures and convenient online solutions underlines the emerging perception of political messages as mere com-

Your
Donation
£20
£0
£2000
£20 could answer 5 calls which may have been left unanswered
Sign up
Donate
Let no cry go unheard

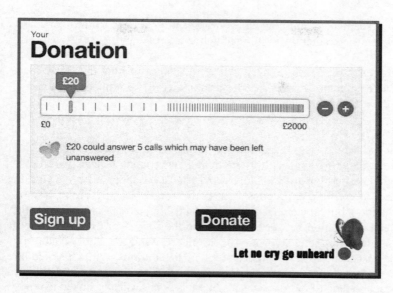

Figure 10.1 NSPCC website donation calculator. Interactive donation calculator showing the potential effect of each donation amount (www.NSPCC.org.uk, accessed 10 October 2008). Used with permission.

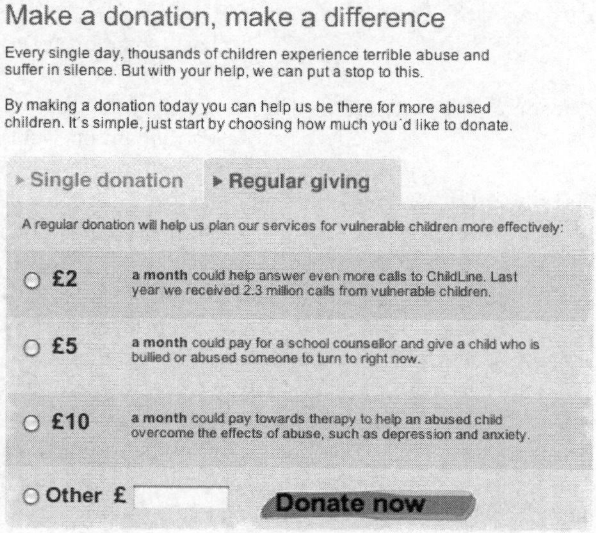

Make a donation, make a difference
Every single day, thousands of children experience terrible abuse and suffer in silence. But with your help, we can put a stop to this.
By making a donation today you can help us be there for more abused children. It´s simple, just start by choosing how much you´d like to donate.
Single donation
Regular giving
A regular donation will help us plan our services for vulnerable children more effectively:
£2
a month could help answer even more calls to ChildLine. Last year we received 2.3 million calls from vulnerable children.
£5
a month could pay for a school counsellor and give a child who is bullied or abused someone to turn to right now.
£10
a month could pay towards therapy to help an abused child overcome the effects of abuse, such as depression and anxiety.
Other £
Donate now

Figure 10.2 NSPCC website donation box allows the user to choose the amount while simultaneously seeing the potential benefits (www.NSPCC.org.uk, accessed 25 November 2011). Used with permission.

petitors in a segmented multimedia environment – a civic culture oriented towards convenience rather than informed deliberation:

> Shocking or sad images (hungry children), images of how the world may look due to climate change. ... The resolutions to the problems – make it sound easy; bitesize chunks.
>
> (Participant no. 3.16)

A third theme, which once again proved particularly salient throughout the study, was the participants' need for emotional engagement, especially through visual material such as images and videos. Our data showed that affective visuals are important in catching an Internet user's attention (especially in the case of first-time visitors), but they are also vital in establishing a more lasting aesthetic and emotional connection between the user and the cause. As Corner and Pels (2003, p. 9) note, 'aesthetic stylisation is an inherent and inevitable feature of mass politics, particularly in its (post)modern mediated form'. While it would be tempting to disregard users' emphasis on aesthetic elements as a sign of dumbing down, a closer reading of our data reveals that this is intrinsically linked to emotions and perhaps, indirectly, to a willingness to step outside the isolated self and connect with others in what could eventually lead to the creation of a collective identity. A clear need for online civic material that creates empathy was evident in the users' responses on expected gratifications:

> Pictures that speak more than words to get you more involved and get involved more efficiently. A lot of things that promote empathy.
>
> (Participant no. 1.06)

> Tries to influence you in some way i.e. pictures that may sway your view.
>
> (Participant no. 4.43)

> Use of images – the PETA website really affects you.
>
> (Participant no. 3.30)

The emotional dimension of online civic engagement also extends to the role of interactive applications, such as message boards and forums, mentioned by half of the sample (although interactive features were relatively less important compared to useful applications and emotive content). Hence, a key quality of a website should be its ability to empower users to express their own feelings or voice, as well as to see how others feel. The expressions used by the respondents were oriented heavily towards the notion of sharing ideas and voices, which could explain the recent meteoric success of content-sharing applications.

Hence, it may be the case that, rather than being disengaged, apathetic or cynical, young people in Britain today need a more direct mode of communication that affects them personally and leads to an emotional connection with public affairs, other citizens or political leaders. Such a mode of communication could be part of a more fundamental shift in the nature of the relationship between citizens and government, what Richards (2007) calls 'emotional governance'.

Having established the participants' civic needs and how these map onto possible web features, the following section pulls together the key themes of their website evaluations.

Young users' evaluations of civic websites

Having completed their first site visit, users were asked to compare their actual impressions to their initial expectations of civic websites. It was assumed that, having been given the opportunity to reflect on what motivates them to engage via such websites, participants would have an additional set of benchmarks by which to evaluate the sampled sites, apart from the obvious and direct assessments emerging from their live user experience.

Challenging perceptions

A key finding immediately emerged from this data: several of the young people taking part in our study had very negative perceptions of charities and civic non-governmental organisations (NGOs) to start with; importantly, however, these negative expectations were challenged by the actual site visits, which in many cases pleasantly surprised them. This was true for all three sites of the first evaluation, but particularly true for Fairtrade and Friends of the Earth. Two thirds of participants made favourable comparisons between initial expectations and post-visit impressions; with half of those stating that they were either (pleasantly) surprised or that the site exceeded their expectations:

> Participant no. 1.01: I thought it was a really good website, perhaps a bit better than I expected it to be, because I didn't know that Fairtrade was such a big organization

> Participant no. 1.04: I agree with [Participant no. 1.01]. I thought it would be a lot more negative. I thought it would be a quite pushy website but I really liked it.

Youth perceptions of civic NGOs are significant for a number of reasons. Firstly, charities and NGOs are supposed to be major agents of emerging forms of youth engagement, such as volunteering and donating, which are arguably replacing more traditional forms of political participation such as voting and joining political parties (e.g. Henn *et al.* 2002; Bell 2005). Therefore, a widespread pattern of negative perceptions could compromise the thesis that such engagement is flourishing and socially conscious. Furthermore, these data can further illuminate our understanding of youth attitudes towards civic engagement altogether (i.e. what is it that they find demotivating about these organisations? And what does this tell us about their attitudes towards participation?). Finally, given the 'pull' nature of the medium and the emerging mode of political communication, the reputation of individual organisations, as well as of the civil society as a whole, is crucial in attracting users to their websites.

Hence, it is significant that several participants expected civic websites to be 'pushy', 'patronising', 'negative', 'depressing', 'inaccessible' and 'boring'. These recurring adjectives indicate a consistent perception of issue organisations as using aggressive tactics, transmitting depressing messages, putting unrealistic demands on citizens and featuring inaccessible discourse that is directed at experts (interestingly, these same allegations are usually directed against politicians).

Efficacy, individualism and civic loneliness

The sample's aversion to 'pushy' messages could be interpreted as a blame-avoidance strategy (i.e., as an inability to assume the fractional share of responsibility that falls upon each individual citizen) or as aversion to commitment and civic duty (i.e. as evidence of a consumerist stance to civic engagement in which the individual chooses if, when and how they will engage):

> It wasn't too pushy that you need to change your entire life to make a difference.
>
> (Participant no. 4.39)

> They weren't, it doesn't seem like that they were forcing you, you could just read it and then get about it if you wanted to, it didn't really say that 'you've got to do this or you will die!'
>
> (Participant no. 3.35)

Having said that, a closer reading of the data reveals that the main factor for this attitude is not so much the need to avoid blame as the anxiety to find positive and effective ways of helping. In other words, these young people are not so much afraid of taking responsibility as keen to produce a useful outcome:

> [The Fairtrade website] didn't make you feel like it was your responsibility – like it was your fault but that you could take some responsibility in helping.
>
> (Participant no. 4.39)

Positive messages of hope and encouragement then become crucial motivators of civic action. Over and over again in the written evaluations and group discussions, practical advice and specific information on how the individual can help (albeit in individualistic rather than collective ways) are contrasted to apocalyptic messages of fear and disaster. In fact, participants themselves often made that direct link between hope and efficacy:

I liked the [Fairtrade] case studies as well. They are a lot more positive and encouraging the user to read more about it, not just to think 'no I'd better get to my mind I'm gonna die'.

(Participant no. 1.04)

[FoE did not feature] something that stops me thinking that it's too late, there's nothing I can do, so I won't do anything [about climate change].

(Participant no. 3.22)

Previous studies in public health campaigns and risk communication have shown that unless accompanied by a strong sense of efficacy, the use of fear through scare or shock tactics can have a 'boomerang effect' or unintended consequences, as it is can lead the public to denial about the threat to their lives (e.g. Kleinot and Rogers 1982; Cho 2003).

Feelings of helplessness may also be linked to the perceived lack of subjective norms around civic participation. That is to say, many young people may not see the relevance of collective action, but they also do not feel motivated or socially driven by the behaviour of others. What emerges, therefore, is a feeling of civic loneliness:

Yeah I'd like to know how ... How ... how it's gonna make a difference, what I do ... as well, that would be important. Sometimes you can just think 'well ... it's just me on my own, what difference am I gonna make?'

(Participant no. 2.10)

There is some tension between the evidence presented here and the view of youth as materially minded self-oriented consumers (e.g. Rahn and Transue 1998). Individualism is definitely present, and even dominant, in these narratives, but it largely appears to be a natural response to an individualistic civic culture that does not provide young people with the necessary social context for the development of trust in broader social and civic structures (Couldry 2006a). It is in (re)building that link between the individual and the collective or global that the use of affective and emotional means of engagement can be particularly crucial. In that sense, the Internet may be a particularly appropriate channel for personalised and affective political communication.

Personalisation and consumerism

The link between efficacy and individualism also re-emerged in the users' evaluations of the sampled civic websites. Participants focused on what the individual can do not in relation to others but in their own lifeworld and thought that websites should provide them with accessible tools that help them make a tangible difference *on their own* – what one user called 'giving the consumer the chance to do something for themselves' (Participant no. 1.01). The reverse was also true: the importance of an issue ought to be demonstrated not with reference to its impact on society at large, but to the individual person:

Like the page I'm looking at now, which is about what you need to know about factory farms and how it affects you doesn't *ever* actually say how it affects you! It says, you know for, like, the antibiotics thing it's quite dangerous to humans but they just mention that it will raise healthcare costs ... and if you didn't care ... you just wouldn't keep reading, would you?

(Participant no. 1.02 on The Meatrix)

In this particular case, not caring about high healthcare costs could be due to either a selfish disregard for the broader community, or – perhaps more likely – to a lack of a cognitive and affective link between higher healthcare costs (abstract macro-political concept) and, for example, higher taxation or lower-quality healthcare (tangible micro-political effect). If this lack of interest in the broader social impact of specific issues were found to be broadly shared, it would support the notion that young people today are faced with a broken cycle of political socialisation which does not allow them to see the interdependence of their individual lifeworld with the broader society.

Our data strongly suggest that this individualistic approach to civic engagement is not necessarily driven by utilitarian or selfish motives, but by a genuine conviction that the individual domain is the only visible one and, subsequently, that individual action is the only possible option. 'Making a difference', 'feeling you can do something' and being given 'practical advice' were almost universally cited as crucial elements of experiencing civic websites and there was a widespread and genuine need for efficacious online tools.

This argument is further supported by a clear divide that many participants drew between political actions (such as lobbying MPs) and non-political actions (consumption) that users can take online. While generally praising the website of FoE, users criticised its mobilisation approach as being remote from their everyday realities:

Because they place a lot of focus on ... whether we think the government is doing enough for climate change, and that's quite a key issue.... I think there was a key focus on the homepage on the political side of it, rather than ... that's what I was looking for, the solutions that *real people* – what real people can do and there was a lot on the political side of it.

(Participant no. 3.22)

This view is consistent with responses from participants in other group sessions (e.g. Participant no. 1.06: 'It says like about how the government wants to attack and cut CO^2 emissions by 2010 but it doesn't say *how* like they're gonna do that, it doesn't say "you can do this" '). The implication is clear: the role and capacity of the government to tackle this issue are questioned, as is the relevance and efficacy of collective action. Representative politics is perceived as almost irrelevant to 'real people's' lives.

This distinction between political and consumer action reflected these young people's scepticism towards large-scale 'changing the world' action as they clearly doubted citizens' ability to bring about social change:

> Also, they were very much you know like ... bringing down conglomerates and bringing down – changing the world ... but they weren't – they didn't have any sections on turning lights off when you leave your house, you know [extended laughs by group] there was no ... there was *no* – it was very much like taking action *for the whole of the world!*
>
> (Participant no. 4.37 on FoE website)

Hence, the participants saw personalisation as the antidote to unrealistically large-scale action. Framing a public affair or social issue with reference to specific cases, communities or 'real people' allowed users to develop an affective relationship with it. The best example of personalisation in the sampled sites was the profiles of product farmers and growers featured on the Fairtrade website (Figure 10.3), which were praised by almost all users:

Figure 10.3 Fairtrade growers' profiles. (www.fairtrade.org.uk, accessed 5 March 2006). Used with permission.

It allows you to read how Fairtrade is helping real people and making their lives better, i.e. Carlos, orange farmer.

(Participant no. 1.04)

It was like this family, the farmer and all that and it makes you realise that it's – they're real lives.

(Participant no. 3.32)

It kind of makes you kind of want to find out more – it's more of a personal touch to the website.

(Participant no. 2.11)

Apart from connecting emotionally with the site's mission, case studies help users see the tangible benefits of the organisation's work. Webb (2007, para. 5.8) takes this point further and argues that Fairtrade labelling builds the symbolism of commodity chain relationships between growers, retailers and consumers into the materialism of a pack of coffee, 'with the "fair trade" product imputing a connection between the lives of low-income farmers and those of affluent consumers' (also see Raynolds 2002).

The themes of convenience and personalisation are also ingrained in the users' preferred site features and applications. As part of the evaluations, participants were given the opportunity to nominate their favourite site elements and those features that pleasantly surprised them (Table 10.3), as well as others that they would have liked to find – a wish-list of sorts (Table 10.4). These responses

Table 10.3 Specific examples of best practice as identified by the users

Site	Feature or application	Motivating factor
Fairtrade	Case studies and profiles of producers	Personalisation
	Images of products	Visual engagement
	Recipes	Everyday life/consumption
	Listings of retailers	Convenience/consumption
Soil Association	'10 Reasons to Choose Organic'	Specific benefits/accessibly succinct
	Listings of local producers	Convenience/consumption
	Celebrity supporters	Personalisation
	Information on Bird Flu	Everyday life/relevance
Friends of the Earth	Vote feature	Interactivity
	'The Big Ask'/'Find your MP'	Convenience/tangible action
	E-petitions	Convenience/tangible action
	'Did you know?'	Accessibly succinct
The Meatrix	Animated clip	Visual engagement/accessibly succinct
	Postcode search engine for local farms	Convenience/consumption

Table 10.4 'Wish-list' of features proposed by the users

Site	Feature or application	Motivating factor
Fairtrade	Detailed info on product availability	Convenience/consumption
	Photos of product packaging/on the shelf	Convenience/consumption /visual
	Self-assessment questionnaire	Personalisation
Soil Association	Insight into farmers' lives	Personalisation
	Online menu	Convenience/consumption
	Restaurant guide	Convenience/consumption
	Real-time chat tool for contacting SA	Interactivity
	E-petitions	Convenience/tangible action
Friends of the Earth	Campaign-related photos/videos	Visual/affective engagement
	Tips on reducing CO_2 emissions	Tangible action/accessibly succinct
	Actions that individual consumers can take	Everyday life/tangible action
The Meatrix	Expand individual country pages	Relevance
	Examples of animal cruelty	Affective engagement

are very useful in gaining a more applied understanding of young people's preferred means of online mobilisation. They rotate primarily around material consumption at the micro-social level (e.g. recipes, menus, restaurant guides, listings
of retailers and local producers).

Furthermore, the embedded role of major supermarkets in youth everyday life
also emerged; for example, realising that Fairtrade-labelled products are available in major supermarkets created a feeling of reassurance amongst participants
that the product or civic action was within the individual's reach. Major retailers
thus appear as crucial spaces that act as mediators between individual consumers
and civically oriented consumer brands:

> They're actually telling you to do it in, like, Tesco's and Sainsbury's and
> things; so you can actually make a difference – it's not just a general site.
> (Participant no. 2.11 on Fairtrade)

This brings us to the final point about the consumerist nature of these young
people's online civic behaviour. A careful reading of the group discussion transcripts reveals a consistent cognitive link between consumption and power.
When responding to questions about empowerment or participation, which did
not contain references to consumption in any form, respondents often translated
getting involved as buying or consuming, e.g.: 'I think it had loads of interesting
stuff on there and stuff that you could do yourself, like where to buy things so
you can get involved' (Participant no. 1.01 on Fairtrade). One participant thought
that The Meatrix was more empowering than the FoE site because:

when it said 'don't buy … sort of … factory meat' sort of … and it said, like, 'buy organic food' or 'buy food from family farms' or 'buy food from local butchers' or 'buy local' … and it's just little things like that, little things like that even [that can help].

(Participant no. 2.13)

It has been argued that websites of consumer organisations can play a critical role in the process of symbolic negotiation and virtual interaction between producers and consumers (e.g. Callon *et al.* 2002). Webb (2007, p. 5.8) argues that '[t]he qualities attributed to products, and their status as "goods" or "bads", are not inherent in the artefacts, but are subject to negotiation, and struggle, between market actors, who may include economists, producers, consumer groups, scientists and international governance bodies'. Bourdieu famously argued that everyday acts carry significant political, social and cultural meanings both for the individual's identity and for social structures: 'consumption practices become important in maintaining the basic structures of power and inequality which characterize our world' (Schor 1999). More recently, thinkers such as Ginsborg (2008) have made the case for the politics of everyday life, illustrating the relevance and interconnectedness between individuals, consumer behaviour and political issues.

While it is important to acknowledge the role of consumption in the process of identity construction, it may be useful to adopt a slightly more critical stance towards the marketised and highly individualised mode of civic engagement outlined so far. Such a critique could aid the development of appropriate civic interventions and structures that avoid the pitfalls created by the fusion between democratic practice and market consumerism.

The limits of civic consumerism

In addition to creating opportunities for greater inclusion and empowerment of citizens and civic actions, the emerging model of civic consumption faces limitations and raises questions about its impact on democracy. Civic consumerism has very diverse, and possibly some contradictory, expressions and consequences: it could be seen as a self-oriented stance towards public life, according to which political leaders have to 'sell' ideas or policies to citizen-consumers who choose whether or not to engage with certain issues; but it can also be defined as a form of participation through the various facets of consumption (e.g. ethically sourced goods). These two phenomena are intrinsically linked to each other, although they are not identical and, in the case of active citizens attempting to make a difference through conscious consumption, they could even be in tension. However, both expressions of civic consumerism were clearly present in the participants' narratives. Given the increasing weight afforded to consumer choice in contemporary liberal democracies, it is important to identify some factors that may limit civic consumerism's democratic potential.

The first such issue is the disputed political significance of symbolic action. The case of Make Poverty History is particularly interesting in that respect. Gorringe and Rosie (2006, para. 9.3) note that demonstrations

> entail symbolic rituals highlighting the cohesion of protestors and communicating their objectives ... MPH voiced concrete demands but relied on heavily symbolic and expressive acts [e.g. white wristband, a minute's silence, etc.] – foremost amongst which was the evocative, expressive invocation to *Make Poverty History*.

Indeed, one could argue that there is a certain tension between the outcome-oriented civic attitudes of our sample as outlined above and the wide range of symbolic or cultural actions that have been embraced by younger generations (such as charity wristbands). The political gravitas of symbolic action has been contested by those who argue that we have lost the distinction between commodity- or culture-oriented actions and end results (e.g. Bey in Bleyer 2004).

A sweeping rejection of the wealth of civic activities that takes place through expressive or even consumerist outlets probably disregards the many positive and empowering spill-over effects that such action can have – not least for citizens' own political socialisation and social capital. However, the lifespan and ultimate impact of such actions in creating a sense of collective identity ought to be probed. Observing civic interactions in Holland after the murder of filmmaker Theo Van Gogh, Herme (2005 cited in Couldry 2006a, p. 323) commented that there was 'curious emptiness at the heart of everyday political talk'. Rhodes (1994) famously described the 'hollowing out of the state' and governance in Britain following the waves of privatisation and deregulation of the 1980s and 1990s. It may not be inappropriate to suggest that we are witnessing the 'hollowing out of citizenship' and political engagement in that individuals are expected to be motivated and feel efficacious within a context of individualism and privatisation of the public sphere. Subsequently, as Edwards (2007, p. 543) notes, the risk is that the impetus to participate is deemed the prerogative of individuals, while the failure to do so is attributed to a flaw of the citizen.

Furthermore, proponents of civic consumerism have argued that the emerging mode of civic interaction allows consumers to use their increasing wealth so as to construct their own lives (Reeves 2008). That is to say, increased affluence gives citizens more choice and power in making important decisions. Yet, Reeves's argument makes a very contestable assumption about the resources available to citizens, especially those of a lower socio-economic status.

The case of Fairtrade is a good example: Webb (2007) criticises the simplistic notion of consumers as passively seduced by the power of marketing and advertising and puts forward the argument that the significant growth in the sales of Fairtrade coffee is consistent with a 'developing politicisation of consumption' and proves the 'market impact of collective consumer agency' (ibid., p. 2.2). Our data supports Webb's point about the potential of Fairtrade to establish a politically charged relationship between foreign suppliers and domestic consumers;

users clearly enjoyed reading the case studies of farmers and reported feeling an emotional connection that also facilitated their cognitive understanding of the more substantive issues. Yet, our participants' civic narrative contests Webb's optimistic view as it shows considerable tension between the theoretically empowering products available to citizen-consumers and the economic realities facing youth groups such as students living on limited means. Table 10.5 draws together some of the main issues emerging from the user evaluations and examines the extent to which they are addressed by the Fairtrade website, as a metaphor of the key barriers to online youth mobilisation.

Participants expressed informed scepticism about the price of Fairtrade products vis-à-vis young people's resources, as well as the recent attempt of major retailers to 'jump on the bandwagon' of ethical trading:

> Participant no. 4.37: There's loads of companies that are now being questioned because they're actually getting into Fairtrade because they're gonna make that much profit. ... Another thing is not just buying these Fairtrade products but maybe trying to bring these Fairtrade prices down...

> Participant no. 4.39: I think that is the main barrier though ... for students ... it is the price difference, when you know you can get something ... um

Table 10.5 Barriers to online youth mobilisation – case study: Fairtrade

Key issues emerging from the user evaluations	Satisfactorily addressed by the Fairtrade website?
1 **Negative perceptions** of Fairtrade as a 'pushy' NGO	**Yes** – users were pleasantly surprised and found the site welcoming, positive and appealing
2 Lack of **awareness** of, and interest in, the **substantive issues** behind Fairtrade (e.g. trade justice, lives of farmers)	**Yes** – users liked the personalised content which allowed them to establish an emotional and cognitive link between the abstract issues and 'real people'
3 **Price difference** between Fairtrade and non-Fairtrade products; subsequent perception of Fairtrade as an expensive brand that students cannot afford	**No** – Barbara Crowther (Director of Communications and Policy) acknowledged that consumers still perceive fairly traded goods as more expensive, although there is no evidence of a slow-down in the growth of ethical consumption due to the recent economic recession (Boyle 2009, p. 39)
4 Lack of **awareness** about the availability, presentation, packaging and range of Fairtrade **products**	**Partly** – many participants were surprised by the range of products and level of information available; others requested more specific consumer details
5 **Site navigation** problems (floating menus, invisibility of homepage link)	**Yes** – these have now been dealt with via the redesigning of the Fairtrade website

crisps or mints or something like that, when you know you can get something cheaper then morally you think 'I should buy that', but that one is half
the price, and I think that's the main barrier for lots of people from
buying...

Therefore, one of the problems with the libertarian and marketised models of
self-empowerment is that 'they may impose new costs and demands on disadvantaged service users, who have to acquire new skills in order to interact successfully with service delivery systems' (Collin 2008, pp. 539–540), as well as
disenfranchise those who are in need of intensive personalised support.

Crucially, the capital required for young people to participate in emerging and
online civic rituals is both economic and socio-cultural. North *et al.* (2008,
p. 895) concluded that 'the link between cultural capital, habitus and cultural
form produces a socially entrenched digital inequality rather than an economically entrenched digital divide'. That is to say, emerging digital inequalities have
not only an economic expression but also a crucial habitual aspect (i.e. lack of
motivation) that can be linked to the particular contexts of individuals' political
socialisation. Thus, online participation strategies that do not cater to disadvantaged groups of young citizens may be aggravating, rather than ameliorating, the
gap between those who are already engaged and those who are socially disen-
franchised. Thus, the limits of civic consumerism are not just economic but also
political, social and cultural.

Conclusions: emerging challenges to the Internet's democratic potential

This study investigated a series of youth civic motivations and their realisation
through users' expected and received gratifications from civic websites. It should
be reiterated that sampling for this research was purposive and focused on a specific community of young people evaluating a small number of websites. Given
the limitations of the sample and of the research design, the findings outlined
above should be treated as tentative and indicative, rather than formally representative of UK youth at large. However, and whilst acknowledging the limits of
this approach, certain interesting patterns emerged which can offer valuable
qualitative insights into the civic and online thought processes of young Internet
users.

It was argued that young people might be willing to participate as long as a
number of 'terms and conditions' are met that would make that engagement
meaningful to them: the benefits of civic action must be highlighted and they
must be tangible; the reasons for engaging in such action should be clear and relevant; the act of participation itself should not stress the individual's resources;
the user-citizen-consumer should be able to choose why, when and how they
will engage with a public affair or cause.

These motivators were further distilled into web features that users themselves consider important, such as visual stimuli that would help establish an

emotional connection between the user and the people behind the civic cause. The participants' evaluations of four issue-oriented civic websites showed that, despite their initially negative perceptions of NGOs, a positive user experience can challenge these notions and attract the attention of website visitors. Features such as micro-political online tools and case studies of communities positively affected by the organisation's work can motivate them to engage with the cause. In terms of civic web design in particular, there was a clear preference among our sample for visual rather than textual or menu-loaded pages. Breaking up the text, introducing visual signposts and reducing the number and size of menus and links were recurring suggestions. While this emphasis on convenience and ease of use may sound like a truism, the premium put by these users on simplicity and the subsequent frustration with a lot of the pages that they evaluated mean that there may well be a gap between current practice and users' needs. Mitra *et al.* (2005) note that a tension may exist between what web designers consider to be state-of-the-art applications in web design and what users actually consider to be attractive. Gibbs also highlights the misperception amongst many designers of information systems, who wrongly perceive a design problem as *information scarcity* rather than *attention scarcity* (2008, p. 130).

However, our study also identified a mode of online youth engagement that is heavily oriented towards consumption and choice. This paradigm of civic consumerism embodies a profound shift in the perceived role of the citizen and could have significant implications for both civic communicators and youth empowerment. With political messages having lost the protected status that they used to enjoy in the 'old' public spheres of the mass media, civic organisations are forced to market their message within a highly fragmented environment competing against a myriad of other products. At the same time, youth notions of citizenship – and the motivations, fears and needs upon which they are based – may be different from the traditional norms upon which the political system and civic culture of liberal democracies are based. Coleman (2004, p. 1) reminds us that 'the lament for old, localised solidarities fails to resonate with twenty-first-century citizens whose interpersonal networks are increasingly a matter of choice rather than a consequence of geography'.

Our data indicate that while citizens' perception of collective responsibility may, indeed, be changing, an alternative form of individual responsibility could be emerging around the notion of empathy. Civic organisations might be able to tap into citizens' moral codes by highlighting, not necessarily the tangible or material benefits of each civic action, but the emotional and aesthetic pleasure that individuals can receive through mobilising on issues that they feel passionate about. Indeed, Schudson (2007) notes that, as political behaviour can be both public-spirited and egocentric, consumer behaviour can also be public-interested as well as self-interested.

However, the emerging paradigm of civic consumerism also raises questions about the political impact of consumer action and, perhaps more importantly, about the inherent assumptions and resource implications that are embedded within this increasingly individualised civic environment, which could lead to new forms of social and civic exclusion. Hence, in addition to established barriers to online youth empowerment, such as the privatised, hierarchical and commodified structures of online interaction and the 'second-level digital divide' (Hargittai and Hinnant 2008), another challenge to the net's democratic potential is emerging, which is not technological, but fundamentally socio-political.

Note

1 For example, UK sales of Fairtrade products rose by 43 per cent year-on-year to £700 million in 2008 (Boyle 2009), while membership of Friends of the Earth (FoE) rose from 1,000 in 1971 to 119,000 in 2002. FoE is a particularly interesting case from a political science perspective as it is one of few NGOs to explicitly identify itself as pursuing democratic objectives (Taylor and Burt 2001, p. 60).

11 Constructing Australian youth online

Empowered but dutiful citizens?

Ariadne Vromen

Introduction

When I started to write this chapter I noticed that it was national Cyber Security Awareness Week in Australia and the federal government agency, the Australian Communication and Media Authority, announced a number of new initiatives: including Cybersmart Hero, a new online anti-cyberbullying activity for students in the last year of primary school; a new SMS spam reporting tool; and Cyber-safety Outreach – a programme to provide pre-service teachers with the skills and confidence they will need to manage cybersafety education and awareness issues in schools today, including a section on e-security. Earlier in the year we celebrated 'Safer Internet Day'. While the Authority's tagline is 'communicating, facilitating, regulating' it is quickly apparent that the discursive energy of local governance structures is mostly spent on discussing risk and safety issues to do with the Internet. While there is a nascent focus on *facilitating* digital literacy this has been overridden by a discourse of *protection* from cyber risks and focus on policy-making (see Osborne 2010). This focus was also seen in the high-profile Australian debate about Internet filtering and blacklisting of particular websites. The federal government proposed this policy in 2007 but due to widespread public and political disquiet, and innovative online campaigns, it has not yet been passed through Parliament or implemented.

There is minimal policy discussion in Australia of a progressive ideal of digital democratic citizenship (see Coleman and Blumler 2009). It is this tension between a democratic ideal (that reflects how young people engage with the Internet) and the discursive context (that reveals a fear of technological change) that provides an important framework for understanding whether and/or how youth-based websites create new spaces for civic and political engagement. This chapter presents a longitudinal content analysis of a mixture of government- and community sector-led sites that are either wholly online or tied to established offline organisations, to establish what kind of citizenship practices and ideals are made available to Australian young people.

Australia provides an appropriate base for analysis as in recent times it has experienced a debate, similar to that in most advanced democracies, about the disengagement of young people from the political process (see Bean 2007). To a large extent the debate has been hidden from the broader comparative context due to compulsory voting in Australia and high turnout rates of the general population. In other nations, especially the UK and USA, low turnout at elections by young people has created cause for concern and generated discussion on civic engagement and a democratic deficit (see for example, Furlong and Cartmel 2007, pp. 21–37). Arguably, Australia has seen a similar level of more generalised political disengagement when attitudes towards the formal political sphere are taken into account (Edwards 2007). Australia also has a government that is prepared to launch interventionist policy-making to change young people's behaviours in general (Bessant 2004; White and Wyn 2008).

The Australian federal government's approach to youth participation is underpinned by the idea that young people need to be enabled through 'empowerment' strategies to become active, 'responsible' citizens (based on Barnes *et al.* 2007). My earlier research found that these ideas or discourses about young people are entrenched in the thinking of high-level government and community decision-makers, and shape youth participation policy practice in both community and government services. That is, decision-makers believe that young people need to be empowered to 'have a say' on both democratic matters and youth services, and that it is young people's civic duty to be engaged in public affairs (Vromen forthcoming; also see Livingstone 2009a; Eliasoph 2009). Overall, it was found in both focus group discussion and a survey of service providers that decision-makers could 'talk the talk' on the need for change in institutional structures to shift participation away from a top-down approach towards the use of more interactive online technology. However, the discursive and actual barriers to doing this are clearly too significant to overcome as there have been few real instances of decision-makers demonstrating to young people that they are heard and are, through their views and actions, able to 'make a difference' in youth policy and service delivery (see Australian Youth Affairs Coalition 2010). Changing youth participation practice necessitates a shift in thinking on the way young people are understood as 'contemporary youth participation policies do not treat young people as active political agents with existing preferences derived from their lived experience' (Vromen forthcoming; see also Horsley and Costley 2008). In this chapter I am interested in building on this earlier research to see what has happened online in youth-oriented websites for civic engagement in Australia. That is, do these websites, which are developed by both government and non-government organisations and are online-only or online representations of established offline organisations, follow this generally institutionalised, top-down approach to young people's civic engagement? Or are they alternate democratic spaces that both engage with young people's everyday lives, and develop young people's capacity for political expression (see Bang 2005; Collin 2008)? For example, Harris *et al.* (2010, p. 27) found in their survey of young Australians that the Internet was a significant part of young people's everyday civic lives, and that they used it 'for leisure, but also to "have a say", especially with their peers, with whom they can make shared social and political meanings out of their individual circumstances'.

This chapter analyses 100 Australian civic youth websites to see if, over time, there has been an expansion in active engagement of young people through Internet-based means, and whether both the style of interactivity and citizenship norms found on sites have changed.

Online civic engagement and young people

Stephen Coleman (2008) theorises about 'autonomous' and 'managed' forms of youth oriented e-citizenship as ideal types. He writes:

> The conflict between the two faces of e-citizenship is between a view of democracy as an established and reasonably just system, with which young people should be encouraged to engage, and democracy as a political as well as cultural aspiration, most likely to be realised through networks in which young people engage with one another.
>
> (Coleman 2008, p. 192)

This work develops a normative model for online democratic citizenship that challenges the state to engage with *new* forms of citizenship practices found on the Internet. In this model it is important for governments to fund, but not control, young people's political expression, and to ensure that there is genuine opportunity for both horizontal and vertical interaction, as well as collaboration. Innovative forms of communication on issues that matter to young people are also core to making it possible and acceptable for young people's e-citizenship to challenge the status quo (Coleman 2008, pp. 202–205). In later work, Stephen Coleman with Jay Blumler (2009 p. 116) acknowledge the inherent contradiction in expecting government to provide more interactive online spaces; they write that 'there is a danger that in following the well-resourced and grandly publicised e-democracy projects run by governments, we will be looking in the wrong place' as it is likely that innovation is happening in the non-government sphere. Yet, grassroots autonomous action, while important, does not replace the state as it needs to find ways of going to where citizens are rather than setting up badly run sites and expecting engagement with people (Coleman and Blumler 2009, pp. 134–137). Other research has found reluctance by electoral campaigning sites to cater their messages and site functionality to younger audiences (Xenos and Bennett 2007a, p. 461). Therefore Sonia Livingstone writes that when seeking to understand civic engagement via the Internet we should note the 'communicative deficit – the gap that exists between the user as imagined by the producers, and the actual users who use the Internet in their real world contexts' (2009a, p. 147).

There are several studies that have collected systematic quantitative data on the 'youth civic web'. One of the first was the survey of over 300 youth directed websites in the US-based study: *Youth as E-Citizens: Engaging the Digital Generation* (Montgomery *et al.* 2004). This study found that sites that engaged with online interaction and creative postings and were either youth-led or youth-controlled were more appealing to participants. Young people also preferred community-related and volunteer activities to electoral-type participation, and they needed to be persuaded that public affairs and governance were relevant to them, and that their action would make a difference (ibid., pp. 17–18). Overall, the study argued that sites were in general failing to exploit the interactive capacity of the web (ibid., p. 105); and that the economy of online information is dominated by a comparative handful of well-connected sites with search engines playing a key role in the consolidation of power of the Internet's marketplace of ideas, thus limiting the vitality of the youth oriented 'civic Internet' (ibid., pp. 127–134). Montgomery has developed this 'youth Internet as marketplace' argument in later work where she documents how commercial business sites are dominant and able to conflate youth civic identity and brand identity under the guise of digital political engagement. Web 2.0 social networking sites such as Facebook, YouTube and MySpace, are key spaces where this kind of commercialisation of youth experience occurs (Montgomery 2008, pp. 33–34).

The Civic Learning Online project (Bennett *et al.* 2009) developed a two-tiered approach to the study of online youth engagement based on contrasting conceptions of ideal types, or norms, of citizenship (dutiful and self-actualising) and related civic skills (knowledge, expression, joining publics and taking action). Broadly, the dutiful citizen has election and government at the core of democratic participation, uses traditional media to follow the news, trusts leaders and joins formal political organisations. The self-actualising citizen has a weaker allegiance to government, focuses on lifestyle politics, mistrusts media and politicians, joins loose networks for social and political action and uses digital media for communication (Bennett, Wells and Rank 2009, p. 107).

This project's analysis of 90 youth websites dedicated to civic engagement found that 76 per cent of the civic learning opportunities observed a dutiful citizenship style (Bennett, Wells and Freelon 2009, p. 19). More specifically, different types of organisations tend to gravitate towards different models of citizenship. For example, 53 per cent of actualising learning opportunities occurred in online-only sites, even though online-only sites made up only one third of the total sample. Indeed, 70 per cent of online-only sites offered some form of expression training in contrast to conventional community, interest and government organisations which were 'disproportionately' concerned with engaging young users in site-defined activities (ibid., p. 19). Government and campaign sites 'offered slightly greater opportunities for actualizing civic learning skills' than other organisations, yet the authors are doubtful that this trend will continue unabated. Community and interest organisations with an offline dutiful citizenship orientation 'overwhelmingly' reproduced this orientation on their website whereas online-only sites tended to communicate a greater mix of self-actualising and dutiful civic skills. Both conventional and online organisations tended to offer highly managed opportunities for joining publics and taking action. It was rare for any type of site to give young people the opportunity to create and promote their own activities (ibid., pp. 20–21). These finding also echo UK-based research on youth websites by Roman Gerodimos (2008).

He suggests that most government and non-governmental organisation (NGO) sites – including those with a traditional youth engagement and those with a social movement orientation – present to young users an 'unimaginative use of the Internet' (p. 984).

Building on the University of Washington Civic Learning Online project Chris Wells (2010) analysed a subset of 36 online-only youth civic engagement websites. A theoretical framework wass created from Lance Bennett *et al's* dutiful versus self-actualising conceptions of citizenship (Bennett, Wells and Rank 2009) and Stephen Coleman's (2008) managed versus autonomous civic communication environments. The sample was coded for the presence of 'managed' and 'autonomous' communicative opportunities and for features that evidence 'dutiful' and 'self-actualising' citizenship norms. Results suggest that online-only youth websites are most commonly 'slightly managed and quite self-actualizing' (Wells 2010, pp. 430–431). It is found that dutiful models of citizenship are correlated with managed styles of interaction but that self-actualising models of citizenship are unrelated to the communication environment (ibid., p. 431). Wells concludes that appealing to young people and delivering conventional civic training at the same time may be as difficult to accomplish with a website as it has proven to be in a classroom (ibid., p. 435).

These studies suggest that there is an increased prevalence of self-actualising citizenship norms emerging through newer, online-only sites, while older established offline organisations maintain a dutiful citizenship disposition. Most sites still however tend to manage young people's interaction with the organisation, and this is demonstrated by limited incidences of opportunities for the promotion of solely youth-led or youth-devised forms of engagement.

Methodology

This project coded and analysed 100 Australian youth-oriented broadly civic websites in April and May 2010, and was partly a longitudinal replication of an unpublished 2006 study and partly a replication of the Civic Learning Online (Bennett, Wells and Freelon 2009) project on mainly US youth sites. The original 2006 population of 96 sites was built from the known universe of youth-led and youth-serving organisations that had a website, partly from lists available from the Australian Clearinghouse for Youth Studies database, and others known to the author and research assistants. The 2006 list was revisited in March 2010 and every site that was inactive, had disappeared, had very low traffic or had not been updated in 12 months (26 sites); or was considered mainly a youth research site (6 sites), were all eliminated from the list. Thus in 2010, 64 of the 2006 sites were used with the addition of 36 new sites. In 2006 very few online-only sites existed, and these types were purposively sampled in 2010 (for example, the new federal government's Australian Youth Forum; and Noise, a young artists' network), and new organisations or sites were also included (for example, the 7pm Project Forums –based on a youth-focused TV news programme – and the Australian Youth Climate Coalition). Government and political party sites were also purposively included in 2010, as they had been largely neglected in the 2006 sample construction. The 100 sites analysed in 2010 are all examples of organisations that engage young people in civic life, broadly conceived. Groups that explicitly foster political engagement (such as most interest groups) are included here, but the promulgation of citizenship norms is not limited to these organisations alone. Youniss and Yates (1999, p. 2) argue that civic organisations are 'norm-bearing institutions' that socialise and integrate young people into society and its traditions, and they include cultural, arts and recreation-based groups. Nina Eliasoph (2009, p. 294), in her study of new approaches to youth empowerment, says civic action is found in ongoing groups that work together to 'create some good that they define as a public one'. Also included are community service groups who use advocacy to influence decision-makers on behalf of young people, and are seeking publicly beneficial social change (see Morales 2009, p. 47; Minkoff 2002; Montgomery *et al.* 2004).

Sampling youth-oriented civic engagement sites is not straightforward (as noted by Gerodimos and Ward 2007, p. 117) and several arbitrary decisions or classifications are necessarily made. For example, even the online-only category is becoming increasingly problematic as, while sites are the major focus of an organisation's civic engagement effort, many interest/activist groups have an offline component that may involved public meet-ups or small activist group formation. I included a handful of sites that do not always overtly present themselves as youth-oriented, but are run by young people (examples include activist group GetUp and media site New Matilda) because they are influential examples of contemporary online civic engagement that young people are creating. While the three groupings of government, community and interest groups seem straightforward, decisions were made to include youth-led news and media type websites in the activist-oriented interest group category where they may not sit comfortably. This distinction is not always clear-cut. I would justify all of these arbitrary choices as significant in creating a sample of sites with breadth and able to tap into a very broad notion of the youth civic web in Australia. The sample of websites analysed here is described in Tables 11.1 and 11.2.

A research assistant and I developed the 2006 quantitative coding schedule originally, and two assistants did most of the coding. In 2010 a new research assistant and I revisited the original coding schedule, keeping over half the questions and categories and then incorporating others from the coding schedules used in the Civic Learning Online project, and analysed in Bennett, Wells and Freelon (2009) and Wells (2010). Note that we were limited by single periods of time for the coding and could not measure site dynamism. As we mostly coded site background, how the site described itself and its functionality rather than, for example, user-posted content, these mostly static features were simpler to code and less likely to undergo rapid change or development. Comparison of site interactivity between 2006 and 2010 is made below, but due to the timing I did not collect data on the citizenship norms or practices of sites in 2006. The study is also limited as its focus is on sites alone and not on users or audience, thus it is impossible to generalise about how sites are actually understood or used by young people (see Gerodimos and Ward 2007). Instead I am interested in the kind of citizenship norms that websites encapsulate to understand how these civic organisations construct their young users.

Tables 11.1 and 11.2 show that most sites overall and the most popular are those that are community service oriented and produced. Government has a very small stake in running civic websites, however it is by far the most significant funder of the organisations included in this sample who reported this type of data online (data on funding sources was not available for 21 sites). Unfortunately, most (77 per cent) organisations did not publicly reveal their *total* revenue. Online-only organisations were twice as likely *not* to receive any government funding; and nearly all of the organisations that did not reveal their funding base were well-established organisations. Community service-type organisations were significantly more likely to have advertising (55 per cent of total) on their sites, but for the majority this was from a partner or sponsoring organisation.

Beyond over-representing online-only sites, the Top 20 in Table 11.2 differ on very few demographics from the overall sample. One exception was for whether they explicitly stated young people were involved in the development of the site. In the Top 20, half of the organisations had young people involved in site development, where this was the case for only a third of the sample overall.

The Top 20 are also interesting due to the diverse range of civic organisations that they represent, and there is no clear pattern. Some organisations are well linked into the progressive community service sector and have emerged in the last 10–15 years (e.g. Orygen, Reach Out and Somazone); while others are well-established, traditional civic organisations (such as Scouts and YMCA). Some are very well known and well funded (e.g. the representative body the Australian Council of Trade Unions' school site), and others are mainly known to the small but active community of interest that they engage with (e.g. Qnet online and Sydney Muslim Youth). The new youth-led organisations that primarily exist online in the Top 20 are mainly a mix of social movement-oriented activism (e.g. the high-profile progressive activist organisation, GetUp, and also the Inspire Foundation-run ActNow) and alternative new media spaces that have precarious financial resources (e.g. Vibewire, Engage Media and New Matilda[1]).

Table 11.1 Overview of 2010 sample (compared to 2006)

Youth website 'demographics'	2010% N = 100	2006% N = 96
Online only?	24	12
Type: Government/formal politics	13	5
Type: Community service	48	58
Type: Interest/activist/new media	39	37
Some government funding?	80	57
Government largest funder	59	54
Advertising on site (inc. partners)	38	23
Young people developed site	34	28
Totally youth-led	25	14
No youth involvement in decisions	43	65

Table 11.2 Top 20 trafficked Australian civic youth sites (June 2010)

Organisation	Organisational type	Online only	Government funded	Youth work on site	Citizenship orientation	Alexa linking sites (10 June 2010)
Get Up!	Interest: progressive issue activist group	Yes	No	Yes	Combination	489
New Matilda	Interest: progressive media commentary	Yes	No	Yes	Self-actualising	557
Reach Out	Community: youth wellbeing service	Yes	Yes	Yes	Combination	27
YMCA	Community: youth and family charity	No	Yes	?	Dutiful	67
Engage Media	Interest: social, environment activist media	Yes	No	Yes	Self-actualising	372
The 7pm Project Forums	Interest: media commentary forums	Yes	No	?	Self-actualising	48
Qnet Online Community	Interest: queer youth space	Yes	Yes	Yes	Combination	720
ActNow	Community: enabling youth engagement	Yes	Yes	Yes	Combination	94
Scouts Australia	Community: outdoor adventure group	No	Yes	?	Dutiful	144
Somazone	Community: youth health information	Yes	No	Yes	Combination	93
Sydney Muslim Youth	Interest: religious activist group	No	No	?	Self-actualising	21
Australian Youth Forum	Government: youth forums portal	Yes	Yes	Yes	Combination	90
Vibewire	Interest: media opinion and commentary	Yes	Yes	Yes	Self-actualising	27
Express Media	Community: youth media development site	No	Yes	Yes	Combination	68
Noise	Community: young artists' network	Yes	Yes	?	Self-actualising	98
Barnardos	Community: child welfare service	No	Yes	?	Self-actualising	69
ACTU worksite for schools	Interest: union peak body	No	No	Yes	Dutiful	392[1]
Youth Off the Streets	Community: homeless youth service	No	Yes	?	Dutiful	81
Young Care	Community: youth living in care advocacy	No	Yes	?	Dutiful	53
Orygen Youth Health	Community: youth mental health service	No	Yes	?	Combination	18
Totals	Interest=8 Government=1 Community=11	11	13	11	Dutiful=5 Combination=8 Self-actualising=7	

Notes
Only YMCA and Orygen had *no* type of public expression on site.
1 Links are for ACTU parent site.

Analysing Australian civic youth websites

This section analyses features of Australian sites through a focus on three dimensions: features and interactivity; how extensively young people's engagement with sites is managed; and the types of citizenship orientation that sites promote. From this analysis it will be possible to identify whether Australian civic youth websites differ from American counterparts, and whether they align with the structured and top-down approach of most offline, Australian youth participation initiatives.

Interactivity

The coding investigated what forms of civic action and communication capacities are developed in each site. Table 11.3 compares 2006 and 2010 data for the scope and use of interactive features on sites. Clearly the level of interactivity and use of web 2.0 features has increased on Australian youth websites. In 2010 only 15 per cent of sites did not have any interactive features (in contrast to 47 per cent of 2006 sites), the median was three features, and a quarter of sites had five or more. There was no relationship between organisational type and total forms of interaction; but online-only sites had a significantly higher median number (five interactive features as compared to two).

However, the features that the majority of sites have offer very little scope for young people's political expression. Providing feedback on site content, looking at YouTube videos posted by the site, and issuing invites to socially networked friends to view the site's content are all highly structured and limited forms of interaction. Importantly, when the Top 20 trafficked sites are singled out they are significantly different in level of interactivity from the rest of the 2010 sample on three important youth-led dimensions of interactivity: making comments, uploading creative material and participating in forums. This suggests that the young people being targeted may repeatedly engage within the site, rather than visit it occasionally to obtain broadcast-style information.

Table 11.3 Interactivity on Australian youth websites (%)

Form of online interaction	2010, N = 100	2006, N = 96	2010 – Top 20
Feedback	53	35	70
Creative by site	53	25	70
Social networking invites	52	n/a	60
Comments	27	n/a	55*
Blogs	22	7	35
Creative by young people	20	n/a	45*
Discussion boards	17	21	25
Polls	16	9	30
Forum	15	17	35*
Wikis	5	n/a	0

Notes
* >0.05; 2010 Top 20 compared to rest of sample with Alexa ratings (N=73).

An examination of the types of interactivity found on the sites in 2010 with site demographics including organisational type and online-only status showed that both interest groups and online-only sites were significantly more likely to offer interactive features including discussion boards, blogs and comments sections. Government and interest groups were equally likely to include polls; government sites were most likely to give users the opportunity to link to social networking sites; online-only sites were significantly more likely to have creative posts by young people; and community groups were most likely to have creative postings created by the site. There were no significant differences in interactivity according to whether the main funder was government or not.

As Table 11.3 confirms, very few sites that aim to shape young people's civic engagement are comfortable offering interactive opportunities for their young Australian users. Despite that, sites that have more interactive features tend to be visited more (as in the case of the Top 20 sites), and all youth-aimed sites could clearly learn from the online-only sites that best understand the web 2.0 environment. Potentially, sites can increase their popularity and profile when they offer interactive opportunities for their target youth audience and do not simply broadcast organisation-specific viewpoints. Most traditional community and government sites are constrained and tend to rely on one-way forms of communication such as creating YouTube videos for users to watch or offering just a feedback page, rather than the more dialogue-friendly comments, forums or discussion boards.

Management of site users

One of the principal ways of understanding the management of site users by the site is to judge whether users are able to *publicly* express viewpoints on the site. Taking the forms of interactivity in Table 11.3, three forms do not lead to young people's public expression on the site: the three most popular of sending feedback, looking at creative postings on the site, and linking to social networking. Thus 55 per cent of sites provide young people with some space to express a point of view, and 55 per cent of those sites expect young people to log in to be able to do so, mostly requiring a combination of name and/or age to register. Unsurprisingly, online-only sites are significantly more likely to give young people space for public expression (phi=0.367), with only three online-only sites not doing so; and similarly there was more public expression when young people were involved in the site development (phi=0.310). Most sites had some sort of moderation of young people's public expression, ranging from explicit filtering before posts went online, to a code of conduct for users and/or moderators. This is not entirely surprising, as for many youth-serving sites a duty of care towards their young users necessitates some form of risk assessment and moderation. Only one site had no moderation whatsoever: the Australian Student Environment Network.

Following Wells (2010) we also examined how sites engage with their members or users. Overall 65 per cent of sites made it possible for users to become members of the organisation, only 5 per cent expected members to pay a fee. On nearly half of all sites users could sign up to receive the organisation's newsletter, and 42 per cent of sites sent out a follow-up email to users once they registered (my research assistant did this) which mainly encouraged users to be active online with the site. Only 18 per cent of sites then proceeded to regularly send emails about site updates and campaigns. Management can also be seen in what the site encourages users to do on it, the recognition of users' role on the site and how much latitude they are given. Of the 100 sites coded here, 29 per cent featured user-generated text or linked directly to user posts from the homepage; only 14 per cent had a customised self-representation such as an avatar; and 35 per cent let users link their involvement on the site with a personal website or social networking page. Online-only organisations were significantly more likely to allow all three of these user-led factors to occur; and sites that had young people's involvement in their development were significantly more likely to both feature user-generated text and links to personal websites. The approaches found toward site management reinforce how sites approach interactivity. That is, more traditional government and community organisations create online spaces that tend to manage young people's citizenship, rather than provide them with new, democratic spaces for civic engagement.

Citizenship orientations

The Civic Learning Online study was directly replicated to identify the type of civic learning goals and overall citizenship orientations sites produced. Table 11.4 summarises what the four main goals are – knowledge, expression, publics and action – and shows how they manifest in either dutiful or self-actualising ideal types of citizenship.

We looked for these citizenship orientations and civic learning goals in two main ways. First, we looked at the discursive construction of citizenship found

Table 11.4 Civic learning goals

Dutiful civic learning goals	Self-actualising civic learning goals
Knowledge: e.g. one-way authoritative information from site producers, news sites and public officials	*Knowledge*: e.g. peer knowledge sharing opportunities
Expression: e.g. training to provide content aimed at institutions, e.g. write an effective letter, etc.	*Expression*: e.g. training in digital participatory media, create a podcast, video, blog, etc.
Join a public: e.g. membership and joining a formal organisation	*Join a public*: e.g. users encouraged to define and start a peer network
Take action: e.g. participate in actions organised by site or affiliates or authorities	*Take action*: e.g. joining or reporting on peer-generated actions

Source: Adapted from Bennett, Wells and Freelon (2009, pp. 20–21).

in the mission statements of websites (usually in the 'About us' section or on the homepage). Based on the descriptive language used we coded sites as broadly promoting an ideal model of dutiful citizenship (58 per cent) or self-actualising citizenship (42 per cent). There are notable tendencies among the organisational websites that claim to provide civic engagement for young people through self-actualisation: they are more likely to be online-only (phi=0.269), be youth led to some extent and, significantly, have had young people develop the website (phi=0.315), and encourage young people's public expression (phi=0.339). The sites tend to mention 'empowerment' and mostly talk about a youth-led space or network for discussion and action. The dutiful citizenship sites tend to focus on notions of communal responsibility, ethics and values, and connect with traditional institutions and services, including a focus on young people's efficacy in improving them. The Top 20 trafficked sites were not significantly more likely to represent themselves as self-actualising, with a 45 per cent dutiful to 55 per cent self-actualising split, thus there is not a clear relationship between the sites most people visit and their citizenship orientation.

The second way we examined citizenship orientations and civic learning goals was by coding the actual presence of the four main learning goals on the websites. This leads to a useful comparison between the discursive and idealised construction of citizenship for young people and the actual practices of citizenship that the site adopts. Codes were made here on the basis of specific opportunities that a site offered to its users, pathways that it identified for them or information that it gave to them. For instance, a positive dutiful 'join a public' code would have been: (a) that the site provided information on adult managed/promoted youth activities in their area; or (b) that the site explained the roles of hierarchical/traditional groups (like political parties, interest or civic groups, etc.) and reasons for joining them. The actualizing 'join a public' code was specific to information on non-hierarchical groups or groups that were not defined/promoted/managed/supervised by non-youth higher authorities. Overall, Table 11.5 shows that there are only three civic learning goals that a majority of websites endorse for Australian young people: dutiful forms of knowledge from

Table 11.5 Civic learning goals on Australian youth websites[1]

Dutiful civic learning goals	% sites	Self-actualising civic learning goals	% sites
Knowledge	90	Knowledge	39
• Expression: online training	20	• Expression: online training	14
• Expression: offline training	29	• Expression: offline training	15
• Expression, without training	12	• Expression, without training	19
Expression *at least one form*	60	Expression *at least one form*	47
Join a public	39	Join a public	47
Take action	77	Take action	34

Note

1 Note that in the coding process we found it necessary to create new categories to differentiate between online and offline expression training, as well as site-based facilitation of expression that did not overtly tell users how to engage in public expression.

authoritative sources; expressing their point of view to authorities; and dutiful forms of action organised by the site, authorities or public officials.

Looking at the relationship between discursive types of citizenship orientation and actual practices, all went the predicted way, that is discursively dutiful sites were more likely to contain dutiful learning goals than self-actualising sites were, and vice versa. All of the actualising civic goals were significantly much more likely to be found on sites that spoke the language of self-actualisation – about empowerment, networks and peer-to-peer exchange. These data tell us two things: first, there is a relationship between citizenship discourse and practice for most organisations; second, a majority of sites that are self-actualising promote distinctive actualising civic learning goals for young people. However, it is also worth examining the mean number of learning goals: the whole sample had an average of 2.7 out of four dutiful goals and 1.7 out of four actualising goals per site which still suggests that dutiful citizenship is the norm for youth websites in their approach to young people's civic engagement.

In classifying sites by their learning goals and actual citizenship practices: four sites had only one learning goal present; 11 had an even combination of dutiful and self-actualising goals; ten sites included nearly all (seven out of eight) learning goals; 20 could be classified as self-actualising sites; and 55 as dutiful sites. Table 11.6 shows the relationship between the demographics and these classifications using just three categories: combination, self-actualising and dutiful sites. That sites with self-actualising civic goals are more likely to be online and have some youth leadership in their organisation is not surprising. The other two findings are of more interest. A majority of 'combination' sites have had young people assist in the site development, furthermore when the sites with youth involvement alone are looked at the split is 38 per cent combination: 35 per cent dutiful: 27 per cent actualising. This suggests that to some extent young people themselves may choose to create sites that foster both kinds of citizenship orientations – dutiful for dealing with authority and power, and self-actualising for creating a peer-led space. Another interpretation could focus on resources available to organisations to invest in a youth participation programme

Table 11.6 Demographics with citizenship orientations of sites (%)

	Dutiful (N = 55)	Combination (N = 21)	Self-actualising (N = 20)	Significance
Online only	9	43	50	Cramers V = 0.429**
Youth developed site	22	62	45	Cramers V = 0.349*
No youth leadership	53	19	35	Cramers V = 0.333*
Some government funding?	71	64	45	Cramers V = 0.382*
Advertising?	31	38	65	Cramers V = 0.427*

Notes
*p < 0.05; **p < 0.001.

that systematically integrates youth involvement in organisational practice and site development. Furthermore, as both a majority of dutiful and combination sites receive government funding it could be an expectation that they include dutiful civic goals in their mandate. The organisations here arguably also differ in terms of their funding base and total revenue, but as 77 per cent did not publish this online I can only surmise. That self-actualising organisations are most likely to have paid advertising on their pages lends credence to Kathryn Montgomery's (2008) argument about the marketisation and commercialisation of young people's online spaces; as well as providing an alternative funding stream from government, in a country like Australia where civic philanthropy is less institutionalised than the USA and the UK.

All of the individual forms of interaction potentially found on websites occurred significantly more often on both self-actualising and combination sites than dutiful sites, with the exception of site posted creative content. Table 11.7 looks at site attributes to see if there are differences among the citizenship orientations in practice. The strongest association here is between the discursive construction of the mission of a website and its practice; notable is that combination sites – that have an equal number of dutiful and actualising civic goals – tend to portray themselves as self-actualising sites. Overall, this finding goes against my suspicion that websites would 'talk' as though they were self-actualising for their young users but in practice give them very little scope for public expression or action. However, as dutiful sites and a dutiful discourse are found on the majority of youth civic sites it remains a centrally important discursive construction of engagement for young Australians.

Table 11.7 Site attributes and citizenship orientations (%)

	Dutiful (N = 55)	Combination (N = 21)	Actualising (N = 20)	Significance
Dutiful discourse/	86	24	20	Cramers V = 0.638**
Actualising discourse	15	76	80	
Public expression on site	35	81	95	Cramers V = 0.541**
Homepage has user-generated content	11	43	70	Cramers V = 0.524**
Encourages users to take part in activities involving government	47	57	10	Cramers V = 0.339*
Encourage political activity not involving government	51	86	75	Cramers V = 0.313*
Links to government sites	73	62	25	Cramers V = 0.306*
Some material aimed at teachers and parents	58	48	30	Not significant

Notes
*$p < 0.05$; **$p < 0.001$.

Overall, the most important point to appreciating the distinctive approach of sites that have a self-actualising approach to young people's citizenship, as the theorisation would expect, is that site users – young people – are at the centre of the site and at the centre of political engagement. This suggests that the discursive construction and actual practices of engagement are aligned; but also that new online spaces are being uniquely used to foster self-actualisation, rather than directing young people to offline action. The vast majority of actualising sites prioritise public expression by young people, and a majority highlight user input on their homepage. Very few dutiful sites do the same, preferring to manage the experience young people can have on their site by mainly being an information source rather than a participatory space. This information tends to be presented as authoritative and links with government action and sites. A majority of dutiful websites target teachers and parents as much as young people, suggesting a latent suspicion of the Internet and its interactive capacities in general.

Empowered but dutiful citizenship in Australian young peoples' online experience?

Most of the Australian youth oriented websites studied here follow a generally institutionalised, discursively top-down and dutiful approach to young people's civic engagement. This reflects the government-led approach to youth participation policy where there is an expectation that young people can 'have a say' but only on the terms set by powerful traditional institutions. Further, only a minority of sites allow young people to express themselves on their sites, preferring instead to provide information, and at most a YouTube video or two as a concession to their intended audience. This prioritisation of dutiful citizenship norms with the management of young people's online experience resonates with the results found in Bennett *et al.* (2011).

However, there is clearly an emerging, albeit still minority, distinctive online experience that focuses on empowering young people in their creation of political space, and encourages them to express political viewpoints. This is similar to what Wells (2010) found in his examination of online-only civic youth sites. The possibility of interactivity on websites, for example, has increased since I surveyed sites in 2006. Young people themselves are increasingly likely to have had a role in shaping civic engagement sites for their peers. There are also some examples of more traditional community service organisations and interest groups changing their citizenship style through their online presence to further target their young audiences (e.g. Barnados, Dusseldorp Skills Forum and Youth Affairs Council of South Australia). Some of the organisations that are fusing citizenship norms, classified as combination sites, provide food for thought about the interdependence between funding, resources and successful appeals to young Internet users. This resonates with Montgomery's (2008) cautionary message on the potential commercialisation of youth citizenship experiences. As some of the newer and popular online-only organisations expand it will be important, through case study analysis, to monitor their commitment, or otherwise, to democratic forms of communication and citizenship, as outlined by Coleman (2008).

Three areas for further discussion emerge in the light of these findings. First, the relationship between youth participation discourses and national context. In Australia the adoption of a discourse of youth empowerment, within an overall ideal of responsibility (or duty) to be active citizens, was made possible by portraying all young people as marginalised. That is: young people have civic deficiencies, they ought to be active citizens and involved in politics, but we need to provide them with the capacities to have a say and express themselves. There has been very little shift towards seeing young people as partners in political decision-making and thus giving them the capacity to make a difference and change policy/politics. This is reflected in the findings here as a minority of sites give young people the capacity to determine (at the core of self-actualisation) how they will express themselves and join with other young people to deliberate and/or take action. Further research could explore the normative dimension of contemporary civic and citizenship practices prescribed for and/or created by young people. That is, do young people want to have a say and effect policymaking; and how do they understand their own efficacious citizenship both online and offline? Recent research suggests that young people's everyday use of the Internet, and social networking sites in particular, shapes all dimensions of their public and private lives, providing 'networked publics' that form 'the civil society of teenage culture' (boyd 2008, p. 121; see also Harris *et al.* 2010). How are public expectations and opportunities for engagement reconciled with these online everyday experiences?

Second, the idea of diversity and structured lived (youth) experience. Marsh *et al.* (2007) use Bourdieu's conceptualisations on the link between economic, social and cultural capital to find that gender, race and class continue to shape how young people understand their lives and their relationship with politics. Under-explored in my data is how sites target particular groups of young people to engage with their lived experience and subsequently construct their citizenship orientation. For example, in my sample there are sites aimed at queer youth, several sites that target religion and ethnicity (e.g. Muslim youth), and young people living in socio-economic disadvantage (in the care of the state or homeless). Do these groups of young people exhibit agency? Are they portrayed online as part of positive social change or are they mainly constructed as marginalised youth needing charitable intervention? Some of the most popular civic sites are those that are shaped by young people's experience of health and wellbeing, especially their mental health (e.g. Reach Out). Many of these sites give at least a cursory acknowledgment of self-actualisation in their citizenship orientation through the availability of peer-to-peer networks and user-generated material on their pages.

Third, what underpins young people's preference for self-actualisation in online political engagement? Has neoliberalism, coupled with individualisation and the diminishing of traditional collective action (see Beck and Beck-Gernsheim 2001), made the emergence of this citizenship orientation more possible? That is, are we no longer duty bound to the state, or grand narratives of mass social and political change; so we network, we DIY, we personalise the political (see Harris 2008)? What does this mean for social movements and for democracy; and how does it change collective action in general? There may be potential in the sites with a 'combination' citizenship orientation to find new experiences in the practice of collective action that can create political change. It is also possible that online-only sites, that are more likely to *not* take government funding, may provide an autonomous democratic space (e.g. linked with social networking sites). But will new, non-government funding bases make commercialisation of youth experience inevitable? While an online presence often lowers the real costs for participation and mobilisation, youth civic engagement spaces (on- and offline) inevitably need reliable resources to be sustained over time. Having a popular Facebook causes page or a well-visited YouTube may seem fleeting, but maybe they are not yet fully understood in terms of the capacity for learning, engagement and political change unfettered by a state-led ideal of responsible and dutiful citizenship.

Note

1 Indeed, New Matilda, a progressive media site and blog, was forced to shut down due to lack of resources not long after we conducted our analysis. At the end of 2010 there is a high-profile fundraising drive occurring to get New Matilda back online.

12 Online participation

New forms of civic and political engagement or just new opportunities for networked individualism

Giovanna Mascheroni

This chapter discusses the findings of a qualitative study aimed at investigating Italian youth's political uses of the web in relation to their civic cultures, that is the shared systems of meaning, values, knowledge, spaces and practices through which young citizens construct collective identities that support or inhibit their political engagement (Dahlgren 2009). Rather than studying Internet-based practices in isolation from offline and other media consumption practices, the use of the Internet as a tool for political information and political participation is here contextualised both in young people's crossmedia diets and in the context of their daily lives and their social networks. It is deemed that the development of web 2.0 and social media potentially expands the opportunities for civic engagement and may represent a remedy for youth disaffection, but studies of the role of the Internet in promoting political engagement among young people are divided in their conclusions. The findings suggest that online participation needs to be contextualized in youth's political socialization and media consumption practices, and that different civic cultures engage in different online activities and forms of participation. On the one hand web 2.0, under certain conditions, seems effective in mobilising participation, at least by those already interested. At the same time, online participation is an outcome of broader social changes, such as the emergence of new patterns of sociality – networked individualism (Castells 2001) and networked collectivism (Baym 2010) – and new citizenship practices.

Introduction

Having its roots in the field of media and Internet studies, this chapter aims at investigating young people's political uses of social network sites (SNS) by contextualising them within youth's 'civic cultures', that is 'cultural patterns in which identities of citizenship, and the foundations for civic agency, are embedded' (Dahlgren 2009, p. 103). Dahlgren's concept of civic cultures, it is argued here, helps understand divides and differences in youth's participation on- and offline.

The concern with younger generations' disaffection for political participation has been a recurrent theme in political and academic debate in the last decades.

Young people, it is argued, are failing to adopt conventional forms of participation such as voting and partisanship and are therefore 'disconnected'. Sociologists and political scientists have identified a number of interrelated socio-cultural changes that result in disengagement from traditional politics and in the parallel rise of new practices of citizenship. Some are more directly related to shifts in the media environment that pervades contemporary youth's everyday lives, and are therefore more relevant here. The most prominent is the networked character of society, and the associated pattern of sociality, namely networked individualism (Castells 2001), that is the development of personalised, ego-centred communities which find a material support in online and mobile technologies. Along with transformed patterns of sociality, more privatised relationships with traditional institutions and agencies of socialisation have emerged, as a further product of the process of individualisation (Beck 1992). These changes, however, generate contradictory outcomes: on the one hand, network sociality and the emphasis upon the individual and the reflexive project of the self (Giddens 1991) result in distrust in traditional institutions which used to provide collective identities and shared meanings; on the other, they promote involvement in new forms of engagement which are related to lifestyle concerns, identity issues and political consumerism (Micheletti 2003).

The debate around youth's disengagement has been increasingly integrated with studies of the Internet as a platform for politics, especially with the development of the so-called web 2.0. Indeed, while supporting the construction of personalised networking (Wellman 2001), the evolving media environment sustains the emergence of a 'convergence culture' (Jenkins 2006) which is significantly altering the boundaries between production and consumption of media content, and, arguably, audiences' relationship not only with cultural industries and their products, but also with politics. In web 2.0 users are involved as co-producers in that they share, manipulate and reassemble cultural products, creating an increasing amount of user-generated content (UGC). Such grassroots practices, some argue, represent new patterns of media and, at times, civic engagement (Bennett 2008). Moreover, new forms of online sociality are emerging, besides networked individualism and personal communities in the shape of ego-centred networks (Castells 2001): not only individuals, but also groups of people are able to network online and through mobile media, and create 'a shared but distributed network identity' following a different sociality pattern that Baym defines as 'networked collectivism' (Baym 2010, p. 91).

In Western democracies the Internet has become an integral part of daily political life, especially, but not solely, during election campaigns. Moreover, there are signs of growing bottom-up political uses of the Internet (Smith *et al.* 2009; Purcell *et al.* 2010; Rainie and Smith 2010), and deinstitutionalised forms of political engagement, such as petitioning and single-issue campaigns, are increasingly enacted through social network sites. Substantially relying on the networking capabilities of Facebook,[1] a group of Italian bloggers and citizens promoted a large demonstration calling for Berlusconi's resignation on 5 December 2009, the 'No-Berlusconi Day',[2] which mobilised around one million people in Italian cities and worldwide. This demonstration gave rise to a citizens' movement called the Popolo Viola (Purple People), still active both on- and offline, and primarily concerned with the defence of the Italian constitution and the monitoring of the prime minister's attempts to finalise a constitutional reform.

It is by drawing on examples like the one described that many argue for the potential of social media to expand the opportunities for civic engagement, and therefore claim that web 2.0 may represent a remedy for youth disaffection. But studies of the role of the Internet in promoting political engagement among young people are divided in their conclusions, claiming that the Internet is effective at mobilising disengaged youth (Montgomery *et al.* 2004; Lusoli *et al.* 2006), or that online initiatives are able to intersect only with those already interested in politics (Livingstone *et al.* 2007).

To what extent and how do Italian youth engage with online political content? What are the meanings attributed to online non-conventional citizenship practices and what is their relationships with offline participation? Why are these participatory practices unevenly taken up by young people? These and other questions remain largely unexplored.

The rise of active audiences and networked communities, it is argued here, calls into question the application of the traditional model of deliberative democracy to the web 2.0:[3] rather than representing an ideal public sphere where formal deliberation takes place, social media are the domain of digital storytelling, cultural remix and informal conversations. However, it is in the context of these informal conversations, online and offline, that people develop their political identities and citizenship practices (Gamson 1992). Following a 'culturalist' approach on issues of citizenship, media and democracy (Dahlgren 2009), this chapter analyses online participation practices within their socio-cultural settings rather than against an ideal model of online deliberation. The study of youth's civic cultures and their incorporation of web practices is deemed capable of shading new light on these issues. Civic cultures can be empirically analysed as comprising six dimensions, insofar as they constitute shared systems of meaning, values, knowledge, spaces and practices through which young citizens define collective identities that support or inhibit their political engagement.

Research methods

Political uses of SNS by young people need to be contextualised within everyday lives and youth cultures, characterised by the growing relevance of peer networks and crossmedia diets in the definition of personal and collective identities. Along with the complexity of changing perceptions of citizenship and participation, these features of contemporary youth lifestyles and mediated communication cultures call for the adoption of qualitative methods for their ability to stimulate interviewees' reflexivity (Couldry and Markham 2007).

The chosen framework, that is the wish to understand participation on- and offline on the basis of youth's civic cultures, and the consideration of people's difficulties in disclosing their political opinions in public contexts encouraged the use of a variant of focus groups, namely those 'peer groups conversation' already profitably employed by Gamson (1992, p. 17) in his study of the construction of shared meanings and 'collective actions frames' through informal political talk. Since 'when most people talk about politics, they tend to do so with people they know and with whom they share basic political assumptions and values' (Dahlgren 2009, p. 89), the closer the group is to natural groups of friends, the easier it is to observe people producing, negotiating and sharing meanings and collective identities.

Overall, eight group interviews, consisting of three to seven participants in the age groups 14–19 and 20–25 years old, were conducted. Peer group conversations, which lasted from one and a half to two hours, took place in natural settings chosen by the participants so as to minimise the asymmetry between the different roles of moderator and participants and put the interaction 'on a more equal footing' (Gamson 1992, p. 17). Settings varied from places where the group's collective practices are usually embedded (a school, a youth centre, a university department, a political party's local office) to public places where they usually gather (two cafés). In some cases, therefore, the place of the interview overlapped with the spatial dimension of the civic culture under investigation. Discussions were initially stimulated by the moderator who asked participants to narrate their habits of news consumption and their engagement with issues on the public agenda, that is their degree of 'mediated public connection' (Couldry et al. 2007). The issues under discussion involved also their attitudes towards institutional politics and related practices (such as turnout or party membership), the place of politics in their daily lives; their practices of civic or political engagement in everyday life, including citizenship practices online; the meanings they attributed to these practices; and the relationship between online and offline participation. However, the list of items was not strictly fixed beforehand nor given in a specific order but, rather, adapted to the characteristics of the group interviewed and the development of each conversation.

In order to untangle the factors that shape online participation, participants were selected through a theoretical sampling. The two sampling criteria were participants' civic cultures, and their engagement in civic or political groups and activities, on the one hand; and the degree of incorporation of the Internet in their everyday life contexts. Behind this choice lies the assumption that online participation is grounded in offline civic cultures, in peer cultures and their media practices, and that young people tend to climb a 'ladder of online opportunities' (Livingstone and Helsper 2007) so that more participatory uses are associated with longer experience and more frequent use of the Internet. The sampling strategy, therefore, led to the selection of eight groups differentiated in terms of age, political socialisation, political affiliation and digital inclusion: some groups are characterised by a strong socialisation to political engagement both at home and in the peer networks (groups 4, 7, 8), and share practices of political or civic engagement (groups 3, 4, 7, 8), that is are active in forms of civic or political engagement; others are mixed, combining individuals who have a strong commitment to citizenship and political engagement and individuals who are not actively engaged in modes of participation (groups 5 and 6), therefore not necessarily belonging to a unique civic culture. These groups, therefore, displayed how different civic cultures are based on different cultural systems, incorporate different practices and result in different degrees of engagement in collective actions. Finally, two groups (1 and 2) were comprised of mostly disengaged individuals, to observe how civic cultures – in this case a civic, or, we would say, an 'uncivic' culture oriented to disengagement – may inhibit participation. As regards digital inclusion, most participants have thoroughly incorporated the Internet in their everyday practices (groups 3, 4, 5, 6, 7); some pursue mainly if not exclusively communication and leisure activities online (1, 2); and a group comprises both frequent and low users.

Table 12.1 shows the composition of each group.

What kind of participation?

In examining how different groups perceive and practise participation, a variety of factors emerge that shape diverse civic cultures and contrasting patterns of citizenship. Cultural background and political socialisation, the degree of 'mediated public connection' (Couldry *et al.* 2007) and interest in issues of public concern, perceived political efficacy and trust or distrust in political institutions all combine and concur to generate the adherence to two main contrasting citizenship patterns, namely the 'dutiful citizen' or the 'actualizing citizen model' (Bennett 2008, p. 14).

Young people's motivation to engage in civic and political activities seems to be strongly embedded in the fabric of everyday life, and in the combination of social and cultural resources. Family, and its culture, represents the first and main context of political socialisation or, conversely, of disinterest and disengagement ('my parents are like me, they don't care and have no interest in politics' says a 19-year-old student from Itis). Participation is then supported and

Table 12.1 Composition of group interviews

Group number	Group features	Number of participants	Age group	Sex
1	Technical high school (Itis) classmates	5	18–19	5 boys
2	Youth centre (CAG)	5	15–17	3 boys, 2 girls
3	Members of the Students' Union (UDS)	4	18–19	3 boys, 1 girl
4	Students' collective (coll.)	3	16–18	3 boys
5	University students (univ.)	7	22–25	6 girls, 1 boy
6	University students (univ.)	6	23–25	6 girls
7	University students (univ.)	3	22–23	3 boys
8	Giovani Comunisti + civic association activist (g.com)[1]	4	20–24	3 girls, 1 boy

Note
1 Giovani Comunisti (Young Communists) is the youth section of Rifondazione Comunista (Communist Party).

facilitated when it is shared within households, peer networks and a set of collective practices that mobilise a consistent investment in time, sociability and identity. As the following excerpts suggest, individuals socialised to politics at home are more likely to belong to civic cultures that promote engagement and that are embedded in friendship ties, cultural values and visions of the world, practices and places:

M, 17, COLL.: My parents transmitted me not much a party identification nor political ideas, but rather the need or the importance of discussion, of being aware of political and social conditions. So fortunately at home – fortunately or unfortunately, it depends on points of view! – we have always discussed a lot about many political issues, or at least social and historical issues. Since I was a child, so ever since I was a child I have been used to listen to that kind of discussion, and to confront with different opinions. And that resulted in my interest in politics

M, 18, COLL.: I think at the beginning it was mainly a matter of friendship, in the sense that having left the Church, those friendship ties have not for political reasons but ... then I joined Rifondazione Comunista, and then I tried to create a node of political activity within my school

M, 16, COLL.: Yes and now the Social Collective we are those ... I mean, we see each other, go out together on Saturdays, for example myself and he go out often together, so politics has made us closer, has made us meet and then turned us into friends, friends or at least people who see each other very often, so politics is also a place for sociability

F, 24, G.COM.: It is participation that builds strong interpersonal relationships, at the end they [the other participants in the peer group conversation] are like my family, an additional piece of my family, because we kind of live together, and do so many things together.

Engagement in public issues is sustained by shared systems of meaning, and has its roots in everyday life practices, among which informal political talk and news consumption play a crucial part. Home is the most popular site where political conversation takes place, especially at dinner time which generates talk among family members watching the news on TV. The second context of political talk is represented by informal conversations among peers, especially in the older age group. In both cases conversations seem to be media-fuelled, in other words, news consumption is closely associated with interest in matters of public concern and with habits of civic and political talk:

M, 22, UNIV.: The three of us [the three participants]? The three of us yes, we talk a lot, very often, every time we meet I would say, at least it is a joke, it is not always a serious discussion, we bet on election results.

F, 24, UNIV.: I talk with my parents and my boyfriend ... and it happens mainly when we watch television together, when we watch talk shows, well, not talk shows, but political talk shows.

That 'public connection' is reinforced by media consumption (Couldry *et al.* 2007) is confirmed also by the opposite link between disaffection and lack of interest in keeping up with the news. Among the peer groups interviewed in this study, it is mainly younger people and those from lower socio-cultural backgrounds who tend to express boredom with political issues and news, and disconnection from society. This lack of interest in what happens beyond one's backyard is related to distrust in political institutions, whose policies are deemed ineffective or irrelevant for their everyday life concerns

(QUESTION): What about politics? Are you interested in politics?

M, 19, ITIS: I don't like politics.

M, 18, ITIS: I don't care.

M, 18, ITIS: I disagree, I am interested in politics.

M, 18, ITIS: Yes, I watch the news sometimes, but I prefer doing other things, too many problems in politics, everyone is concerned with oneself and with gaining what he wants.

M, 18, ITIS: Yes, that's the same reason I am not involved neither, because it is all the same.

F, 15, CAG: We are more interested in news that ...

M, 17, CAG: that affects us personally, or maybe not personally but that involves our parents and family, our neighbourhood ... it is your everyday life problems that make you think and do something, I guess.

Informal political conversations offer symbolic resources to be employed in the development of political identities, which are at the core of civic cultures (Dahlgren 2009). Since collective identities are defined in we–they terms, the boundary that supports identification in a shared 'we-ness' is the distinction between engaged and disaffected youth. Younger interviewees, when involved in political activities and social movements, define themselves in opposition to the recognition of their generation as a disengaged generation:

M, 18, UDS: Young people are more, it is not difficult to engage them because they don't want to, it is more a matter of disaffection, they say 'we cannot change anything, everything will remain the same'. And so it is difficult to engage them because they have already lost any hope. When you talk to them they understand the meaning of what you do, and they are positively impressed. But the main problem is that people keep on saying that 'it is all useless, you can't change things'. That is, everyone is concerned only with his own backyard 'my neighbour's backyard is all dry, but mine is fine so I don't care'.

F, 18, UDS: Yes, and it requires some kind of commitment, a small commitment but still it means going to weekly meetings, engage new people, give leaflets, find new contacts, organize meetings and demonstrations, so if you don't believe in this kind of participation you are not willing to commit yourself.

M, 17, COLL.: We are aware of how people of our age perceive political issues, there's a generalized disinterest, a sort of apathy. And we are trying to fight this apathy, because we strongly believe in the opposite. I mean, political disaffection leads to be unaware of your own rights, your freedom, and everything that deals with political life. Political life is all that deals with, it is how society is organised, so how we live, which rights do we have, which freedom are we guaranteed. So we are involved in rowing against because the citizen, and the student as well, as a future citizen, should be aware of political life, not let that decisions over his own life and his own freedom are taken by someone else without even being aware of it.

M, 16, COLL.: Yes, as he said, our generation's apathy is something we face everyday, we face it every time we leaflet.

As the above excerpts suggest, young people's motivations to engage in the public world depend also on their perceived political efficacy and on social expectations regarding the role of these citizens-in-the-making in society (Livingstone 2009a). Young people express considerable disillusionment concerning the opportunities for being listened to, and distrust of traditional party politics, perceived as distant from their everyday lives. This distance is often framed as a 'generational gap'. Politicians, they argue, have disengaged from young people (Coleman 2007), because they are too self-referential, and too old to understand younger generations:

F, 24, UNIV.: We, as young people, are still too far from institutional politics. The point is that institutional politics is in the hands of parties, because what you vote is parties ... so the point is that participation, becoming a member of a party is not perceived as meaningful anymore since those who get elected in Parliament, it is not transparent how it works.

M, 22, UNIV.: There used to be more young people involved in political groups or members of political parties, but now parties have lost their connection to youth, they cannot understand what we want any more, nor how we want to be addressed.

F, 25, UNIV.: Politicians are on average over 60, we really belong to different generations, dialogue is impossible, they have a far different mentality.

F, 24, UNIV.: They are not reliable, how can I think that Berlusconi, who is 75, shares my interests, and is committed for my future?

So lack of engagement does not necessarily mean indifference towards political issues: rather, as the empirical evidence discussed here suggests, some youth miss the socio-cultural resources that enable civic agency and promote the opportunities to 'have their say'. Political efficacy is closely related to models of citizenship: since distrust tends to be restricted to party politics and government, those civic cultures that still adhere to the idea of a dutiful citizen engaged in conventional participation such as voting and party membership are those that suffer most from this sense of inefficacy, that are characterised by a lack of opportunities to engage in forms of collective action and are, therefore, more 'uncivic'. Relying on a strict definition of what constitutes participation, these young people tend to express a strong disaffection, and to play their civic role in a routine manner

QUESTION: So, why will you vote at next regional elections?

M, 18, ITIS: Because it's my duty.

M, 19, ITIS: I've been told, I am not sure, that employers ask you if you voted.

M, 18, ITIS: Yes, they keep a kind of list, and check how many times you voted.

M, 18, ITIS: It is not mandatory, but it's right.

M, 19, ITIS: After all, they made such a mess in the past in order to gain the right to vote.

M, 18, ITIS: Besides that, voting is a way to let the people have their say.

M, 18, ITIS: You have the power to vote, but then people mind their own business, they don't care

While those who frame participation as a duty seem to adhere to the 'disaffected citizen perspective' (Loader 2007), most young people, even those engaged in traditional political activities such as party membership, tend to embrace a broader definition of what constitutes participation, which includes deinstitution-alised practices of engagement associated with lifestyle concerns. Within a model of the 'self-actualized citizen' (Dahlgren 2009, p. 81), citizenship is something actively performed in day-to-day contexts, not passively received from above, and is closely associated with public connection

F, 24, G.COM.: Participation, as she said, means being an actor in what happens around you, not merely a spectator, participation requires a certain amount of commitment and engagement, I mean, I started being involved in 'poli-tics' when I was 16 in social centres. It implied to dedicate the majority of Saturday nights to the activities of the social centre, the various initiatives and countercultural events, so not exactly how I would have wanted to spend my Saturdays ... so to me the word participation means lot of effort and work, because since I started to form my political consciousness partici-pation meant being personally involved in what was going on and then making an effort to engage the others.

F, 23, G.COM.: I think participation means being active in the place you live, so being informed and contributing to make it a better place.

F, 25, UNIV.: Active citizenship has largely to do with politics, and so feeling part of a shared sense, not feeling simply acted but actively participating ... you can live politically your everyday life, through the choices you make ... such as, I don't know, boycotting that global brand or riding a bike instead of driving a car. It is small, everyday choices that I think we can engage in. So for example I chose to ride a bike for political reasons. I have a sort of ... broad sense of what politics is and I think that, for example, vegetarian-ism may represent a political choice.

Participation is broadened out so as to include non-conventional, deinstitutional-ized, and peer-to-peer forms of political engagement, practised at both individual and collective level, such as demonstrations and rallies, petitions, single-issue campaigns, flash mobs and political consumerism. The emergence of a 'social movement citizenship' (Bennett 2008, p. 8) marks, and is perceived as, a genera-tional change. Young political activists express the need for reinventing the rep-ertoires of action and communication in order to mobilise their disengaged peers. In this respect, the Internet is deemed effective in sustaining more personalized, flexible and lifestyle-related forms of engagement

M, 19, UDS: It is a matter of actual issues versus ideological issues. Traditional issues are the more ideological, such as antifascism. It is not that I am against these issues but they require traditional forms of collective action such as the classical assembly and classical demonstration. These issues need to be updated and combined with new and less ideological issues, such as environmentalism, freedom of information, fight against Mafia, through new forms of mobilisation, that may be online, it may be flash mobs, that we use more than traditional rallies, in that they are more funny, more immediate, and communication is more direct. So new issues and new prac-tices. Because old methods, such as leaflets and the traditional boring meet-ings, youth don't get involved in them any more.

To sum up, participation and engagement are clearly rooted in specific civic cul-tures and specific patterns of citizenship. The definition of civic identities and related systems of meanings and activities, though, seems also a matter of age, with older interviewees generally more engaged than the younger, who are strongly disaffected unless actively engaged in associations, movements and collectives.

Online participation: attitudes and practices

The role of the Internet with regard to mediated public connection and con-temporary non-conventional citizenship practices is clearly shaped by the sym-bolic, social and material resources that define civic identities. However, since opportunities for civic engagement online are not taken up equally (Livingstone and Helsper 2007), digital literacy and digital inclusion are also at play here.

The conclusion that the Internet seems less effective than traditional media in engaging the disengaged (Livingstone *et al.* 2007) is supported by our findings. Concerning mediated public connection, reliance on the Internet as a source of political information is contextualised within already articulated and defined pat-terns of news consumption that combine the Internet with press and television. More sophisticated news consumption online, such as including blogs and other non-mainstream media among the preferred platforms for news, is positively associated not only with engagement in news, but also with frequency of Internet use and level of domestication of online media. Among those who express a stronger mediated public connection, the more skilled users, and the more confident in the Internet as an independent source of information,[4] are those who develop complex patterns of news consumption online.

Offline civic and political engagement and digital literacy are also the precondition for more participatory uses of the Internet, from mailing lists for internal coordination of associations and movements and for keeping up with the latest news, to the production of websites and blogs to inform, engage and mobilise Internet users, practices that Castells (2007) has named 'mass self-communication'.

F, 23, G.COM.: The way we participate has changed because we have the means of participating in a time-saving manner. Our association for example, we don't meet weekly. We share information via email, we keep updated with the latest news in the mailing list and then we meet when we have something important to discuss that requires face-to-face proximity. So it is much easier, I can get involved in different working groups because I can follow three discussion in the same night simply sitting in front of my computer.

M, 18, UDS: Now we have created the Pomodoro[5] web page, and left a section free for citizens' contributions, every citizen can email us his article and we publish it.

M, 19, UDS: Yes, the good thing with the Internet is that every individual citizen, every individual student has access to news media ... every individual has a very powerful medium to inform other people.

The divide in the take-up of the Internet as a resource for civic identities and a place for political participation is sometimes framed as a generational gap. When different attitudes towards online practices take place within the same age cohort, however, the key factor at play is the practised model of citizenship: young people who are accustomed to engage in traditional party politics still think of online participation as opposed to offline, face-to-face and more valued forms of engagement, rather than as a continuity of online and offline citizenship practices.

F, 24, G.COM.: In our party, the web is underestimated, they have a prejudice ... it is hard to make them understand that you can reach people also beyond the cultural event, the public event. It is a generational issue, I think, because for us it is normal to use the Internet to get the news. But older people perceive it ... as a game, they don't take it seriously enough, especially Facebook, there is also this common sense that Facebook is a teenagers' thing.

M, 19, UDS: Within the different components of the students' movement there are quite a lot of people who say 'no, online mobilisation is a marginal thing' or boring 'face-to-face meeting are still needed', or 'we have to return to more traditional methods'. Within the very UDS, we use Facebook, another guy, from the UDS as well, who is fanatic with 20 years ago methods, like asking for personal details, name and phone number, then organize a meeting, and then calling people to tell them to attend.

F, 24, G.COM.: We are really prehistoric, we still live in the Middle Ages, because we still meet every week, more than once a week because we have ... kind of rituals: we have the meeting of the local node every Wednesday, and the meeting of the youth section on Fridays. I think this habit dates back to ... some parties tend to use the same relationship methods. And after all I don't dislike it, because if it is true that the ability to participate in more working groups through mailing lists is a godsend, since the day is made of 24 hours, and the week of seven days ... from another perspective the construction of a political community relies also on the time you spend doing things together.

To briefly summarise, civic cultures differ in terms of citizenship models and practices, and online forms of engagement are no exception in this respect, being variously integrated and adopted by different groups.

How different civic cultures participate in SNS

Social network sites are the places where the connections with one's 'extended social networks' (boyd and Ellison 2007, p. 211) are maintained and reinforced. Worldwide, young people 'commit to these networks a considerable investment in time, motivation, sociability and identity' (Livingstone 2009a, p. 127).

Though relational and entertainment uses of SNS are predominant and normative, some forms of civic and political engagement are emerging.

First, Facebook is becoming an important news platform where users disseminate and comment about news. Not only does Facebook become a support of 'public connection' but it turns news consumption into a shared social experience. Social networks and SNS are used to filter news (Purcell *et al.* 2010), to make sense of and interpret media content through mediated social interaction

M, 18, UDS: Besides jokes that we share, I feel a sort of a duty to form people's opinion. So sometimes I post some articles, I send news to those disengaged with news ... in case they want to read it. So at times I post some interesting news, I am involved in some counterinformation activity. Besides that yes, some jokes, some laughs

F, 18, UDS: There are two groups on Facebook that post articles of counterinformation, and so we like to share also such content.

F, 24, G.COM.: I find it very useful, because I am connected to so many people that share my own interests, and so I can browse what they post. It is an excellent tool, because you know that you can find interesting news there.

F, 23, G.COM: It is even easier than with blogs.

F, 24, G.COM: Yes, you have to search for blogs.

F, 23, G.COM: Some bloggers used to post their articles on their profiles too, so I've noted that since I am on Facebook – around one year and a half ago – I use blogs less, since I have some 20 profiles which check more often, some of whom are journalists, and so I check their profiles.

F, 24, G.COM: It is a filter.

F, 23, G.COM: That's right, a filter by people you trust, because you know you share their opinions, or that you are interested in their point of view even if you don't share it ... and I'm quite active, I also comment at times.

As in relation to offline news consumption, these practices represent a precondition for more participatory forms of engagement, that may lead to offline mobilisation. However, engagement with (pre)political[6] content on Facebook acquires different meanings for different civic cultures and is variously incorporated in the process of defining collective identities. The youngest and the more disengaged tend to dismiss (pre)political groups and causes as a matter of entertainment, a sort of political fandom, or as tools for patterns of 'identity as display' (Livingstone 2008). Others, instead, consider groups as markers and supporters of identity, places to share lifestyle concerns with like-minded people, but deny Facebook's role in engaging and promoting awareness on single-issue campaigns

F, 23, UNIV.: I tend to compromise myself a lot on Facebook about some specific issues, that is environmental issues and animal rights, that is what I care most, so I joined groups as 'against whale hunting' or 'against eating meat'.

F, 25, UNIV.: I guess she joined these groups to get in touch with like-minded persons from all over Italy, it is the chance to share something.

F, 23, UNIV.: I agree with what she says, it is a somewhat private issue, sometimes I feel depressed when I see so many people in winter wearing a fur coat, disgusting I think, and so going on a group and seeing that you are not alone, other people share your opinions ... is comforting. But I think it is not with Facebook groups that you persuade other people, it is more personal.

What is lacking here is the understanding that the prevailing identity model in Facebook, that is 'identity through connection' (Livingstone 2008) may serve as a basis for defining civic identities and sharing knowledge, values, practices of online engagement and a social space online. In other words, engagement in single-issue groups does not automatically turn into participation, and though individuals belong to civic cultures built around single issues and lifestyle concerns, Facebook is not incorporated as a place for networking, defining shared practices and mobilising; rather, as the last excerpt suggests, for some people it is mainly a matter of representing one's identity online.

Conversely, young activists in associations, collectives and parties use Facebook in a more active way, first of all as a place for engaging the youngest and promoting their offline activities. They appropriate the practice of using Facebook as a search engine, and give rise to forms of 'mass self communication':

F, 23, G.COM.: I've noticed that those aged 16 to 26 rather than searching for 'Libera Milano' in Google, they look for it in Facebook, and if they find it they add to their friends' list. So it can help to reach young people … even just to let people know your association, or to reach new young people it's a good medium. In my little experience, many contacts to my association came from Facebook, and through Facebook we engaged people in our initiatives.

M, 18, UDS: On Facebook they find you. Once you tell them that UDS is on Facebook, they pass it over through word of mouth, and all this sharing makes it easer for them to find you

The case of the UDS students is paradigmatic of emerging uses of SNS to engage young people

> M, 18, UDS: Well the Pomodoro was born as a challenge to Berlusconi's popularity on Facebook, he has over 200,000 fans, so I created this group 'I bet this Tomato will have more fans than Berlusconi', and the second day we had already 270,000 fans, we have already beaten him. And then it kept growing until it reached the around 600,000 fans we have now … and it was more from below than from UDS, fans started asking 'Now that we are so many what are we going to do? Let's do something together.' That's how we decided to have a meeting, and we started to launch some issues to discuss on the page. Then we created the website, and two offline events, that were the meeting and the flash mob.

Experiences like the Pomodoro, however, raise questions about the link between online and offline participation, and the efficacy of Facebook in mobilising audiences. Interviewees agree that the main limit of these practices of online engagement is their low efficacy in terms of offline participation and their ephemeral character, when not supported by pre-existing relationships and not re-embedded in physical places. Young activists express considerable concern for forms of 'clicktivism' such as attending a Facebook event, clicking 'Like' on a fan page, signing an online petition: activities which reinforce the individual's sense of being mobilised, but result in no durable, focalised and active interest for a political issue:

M, 19, UDS: This is a way to socialise and engage. It is not simply a matter of preferring the virtual agora instead of physical places, it is a new kind of engagement, of being locally active in new, innovative ways. Both the virtual and the physical are important, and both have to be used. It is meaningless to underestimate one of the two.

M, 18, UDS: There's no point in using them separately even because if I make something online then I get 2 billion clicks, and when I do it offline I do not involve the same amount of people. Because on Facebook it is just a matter of a click but once you have clicked you don't automatically go and join the meeting.

F, 18, UDS: That's right, a lot of people joined the flash mob call online, and then
we ended up ...

M, 19, UDS:... in forty people.

F, 24, G.COM.: The problem with Facebook, and with websites and mailing lists
too, is that it doesn't cost you anything: you click, send your email and the
information is pushed towards you. It is information, it is not real participation ... it costs you so little effort, so little commitment, that you don't take
it seriously. Facebook is helpful for disseminating and sharing information
on things and among people that you meet offline. Otherwise it is sterile,
unproductive. Participation is something you practice daily, face-to-face,
building a community.

F, 23, G.COM.: Communities from virtual have to become real.

Involvement in Facebook groups and causes does not imply, per se, engagement
in forms of collective activities offline. For this to happen it requires the development of collective identities that are embedded also in offline practices and
places. Facebook works as long as it sustains the coordination of dispersed
people in modes of participation, providing a place for re-embedding disembed-
ded relationships

F, 24, UNIV.: It works as long as people organize, it needs to be practical ... it may
be helpful, for example, to gather people, to promote meetings besides official demonstrations, it helps criticize, do something ... in the protest against
the reform of education the movement organized online, the word of mouth
spread online and the outcome was a massive demonstration.

The Popolo Viola itself, though capable of raising attention and mobilisation
around the call for Berlusconi's resignation, could not maintain the same degree
of interest and participation for long. Their mobilisation online and on SNS was
effective in coordinating a number of individuals who gave rise to smaller local
groups, that is to an offline re-embedding of online ties.

In conclusion, young activists are divided in their uses of and the values and
meanings they attribute to forms of engagement on SNS, and the origins of different attitudes have to be found in their overall civic cultures.

Discussion

This chapter was aimed at exploring emerging practices of participation on SNS
by contextualising them in young people's civic cultures. This contextualisation,
it is argued, provides a route to avoid easy generalisations and enthusiasm for
the Internet as the remedy for youth's disengagement.

Inequalities in the take-up of online participatory practices are embedded in
young people's socio-cultural backgrounds – including their digital literacy and
digital inclusion, their conceptualisation and practice of participation and the
specific subcultures and civic identities they belong to.

Overall, the use of SNS for political purposes is overshadowed by other uses, such as social networking and entertainment. Moreover, most of the (pre)political content on Facebook has more to do with the development of personal identity 'through connection' with like-minded individuals or 'through display' (Livingstone 2008), thus supporting networked individualism (Castells 2001) as the dominant pattern of sociality. That participation on SNS is often a marker of identity, functional to the development of one's profile and personalised communities, suggests that participatory practices are both the outcome and the drive to increasing individualisation and shifting of the boundaries between the personal and the political.

On the other side, however – though ordinary users only to a small extent act as content producers and are mainly consumers of information and cultural products online – participatory practices do emerge, mainly in the form of non-conventional citizenship practices such as petitioning, single-issue campaigns, contention over cultural products, in a word, lifestyle politics. The impact and meaning of such practices is contingent and largely dependent on the civic cultures of the participants.

Among young activists, Facebook represents a further resource for the continuous construction of pre-existing offline collective identities and cultures. It is a means for 'mass self-communication' (Castells 2007) and supports also the networking with associations, groups and social movements who belong to similar civic cultures. Networked collectivism (Baym 2010) may provide a route to promote awareness on certain issues by engaging wider dispersed audiences and to coordinate single issue campaigns online. The Popolo Viola's visibility on SNS, blogs and websites helped to push the issue of Berlusconi's legitimacy onto the media and public agenda. Besides this agenda-amplifying function of online social discourses, what the Popolo Viola shows, moreover, is how participation on SNS can serve as a basis for offline mobilisation: what can be viewed as latent civic cultures, insofar as they are comprised of fragmented and isolated individuals who lack resources for mobilisation in their everyday life contexts, were provided with a place to build a sense of belonging to a network, a perceived common identity symbolised by the purple colour, and shared meanings, values and practices. These civic cultures may lack a formal and long-term structure, but are effective for mobilising people, as the recurrent demonstrations, rallies and mobs called by the Popolo Viola show.

To conclude, the findings of the study presented here are mainly supportive of the reinforcement thesis, suggesting that offline divides in political participation are reproduced and reinforced online. As far as participants in our peer group conversations are concerned, online political users tend to be young people who are already politically active offline. That is to say, networked collectivism is mainly rooted in offline civic cultures; at times, however, it may serve as the basis for the rise of new civic cultures that, initiated online, are then actively reproduced in participants' offline daily lives. Though still emerging, networked collectivism may therefore have a significant role in the shaping of new modes of citizenship, thus challenging the assumption that non-conventional participation represents an outcome and a further drive towards individualisation.

Notes

1 At the end of October 2011 there were over 20 million Facebook users in Italy (Facebook Advertising), corresponding to 76 per cent of active Internet users (Audiweb).
2 The main group on Facebook counted 370,519 members.
3 On the limits of the normative concept of deliberative democracy see for example: Dahlgren 2009; Silverstone 2007; Young 1996. On the potentials of online deliberation see for example Coleman and Blumler 2009.
4 According to a recent survey on Italians' news engagement (available at www.demos. it/a00355.php) 58.9 per cent of those aged 15–24, and 60.2 per cent of those aged 25–34 years old (34.7 per cent of the entire population) trust the Internet as the most independent source of information.
5 The UDS invented a Facebook page called 'I bet this tomato will get more fans than Silvio Berlusconi' which attracted over 600,000 fans. After that unexpected success they also created a web page (www.ilpomodoro.weebly.com).
6 The concept of prepolitical is used here to refer to online mobilisations and discussions that acquire a political meaning but are born around products of popular culture; and online social discourses around political actors which draw on popular culture's narratives and resources, and thus represent a popularisation of politics.

13 How the Internet is giving birth (to) a new social order

Jodi H. Cohen and Jennifer M. Raymond

Introduction

Mullin and MacLean (2005) note that pregnancy is crafted and socially proscribed as private, and therefore somewhat embarrassing to women, which encourages the dismissal of that lived experience as inappropriate for public discourse. While it may be appropriate to narrate the experiences of women medically, those narrations are limited to breast cancer experience and survival, loss of a child, loss of a pregnancy or issues with conception. Often recountings of birth experiences are available to readers, noting here that birth is created as less private due to the witnessing of birthing itself in medical facilities, and even this is a dramatic shift in the last 30 years. Early feminist writing chastising the medical establishment for their medicalization of birth led to vibrant and public discussions of the role of doctors (often versus midwives) in childbirth. Yet these discussions do not touch on the experiences of the 40 weeks leading up to birth, pregnancy. Mullin and MacLean (2005) note that women's stories and experiences of pregnancy have more recently entered the public arena in books for pregnant women and in academic studies, but this research limits itself to looking at the medical experiences and emotional stressors, and not at women's seeking of information in what is often considered the world's largest library, the Internet.

While support groups and forums online have been researched for breast cancer suffers and survivors, as well as other "ill" communities, pregnancy falls to a unique divide between infirm and well. Pregnant women are not ill based on their status as pregnant, but many suffer different ailments as a result of their pregnancies. These ailments are often cast as side-effects of pregnancy, belittled as unimportant and "nothing to worry about." Yet, for the women experiencing them, they are often more than simple discomforts, instead they include fearsome experiences that threaten both their physical and psychological selves. For these reasons, women in the millions are turning to online forums and chat spaces seeking out peer support from other pregnant and recently pregnant women during their times of greatest discomfort and fear. Some women open a search engine and type in words that express their experiences, seeking help and advice, leading to the responses of peers, and then voting for the best-suited answer. Others directly access boards and forum spaces, and start or search for subgroup discussions to find answers to postings resembling their experiences.

Literature review

Health and the Internet

Fox and Rainie (2000) stated that, in the US, the Internet has grown to become one of the most commonly used sources for health information. Previous research suggests that more than half and as much as 80 percent of adults with Internet access search for healthcare information online, and that the Internet is clearly an important tool with the potential to improve information dissemination (Baker *et al.* 2003). On any given day in August 2006, approximately eight million Americans were online searching for health information (Fox 2006). Yet, the Pew Report of Health Topics for 2006 did not ask about use of the Internet for information on pregnancy. Related topics included: sexual health and specific disease or medical problems, but pregnancy was not included in the Pew study as a specific reason to look online for medical information (ibid.).

Illness versus health

Outside of random searching for health information, groups with specific ailments or experiences seek out spaces for discussion and support from peers. Much of this research has examined the Internet's use by cancer patients, and most commonly for women breast cancer patients. Fogel *et al.* (2002) found in their interviews of 188 US women with breast cancer that 41.5 percent used the Internet for breast health information, and Satterlund *et al.* (2003) found that the Internet was the most frequently cited source of breast cancer and breast health information 16 months post-diagnosis. Høybye *et al.* (2005) found that women using an Internet-based support group/list reported that the list worked to empower them, and that it provided a space in which their experiences could be voiced and shared through telling their personal stories, where these stories ranged from serious to humorous, bringing relief to both the writer and the reader. Research has shown that discussion groups for breast cancer fulfill the functions of a community (Sharf 1997).

Although there is limited research on the Internet usage of pregnant women, there is more research on the use of Internet as an outlet for those struggling with infertility (see Kahlor and Mackert 2009; Rawal and Haddad 2006; Epstein *et al.* 2002; Weissman *et al.* 2000). Again, whereas infertility is a medical problem or condition, pregnancy is socially constructed as a natural state and condition and therefore those who are pregnant are not in need of solace and support. Yet, in much the same way that disease or illness-focused groups converge online for mutual support and the exchange of information, it appears that pregnant women too seek out and benefit from support and information through online forums (Madge and O'Connor 2005; Drentea and Moren-Cross 2005).

Pregnancy discourses

Despite an ever-increasing literature on women's use of the Internet to find medical information, there still exists a gap in information about pregnant women's use of the Internet to find information on their pregnancies. Lagan *et al.* (2010) found that 97 percent of pregnant women in their study used search engines such as Google to access pregnancy-related information online, and for pregnancy-related social networking and support. Additionally, 94 percent of pregnant women reported using the Internet to supplement information already provided by their doctors, and 48.6 percent reported dissatisfaction with the information that they received from their doctors and a lack of opportunity and time to ask questions (46.5 percent). Larsson (2009) and Declercq *et al.* (2006) also offered some insight into pregnant women's Internet usage, but unlike the findings of Lagan *et al.* (2010), both Larsson (2009) and Declercq *et al.* (2006) only looked at usage for pregnancy information, and did not include pregnancy-related social networking and support in forums. Also, they did not look at pregnant women's levels of dissatisfaction with information provided by their doctors.

Although there is much research on pregnancy itself, and the social issues embedded within, there again is limited research constructing the lived experiences of women while pregnant. One notable exception is Bessett's (2010) work examining the normalization of pregnancy symptoms in 64 pregnant women in metropolitan New York. This work is key to understanding why women seek additional support, potentially in online venues, as the doctor–patient relationship often provides little more than a patriarchal pat on the hand for support, with statements such as "well, that's normal." The potential for understanding why women choose to report or not report pregnancy symptoms is firmly rooted in both the universality of prenatal care in the US and maternal sacrifice (Bessett 2010). Historically, pregnancy was not cast as "disease," requiring medical monitoring. It was not until into the twentieth century that a shift toward requisite prenatal care, notably hegemonic, occurred (Barker 1998).

The fight for control over information between care recipients and providers has a long history for women, and continues to be a struggle because of social expectations of women's behaviors, including deference toward authority figures such as doctors. And because women are socialized by their medical practitioners and society not to ask too many questions during and between appointments, or risk being negatively labeled, they are not likely to receive information that they both want and need (Bessett 2010; Barker 1998). Bessett (2010) found that women also sought to minimize appearing foolish, fearing that their experiences were "probably nothing." Additionally, where prenatal appointments are typically 15 minutes or less in length, women are further socialized to be conscious of taking up too much of the doctor's time. Furthermore, the creation of a culture of maternal sacrifice and normalization of suffering, where women are meant to believe that their suffering during pregnancy is for the good of the baby, leads women to feel internally conflicted about sharing their pregnancy symptoms for fear of being judged negatively in their future ability as a "good" mother, willing and able to sacrifice for her children. Bylund (2005) examined women's birth stories posted to a birth stories website, and reports that the site gives the following directions to potential storytellers: "Things to think about when sharing your story: the duration of the various stages of your labor, how you felt about the experience, how you coped with the labor and birth" (p. 29). This invitation gives women permission to talk about their pain, yet only again in the context of perseverance, and in the coping with that pain they therefore become good and worthy mothers.

Women, pregnancy and the Internet

Lagan *et al.* (2009) found that two thirds of midwives in their study believe that the Internet provides women with information that they otherwise would not receive, and 73 percent of midwives in their study agreed that the Internet improved women's understanding of conditions associated with their pregnancies and gave women more control. Pandey *et al.* (2003) state that in their view, healthcare professionals need to "be more responsive to the democratizing effects of the Internet (p. 188)," in particular noting the long history of struggle between women and healthcare providers for control of information in women's health. Larsson (2009) found that 84 percent of women in her study in Sweden used the Internet on one or more occasions to access information on pregnancy and childbirth, although only 6 percent of women in her study sought out chat forums. A national survey of women in the US who gave birth in 2005 revealed that more than 75 percent of pregnant women were using the Internet for information about pregnancy and birth (Declercq *et al.* 2006).

Issues of maternal sacrifice are linked to constructions of privacy, where women are expected to "grin and bear it" throughout their pregnancies without complaint. Much related fear and disgust about changing pregnant bodies stems from a culture of airbrushed beauty shown in magazines, where women are not even projected to sweat, let alone expel "unusual" body fluids. As Romano (2007) states, "women may turn to the Internet when they have questions about breast changes, bowel and bladder concerns, sex and sexuality, vaginal bleeding and discharge, or emotional changes in pregnancy and early parenthood" (p. 19). She also reports that often questions posted online to forums are by anonymous women who apologize for potentially including "TMI" (too much information). Online support groups provide an anonymous place for asking questions that might be viewed as too personal or too embarrassing (Romano 2007; Drentea and Moren-Cross 2005; Sharf 1997). These are places where users can support each other and check up on the status of individuals with whom they have fostered a bond. Previous research has shown that women's sites, such as these forums, are much more likely to be supportive (Madge and O'Connor 2006, 2002; Drentea and Moren-Cross 2005; Sharf 1997).

Community seeking and online support

Romano (2007) notes "women naturally seek support and a sense of community in pregnancy and motherhood" (p. 20). This is in part because contemporary demographic trends have eliminated home-based communities in which women were primarily at home raising children, and could rely on this propinquity for advice. As neighborhoods are no longer filled with women and young children interacting throughout the day, these geographic networks are lost and so is the informal support that was once afforded to pregnant women (Ley 2007; Drentea and Moren-Cross 2005). The argument is then that geographical dispersal of women causes a decrease in familiarity with pregnancy, and less contact with those experiencing it simultaneously or in the very recent past, in their neighborhoods. Drentea and Moren-Cross (2005) discuss that one method of uniting pregnant mothers, and therefore also pregnant women, is on the Internet where geographic location is not a disqualification to relationship-building and information-sharing. This parallels Eble and Breault's (2002) discussion of online communities for women as not only granting agency in the production of knowledge, but also creating space where women are free to create the knowledge and judge what is knowledge within their own communities.

Romano (2007) and Drentea and Moren-Cross (2005) note that Internet discussion forums and chat rooms allow for women to connect over common circumstances and interests, and create a system of support and camaraderie. Shared experiences, such as pregnancy complications and depression, also bring women together who are seeking support, fostering connection with others believed to understand. Raymond (2009) found that antenatal depression sufferers had lessened effects of depression with increased social support. Emotional isolation and lack of support were central themes in the reported experiences of women suffering from depression while pregnant. As Ley (2007) explains further, "functioning as *biosocialities* (Rabinow 1996) and *technosocialities* (Escobar 1994), online support groups are simultaneously social, cultural, technical, and therapeautic spaces" (p. 2). Advice and information offered by pregnant or recently pregnant women is valued as shared experience, and this is central to why women seek out these online forums (Drentea and Moren-Cross 2005), as seen in previous research about mothers using the Internet for parenting information (Madge and O'Connor 2005, 2006).

Methodology

This study uses participant observation to explore the communication on three pregnancy forum sites. Both authors joined the three boards where required, creating a shared username and entered as members, though neither of us posted on the forums, nor participated in locked forums that required an invitation. Three central themes were identified: the exchange of information, peer support, and self-empowerment. On these forums, information seeking and peer support often run together, where those seeking information are frequently offered support by those with similar experiences. Self-empowerment centers on seeking information when the medical community has either not offered it, or has been believed to blatantly withhold it. There are thousands of pregnancy information sites with chat rooms and forums, many of which have a global user base. For this study we chose to focus only on sites written in English, with what appeared to be a US-centered user base.

The forum sites used for this study were selected using Google, where Nielsen NetRatings for Search Engines rated Google in 2006 as the most used search engine with 49.2 percent of searches internationally undertaken using its website in a study of 500,000 people worldwide (Sullivan 2006). Shannon (2010) notes that as of December 2009, Google has captured 85.35 percent of the search engine market.

After selecting Google as the search engine, five search phrases were used to select the three forums: pregnancy forum, pregnancy board, pregnancy message board, pregnancy chat room and pregnancy chat. These search terms were entered into Google as regular searches, and again in the Google Directory. With each of the regular searches we consulted the first page of results only, looking for the most frequently found among the five searches. Those sites that were listed on the first page of each search were then compared with the listings in Google Directory. From these two sets of lists we chose the most frequently listed sites as the most popular. The three most popular sites using this method of selection were: www.cafemom.com (CafeMom), www.i-am-pregnant.com (I-Am-Pregnant), www.justmommies.com (JustMommies). It is also of interest to note that I-Am-Pregnant is the first site that comes up when a user types the phrase: "I am pregnant" into Google.

After selecting the three sites, we then selected similar forums on each site to look for discussions posted by pregnant women and answered by peers. Each site included forums linked to expected due date for those already pregnant, for those trying to conceive (TTC), miscarriage and loss, pregnancy issues, and general pregnancy, along with forums related to subgroup identities, such as those based on age – teens and women of "advanced age" (over 35), as well as groups for lesbians, single mothers, and mothers in biracial relationships. There are also many more specific groups for C-section (cesarean births), baby names, and infertility, among many others. This study focuses on forums for pregnancy issues, general pregnancy and some subgroup identities, primarily "advanced age" women over 35. The inclusion of the advanced age forums was to look for more community formation than may exist in the general forums. We then read and tracked daily postings through March 2010, and used the discussions that were from that month or began before that where postings on these dates were a part of discussion threads that began in months prior but were continuously added to.

The forum sites

Each of the forums has a tagline to describe its function and offer a description to potential users that is visible underneath the URL when potential users perform a search in Google.

CafeMom: "Talk to Other Pregnant Moms about Pregnancy Who Are Just Like You." (www.cafemom.com/group/pregnancy/).

I-Am-Pregnant: "I-am-pregnant.com is your first source of pregnancy and baby information. It's a forum based community of other pregnant women and new mothers." (www.i-am-pregnant.com/encyclopedia/).

JustMommies: "JustMommies is the friendliest message board for moms and moms-to-be! Discuss getting pregnant, pregnancy and prenatal care, parenting, and more." (www.justmommies.com/forums/).

Findings and discussion

The content of posts in each of these forums primarily consisted of statements and questions looking to establish whether symptoms or experiences are normal or not. Frequently the posting member asks: "Is this normal?" or "Have you experienced this?" In other postings there are direct requests for help with a current situation or experience where the member posts "Needing advice." Finally, the third type of posting is about needing support for a decision that has more or less been made by the posting member: "Needing to vent." These ventings were frequently frustrations over doctors, bosses and coworkers, partners, children, and other friends and family members. Many of the postings fall into multiple types, both needing advice and help and asking if a situation is normal, or needing advice while simultaneously needing to vent. Within each thread members of the boards would post support and answers, and less frequently would post disagreement, pass judgment or express anger with the original poster (OP). These statements are typically responded to with varying degrees of outrage in an attempt to protect the OP. On rare occasions, posts within threads were not responded to, either to avoid conflict or potentially out of lack of interest. The former is more likely, as previous research has demonstrated that women in online spaces primarily seek to protect and support than to flame or create conflict (Ley 2007; Drentea and Moren-Cross 2005; Sharf 1997).

Additionally it is important to note that there were forums where fewer members participated. This potentially leads to fewer responses to questions and calls for help and support. The design of the forums is such that many were likely to draw smaller groups of participants, and in those cases it is possible for a posting to languish for an extended period of time without a response. This is a potential drawback of the site design, where there were both overlapping forum themes and forums with narrowly directed topics. While a forum on cramping may receive dozens to hundreds of visits in a day, a forum on depression may receive fewer visits, and even fewer postings, either due to fear of labeling or lack of identification with that particular issue. This can be problematic for posters looking for support about their depression, but only if they rely solely on the more narrowly described topic forums.

Is this normal?

In looking to fit into a known and understood schematic of what pregnancy should look like, women often turn to other women for feedback and advice on the changes in their bodies, valued as shared experience (Drentea and Moren-Cross 2005; Madge and O'Connor 2006, 2005). Historically, women would have turned to other women within their immediate communities, and this has shifted to include online spaces where pregnant women and women who have previously been pregnant congregate (Ley 2007; Drentea and Moren-Cross 2005). Where many might like to ask their doctors more questions and for more information, previous research has shown that doctors are either unsympathetic to what might be referred to as expected discomforts of pregnancy, or nod their way through appointments never really answering the questions of their patients (Bessett 2010; Madge and O'Connor 2006). Bessett (2010) notes that "while women were charged to report everything to their providers *in theory*, institutional obstacles, provider ambivalence, or the sheer volume of symptoms meant that women had to learn to share their symptoms selectively with their providers" (p. 3). In the forums women often reported that symptoms might include TMI (too much information) or sound silly or frivolous in some way, almost an apology for asking for help and advice, as seen in Romano's (2007) research. Social conditioning during pregnancy has taught women to apologize for admitting to experiencing pain, discomfort, and strange changes to the body, all in an attempt to socialize them toward maternal sacrifice where they are expected to suppress their needs to the baby's needs, and to do it while pregnant as training to be a good mother (Bessett 2010). One example of this, out of the hundreds we read on the forums, is from Preggo-Eggo on the JustMommies forums. She notes her status as newly pregnant and her concerns over cramping:

> Hi. I am newly pregnant and I have been having cramps. Most of them are really subtle and painless, but today I had one that hurt a lot. I was wondering if anyone could tell me if this is normal if anyone has experienced this? I have a doctors appointment in a few days and I was planning on asking the doctor, but I am kind of worried now.

There were 117 views of this posting and nine replies. All of the women replying discussed their experience with cramping in their pregnancies, and two of the posters used the word "normal" to set Preggo-Eggo at ease. The feedback of these women is seen as valued shared experience, where their authority of their own experiences is considered authentic (Drentea and Moren-Cross 2005; Madge and O'Connor 2006, 2005) Preggo-Eggo herself uses the phrase "tell me if this is normal," looking for that reassurance. Responses also focused on telling Preggo-Eggo that she should call her doctor, and that cramping of any kind is worthy of medical attention. Dragonfish replied:

> I would call your OB [obstetrician] if they are more painful then a period cramp expecially if there is any type of blood involved. With the twins I cramped a lot. Just to be on the safe side always call.

Other replies included:

> Hi. I had cramping with my girls. I know it can be quiet normal. If they are really painful I would get checked just to be on the safe side.
>
> Take care hun.
>
> (Mega Super Mommy)

> i had alot of cramping early on … wayyyyy more than my usualy period cuz i dont really get much cramping w a period and these had me so miserable … then day i missed my period they eased up and turned into more suttle cramping … one type i know was my ovary … on my left side and suposedly you will have some cramping often times as when you are newly preg there is a cyst on your ovary that will pump out progesterone until the placenta forms and takes over. and then the other cramping is just your uterus stretching and the ligaments around it … all very normal!
>
> (Missy11)

The desire of posters to reassure and support Preggo-Eggo is what previous researchers have found with discussion forums linked to parenting (Drentea and Moren-Cross 2005; Madge and O'Connor 2005) and breast cancer (Høybye *et al.* 2005). Drentea and Moren-Cross (2005) report that women on the parenting boards were constantly asking if they were alone in their experiences, and that much of the function of the forums was to put mothers' minds as ease. Likewise, with the pregnancy forums, the focus is on bringing support and easing the minds of fellow posters on the website, and also in providing a push toward entitlement to information. The teaching or training toward entitlement here is focused on access to power. As previous research has shown (Bessett 2010; Madge and O'Connor 2006), women often do not feel entitled to ask for more information from doctors who offer them limited time and access. The empowerment that comes from seeking information and receiving support to request or demand that information is as central to these forums as the information shared about their experiences and conditions.

Posting after posting demonstrates the desire of women to find that their circumstances are normal or, when not normal, so outrageous as either to bring out the ire of other posters toward the persons creating the problem or damage for the OP, or to bring out the sympathy of other posters where the loss experienced is so great that it is sometimes just not possible to bear it alone. One poster on CafeMom, ColleO, writes to the forum with a question that many women have faced, bleeding, but she faces it in the wake of limited doctor access because her health insurance is not yet available. Her posting is titled: "Question about bleeding":

> I did try calling and asking the doctor but they said they couldn't answer questions over the phone. My insurance policy doesn't go in effect til wednesday. I'm having some very slight cramping, but nothing really painful. Just sort of a dull ache. And I just went to the bathroom and there was some blood when I wiped. Not too much. So far. Has anyone experienced this and was it ok? I'll be keeping an eye out. I just wanted to see if it was ok sometimes.

She receives 17 postings with a range of feedback, most sharing experiences with bleeding at the same stage of pregnancy and offering various reasons for that bleeding. Throughout the exchange ColleO responds to questions about the status of her bleeding, the color and amount, as well as requests for additional medical information. The women that respond to her are supportive, seek to assure her that everything will be fine, and most recommended that she talk to a doctor as soon as she has access. In posting 16, ColleO updates the forum members:

> Called the doctor that told me I was pregnant. Said its usually normal, even if its bright red. Even the cramping may not be a problem. If it gets worse she said to call back and they'd get me in today to see if things were alright.

Immediately following this post she receives a supportive post from Joywalz:

> I had bleeding from weeks 2–6 with this pregnancy.... And then at 10 weeks I went to the walk in clinic for IV fluids, and randomly started bleeding bright red blood, I was so scared!!! I was crying thinking it was a m/c. Luckely they did a U/S and the baby came up right away just kicken like crazy and rolling around lol. I then had tears of joy. I know they say to come in when you have been bleeding enough to fill a pad an hour, but if it were me I would go in for a peice of mind! I am sure you would feel better if you do. Good luck!!

ColleO logs in twice more with postings 18 and 19:

> Bleeding just now got worse. FML [fuck my life].

> Lots of blood. Big clot. Thinking journey here is over. I'll take morning sickness. I'll take bed rest. This fucking sucks. At least I'm at the doctors when it happened.

This is her last posting on the forum, she does not return with more information and it is unknown whether she returns to hear the sympathetic responses from the final posters, including BraedynsMama409, stating "I am so sorry. ☹"

What is important is that during these intensely personal moments in their experiences, women are posting to these spaces where their voices are heard often by people who are unknown to them, and often by those who will not respond. This particular forum posting was viewed 262 times, but only received 21 total replies, including the postings throughout by ColleO. Her painful experience is witnessed again and again, and is continuously consumed by readers of the forum. We project that others logged in and typed in the words "I am bleeding" only to come across this posting and experience both fear and revulsion that this too could be their story and the end of their pregnancy. The normalization of her experience of bleeding is not considered a normal experience after all, as most will hope that this is an atypical experience, but all experiences posted (that do not appear to be outlandish) hold the potential to become the readers' reality. Does this then mean that the forums are more disempowering than empowering? Here, we argue no, because although some posted experiences end in premature pregnancy termination, for most others the information gathered is a further demonstration that their fears are warranted, and seeking medical attention is not only recommended but imperative. And even when the experience may not be seen as normal, the peer voices directing the poster to seek medical attention help to legitimize her fears, which then empowers her to demand further medical access, even when society may be seen to accuse her of being overly dramatic or sensitive. Here, instead of the dictates of maternal sacrifice that force women to ignore their fears (Bessett 2010), the forums become places to undo the social pressures of conformity to actions that are potentially dangerous in their silencing. It is the legitimization of seeking medical support that leads to empowerment during pregnancy, where previous research has shown that women are often bullied into silencing behaviors, leaving them at risk and fearful, often isolated, when medical advice and access should be available (Bessett 2010; Madge and O'Connor 2006; Raymond 2009).

Fighting for control

Of the central posting types, needing advice and needing to vent are clear demonstrations of fighting for control and empowerment. Maria2008, a posting member of CafeMom sought advice and vented about her doctor in a post that she titled "Dr. changed his mind and wants to do a C-section! Please help me!":

> Im so disappointed right now! He said that since baby estimated 8 lbs 13 ounces at 34½ weeks that it would be dangerous to try for a vaginal birth due to shoulder dystocia. But what if the ultrasound was off??? I asked him that and he said it very well could have been but what if its off by bigger lbs. He said it's a big risk if I decide to go on with the induction and try a vaginal birth … but I am so torn what to do. I want to try a vaginal birth but I want my baby to be safe!!

Here, what we see is the medical establishment creating rules about birth that are more about control, and in this case controlling the patient, than about her ability and desire to birth her child vaginally. She turns to her online community for advice and help, and if nothing else, support.

There were 156 responses in this thread and 2,522 views of the thread. Responses included outrage at the doctor, and a number of women posting stories that are similar with outcomes resembling the one that Maria2008 desires:

> I'd tell him you at least want to TRY! If it sees like it's going nowhere or baby is getting stuck then have a c-sec. JMO [Just my opinion]!
>
> (orange4agua72)

> First off it sounds like the ultrasound measurement is way off if they are saying at 34 weeks that the baby is over 8 pounds. If you do not want a C-section, simply do not agree to one, you can also switch providers.
>
> (MonroeLoves82)

> I would try vaginal then and hope it goes perfectly. He can't force you to do a C-section!
>
> (mmoleader)

> Dangerous?? I gave birth at 38 weeks with a 9.3 lb chubby baby!! Some women give birth to 10/11 even 12 lbs. Your doctor is crazy!
>
> (Charlene_x)

> Tell him flat out that you want to try a vaginal birth. he cannot force you to do a C-section, and don't let him intimidate you! Women have given birth to 9–10 lbs babies vaginally, you can push out an 8 lb baby.
>
> (Pandapanda)

Clearly the theme of these select responses (out of a total of 156 replies) is that the doctor cannot insist on medical interventions, in this case surgery, if the patient does not acquiesce and comply. The empowerment language offered by members of the forum community is not based in medical rhetoric or scare tactics, instead it is about body-ability and personal experiences with doctors and their sometimes incorrect diagnoses. Other posters recommended finding a provider who would not look to strong arm her with scare tactics and to stand up for what she wants. Some postings included extensive medical information, though from non-medically established sources, to soothe the concerns and support Maria2008. The outrage expressed by community members that her doctor would take on tactics to scare her about potential permanent brain damage to her child to force the C-section seemed unconscionable to many.

Through those few who posted in favor of following doctor's orders though, we can see that not all pregnant women are interested in looking for advice beyond what they are told by doctors, and that those who self-advocate are more likely to be painted as the difficult patients seen in Bessett's (2010) work. One such poster, Destiny1403 stated:

> I personally think that the OP should listen to her Drs. This seems like a serious situation and if she has 2 Drs telling her that it is a good idea for a C-section, then I would do that. One of those Drs isnt going to make a penny on that C-section so why is he recommending it? I think that if the OP really wants to try to deliver vaginally, then go for it. I just dont think I would be able to live with myself after being warned if something were to happen.... The women here on CafeMom do not know the details of your pregnancy. Many are advocates for Vbacs [vaginal birth after a cesarean section] and absolutely despise Drs, but in the long run, the women here ARENT delivering your child.

Here, Destiny1403 attempts to take the power back from both Maria2008 and all of the other posters on the site. This strike to disempower though was ignored by most posters, and those responding, instead of flaming, continued to offer support to Maria2008, as is seen in previous research examining women's behaviors in online forums (Ley 2007; Drentea and Moren-Cross 2005; Sharf 1997). It is important to note that of the 156 replies to Maria2008, 101 women supported her desire to avoid a C-section and make her own decisions about her impending birth, and 15 posters felt that she should listen to her doctor. The other 40 postings on the forum were either about the medical information offered by other posters, comments on the content of other posts, or Maria2008 commenting on the responses. The uneasy position of accepting medical information from non-medical providers is a challenge when examining the responses to posters. While none would recommend ignoring doctor's expertise altogether, the intent is most often to encourage the women to ask more questions, and to feel entitled to ask those questions. This response of Destiny1403 is not disempowering in her disagreement with other responders, but in her dismissal of the poster's frustrations in stating that "I think that if the OP really wants to try to deliver vaginally, then go for it. I just dont think I would be able to live with myself after being warned if something were to happen." Maria2008 becomes the bad patient and the bad mother, lacking the requisite maternal sacrifice, by not obeying her doctor without question and without challenge.

Three days later at the end of the posting, Maria2008 reports back with an update, a "bump" (meaning to go back to the top of chronologically sorted discussion for information or an update), where she reports that a second ultrasound showed the baby at 9 lbs 13 oz, and that she decided to go ahead with the vaginal delivery because she expressed having faith in herself and her ability to birth the baby. After six hours of labor and 45 minutes of pushing she delivered a healthy baby. This led to a round of congratulatory postings on both the healthy baby and getting to achieve her wish for a vaginal birth.

Identity claiming and community building

On the forums there are spaces where women can choose to move along through their pregnancies with others expecting to give birth in the same month, often referred to as due date clubs, or seek out others with similar life-stage or demographic characteristics, such as the Mommies Like You forums on JustMommies including: teen, LGBT (lesbian, gay, bisexual and transgender), single mothers, age groups, and interracial. Within these smaller communities a sense of camaraderie is more frequently built over time than in some of the larger and more general forums. One example of these relationships is seen in I-Am-Pregnant's forum for Advanced Age. The women participating in this forum are all over the age of 35, which means that they are considered by the medical community to have additional potential risks in their pregnancies. This particular forum group had between 12 and 15 regular members posting almost daily, with occasional posts from others who were less active but were familiar with active members, along with some new posters just joining the group. Collectively they checked in with each other about amniocentesis (amnio – a procedure used to test amniotic fluid to diagnose chromosomal abnormalities), fetal development, pregnancy problems, fears, and efforts to become pregnant. This particular thread is a discussion starting with RoseyGirl talking about her amnio:

> Well everyone I had my amnio this morning ... the procedure itself was quite painless and quick – and I got to see bubs again, looking like a normal baby (no external defects) and solid heartbeat. I haven't had any physical after effects (phew!), just the emotional rollercoaster of anxiety and helplessness. I thank you all for your support and well wishes – truly has helped me mentally. xx We now have a 2 week for the results – gonna be a long two weeks...

Titangoddess responds:

> Rosey~ Yay, it is done. The wait is not going to be so much fun but just remember that the chances are very very low. You will be great.... Beetle~ Let us know what is going on. I would not get too upset about it. I mentioned this before but I will touch on it again. I did an IVF cycle with a lady who just naturally had small babies. Her first one was only 4 lbs at birth full term and her second one was only a few ounces more. It happens and it does not mean it is a bad thing at all.

In this post Titangoddess is referring to an earlier discussion on the forum about fears of lower birth weights and fetus size, offering medical information through personal story, considered authentic in that it is shared experience (Drentea and Moren-Cross 2005; Madge and O'Connor 2006, 2005). Further responses included a discussion about the three women who are going through their amnio testing and awaiting results together, RoseyGirl, Beetle, and 2ksMommy. RoseyGirl reports back in with an update (before her results), and a second response immediately after that post:

Ok – a long story ... I had my amnio yesterday, and had leakage in the afternoon ... slept on it and rang the women's clinic this morning and was told to go to emergency straight away. So 4 hours later and some fabulous care, I am not leaking amnio fluid it just may be thrush ... silly me right???? But I did get to have another u/s and bubs was somersaulting and was wriggling everywhere – oh and it's a BOY!!! Go team blue:):):)

2ksmommy – thinking of you xo thanks everyone – appreciate your input and care:) xo

Ssl responds to her, both to reassure her of her decision to call the doctor – taking note of RoseyGirl's self-effacement about "silly me", nudging her to respect her own decision, and to joke with her:

Thanks Roseygirl. Glad everything is ok. And no not silly you. You should always check if you are worried. That little boy of yours is relying on you;o) Congratulations by the way. xx.

It is important to note that even in forums where a longer relationship between posters has been established, there are personal self-effacing comments that again illuminate the fear of being the problem patient, as discussed by Bessett (2010). When RoseyGirl says "silly me," apologizing for her fears and decision to call the doctor for further confirmation on what ended up not being a leak of fluid, she is chided by Ssl for not fully respecting that she (RoseyGirl) is entitled to continued care when faced with questions, uncertainty, and fear. It is the checking of oneself within the culture of the board, as if to reassure herself that she is not demanding more than she deserves.

This conversation wraps up with good news from RoseyGirl and supportive responses from her forum friends:

Fabulous news today – the baby is perfect:):):) the amnio came back with no chromosonal defects and it's a girl!!!!! So much for seeing the willy at the ultrasound.... I haven't stopped crying since I found out, we are both soooooo happy.

(RoseyGirl)

well done RoseyGirl – and 2ksmommy – I have to say I am very envious you did the amnio – because now you can truly relax and make plans fully!

(beetle)

rosey, thats awesome!!!!! CONGRATS!!! a little girl. yay!!

(dawnp)

What is of particular interest to this series of posts, is that compared to many of the other forums, the Advanced Age forum most represents an ongoing supportive community. As illustrated by their discussion, these women have formed a relationship together, showing both familiarity and friendship. Perhaps this comes from being a subgroup within the larger population of pregnant women, in particular for a group that claims their age as a central element of their pregnant identity – members of the "old girls club," a title many used when welcoming new members to their forum. Unlike the format of posting a particular question at a specific moment in time or with a specific occurrence or concern about their bodies, this group discusses their daily lives, along with their pregnancies, and they post more regularly, committing both to the needs of others in the group and to the relationships overall, a space that is both social and therapeutic simultaneously (Ley 2007).

Conclusions

An exploration of CafeMom, I-Am-Pregnant, and JustMommies forums suggests that these sites can offer support and create access to empowerment. Digital networks, such as online forums, create opportunities for exchange that typically would be limited by geography. Shifting American living and work patterns leave women without the communities they historically would have accessed for information about pregnancy. No longer are there neighborhoods filled with women, home for much of the day, raising small children; where these geographic patterns shift, women now seek out communities that are unencumbered by demands of propinquity. Online forums offer access to communities of women who can offer shared experiences otherwise unavailable to pregnant women. The role that these forums play in their lives is central, as they receive emotional support, information about pregnancy, and, more specifically, a social outlet where others too are experiencing similar issues over their life course position, pregnancy. Seeking a barometer for the normalcy of physical and mental experiences during pregnancy potentially allows women to be less fearful and more self-assured about their bodies and their experiences.

Women are socialized by the medical community to limit their questioning and reporting of symptoms through subtle messages that they are either bothering the doctor or simply listing off experiences that are "probably nothing." This coupled with expected 15-minute doctors' appointments leaves women with the choice either to accept that their experiences are unimportant and too typical for consideration, or to become the "bad" patient, demanding more access and information than they are entitled to (Bessett 2010). Even as the medical community appears to ignore the ailments of pregnant women as merely side-effects of their current status, and women begin to seek each other out online for both camaraderie and support, there is a continuous referencing of doctors, medical procedures, and self-diagnosed medical problems. The influence of the medical community is everywhere on the forums, and there does not appear to be any real desire to escape from it. Instead, there is in many ways a desire for more access to it – space to ask more medical questions, and to feel entitled to ask more questions without censure. The forums become places to undo the social pressures of conformity and undermine the silence that women have been bullied into accepting. The forums, and the women posting on them, frequently encourage the asking of questions that previously would have been off-limits socially as seemingly frivolous or excessive. These spaces also encourage venting, and fighting for increased access to both information and a voice in the decision-making process about their pregnancies. In these forums women reveal the burden of their uncertainty, their fears about failure and of making a mistake that will somehow be *their* mistake alone, leading to the untimely end of their pregnancy. Yet, these forums serve to empower pregnant women to ask more questions, and receive both answers and support in an environment that is largely free of negative judgment. In the spirit of that empowerment, pregnant women are asking hundreds of thousands of questions in tens of thousands of online forums in a myriad of languages from living rooms to libraries across the world, and in doing so are shifting the politics of pregnancy and challenging the social order.

References

Abel-Smith, B. (1992) 'The Beveridge Report: Its Origins and Outcomes', *International Social Security Review*, vol. 45, no. 1–2, pp. 5–16.

Ajzen, I. (1991) 'The Theory of Planned Behavior', *Organizational Behavior and Human Decision Processes*, vol. 50, pp. 179–211.

Ajzen, I. and Fishbein, M. (1980) *Understanding Attitudes and Predicting Social Behavior,* Englewood Cliffs, NJ: Prentice Hall.

Alderman, K. (1999) 'Parties and Movements', *Parliamentary Affairs,* vol. 52, no. 1, pp. 128–130.

Almond, G. and Verba, S. (1963) *The Civic Culture: Political Attitudes and Democracy in Five Nations*. Princeton, NJ: Princeton University Press.

Althaus, S. (1996) 'Opinion Polls, Information Effects, and Political Equality: Exploring Ideological Biases in Collective Opinion', *Political Communication*, vol. 13, pp. 3–21.

Altheide, D. L. and Snow, R. P. (1979) *Media Logic*. Beverly Hills, CA: Sage.

Anderson, T. and Kanuka, H. (2003) *E-Research: Methods, Strategies and Issues*. Boston: Pearson Education.

Andrews, P. (2003) 'Is Blogging Journalism?' *Nieman Reports*. Available at www.nieman.harvard.edu/reportsitem.aspx?id=101027

Angus, R. (2010, 22 April) 'Clegg and Cameron Share Spotlight in Britain's Second Televised Debate'. Available at www.angus-reid.com/polls/43046/clegg-and-cameron-share-spotlight-in-britains-second-televised-debate/ (accessed 8 March 2011)

Anstead, N. and Chadwick, A. (2008) 'Parties, Election Campaigning and the Internet: Toward a Comparative Institutional Approach', in *The Routledge Handbook of Internet Politics*, ed. A. Chadwick and P. Howard. London and New York: Routledge, pp. 56–71.

Anstead, N. and O'Loughlin, B. (2011) *The Emerging Viewertariet and BBC Question Time: Television Debate and Real-Time Commenting Online, The International Journal of Press/Politics*, vol. 16, no. 4, pp. 440–462.

Arat-Koc, S. (1999) 'Neo-liberalism, State Restructuring and Immigration: Changes in Canadian Politicies in the 1990s', *Journal of Canadian Studies,* vol. 2, no. 34, pp. 31–56.

Asbjørnsen, N. and Vogt, G. (1992) 'Measuring Political Competence: An Analysis with Reference to Gender', *Scandinavian Political Studies*, vol. 15, no. 1, pp. 61–76.

Atkinson, J. D. (2010) *Alternative Media and Politics of Resistance*. New York: Peter Lang.

Atton, C. (2002) 'News Cultures and New Social Movements: Radical Journalism and the Mainstream Media', *Journalism Studies*, vol. 3, no. 4, pp. 491–505.

Atton, C. (2004) *An Alternative Internet*, Edinburgh: Edinburgh University Press.

Australian Youth Affairs Coalition (2010) *Where Are You Going with That? Maximising Young People's Impact on Organisation and Policy.* Sydney: AYAC. Available at www.ayac.org.au (accessed 30 August 2010).

Ayers, J. M. (1999) 'From the Streets to the Internet: The Cyber-Diffusion of Contention', *Annals of the American Academy of Political and Social Science*, vol. 566, pp. 132–143.

Babb, P. (2005) 'A Summary of *Focus on Social Inequalities*', Office of National Statistics. Available at www.statistics.gov.uk/cci/article.asp?id=1223.

Bae Brandtzaeg, P. and Heim, J. (2009) 'Why People Use Social Network Sites', in *Online Communities, LNCS 5621*, ed. A. A. Ozok and P. Zaphiris. Berlin and Heidelberg: Springer-Verlag, pp. 143–152.

Baker, L., Wagner, T. H., Singer, S. and Bundorf, M. K. (2003) 'Use of the Internet and E-Mail for Health Care Information', *Journal of the American Medical Association*, vol. 289, no. 18, pp. 2400–2406.

Banaji, S. (2008) 'The Producers of Civic Websites for Young People in the UK', in *Young People, the Internet and Civic Participation*. London: CIVICWEB, Institute of Education, University of London.

Bang, H. (2005) 'Among Everyday Makers and Expert Citizens', in *Remaking Governance: Peoples, Politics and the Public Sphere* ed. Janet Newman. Bristol: Policy Press, pp. 159–178.

Barabasi, A. (2011) 'Introduction and Keynote to a Networked Self', in *A Networked Self: Identity, Community, and Culture on Social Network Sites*, ed. Z. Papacharissi. London: Routledge, pp. 1–14.

Barber, B. (1984) *Strong Democracy: Participatory Politics for the New Age.* Berkeley: University of California Press.

Barker, K. K. (1998) '"A ship upon a stormy sea": The Medicalization of Pregnancy', *Social Science and Medicine*, vol. 47, no. 8, pp. 1067–1076.

Barlow, J. P. (1996) 'Declaration of the Independence of Cyberspace'. Available at http://projects.eff.org/~barlow/Declaration-Final.html (accessed 3 February 2011).

Barnes, M., Newman, J. and Sullivan, H. (2007) *Power, Participation and Renewal: Case Studies in Public Participation.* Bristol: Policy Press.

Barnhurst, K. (2002) 'News Geography and Monopoly: The Form of Reports on US Newspaper Internet Sites', *Journalism Studies*, vol. 3, no. 4, pp. 477–489.

Baron, N. (2008) *Always On: Language in an Online and Mobile World.* Oxford: Oxford University Press.

Bashevkin, S. B. (2002) *Welfare Hot Buttons: Women, Work, and Social Policy Reform.* Toronto: University of Toronto Press.

Bauder, H. (2008) 'Immigration Debate in Canada: How Newspapers Reported, 1996–2004', *Journal of International Migration and Integration*, vol. 9, no. 3, pp. 289–310.

Baum, M. and Groeling, T. (2008) 'New Media and the Polarization of American Political Discourse', *Political Communication*, vol. 25, no. 4, pp. 345–365.

Bauman, Z. (1998) *Work, Consumerism and the New Poor.* Buckingham: Open University Press.

Bauman, Z. (2000) *Liquid Modernity*. Cambridge: Polity Press.

Baym, N. K. (2010) *Personal Connections in the Digital Age*, Cambridge: Polity Press.

BBC News Online (2009, 2 October) 'TV Firms Propose Election Debates'. Available at http://news.bbc.co.uk/1/hi/8287620.stm (accessed 8 March 2011).

Bean, C. (2007) 'Young People's Voting Patterns', in *Youth and Political Participation* ed. Lawrence Saha, Murray Print and Kathy Edwards. Rotterdam: Sense Publishers, pp. 33–50.

Beaumont, C. (2008, 27 November) 'Mumbai Attacks: Twitter and Flickr Used to Break News', *Daily Telegraph*. Available at www.telegraph.co.uk/news/worldnews/asia/india/3530640/Mumbai-attacks-Twitter-and-Flickr-used-to-break-news-Bombay-India.html (accessed 25 May 2010).

Beck, U. (1992) *Risk Society: Towards a New Modernity*, London: Sage.

Beck, U. and Beck-Gernsheim, E. (2002) *Individualization: Institutionalized Individualism and its Social and Political Consequences*. London: Sage.

Bednarek, M. (2006) *Evaluation in Media Discourse Analysis: An Analysis of a Newspaper Corpus*. London: Continuum.

Bell, A. (1991) *The Language of News Media*, Oxford: Basil Blackwell Ltd.

Bell, B. L. (2005) *Children, Youth and Civic (Dis)Engagement: Digital Technology and Citizenship*, Working Paper No. 5, Canadian Research Alliance for Community Innovation and Networking (CRACIN). Available at www3.fis.utoronto.ca/iprp/cracin/publications/workingpapersseries.htm (accessed on 21 May 2008).

Benford, R. D. and Snow, D. A. (2000) 'Framing Processes and Social Movements: An Overview and Assessment', *Annual Review of Sociology*, vol. 26, pp. 611–39.

Bengtsson, Å. and Christensen, H. S. (2009) 'Politiskt deltagande i Finland – spridning och drivkrafter', *Politiikka*, vol. 51, no. 2, pp. 77–95.

Bengtsson, Å., and Grönlund, K. (2005) 'Muu poliittinen osallistuminen'. In *Vaalit ja demokratia Suomessa*, ed. H. Paloheimo. Helsinki: WSOY, pp. 147–168.

Benkler, Y. (2006) *The Wealth of Networks: How Social Production Transforms Markets and Freedom*, New Haven, CT: Yale University Press.

Bennett, E. (2003) 'Communicating Global Activism, Strengths and Vulnerabilities of Networked Politics', *Information, Communication and Society*, vol. 6, no. 2, pp. 143–168.

Bennett, W. L. (1998) 'The Uncivic Culture: Communication, Identity, and the Rise of Lifestyle Politics', *Political Science and Politics*, vol. 31, no. 4, pp. 41–61.

Bennett, W. L. (2003a) 'Communicating Global Activism: Strengths and Vulnerabilities of Networked Politics', *Information, Communication and Society*, vol. 6, no. 2, pp. 143–168.

Bennett, W. L. (2003b) 'Lifestyle Politics and Citizen-Consumers: Identity, Communication and Political Action', in *Media and the Restyling of Politics: Consumerism, Celenrity and Cynicism*, ed. John Corner and Dick Pels. London: Sage, pp. 137–150.

Bennett, W. L. (2003c) 'New Media Power, The Internet and Global Activism', in *Contesting Media Power: Alternative Media in a Networked World*, ed. Nick Couldry and James Curran. Lanham, MD: Rowman and Littlefield, pp. 17–37.

Bennett, W. L. (2005) 'Social Movements beyond Borders: Understanding Two Eras of Transnational Activism', in *Transnational Protest and Global Activism*, ed. D. della Porta and S. Tarrow. Lanham, MD: Rowman and Littlefield, pp. 203–226.

Bennett, W. L. (2008) 'Changing Citizenship in the Digital Age', in *Civic Life Online: Learning How Digital Media Can Engage Youth*, ed. W. L. Bennett. Cambridge, MA: MIT Press, pp. 1–24.

Bennett, W. L. and Xenos, M. (2005) *Young Voters and the Web of Politics 2004: The Youth Political Web Sphere Comes of Age*. Circle Working Paper 42, Medford, MD: Center for Information and Research on Civic Learning and Engagement. Available at www.civicyouth.org/PopUps/WorkingPapers/WP42BennettXenos.pdf

Bennett, W. L., Breunig, C. and Givens, T. (2008) 'Communication and Political Mobilization: Digital Media Use and Protest Organization among Anti-Iraq War Demonstrators in the US', *Political Communication*, vol. 25, pp. 269–289.

Bennett, W. L., Foot, K. and Xenos, M. (2011) 'Narratives and Network Organization: A Comparison of Fair Trade Systems in Two Nations', *Journal of Communication*, vol. 61, pp. 219–245.

Bennett, W. L., Wells, C. and Freelon, D. (2009) *Communicating Civic Engagement: Contrasting Models of Citizenship in the Youth Web Sphere*. Seattle: Center for Communication and Civic Engagement. Available at www.engagedyouth.org/research/reports/#comcit (accessed 30 August 2010).

Bennett, W. L., Wells, C. and Freelon, D. (2011) 'Communicating Civic Engagement: Contrasting Models of Citizenship in the Youth Web Sphere', *Journal of Communication*, vol. 6, no. 5, pp. 835–856.

Bennett, W. L., Wells, C. and Rank, A. (2009) 'Young Citizens and Civic Learning: Two Paradigms of Citizenship in the Digital Age', *Citizenship Studies*, vol. 13, no. 2, pp. 105–120.

Bentivegna, S. (1999) *La politica in rete*. Rome: Meltemi.

Bentivegna, S. (2002) 'Politics and the New Media', In *The Handbook of New Media*, ed. Leah A. Lievrouw and Sonia M. Livingstone. London: Sage, pp. 50–61.

Bessant, J. (2004) 'Mixed Messages: Youth Participation and Democratic Process', *Australian Journal of Political Science*, vol. 39, no. 2, pp. 387–405.

Bessett, D. (2010) 'Negotiating Normalization: The Perils of Producing Pregnancy Symptoms in Prenatal Care', *Social Science and Medicine*, vol. 71, no. 2, pp. 370–377. doi: 10.1016/j.socscimed.2010.04.007.

Best, S. J. and Krueger, B. S. (2005) 'Analyzing the Representativeness of Internet Political Participation', *Political Behaviour*, vol. 27, no. 2, pp. 183–216.

Bijker, W. E., Hughes, T. P. and Pinch, T. J. (eds) (1987) *The Social Construction of Technology Systems: New Directions in the Sociology and History of Technology*. Cambridge, MA: MIT Press.

Bimber, B. (2001) 'Information and Political Engagement in America: The Search for Effects of Information Technology at the Individual Level', *Political Research Quarterly*, vol. 54, no. 1, pp. 53–67.

Bimber, B. (2003) *Information and American Democracy: Technology in the Evolution of Political Power*. New York: Cambridge University Press.

Bimber, B., Flanagin, A. and Stohl, C. (2005) 'Reconceptualizing Collective Action in the Contemporary Media Environment', *Communication Theory*, vol. 15, pp. 389–413.

Blair, T. (2010) *The Journey*. London: Random House.

Blevis, M. (2010, 25 February) 'House of Tweets: Twitter and the House of Commons'. Available at http://politicalview.ca/2010/02/house-of-tweets-twitter-and-the-house-of-commons/ (accessed 25 May 2010).

Bleyer, J. (2004, 31 July) Interview with Peter Lamborn Wilson (Hakim Bey), available from: www.oekonux.org/list-en/archive/msg02568.html (accessed on 22 February 2010).

Blumler, J. and Gurevitch, M. (2001) 'The New Media and our Political Communication Discontents: Democratizing Cyberspace', *Information, Communication and Society*, vol. 4, no. 1, pp. 1–13.

Bowler, S. and Donovan, T. (2002) 'Democracy, Institutions and Attitudes about Citizen Influence on Government', *British Journal of Political Science*, vol. 32, pp. 371–390.

boyd, d. (2008) 'Why youth © social network sites', in *Youth, Identity and Digital Media*, ed David Buckingham. Cambridge, MA: MIT Press, pp. 112–135.

boyd, d. and Ellison, N. (2007) 'Social Network Sites: Definition, History, and Scholar-ship', *Journal of Computer-Mediated Communication*, vol. 13, no. 2, pp. 210–230. Available at http://jcmc.indiana.edu/vol. 13/issue1/boyd.ellison.html

boyd, d. and Heer, J. (2006) 'Profiles as Conversation: Networked Identity Performance on Friendster', in *Proceedings of Thirty-Ninth Hawai'i International Conference on System Sciences*. Los Alamitos, CA: IEEE Press, pp. 59–69.

boyd, d., Golder, S. and Lotan, G. (2010, 6 January) 'Tweet, Tweet, Retweet: Conversa-tional Aspects of Retweeting on Twitter', presented at the Forty-Third Hawai'i Interna-tional Conference on System Sciences, Kauai, HI.

Boyle, C. (2009, 22 July) 'Fairtrade Chocolate Sales Set to Treble as Cadbury's Dairy Milk Carries Ethical Logo', *The Times*, p. 39.

Brandolini, A. and Smeeding, T. M. (2007) *Inequality Patterns in Western-Type Demo-cracies: Cross-Country Differences and Time Changes*, *Child Working Papers*, Italy: Centre for Household, Income, Labour and Demographic Economics. Available at www.child-centre.unito.it/papers/child08_2007.pdf (accessed 10 October 2009).

Brants, K. and Neijens, P. (1998) 'The Infotainment of Politics', *Political Communica-tion*, vol. 15, no. 2, pp. 149–164.

Breindl, Y. and Francq, P. (2008) 'Can Web 2.0 Applications Save E-Democracy? A Study of How New Internet Applications May Enhance Citizen Participation in the Political Process on-Line', *International Journal of Electronic Democracy*, vol. 1, no. 1, pp. 14–31.

Brewer, M., Sibieta, L. and Wren-Lewis, L. (2008) *Racing Away? Income Inequality and the Evolution of High Incomes*. London: Institute for Fiscal Studies. Available at www. ifs.org.uk/bns/bn76.pdf (accessed 1 May 2008).

British Polling Council (2011) 'About the BPC'. Available at www.britishpollingcouncil. org (accessed 4 March 2011).

Broh, C. A. (1980) 'Horse-Race Journalism: Reporting the Polls in the 1976 Presidential Election', *Public Opinion Quarterly*, vol. 44, no. 4, pp. 514–529.

Brown, P., and Tannock, S. (2009) 'Education, Meritocracy and the Global War for Talent', *Journal of Education Policy*, vol. 24, no. 4, pp. 377–392.

Brown, W. (2005) 'Neoliberalism and the End of Liberal Democracy', in *Edgework: Critical Essays on Knowledge and Politics*. Princeton, NJ: Princeton University Press, pp. 37–59.

Bruns, A. (2005) *Gatewatching: Collaborative Online News Production*. New York: Peter Lang.

Bryman, A. (2001) *Social Research Methods*. Oxford: Oxford University Press.

Bullock, H. E., Wyche, K. F. and Williams, W. R. (2001) 'Media Images of the Poor', *Journal of Social Issues,* vol. 57, no. 2, pp. 229–246.

Burt, E. and Taylor, J. (2008) 'How Well Do Voluntary Organizations Perform on the Web as Democratic Actors? Towards an Evaluative Framework', *Information, Com-munication and Society*, vol. 11, no. 8, pp. 1047–1067.

Bylund, C. L. (2005) 'Mothers' Involvement in Decision Making During the Birthing Process: A Quantitative Analysis of Women's Online Birth Stories', *Health Communi-cation*, vol. 18, no. 1, pp. 23–39.

CAFOD (2009) Available at www.cafod.org.uk/resources/videogalleries/put-people-first (accessed 7 October 2010).

Callon, M., Meadel, C. and Rabeharisoa, V. (2002) 'The Economy of Qualities', *Economy and Society*, vol. 31, pp. 194–217.

Cameron, D. (2008, 29 October) 'Free Markets Fail'. Available at http://rabble.ca/col-umnists/free-markets-fail (accessed June 2010).

Campbell, A. (2007) *The Blair Years: The Alastair Campbell Diaries*. London: Hutchinson.

Campus, D., Pasquino, G. and Vaccari, C. (2008) 'Social Networks, Political Discussion and Voting in Italy: A Study of the 2006 Election', *Political Communication*, vol. 25, no. 4, pp. 423–444.

Canadian Newspaper Association (April 2010) *Circulation Data Report*. Available at www.newspaperscanada.ca/about-newspapers/circulation

Cardon, Domenique and Granjou, Fabien (2003) 'Peut-on se libérer des formats médiatiques? Le mouvement alter-mondialisation et l'Internet,' *Mouvements*, vol. 25, pp. 67–73.

Carlson, T. and Strandberg, K. (2007) 'Finland: The European Parliament Election in a Candidate-Centered Electoral System', in *The Internet and National Elections*, ed. R. Kluver, N. W. Jankowski, K. A. Foot and S. M. Schneider. London and New York: Routledge, pp. 29–42.

Castells, M. (2001) *The Internet Galaxy. Reflections on the Internet, Business and Society*. Oxford: Oxford University Press.

Castells, M. (2007) 'Communication, Power and Counter-power in the Network Society', *International Journal of Communication*, vol. 1, no. 1, pp. 238–266.

Castells, M. (2009) *Communication Power*. Oxford: Oxford University Press.

Chadwick, A. (2006) *Internet Politics: States, Citizens, and New Communication Technologies*. New York, Oxford University Press.

Chadwick, A. (2007) 'Digital Network Repertoires and Organizational Hybridity', *Political Communication*, vol. 24, no. 3, pp. 283–301.

Chadwick, A. (2009) 'Web 2.0: New Challenges for the Study of e-Democracy in an Era of Informational Exuberance', *I/S: Journal of Law and Policy for the Information Society*, vol. 5, no. 1, pp. 9–41.

Chadwick, A. (2011a) 'Britain's First Live Televised Party Leaders' Debate: From the News Cycle to the Political Information Cycle', *Parliamentary Affairs*, vol. 64, no. 1, pp. 24–44.

Chadwick, A. (2011b) 'The Political Information Cycle in a Hybrid News System: The British Prime Minister and the "Bullygate" Affair', *International Journal of Press/Politics*, vol. 16, no. 1, p. 3.

Cheng, A., Evans, M. and Singh, H. (2009) 'Inside Twitter An In-Depth Look Inside the Twitter World'. Available at www.sysomos.com/insidetwitter/ (accessed 25 May 2010).

Cho, H. (2003) 'Communicating Risk Without Creating Unintended Effects', *American Journal of Health Studies*, vol. 18, no. 2/3, pp. 104–110.

Chu, D. (2010) 'In Search of Prosumption: Youth and the New Media in Hong Kong', *First Monday*, vol. 15, no. 2. Available at www.uic.edu/htbin/cgiwrap/bin/ojs/index.php/fm/article/view/2772/2451

Coleman, R., Lieber, P., Mendelson, A. L. and Kurpius, D. D. (2008) 'Public Life and the Internet: If You Build a Better Website, Will Citizens Become Engaged?', *New Media and Society*, vol. 10, no. 2, pp. 179–201.

Coleman, S. (2004, 30 November) 'The Network-Empowered Citizen: How People Share Civic Knowledge Online', paper delivered at the Institute for Public Policy Research event 'From Grass Roots to Networks: The Role of Social Capital in Increasing Political Participation', Houses of Parliament, London.

Coleman, S. (2005) 'Blogs and the New Political Listening', *Political Quarterly* vol. 76, no. 2 pp. 272–280.

Coleman, S. (2007) 'How Democracies Have Disengaged from Young People', in *Young Citizens in the Digital Age: Political Engagement, Young People and New Media*, ed. B. Loader. London: Routledge, pp. 166–185.

Coleman, S. (2008) 'Doing IT for Themselves: Management Versus Autonomy in Youth E-Citizenship', in *Civic Life Online: Learning How Digital Media Can Engage Youth*, ed. W. L. Bennett. Cambridge, MA: MIT Press, pp. 189–206.

Coleman, S. and Blumler, J. G. (2009) *The Internet and Democratic Citizenship*. Cambridge: Cambridge University Press.

Coleman, S. and Gøtze, J. (2002) *Bowling Together: Online Public Engagement in Policy Deliberation*, London, Hansard Society.

Coleman, S. and Rowe, C. (2005) *Remixing Citizenship: Democracy and Young People's Use of the Internet*, Research Report. London: Carnegie Young People Initiative.

Coleman, S., Anthony, S. and Morrison, D. E. (2009) *Public Trust in the News*. Oxford: Reuters Institute for the Study of Journalism, University of Oxford.

Collin, P. (2008) 'The Internet, Youth Participation Policies, and the Development of Young People's Political Identities in Australia', *Journal of Youth Studies*, vol. 11, no. 5, pp. 527–542.

ComRes. (2010, 22 April) 'ITV News Instant Debate Poll'. Available at www.comres.co.uk/page16539431.aspx (accessed 8 March 2010).

Corner, J. and Pels, D. (2003) *Media and the Restyling of Politics: Consumerism, Celebrity and Cynicism*, London: Sage.

Cornia, G. A., Addison, T. and Kiiski, S. (2004) 'Income Distribution Changes and their Impact in the Post-Second World War Period', in *Inequality, Growth and Poverty in an Era of Liberalization and Globalization*, ed. G. A. Cornia. Oxford: Oxford University Press, pp. 26–55.

Cottle, S. (2006) *Mediatized Conflict: Developments in Media and Conflict Studies*. Maidenhead: Open University Press.

Couldry, N. (2000) *The Place of Media Power: Pilgrims and Witnesses of the Media Age*. London: Routledge.

Couldry, N. (2003) 'Beyond the Hall of Mirrors? Some Theoretical Reflections on the Global Contestation of Media Power', in *Contesting Media Power: Alternative Media in a Networked World*, ed. Nick Couldry and James Curran. Lanham, MD: Rowman and Littlefield, pp. 39–55.

Couldry, N. (2006a) 'Culture and Citizenship: The Missing Link?', *European Journal of Cultural Studies*, vol. 9, no. 3, pp. 321–339.

Couldry, N. (2006b) *Listening Beyond the Echoes: Media, Ethics and Agency in an Uncertain World*. New York: Paradigm.

Couldry, N. (2008) 'Mediazation or Mediation? Alternative Understandings of the Emerging Space of Digital Story Telling', *New Media and Society*, vol. 10, no. 3, pp. 373–391.

Couldry, N. (2010) *Why Voice Matters: Culture and Politics after Neoliberalism*. London: Sage.

Couldry, N. and Markham, T. (2007) 'Tracking the Reflexivity of the (Dis)Engaged Citizen. Some Methodological Reflections', *Qualitative Enquiry*, vol. 13, no. 5, pp. 675–695.

Couldry, N., Livingstone, S. and Markham, T. (2007), *Media Consumption and Public Engagement: Beyond the Presumption of Attention*. Basingstoke: Palgrave Macmillan.

Creswell, J. W. (1998) *Qualitative Inquiry and Research Design: Choosing Among Five Traditions*, London: Sage.

Croghan, R., Griffin, C., Hunter, J. and Phoenix, A. (2006) 'Style Failure: Consumption, Identity and Social Exclusion', *Journal of Youth Studies*, vol. 9, no. 4, pp. 463–478.

Crouch, C. (2005) *Postdemocracy*, Cambridge: Polity Press.

Curran, J. (1991) 'Mass Media and Democracy', in *Mass Media and Society*, ed. J. Curran and M. Gurevitch. London: Edward Arnold, pp. 82–117.

Curran, J. (1998) 'Communications, Power and Social Order', in *Culture, Society and the Media*, ed. M. Gurevitch, T. Bennett, J. Curran and J. Woollacott. London: Routledge, pp. 202–235.

Curran, J. (2003a) 'Global Journalism: A Case Study of the Internet', in *Contesting Media Power: Alternative Media in a Networked World*, ed. N. Couldry and J. Curran. Lanham, MD: Rowman and Littlefield, pp. 227–241.

Curran, J. (2003b) 'Part I: Press History', in *Power Without Responsibility: The Press, Broadcasting, and New Media in Britain*, ed. J. Curran and J. Seaton. London: Routledge, pp. 1–104

Curran, J. (2010) 'Future of Journalism', *Journalism Studies*, vol. 11, no. 4, pp. 1–13.

Curtis, P. (2010, 19 April) 'Mystery Yougov Poll Looks for Nick Clegg's Weaknesses', *Guardian*. Available at www.guardian.co.uk/politics/2010/apr/19/yougov-survey-nick-clegg-attack

Dahl, R. (1998) *On Democracy*. New Haven, CT: Yale University Press.

Dahlgren, P. (2003) 'Reconfiguring Civic Culture in the New Media Milieu'. In *Media and the Restyling of Politics: Consumerism, Celebrity, Cynicism*, ed. J. Corner and D. Pels. London: Sage, pp. 151–170.

Dahlgren, Peter (2009) *Media and Political Engagement: Citizens, Communication and Democracy*. Cambridge: Cambridge University Press.

Daily Show (2009, 1 October) 'Tea Parties Advise G20 Protesters'. Available at www.thedailyshow.com/watch/thu-october-1–2009/tea-partiers-advise-g20-protesters (accessed 6 October 2010).

Dalrymple, K. and Scheufele, D. A. (2007) 'Finally Informing the Electorate? How the Internet Got People Thinking About Presidential Politics in 2004', *Harvard International Journal of Press/Politics*, vol. 12, no. 3, pp. 96–111.

Dalton, R. J. (2006) *Citizen Politics: Public Opinion and Political Parties in Advanced Industrial Democracies*, 4th edn. Washington DC: CQ Press.

Danso, R. (2009) 'Emancipating and Empowering De-Valued Skilled Immigrants: What Hope Does Anti-Oppressive Social Work Practice Offer?' *British Journal of Social Work*, vol. 39, pp. 539–555.

Davis, A. (2007a) 'Investigating Journalist Influences on Political Issue Agendas at Westminster', *Political Communication*, vol. 24, no. 2, pp. 181–199.

Davis, A. (2007b) *The Mediation of Power*. London: Routledge.

Davis, A. (2010a) 'New Media and Fat Democracy: The Paradox of Online Participation', *New Media and Society*, vol. 12, no. 5, pp. 745–761.

Davis, A. (2010b) *Political Communication and Social Theory*. London: Routledge.

Davis, R. (2009) *Typing Politics: The Role of Blogs in American Politics*. New York: Oxford University Press.

Davis, R. and Owen, D. (1998) *New Media and American Politics*. New York: Oxford University Press.

de Goede, M. (1996) 'Ideology in the US Welfare Debate: Neo-Liberal Representations of Poverty', *Discourse and Society*, vol. 7, no. 3, pp. 317–357.

de Vreese, C. H. (2007) 'Digital Renaissance: Young Consumer and Citizen?' *Annals of the American Academy of Political and Social Science*, vol. 611, pp. 207–216.

Dean, J. (2009) *Democracy and Other Neoliberal Fantasies: Communicative Capitalism and Left Politics*, Durham, NC: Duke University Press.

Declercq, E. R., Sakala, C., Corry, M. P. and Applebaum, S. (2006) *Listening to Mothers II: Report of the Second National US Survey of Women's Childbearing Experiences.* New York: Childbirth Connections.

della Porta, D. (2005a) 'Deliberation in Movement: Why and How to Study Deliberative Democracy and Social Movements,' *Acta Politica*, vol. 40, pp. 336–350.

della Porta, D. (2005b) 'Multiple Belongings, Flexible Identities and the Construction of "Another Politics": Between the European Social Forum and the Local Social Fora', in *Transnational Protest and Global Activism*, ed. D. della Porta and S. Tarrow. Boulder, CO: Rowman & Littlefield, pp. 175–202.

della Porta, D. (ed.) (2009a) *Democracy in Social Movements*. London: Palgrave Macmillan.

della Porta, D. (ed.) (2009b) *Another Europe*. New York and London: Routledge.

della Porta, D. (2009c) *I partiti politici*, 2nd updated and expanded edn. Bologna: Il Mulino.

della Porta, D. and Diani. M. (2006) *Social Movements: An Introduction*, 2nd expanded edn. Oxford: Blackwell.

della Porta, D. and Mosca, L. (2005) 'Global-Net for Global Movements? A Network of Networks for a Movement of Movements', *Journal of Public Policy*, vol. 25, pp. 165–190.

della Porta, D. and Mosca, L. (2007) '*In movimento*: "Contamination" in Action and the Italian Global Justice Movement', *Global Networks: A Journal of Transnational Affairs*, vol. 7, pp. 1–27.

della Porta, D. and Mosca, L. (2009) 'Searching the Net', *Information, Communication and Society*, vol. 12, no. 6, pp. 771–792.

Delli Carpini, M. X. (2000) 'Gen.Com: Youth, Civic Engagement, and the New Information Environment', *Political Communication*, vol. 17, no. 4, pp. 341–349.

Delli Carpini, M. X. and Keeter, S. (1993) 'Measuring Political Knowledge: Putting First Things First', *American Journal of Political Science*, vol. 37, no. 4, pp. 1179–1206.

Delli Carpini, M. X. and Keeter, S. (1996) *What Americans Know about Politics and Why It Matters*, New Haven, CT: Yale University Press.

Deutsch, K. W. (1964) *The Nerves of Government: Models of Political Communication.* New York: Free Press.

Deuze, M. (2011) 'Media Life', *Media, Culture and Society*, vol. 33, no. 1, pp. 137–148.

Diani, M. (1995) *Green Networks: A Structural Analysis of the Italian Environmental Movement*. Edinburgh: Edinburgh University Press.

Diani, M. (2001) 'Social Movement Networks: Virtual and Real', in *Culture and Politics in the Information Age*, ed. F. Webster. New York: Routledge, pp. 117–128.

Diani, M. (2003) 'Networks and Social Movements: A Research Programme', in *Social Movements and Networks: Relational Approaches to Collective Action*, ed. M. Diani and D. McAdam. Oxford: Oxford University Press, pp. 299–319.

Diani, M. (2004) 'Networks and Participation', in *The Blackwell Companion to Social Movements*, ed. D. Snow, S. A. Soule, and H. Kriesi. Malden, MA: Blackwell, pp. 339–359.

Diani, M. and McAdam, D. (eds) (2003) *Social Movements and Networks: Relational Approaches to Collective Action*, Oxford: Oxford University Press.

Dickens, R. and McKnight, A. (2008) *The Changing Pattern of Earnings: Employees, Migrants and Low-Paid Families*. York: Joseph Rowntree Foundation. Available at www.jrf.org.uk/publications/changing-pattern-earnings-employeesmigrants-and-low-paid-families (accessed February 2011).

Dickerson, J. (2008) 'Don't Fear Twitter', *Nieman Reports*. Available at www.nieman.harvard.edu/reports.aspx?id=100006 (accessed 25 May 2010).

DiMaggio, P., Hargittai, E., Neuman, W. R. and Robinson, J. P. (2001) 'Social Implications of the Internet', *Annual Review of Sociology*, vol. 27, pp. 307–336.

Doctor, S. and Dutton, W. H. (1998) 'The First Amendment Online: Santa Monica's Public Electronic Network', in *Cyberdemocracy: Technology, Cities and Civic Networks*, ed. R. Tsagarousianou, D. Tambini and C. Bryon. London: Routledge. pp. 125–151.

Donath, J. (2008) 'Signals in Social Supernets', *Journal of Computer-Mediated Communication*, vol. 13, no. 1, pp. 231–251.

Downes, E. J. and McMillan, S. J. (2000) 'Defining Interactivity: A Qualitative Identification of Key Dimensions', *New Media and Society*, vol. 2, pp. 157–179.

Downey, L. L. (2007) 'Group Usability Testing: Evolution in Usability Techniques', *Journal of Usability Studies*, vol. 2, no. 3, pp. 133–144.

Downing, J. D. H., with Tamara Villareal Ford, Genève Gil and Laura Stein (2001) *Radical Media: Rebellious Communication and Social Movements*. London, Sage.

Drentea, P. and Moren-Cross, J. L. (2005) 'Social Capital and Social Support on the Web: The Case of an Internet Mother Site', *Sociology of Health and Illness*, vol. 27, no. 7, pp. 920–943.

Drezner, D. W. and Farrell, H. (2004) 'Web of Influence', *Foreign Policy*, vol. 145, pp. 32–40.

Druckman, J. and Kjersten, N. (2003) 'Framing and Deliberation: How Citizens' Conversations Limit Elite Influence', *American Journal of Political Science*, vol. 47, no. 4, pp. 729–745.

Dustmann, C. and Fabbri, F. (2005) 'Immigrants in the British Labour Market', *Fiscal Studies*, vol. 26, no. 4, pp. 423–470.

Dustmann, C., Frattini, T. and Halls, C. (2009) *Assessing the Fiscal Costs and Benefits of A8 Migration to the UK*, Centre for Research and Analysis of Migration, Department of Economics, University College London. Available at www.econ.ucl.ac.uk/cream/pages/CDP/CDP_18_09.pdf (accessed February 2011).

Eble, M. and Breault, R. (2002) 'The Primetime Agora: Knowledge, Power and "Mainstream" Resource Venues for Women Online', *Computers and Composition*, vol. 19, no. 3, pp. 315–329.

Edelman, M. J. (1977) *Political Language: Words That Succeed and Policies That Fail*. New York: Academic Press.

Edwards, K. (2007) 'From Deficit to Disenfranchisement: Reframing Youth Electoral Participation', *Journal of Youth Studies*, vol. 10, no. 5, pp. 539–555.

Eliasoph, N. (2009) 'Top Down Civic Projects Are Not Grassroots Associations: How the Differences Matter in Everyday Life', *Voluntas*, vol. 20, no. 2, pp. 291–308.

Elving, R. D. (1996) 'Accentuate the Negative: Contemporary Congressional Campaigns', *PS: Political Science and Politics*, vol. 29, no. 3, pp. 440–446.

Emmett, A. (2008) 'Networking News: Traditional News Outlets Turn to Social Networking Web Sites in an Effort to Build Their Online Audience', *American Journalism Review*. Available at www.ajr.org/article.asp?id=4646 (accessed 25 May 2010).

Epstein, Y. M., Rosenberg, H. S., Grant, T. V. and Hemenway, N. (2002) 'Use of the Interent as the Only Outlet for Talking About Infertility', *Fertility and Sterility*, vol. 78, no. 3, pp. 507–514.

Esser, F., Reinemann, C. and Fan, D. (2001) 'Spin Doctors in the United States, Great Britain, and Germany: Metacommunication about Media Manipulation', *Harvard International Journal of Press/Politics*, vol. 6, no. 1, pp. 16–45.

Eurostat (2010) 'Information Society Statistics'. Available at http://epp.eurostat.ec. europa.eu/portal/page/portal/information_society/data/main_tables (accessed 12 May 2010).

Fenton, N. (2008) 'Mediating Solidarity', *Global Media and Communication,* vol. 4, pp. 37–57.

Fenton, N. (2010) 'NGOs, New Media and the Mainstream News: News from Everywhere', in *New Media, Old News: Journalism and Democracy in the Digital Age*, ed. N. Fenton. London: Sage, pp. 153–168.

Ferree, M. M., Gamson, W. A., Gerhards, J. and Rucht, D. (2002) *Shaping Abortion Discourse: Democracy and the Public Sphere in Germany and the United States*. Cambridge: Cambridge University Press.

Ferrie, J. E., Marmot, M. G., Griffiths, J. and Ziglio, E. (1999) *Labour Market Changes and Job Insecurity: A Challenge for Social Welfare and Health Promotion*. World Health Organization Regional Publications, European Series, No 81. Copenhagen: World Health Organization.

Finkel, A. (2006) *Social Policy and Practice in Canada: A History.* Waterloo, Ontario: Wilfrid Laurier University Press.

Fitton, L., Gruen, M. and Poston, L. (2009) *Twitter for Dummies*. Hoboken, NJ: Wiley.

Flanagin, A., Stohl, C. and Bimber, B. (2006) 'Modeling the Structure of Collective Action', *Communication Monographs*, vol. 73, no. 1, pp. 29–54.

Fleury, D. (2007) *A Study of Poverty and Working Poverty Among Recent Immigrants to Canada*. Ottawa: Human Resources and Social Development Canada.

Fogel, J., Albert, S., Schnabel, F., Ditkoff, B. A. and Neugut, A. (2002) 'Use of the Internet by Women with Breast Cancer', *Journal of Medical Internet Research*, vol. 4, no. 2, p. e9.

Foot, K. and Schneider, S. (2006) *Web Campaigning*. Cambridge, MA: MIT Press.

Foucault, M. (2008) *The Birth of Biopolitics: Lectures at the Collège de France 1978–1979*. New York: Palgrave Macmillan.

Fox, S. (2006, 29 October) 'Most Internet Users Start at a Search Engine When Looking for Health Information Online: Very Few Check the Source and Date of the Information They Find'. Available at http://pewinternet.org (accessed 13 May 2010).

Fox, S. and Rainie, L. (2000) *The Online Health Care Revolution: How the Web Helps Americans Take Better Care of Themselves*. Washington, DC: Pew Internet and American Life Project. Available at http://pewinternet.org (accessed 15 May 2010).

Franklin, M. N. (2004) *Voter Turnout and the Dynamics of Electoral Competition in Established Democracies since 1945*, Cambridge University Press, New York.

Fraser, N. (1990) 'Rethinking the Public Sphere: A Contribution to the Critique of Actually Existing Democracy', *Social Text*, vol. 25/26, pp. 56–80.

Fraser, N. (1999) 'Social Justice in the Age of Identity Politics: Redistribution, Recognition, and Participation', in *Culture and Economy After the Cultural Turn*, ed. J. R. Lawrence and A. Sayer. London: Sage, pp. 25–52.

Fraser, N. and Gordon, L. (1994) '"Dependency" Demystified: Inscriptions of Power in a Keyword of the Welfare State', *Social Politics*, vol. 1, no. 1, pp. 4–31.

Freschi, A. C. (2003) 'Dalla rete delle reti al movimento dei movimenti: Gli hacker e l'altra comunicazione', in *Globalizzazione e movimenti sociali*, ed. D. della Porta and L. Mosca. Rome: Manifestolibri, pp. 49–75.

Fuchs, C. (2010) 'Alternative Media as Critical Media', *European Journal of Social Theory*, vol. 13, pp. 173–192.

Furlong, A. and Cartmel, F. (2007) *Young People and Social Change: New Perspectives*, 2nd edn. Maidenhead: Open University Press.

Fuster, M. (2010) 'Governance of Online Creation Communities: Provision of Infrastructure for the Building of Digital Commons'. PhD thesis, European University Institute, Florence.

G20 Meltdown (2009) Available at www.g-20meltdown.org/ (accessed 1 April 2009).

Gabrielatos, C. and Baker, P. (2008) 'Fleeing, Sneaking, Flooding: A Corpus Analysis of Discursive Constructions of Refugees and Asylum Seekers in the UK Press, 1996–2005', *Journal of English Linguistics*, vol. 36, no. 1, pp. 5–38.

Galabuzi, G.-E. (2006) *Canada's Economic Apartheid: The Social Exclusion of Racialized Groups in the New Century*. Toronto: Canadian Scholars Press.

Gallup, G. (1939) *Public Opinion in a Democracy*. Princeton, NJ: Princeton University Press.

Galston, W. A. (2001) 'Political Knowledge, Political Engagement, and Civic Education', *Annual Review of Political Science*, vol. 4, pp. 217–234.

Gamson, W. A. (1992) *Talking Politics*. Cambridge: Cambridge University Press.

Gamson, W. A. (2004) 'Bystanders, Public Opinion and the Media', in *The Blackwell Companion to Social Movements*, ed. David A. Snow, Sarah H. Soule and Hanspeter Kriesi. Oxford: Blackwell, pp. 242–261.

Gamson, W. A. and Modigliani, A. (1989) 'Media Discourse and Public Opinion on Nuclear Power', *American Journal of Sociology*, vol. 95, pp. 1–37.

Gamson, W. A. and Wolfsfeld, G. (1993) 'Movements and Media as Interacting Systems', *Annals of the American Academy of Political and Social Science*, vol. 528, p. 114.

Gamson, W. A., Croteau, D., Hoynes, W. and Sasson, T. (1992) 'Media Images and the Social Construction of Reality', *Annual Review of Sociology*, vol. 18, pp. 373–393.

Gans, H. J. (1995) *The War Against the Poor: The Underclass and Antipoverty Policy*. New York: Basic Books.

George Washington University and Cision (2009) *2009 Social Media and Online Usage Study*. Available at http://insight.cision.com/content/GWU-request (accessed 25 May, 2010).

Gerhard, J. and Neidhardt, F. (1990) *Strukturen und Funktionen moderner Oeffentlighkeit: Fragestellung und Ansaetze*. WZB Discussion Paper FS III. Berlin: Wissenschaftszentrum Berlin für Sozialforschung.

Gerodimos, R. (2005a) 'Democracy Reloaded: Generation Y and Online Civic Engagement'. Paper presented at the Association of Internet Researchers (AoIR) Conference, 5–9 October, Chicago.

Gerodimos, R. (2005b) 'Democratic Engagement and Media Uses Amongst the Internet Generation'. Paper presented at the 55th Annual Conference of the Political Studies Association (PSA), April, University of Leeds.

Gerodimos, R. (2008) 'Mobilising Young Citizens in the UK: A Content Analysis of Youth and Issue Websites', *Information, Communication and Society*, vol. 11, no. 7, pp. 964–988.

Gerodimos, R. and Ward, J. (2007) 'Rethinking Online Youth Civic Engagement: Reflections on Web Content Analysis', in *Young Citizens in the Digital Age: Political Engagement, Young People and New Media,* ed. Brian Loader. London: Routledge, pp. 114–126.

Gibbs, W. J. (2008) 'Examining Users on News Provider Web Sites: A Review of Methodology', *Journal of Usability Studies*, vol. 3, no. 3, pp. 129–148.

Gibson, R., Ward, S. and Nixon, P. (2003) *Political Parties and the Internet: Net Gain?* London: Routledge.

Giddens, A. (1990) *The Consequences of Modernity*. Stanford, CA: Stanford University Press.

Giddens, A. (1991) *Modernity and Self Identity: Self and Society in the Late Modern Age*. Stanford, CA: Stanford University Press.

Gidengil, E., Blais, A., Nadeau, R. and Nevitte, N. (2004) *Citizens*. Vancouver: UBC Press, 2004.

Gilens, M. (1999) *Why Americans Hate Welfare: Race, Media, and the Politics of Antipoverty Policy*. Chicago: University of Chicago Press.

Gillan, K., Pickerill, J. and Webster, F. (2008) *Anti-War Activism: New Media and Protest in the Information Age*. Basingstoke: Palgrave Macmillan.

Gillespie, M. and O'Loughlin, B. (forthcoming) *Ethnographies of Citizenship: Insecurity, Media and Multiculturalism*. Basingstoke: Palgrave Macmillan.

Ginsborg, P. (2008, 1 July) 'Democracy: Participation to Passivity – Can Things Change?', speech at the Royal Society of Arts seminar. Available at www.thersa.org/events/audio-and-past-events/2008/democracy-participation-to-passivity--can-things-change (accessed: 22 February 2010).

Gitlin, T. (1980) *The Whole World Is Watching: Mass Media in the Making and Unmaking of the New Left*. Berkeley and Los Angeles: University of California Press.

Golding, P. and Middleton, S. (1982) *Images of Welfare: Press and Public Attitudes to Welfare*. Oxford: Martin Robertson.

Gorringe, H. and Rosie, M. (2006) '"Pants to Poverty"? Making Poverty History, Edinburgh 2005', *Sociological Research Online*, vol. 11, no. 1. Available at www.socresonline.org.uk/11/1/gorringe.html (accessed 9 July 2009).

Gould, R. (1991) 'Multiple Networks and Mobilization in the Paris Commune, 1871', *American Sociological Review*, vol. 56, no. 6, pp. 716–729.

Gould, R. (1993) 'Collective Action and Network Structure', *American Sociological Review*, vol. 58, no. 2, pp. 182–196.

Gowing, N. (2009) '*Skyful of Lies' and Black Swans: The New Tyranny of Shifting Information Power in Crises*. Oxford: Reuters Institute for the Study of Journalism, University of Oxford.

Grandi, R. and Vaccari, C. (2009) 'Election Campaigning and the New Media', in *Resisting the Tide: Cultures of Opposition under Berlusconi (2001–06)*, ed. D. Albertazzi, C. Brook, C. Ross and N. Rothenberg, New York: Continuum, pp. 46–56.

Greenslade, R. (2005) *Seeking Scapegoats: The Coverage of Asylum in the UK Press*, Asylum and Migration Working Paper 5. London: Institute for Public Policy Research. Available at www.ippr.org.uk/publicationsandreports/ publication.asp?id=288 (accessed 21 January 2011).

Grönlund, K. (2007) 'Knowing and Not Knowing: The Internet and Political Information', *Scandinavian Political Studies*, vol. 30, no. 3, pp. 397–418.

Grossman, L. (2009, 17 June) 'Iran Protests: Twitter, the Medium of the Movement', *Time* magazine. Available at www.time.com/time/world/article/0,8599,1905125,00.html (accessed 25 May 2010).

Gunter, B. (2003) *News and the Net*. London: Lawrence Erlbaum.

Gunther, R. and Mughan, A. (eds) (2000) *Democracy and the Media: A Comparative Perspective*. Cambridge: Cambridge University Press.

Habermas, J. (1962/1989) *The Structural Transformation of the Public Sphere*. Cambridge: Polity Press.

Habermas, J. (1996) *Between Facts and Norms: Contribution to a Discursive Theory of Law and Democracy*. Cambridge, MA: MIT Press.

Hackett, R. A., Gruneau, R. S. and Canadian Centre for Policy (1999) *The Missing News: Filters and Blind Spots in Canada's Media*. Ottawa: Canadian Centre for Policy Alternatives.

Hague, B. and Loader, B. D. (1999) *Digital Democracy: Discource and Decision-Making in the Information Age*,. London: Routledge.

Halavias, A. (2009) *Search Engine Society*. Cambridge: Polity Press.

Hall, S. (1993) 'Encoding, Decoding', in *The Cultural Studies Reader*, ed. S. During, Routledge, London, pp. 90–103.

Hallin, D. and Mancini, P. (2004) *Comparing Media Systems: Three Models of Media and Politics*. Cambridge: Cambridge University Press.

Hargittai, E. and Hinnant, A. (2008) 'Digital Inequality: Differences in Young Adults' Use of the Internet', *Communication Research*, vol. 35, no. 5, pp. 602–621.

Harris, A. (2008) 'Young Women, Late Modern Politics and the Participatory Potential of Online Cultures', *Journal of Youth Studies*, vol. 11, no. 5, pp. 481–495.

Harris, A., Wyn, J., and Younes, S. (2010) 'Beyond Apathetic or Activist Youth: "Ordinary" Young People and Contemporary Forms of Participation', *Young*, vol. 18, no. 9, pp. 9–32.

Harris, J. (1999) 'Political Thought and the Welfare State 1870–1940: An Intellectual Framework for British Social Policy', in *Before Beveridge: Welfare Before the Welfare State*, ed. D. Gladstone. London: Cromwell Press, pp. 116–141.

Hartley, J. (2009) *The Uses of Digital Literacy*, St Lucia: University of Queensland Press.

Harvey, D. (2007) *A Brief History of Neoliberalism*. Oxford: Oxford University Press.

Hatfield, M. (2004) 'Vulnerability to Persistent Low Income, Policy Research Initiative', *Horizons*, vol. 7, no. 2, pp. 19–26. Available at www.horizons.gc.ca/doclib/HOR_v7n2_200712_e.pdf (accessed August 2010).

Heaney, M. and Rojas, F. (2006) 'The Place of Framing: Multiple Audiences and Antiwar Protests near Fort Bragg', *Qualitative Sociology*, vol. 29, pp. 485–505.

Henn, M., Weinstein, M. and Wring, D. (2002) 'A Generation Apart? Youth and Political Participation in Britain', *British Journal of Politics and International Relations*, vol. 4, no. 2, pp. 167–192.

Hick, S. and McNutt, J. (2002) 'Communities and Advocacy on the Internet: A Conceptual Framework', in *Advocacy, Activism and the Internet*, ed. S. Hick and J. McNutt. Chicago: Lyceum Books, pp. 3–18.

Hill, K. A. and Hughes, J. E. (1998) *Cyperpolitics: Citizen Activism in the Age of the Internet*. Oxford: Rowman and Littlefield.

Hippel, E. von (2005) *Democratizing Innovation*, Cambridge, MA: MIT Press.

Hjavard, S. (2008) 'The Mediazation of Religion: A Theory of the Media as Agents in Religious Change', *Northern Lights*, vol. 6, no. 1, pp. 9–26.

Hobsbawm, J. and Lloyd, J. (2008) *Power of The Commentariat: How Much Do Commentators Influence Politics and Public Life?* London: Editorial Intelligence Ltd.

Hoffman, L. H. (2006) 'Is Internet Content Different After All? A Content Analysis of Mobilizing Information in Online and Print Newspapers', *Journalism and Mass Communication Quarterly*, vol. 83, no. 1, pp. 58–76.

Hogan, B. and Quan-Hasse, A. (2010) 'Persistence and Change in Social Media', *Bulletin of Science and Technology*, vol. 30, no. 5, pp. 309–315.

Honeycutt, C. and Herring, S. C. (2009) 'Beyond Microblogging: Conversation and Collaboration via Twitter', in *Proceedings of the Forty-Second Hawai'i International Conference on System Sciences*. Los Alamitos, CA: IEEE Press, pp. 1–10.

Hoofd, I. M. (2009) 'Activism, Acceleration, and the Humanist Aporia: Indymedia Intensified in the Age of Neoliberalism', *Cultural Politics*, vol. 5, no. 2, pp. 199–228.

Horsley, M. and Costley, D. (2008) *Young People Imagining a New Democracy: Young People's Voices*. University of Western Sydney: Whitlam Institute. Available at www.whitlam.org/__data/assets/pdf_file/0010/82972/focus_groups_report.pdf (accessed 30 August 2010).

Hoskins, A. (2009) 'The Mediatization of Memory', in *Save As... Digital Memories*, ed. J. Garde-Hansen, A. Hoskins and A. Reading. Basingstoke: Palgrave Macmillan, pp. 27–43.

Hoskins, A. and O'Loughlin, B. (2007) *Television and Terror: Conflicting Times and the Crisis of News Discourse*. Basingstoke: Palgrave Macmillan.

Howard, P. (2006) *New Media Campaigns and the Managed Citizen*. Cambridge: Cambridge University Press.

Høybye, M. T., Johansen, C. and Tjørnhøj-Thomsex, T. (2005) 'Online Interaction: Effects of Storytelling in an Internet Breast Cancer Support Group', *Psycho-oncology*, vol. 14, no. 3, pp. 211–220.

Human Highway (2010) 'Raiperunanotte: Misura dell'audience live e differita dell'evento, complessiva e per singolo mezzo di diffusione'. Available at www.human-highway.it/index.php?fase=printRaiperunanotte02 (accessed 14 May 2010).

ICM. (2010) ICM post-debate poll for the *Guardian* available at www.icmresearch.co.uk/pdfs/2010_apr_guardian_post_debate2_poll.pdf#search="debate" (accessed 8 March 2011).

Indymedia (2007) 'Indymedia's Frequently Asked Questions', Indymedia Documentation Project. Available at https://docs.indymedia.org/Global/FrequentlyAskedQuestionEn#1 anguages (accessed 2 February 2009).

Indymedia London (2009, 28 March) 'Pics from Today's "Put People First" March'. Available at http://london.indymedia.org/articles/913 (accessed 7 October 2010).

Inglehart, R. (1997) *Modernization and Post-modernization: Cultural, Economic and Political Change in 43 Societies*. Princeton, NJ: Princeton University Press.

Ingram, M. (2008) 'Yes, Twitter Is a Source of Journalism'. Available at www.mathewingram.com/work/ (accessed 25 May 2010).

Ipsos Reid. (2009, 11 June) 'What's All That Twitter About – A Lot About Nothing?' Available at www.ipsos-na.com/news/pressrelease.cfm?id=4423 (accessed 2 October 2009).

Iyengar, S. (1994) *Is Anyone Responsible? How Television Frames Political Issues*. Chicago: University of Chicago Press.

Iyengar, S. and McGrady, J. (2007) *Media Politics: A Citizen's Guide*. New York and London: W. W. Norton.

James, F. (2009, 17 June) 'Which Tweets from Iran Are True?' NPR (National Public Radio). Available at www.npr.org/blogs/thetwo-way/2009/06/which_tweats_from_iran_are_tru.html (accessed 25 May 2010).

Jansen, B. J. and Spink, A. (2005) 'An Analysis of Web Searching by European AlltheWeb.com Users', *Information Processing and Management*, vol. 41, no. 2, pp. 361–81.

Jansen, B. J. and Spink, A. (2006) 'How Are We Searching the World Wide Web? A Comparison of Nine Large Search Engine Transaction Logs', *Information Processing and Management*, vol. 42, no. 2, pp. 248–263.

Jansen, B. J., Zhang, M., Sobel, K. and Chowdury, A. (2009) 'Micro-Blogging as Online Word of Mouth Branding', *Proceedings of the International Conference on Human Factors in Computing Systems*, pp. 3859–3864.

Jansky, L. J. and Huang, J. C. (2009) 'A Multi-Method Approach to Assess Usability and Acceptability: A Case Study of the Patient-Reported Outcomes Measurement System (PROMIS) Workshop', *Social Science Computer Review*, vol. 27, no. 2, pp. 262–270.

Jasper, J. (1997) *The Art of Moral Protest: Culture, Biography, and Creativity in Social Movements*. Chicago: University of Chicago Press.

Java, A., Finin, T., Song, X. and Tseng. B. (2007) 'Why We Twitter: Understanding Microblogging Usage and Communities', in *Proceedings of the 9th WEBKDD and 1st SNA-KDD Workshop on Web Mining and Social Network Analysis*, pp. 56–65.

Jenkins, H. (2006) *Convergence Culture*. New York: New York University Press.

Jennings, M. K. and Zeitner, V. (2003) 'Internet Use and Civic Engagement', *Public Opinion Quarterly*, vol. 67, pp. 311–334.

Jewitt, R. (2009) 'The Trouble with Twittering: Integrating Social Media Into Mainstream News', *International Journal of Media and Cultural Politics*, vol. 5, no. 3, pp. 233–240.

Jones, B., Kavanagh, D. and Moran, M. (2007) *The Mass Media and Political Communication*. Harlow: Pearson Education.

Jordan, T. (2002) *Activism! Direct Action: Hacktivism and the Future of Society*, London: Reaktion Books.

Jordan, T., and Taylor, P. A. (2004) *Hactivism and Cyberwars: Rebels with a Cause?* New York: Routledge.

Jørgensen, M. and Phillips, L. (2002) *Discourse Analysis as Theory and Method*. Thousand Oaks, CA: Sage.

Juris, J. S. (2008) *Networking Futures*. Durham, NC: Duke University Press.

Kahlor, L. and Mackert, M. (2009) 'Perceptions of Infertility Information and Support Sources Among Female Patients who Access the Internet', *Fertility and Sterility*, vol. 91, no. 1, pp. 83–90.

Karpf, David. 2009. 'The MoveOn Effect: Disruptive Innovation within the Interest Group Ecology of American Politics', paper presented at the annual meeting of the American Political Science Association, 2–6 September, Toronto.

Katz, M. B. (1990) *The Undeserving Poor: From the War on Poverty to the War on Welfare*. New York: Pantheon Books.

Kavada, A. (2009) 'Engagement, Bonding and Identity across Multiple Platforms: Avaaz on Facebook, YouTube and MySpace'. Paper presented at ECPR General Conference, 10–12 September, Potsdam.

Kavanagh, D. and Cowley, P. (2010) *The British General Election of 2010*. Basingstoke: Palgrave Macmillan.

Kavanaugh, A., Reese, D., Carroll, John and Rosson, M. (2005) 'Weak Ties in Networked Communities', *Information Society*, vol. 21, pp. 119–131.

Keck, M. E. and Sikkink, K. (1998) *Activists beyond Borders*, Ithaca, NY: Cornell University Press.

Kenix, L. J. (2007) 'In Search of Utopia: An Analysis of Non-Profit Web Pages', *Information, Communication and Society*, vol. 10, no. 1, pp. 69–94.

Kenix, L. J. (2008) 'Nonprofit Organizations' Perceptions and Uses of the Internet', *Television and New Media*, vol. 9, no. 5, pp. 407–428.

Kensicki, L. J. (2004) 'No Cure for What Ails Us: The Media-Constructed Disconnect between Societal Problems and Possible Solutions', *Journalism and Mass Communications Quarterly*, vol. 81, no. 1, p. 53.

Kidd, D. (2002) 'Indymedia.org: The Development of the Communication Commons', *Democratic Communiqué*, vol. 18, no. 1, pp. 65–86.

Kielbowicz, R. B., and Scherer, C. (1986) 'The Role of the Press in the Dynamics of Social Movements', *Research in Social Movements, Conflict and Change*, vol. 9, pp. 71–96.

Kirshner, B., Strobel, K. and Fernandez, M. (2003) 'Critical Civic Engagement Among Urban Youths', *Penn GSE Perspectives on Urban Education*, vol. 2. Available at www.urbanedjournal.org/archive/Issue3/articles/article0010.html (accessed 21 May 2008).

Kitzinger, J. (2007) 'Framing and Frame Analysis', in *Media Studies, Key Issues and Debates*, ed. E. Devereux. London: Sage, pp. 134–161.

Klein, N. (2002) *Fences and Windows: Dispatches from the Front Lines of the Globalization Debate*. London: Flamingo.

Kleinot, M. C. and Rogers, R. W. (1982) 'Identifying Effective Components of Alcohol Misuse Prevention Programs', *Journal of Studies on Alcohol*, vol. 43, pp. 802–811.

Knight, G. (1982) 'News and Ideology', *Canadian Journal of Communication, vol.* 8, no. 4, pp. 15–41.

Kofman, E., Lukes, S., D'Angelo, A. and Montagna, N. (2009) *The Equality Implications of Being a Migrant in Britain*, Research Report 19. Equality and Human Rights Commission, Social Policy Research Centre, Middlesex University.

König, T. (2004) 'Frame Analysis: A Primer'. Available at www.lboro.ac.uk/research/mmethods/resources/links/frames_primer.html (accessed 21 March 2009).

Koop, R. and Jansen, H. (2009) 2009. 'Political Blogs and Blogrolls in Canada: Forums for Democratic Deliberation?' *Social Science Computer Review*, vol. 27, no. 2, pp. 155–173.

Krishnamurthy, B., Gill, P. and Arlitt, M. (2008) 'A Few Chirps about Twitter', in *Proceedings of the First Workshop on Online Social Networks (WOSN)*. New York: Association for Computing Machinery, pp. 19–24.

Kuhn, R. (2002) 'The First Blair Government and Political Journalism', in *Political Journalism: New Challenges, New Practices*, ed. R. N. Kuhn and E. Neveu. London: Routledge, pp. 47–68.

Lagan, B. M., Sinclair, M. and Kernohan, W. G. (2009) 'A Web-Based Survey of Midwives' Perception of Women Using the Internet in Pregnancy: A Global Phenomenon', *Midwifery*, vol. 27, no. 2, pp. 273–281. doi:10.1016/j.midw.2009.07.002.

Lagan, B. M., Sinclair, M. and Kernohan, W. G. (2010) 'Internet Use in Pregnancy Informs Women's Decision Making: A Web-Based Survey', *Birth: Issues in Perinatal Care*, vol. 37, no. 2, pp. 106–115.

Larsson, M. (2009). 'A Descriptive Study of the Use of the Internet by Women Seeking Pregnancy-Related Information', *Midwifery*, vol. 25, pp. 14–20.

Lasica, J. D. (2003) 'Blogs and Journalism Need Each Other', *Nieman Reports*. Available at www.nieman.harvard.edu/reportsitem.aspx?id=101042 (accessed 25 May 2010).

Leadbeater, C. (2008) *We-Think*, London: Profile Books.

Lee-Wright, P. (2010) 'Culture Shock: New Media and Organizational Change in the BBC', in *Futures of the News: Journalism and Democracy in a Digital Age*, ed. N. Fenton. London: Sage, pp. 71–86.

Legnante, G. (2007) 'Cittadini, mezzi di comunicazione e politica', in *Gli italiani e la politica*, ed. M. Maraffi. Bologna: Il Mulino, pp. 265–296.

Leigh, D. and Harding, L. (2011) *Wikileaks: Inside Julian Assange's War on Secrecy*. London: Guardian Books.

Lemke, T. (2001) '"The Birth of Bio-Politics": Michel Foucault's Lecture at the Collège de France on Neoliberal Governmentality', *Economy and Society*, vol. 30, no. 2, pp. 197–207.

Lenhart, A. and Fox, S. (2009) *Twitter and Status Updating*. Pew Internet and American Life Project. Available at www.pewinternet.org/Reports/2009/Twitter-and-status-updating.aspx (accessed 25 May 2010).

Ley, B. (2007) '"Vive les roses!" The Architecture of Commitment in an Online Pregnancy and Mothering Group', *Journal of Computer-Mediated Communication*, vol. 12, no. 4, pp. 1388–1408.

Li, X. (1998) 'Web Page Design and Graphic Use of Three US Newspapers', *Journalism and Mass Communication Quarterly*, vol. 75 (summer), pp. 352–65.

Linton, M. (1996) 'Maybe *The Sun* Won It After All', *British Journalism Review*, vol. 7, no. 2, pp. 20–26.

Lister, R. (2004) *Poverty*. Cambridge: Polity Press.

Livingstone, S. (2002) *Children's Use of the Internet: A Review of the Research Literature*. London, National Children's Bureau.

Livingstone, S. (2008) 'Taking Risky Opportunities in Youthful Content Creation: Teenagers' Use of Social Networking Sites for Intimacy, Privacy and Self-Expression', *New Media and Society*, vol. 10, no. 3, pp. 393–411.

Livingstone, S. (2009a) *Children and the Internet*. Cambridge: Polity Press.

Livingstone, S. (2009b) 'On the Mediation of Everything', ICA Presidential Address, *Journal of Communication*, vol. 59, no. 1, pp. 1–18.

Livingstone, S. and Helsper, E. (2007) 'Gradations in Digital Inclusion: Children, Young People and the Digital Divide', *New Media and Society*, vol. 9, no. 4, pp. 671–696.

Livingstone, S., Couldry, N. and Markham, T. (2007) 'Youthful Steps towards Participation: Does the Internet Help?' in *Young Citizens in the Digital Age: Political Engagement, Young People and New Media*, ed. B. Loader. London: Routledge, pp. 21–34.

Livingstone, S., Olaffson, K. and Staksrud, E. (2011) 'Social Networking, Age and Privacy', in *EU Kids Online: Enhancing Knowledge Regarding European Children's Use, Risk and Safety Online*, LSE Department of Media and Communications. Available at www2.lse.ac.uk/media@lse/research/EUKidsOnline/Home.aspx (accessed 9 May 2011).

Loader, B. D. (1997) (ed.) *The Governance of Cyberspace: Politics, Technology and Global Restructuring*. London: Routledge.

Loader, B. D. (2007) (ed.) *Young Citizens in the Digital Age: Political Engagement, Young People and New Media*. London: Routledge.

Lusoli, W., Ward, S., and Gibson, R. (2006) '(Re)connecting Politics? Parliament, the Public and the Internet', *Parliamentary Affairs*, vol. 59, no. 1, pp. 24–42.

Macefield, R. (2007) 'Usability Studies and the Hawthorne Effect', *Journal of Usability Studies*, vol. 2, no. 3, pp. 145–154.

MacInnes, T., Kenway, P. and Parekh, A. (2009) *Monitoring Poverty and Social Exclusion 2009*. York: Joseph Rowntree Foundation. Available at www.jrf.org.uk/publications/monitoring-poverty-2009

Madge, C. and O'Connor, H. (2002) 'On-Line with E-Mums: Exploring the Internet as a Medium for Research', *Area*, vol. 34, no. 1, pp. 92–102.

Madge, C. and O'Connor, H. (2005) 'Mothers in the Making? Exploring Liminality in Cyber/Space', *Transactions of the Institute of British Geographers*, vol. 30, no. 1, pp. 83–97.

Madge, C. and O'Connor, H. (2006) 'Parenting Gone Wired: Empowerment of New Mothers on the Internet?', *Social and Cultural Geography*, vol. 7, no. 2, pp. 199–220.

Manin, B. (1995) *Principes du gouvernement représentatif.* Paris: Flammarion.

Manning Centre for Democracy (n.d.) *A rightoftwitter.ca Guide to Twitter.* www.rightoft-witter.ca/twitterguide.php (accessed 25 May 2010).

Margolis, M., and Resnick, D. (2000) *Politics as Usual: The Cyberspace 'Revolution.'* Thousand Oaks, CA: Sage.

Marletti, C., and Roncarolo, F. (2000) 'Media Influence in the Italian Transition from a Consensual to a Majoritarian Democracy', in *Democracy and the Media: A Comparative Perspective*, ed. R. Gunther and A. Mughan. Cambridge and New York: Cambridge University Press, pp. 195–240.

Marsh, D., O'Toole, T. and Jones, S. (2007) *Young People and Politics in the UK: Apathy or Alienation?* Basingstoke: Palgrave Macmillan.

Mattoni, A. (2009) 'Multiple Media Practices in Italian Mobilizations against Precarity of Work'. PhD thesis, European University Institute, Florence.

Mayring, P. (2000) 'Qualitative Content Analysis', Forum qualitative sozialforschung/ Forum, *Qualitative Social Research*, vol. 1, no. 2. Available at www.qualitative-research.net/fqs-texte/2–00/2–00mayring-e.pdf

Mazzoleni, G. (2000) 'The Italian Broadcasting System between Politics and the Market', *Journal of Modern Italian Politics*, vol. 5, no. 2, pp. 157–168.

McAdam, D. (1988) 'Micromobilisation Contexts and the Recruitment to Activism', in *From Structure to Action: Comparing Social Movement Research across Cultures*, ed. B. Klandermans, H. Kriesi, and S. Tarrow. Greenwich, CT: JAI Press, pp. 125–154.

McAdam, D., Tarrow, S. and Tilly, C. (2001) *Dynamics of Contention.* Cambridge: Cambridge University Press.

McCombs, M. E. and Bell, T. (1996) 'The Agenda-Setting Role of Mass Communication', in *An Integrated Approach to Communication Theory and Research*, ed. M. B. Salwen and D. W. Stacks. Philadelphia, PA: Lawrence Erlbaum Associates, pp. 93–110.

McCombs, M. E. and Shaw, D. L. (1972) 'The Agenda-Setting Function of Mass Media', *Public Opinion Quarterly*, vol. 36, pp. 176–187.

McDonald, K. (2002) 'From Solidarity to Fluidiarity: Social Movements beyond "Collective Identity": The Case of Globalization Conflicts', *Social Movement Studies*, vol. 1, no. 2, pp. 109–128.

McGiboney, M. (2009, 18 March) 'Twitter's Tweet Smell Of Success'. Available at http://blog.nielsen.com/nielsenwire/online_mobile/twitters-tweet-smell-of-success (accessed 1 May 2009).

McKee, A. (2005) *The Public Sphere: An Introduction.* Cambridge: Cambridge University Press.

McKendrick, J. H., Sinclair, S., Irwin, A., O'Donnell, H., Scott, G. and Dobbie, L. (2008) *The Media, Poverty and Public Opinion in the UK.* York: Joseph Rowntree Foundation.

McKenna, L. and Pole, A. (2008) 'What Do Bloggers Do: An Average Day on an Average Political Blog', *Public Choice*, vol. 134, nos 1–2, pp. 97–108.

McMillan, S. (2002) 'Exploring Models of Interactivity from Multiple Research Traditions: Users, Documents, and Systems.' in *The Handbook of New Media*, ed Leah A. Lievrouw and Sonia M. Livingstone. London: Sage, pp. 164–175.

McNair, B. (2009) *News and Journalism in the UK.* London: Routledge.

Mesch, G. S. and Coleman, S. (2007) 'New Media and New Voters: Young People, the Internet and the 2005 UK Election Campaign', in *Young Citizens in the Digital Age: Political Engagement, Young People and New Media*, ed. B. Loader. London: Routledge, pp. 35–47.

Meyer, T. (2002) *Media Democracy: How the Media Colonize Politics*. Cambridge: Polity Press.

Micheletti, M. (2003) *Political Virtue and Shopping: Individuals, Consumerism, and Collective Action*. New York: Palgrave Macmillan.

Milan, Stefania (2009) 'Stealing the Fire. a Study of Emancipator Practices in the Field of Communication', PhD Thesis, European University Institute, Florence.

Milner, H. (2002) *Civic Literary: How Informed Citizens Make Democracy Work*. Hanover, NH: Tufts University Press.

Minkoff, D. (2002) 'The Emergence of Hybrid Organizational Forms: Combining Identity-Based Service Provision and Political Action', *Nonprofit and Voluntary Sector Quarterly* vol. 31, no. 3, pp. 377–401.

Misra, J., Moller, S. and Karides, M. (2003) 'Envisioning Dependency: Changing Media Depictions of Welfare in the Twentieth Century', *Social Problems*, vol. 50, no. 4, pp. 482–504.

Mitra, A., Willyard, J., Platt, C. A. and Parsons, M. (2005) 'Exploring Web Usage and Selection Criteria Among Male and Female Students', *Journal of Computer-Mediated Communication*, vol. 10, no. 3. Available at http://jcmc.indiana.edu/vol. 10/issue3/mitra.html

Mondak, J. J. (2001) 'Developing Valid Knowledge Scales', *American Journal of Political Science*, vol. 45, no. 1, pp. 224–238.

Monge, P. and Contractor, N. (2003). *Theories of Communication Networks*. New York: Oxford University Press.

Montgomery, K. (2008) 'Youth and Digital Democracy: Intersections of Practice, Policy and Marketplace', in Civic Life Online: Learning How Digital Media Can Engage Youth, ed. W. L. Bennett. Cambridge, MA: MIT Press, pp. 25–50.

Montgomery, K., Gottlieb-Robles, B. and Larson, G. O. (2004) *Youth as E-Citizens: Engaging the Digital Generation*. Report from the Center for Social Media, School of Communication, American University, Washington, DC. Available at http://aladinrc.wrlc.org/bitstream/1961/4649/1/youthreport.pdf (accessed 19 October 2010).

Mooney, G. (2010) 'The "Broken Society" Election: Class Hatred and the Politics of Poverty and Place in Glasgow East', *Social Policy and Society*, vol. 8, no. 4, pp. 437–50.

Morales, L. (2009) *Joining Political Organisations: Institutions, Mobilisation and Participation in Western Democracies*. Colchester: ECPR Press,.

Morissette, R. and Zhang, X. Z. (2006, December) 'Canada, Revisiting Wealth Inequality'. Available at www.statcan.ca/english/freepub/75–001-XIE/11206/art-1.pdf (accessed February 2008).

Mosca, L. (2010) 'From the Streets to the Net? The Political Use of the Internet by Social Movements', *International Journal of E-Politics*, vol. 1, no. 1, pp. 1–21.

Mosca, L. and della Porta, D. (2009) 'Unconventional Politics Online', in *Democracy in Social Movements*, ed. D. della Porta. London: Palgrave Macmillan, pp. 194–216.

Mosca, L., and Santucci, D. (2009) 'Petitioning Online: The Role of E-Petitions in Web Campaigning', in *Political Campaigning on the Web*, ed. S. Baringhorst, V. Kneip and J. Niesyto. Bielefeld: Transcript Verlag, pp. 121–146.

Mosco, V. (2005) *The Digital Sublime: Myth, Power and Cyberspace*, Cambridge, MA: MIT Press.

Mossberger, K., Tolbert, C. J. and McNeal, R. S. (2008) *Digital Citizenship: The Internet, Society, and Participation*. Cambridge, MA: MIT Press.

Mullin, A. and MacLean, D. (eds) (2005) *Reconceiving Pregnancy and Childcare: Ethics, Experience, and Reproductive Labor*. Cambridge: Cambridge University Press.

Murray, C. (2010, 18 April) 'YouGov/Murdoch Distort Poll To Stop Lib Dem Momentum'. Available at www.craigmurray.org.uk/archives/2010/04/yougovmurdoch _d.html

Mutz, D. C. (1995) 'Effects of Horse-Race Coverage on Campaign Coffers: Strategic Contributing in Presidential Primaries', *Journal of Politics*, vol. 57, no. 4, pp. 1015–1042.

Myers, D. J. (2001) 'Social Activism through Computer Networks', in *Computing in the Social Science and Humanities*, ed. Orville Vernon Burton. Urbana: University of Illinois Press, pp. 124–139.

Nakache, D. and Kinoshita, J. (2010) *The Canadian Temporary Foreign Worker Program: Do Short-Term Economic Needs Prevail Over Human Rights Concerns? IRPP Study No. 5*. Montreal: IRPP, vailable at www.irpp.org/pubs/IRPPStudy/IRPP_ study_no5.pdf (accessed 3 October 2010).

National Council of Welfare (1973) *The Press and the Poor: A Report by the National Council of Welfare on How Canada's Newspapers Cover Poverty*. Ottawa: National Council of Welfare.

Neuman, W. L. (1997) *Social Research Methods: Qualitative and Quantitative Approaches*, 3rd edn. Boston: Allyn and Bacon.

Neveu, E. (1999) 'Média, mouvements sociaux, espace public', *Réseaux*, vol. 98, pp. 17–85.

Nielsen, J. (2007, 15 October) 'Multiple-User Simultaneous Testing (MUST)', *Jakob Nielsen's Alertbox*. Available at www.useit.com/alertbox/multiple-user-testing.html (accessed 9 July 2009).

Nielsen, J. (2008, 6 October) 'When to Use Which User Experience Research Methods', *Jakob Nielsen's Alertbox*, available from: www.useit.com/alertbox/user-research-methods.html (accessed on 9 July 2009).

Niemi, R. G., Craig, S. C. and Mattei, F. (1991) 'Measuring Internal Political Efficacy in the 1988 National Election Study', *American Political Science Review*, vol. 85, no. 4, pp. 1407–1413.

Norris, P. (ed.) (1999) *Critical Citizens – Global Support for Democratic Government*. Oxford: Oxford University Press.

Norris, P. (2000a) 'The Impact of Television on Civic Malaise', in S. J. Pharr and R. D. Putnam (eds), *Disaffected Democracies: What's Troubling the Trilateral Countries?* Princeton, NJ: Princeton University Press, pp. 231–251.

Norris, P. (2000b) *A Virtuous Circle: Political Communication in Postindustrial Societies*. Cambridge: Cambridge University Press.

Norris, P. (2001) *Digital Divide? Civic Engagement, Information Poverty and the Internet Worldwide*. New York: Cambridge University Press.

Norris, P. (2002) *Democratic Phoenix: Reinventing Political Activism*. Cambridge: Cambridge University Press.

Norris, P. (2003) 'Preaching to the converted? Pluralism, participation and party websites', *Party Politics*, vol. 9, no. 1, pp. 21–45.

North, S., Snyder, I. and Bulfin, S. (2008) 'Digital Tastes: Social Class and Young People's Technology Use', *Information, Communication and Society*, vol. 11, no. 7, pp. 895–911.

O'Loughlin, B. and Linguamatics. (2010) *Monitoring of Complex Information Infrastructure by Mining External Signals*. Project Report, Technology Strategy Board, Award Ref: TP No: BK067C.

O'Reilly, T. (2005, 30 September) 'What Is Web 2.0? Design Patterns and Business

Models for the Next Generation of Software'. Available at http://oreilly.com/web2/archive/what-is-web-20.html

O'Reilly, T. and Milstein, S. (2009) *The Twitter Book.* Sebastopol, CA: O'Reilly Media, Inc.

Ofcom (2007) *New News, Future News: The Challenges for Television News After Digital Switch-over.* London: Ofcom.

Office of National Statistics (2009) *Internet Access*, London: Office of National Statistics.

Olesen, T. (2005) *International Zapatismo: The Construction of Solidarity in the Age of Globalization.* London: Zed Books.

Osborne, L. (2010, February) 'Digital Communications Literacy', presented on behalf of Australian Communications and Media Authority (ACMA) at the International Institute of Communications Digital Communications Literacy, Qatar. Available at www.acma.gov.au/webwr/_assets/main/lib310665/digital%20communications%20literacy%20iic%20qatar.pdf (accessed 20 June 2010).

Oudshoorn, N. and Pinch, T. (2005) *How Users Matter: The Co-construction of Users and Technology,* Cambridge, MA: MIT Press.

Oxfam (2009) *Close to Home: UK Poverty and the Economic Downturn.* Oxford: Oxfam GB.

Painter, A. (2010) *A Little Less Conversation, a Little More Action.* London: Orange.

Pandey, S. K., Hart, J. J. and Tiwary, S. (2003) 'Women's Health and the Internet: Understanding Emerging Trends and Implications', *Social Science and Medicine*, vol. 56, pp. 179–191.

Papacharissi, Z. (2010) *A Private Sphere: Democracy in a Digital Age.* Cambridge: Polity Press.

Paris Declaration (2009) available at Indymedia UK: www.indymedia.ie/article/90666 (accessed 10 May 2010).

Park, A., Phillips, M. and Robinson, C. (2007) *Attitudes to Poverty; Findings from the British Social Attitudes Survey.* York: Joseph Rowntree Foundation. Available at www.jrf.org.uk/bookshop/eBooks/1999-poverty-attitudes-survey.pdf (accessed February 2008).

Parvez, Z. and Ahmed, P. (2006) 'Towards Building an Integrated Perspective on E-Democracy', *Information, Communication and Society*, vol. 9, no. 5, pp. 612–632.

Pasma, C. (May 2010) *Bearing the Brunt: How the 2008–2009 Recession Created Poverty for Canadian Families.* Toronto: UNICEF Canada. Available at www.unicef.ca/portal/Secure/Com   munity/502/WCM/Get%20Involved/Advocacy/Bearing_the_Brunt.pdf

Pateman, C. (1970) *Participation and Democratic Theory.* Cambridge: Cambridge University Press.

Pateman, C. (1989) *The Disorder of Women: Democracy, Feminism and Political Theory.* Cambridge: Polity Press.

Pattie, C., Seyd, P. and Whiteley, P. (2003) 'Citizenship and Civic Engagement: Attitudes and Behaviour in Britain', *Political Studies*, vol. 51, no. 3, pp. 443–468.

Pattie, C., Seyd, P. and Whiteley, P. (2004) *Citizenship in Britain: Values, Participation and Democracy.* Cambridge: Cambridge University Press.

Pavlik, J. V. (2001) *Journalism and New Media.* New York: Columbia University Press.

Peretti, J. (with Micheletti, M.) (2004) 'The Nike Sweatshop Email: Political Consumerism, Internet, and Culture Jamming', in *Politics, Products and Markets: Exploring Political Consumerism Past and Present*, ed. Michele Micheletti, Andreas Follesdal and Dietlind Stolle. New Brunswick, NJ: Transaction Publishers, pp. 127–142.

Pharr, S. J. and Putnam, R. D. (eds) (2000) *Disaffected Democracies: What's Troubling the Trilateral Countries?* Princeton University Press, Princeton.

Phillips, A. (2010) 'Old Sources: New Bottles', in *New Media, Old News*, ed. N. Fenton. London: Sage, pp. 000–000.

Pickard, V. (2006) 'United Yet Autonomous: Indymedia and the Struggle to Sustain a Radical Democratic Network', *Media Culture and Society*, vol. 28, no. 3, pp. 315–336.

Pickerill, J. (2003) *Cyberprotest: Environmental Activism Online*. Manchester: Manchester University Press.

Picot, G. and Sweetman, A. (2005) *The Deteriorating Economic Welfare of Immigrants and Possible Causes: Update 2005*. Ottawa: Statistics Canada.

Picot, G., Hou, F., and Coulombe, S. (2008) 'Poverty Dynamics Among Recent Immigrants to Canada', *International Migration Review*, vol. 42, no. 2, pp. 393–424.

Piven, F. F. and Cloward, R. A. (1997) *The Breaking of the American Social Compact*. New York: New Press.

Platon, S. and Deuze, M. (2003) 'Indymedia Journalism: A Radical Way of Making, Selecting and Sharing News?', *Journalism*, vol. 4, no. 3, pp. 336–355.

Platt, L. (2005) *Discovering Child Poverty: The Creation of a Policy Agenda from 1800 to the Present*. Bristol: Policy Press.

Platt, L. (2007) *Poverty and Ethnicity in the UK*. Bristol: Policy Press.

Polletta, F. (1998) '"It Was Like a Fever…" Narrative and Identity in Social Protest', *Social Problems*, vol. 45, no. 2, pp. 137–159.

Populus. (2010, 29 April) '*Times* Post-Debate Poll', available from http://popululuslimited. com/uploads/download_pdf-220410-The-Times-Post-Debate-Poll–April-22–2010.pdf (accessed 8 March 2011).

Prensky, M. (2001) 'Digital Natives, Digital Immigrants', *On the Horizon*, vol. 9, no. 5, pp. 1–6.

Purcell, K., Rainie, L., Mitchell, A., Rosenstiel, T. and Olmestead, K. (2010) *Understanding the Participatory News Consumer*. Pew Internet and American Life Project. Available at www.pewinternet.org/Reports/2010/Online-News.aspx (accessed 23 October 2011).

Put People First (2009) Available at www.putpeoplefirst.org.uk/ (accessed 28 March 2009).

Putnam, R. D. (2000) *Bowling Alone: The Collapse and Revival of American Community*. New York: Simon and Schuster.

Rafaeli, S. (1988) 'Interactivity: From New Media to Communication', in *Advancing Communication Science: Merging Mass and Interpersonal Process*, ed. R. P. Hawkins, J. M. Wiemann and S. Pingree. Newbury Park, CA: Sage, pp. 110–134.

Rahn, W. M. and Transue, J. E. (1998) 'Social Trust and Value Change: The Decline of Social Capital in American Youth, 1976–1995', *Political Psychology*, vol. 19, no. 3, pp. 545–564.

Rainie, L. and Smith, A. (2010) *Politics Goes Mobile*. Pew Internet and American Life Project. Available at www.pewinternet.org/Reports/2010/Mobile-Politics.aspx (accessed 23 October 2011).

Raphael, D. (2007) *Poverty and Policy in Canada: Implications for Health and Quality of Life*. Toronto: Canadian Scholars Press.

Rawal, N. and Haddad, N. (2006) 'Use of Internet in Fertility Patients', *Internet Journal of Gynecology and Obstetrics*, vol. 5, no. 2. Available at www.ispub.com/ostia/index. php?xmlFilePath=journals/ijgo/vol. 5n2/internet.xml (accessed 15 May 2010).

Raymond, J. E. (2009) '"Creating a Safety Net": Women's Experiences of Antenatal

Depression and Their Identifiation of Helpful Community Support and Services During Pregnancy', *Midwifery*, vol. 25, pp. 39–49.

Raynolds, L. (2002) 'Consumer/Producer Links in Fair Trade Coffee Networks', *Sociologia Ruralis*, vol. 42, pp. 404–424.

Redden, J. (2007) 'Locating the "Unthinkable" in Canadian Poverty Coverage: A Discourse and Content Analysis of Two Mainstream Dailies', unpublished master's thesis, Ryerson University, Toronto.

Reeves, R. (2008, 1 July) 'Democracy: Participation to Passivity – Can Things Change?' Speech at the Royal Society of Arts seminar, available from: www.thersa.org/events/audio-and-past-events/2008/democracy-participation-to-passivity-can-things-change (accessed 22 February 2010).

Reitan, R. (2007) *Global Activism*. New York and London: Routledge.

Rettberg, J. W. (2008) *Blogging*, Cambridge: Polity Press.

Reutter, L. I., Veenstra, G., Stewart, M. J. and Raphael, D. (2006) 'Public Attributions for Poverty in Canada', *Canadian Review of Sociology and Anthropology, vol.* 43, no. 1, pp. 1–22.

Reutter, L. I., Veenstra, G., Stewart, M. J., Raphael, D., Love, R., Makwarimba, E. and McMurray, S. (2005) 'Lay Understandings of the Effects of Poverty: A Canadian Perspective', *Health and Social Care in the Community*, vol. 13, no. 6, pp. 514–30.

Rhodes, R. (1994) 'The Hollowing Out of the State: The Changing Nature of the Public Service in Britain', *Political Quarterly*, vol. 65, pp. 138–151.

Richards, B. (2007) *Emotional Governance: Politics, Media and Terror*, Basingstoke: Palgrave Macmillan.

Robinson, D. (2010) 'Migration in the UK: Moving Beyond Numbers', *People, Place and Policy Online*, vol. 4, no. 1, pp. 14–18.

Robinson, S. (2006) 'The Mission of the J-Blog: Recapturing Journalistic Authority Online', *Journalism*, vol. 7, pp. 65–83.

Rogers, R. (2004) *Information Politics on the Web*. Cambridge, MA: MIT Press.

Rokeach, M. (1968) 'The Role of Values in Public Opinion Research', *Public Opinion Quarterly*, vol. 32, pp. 547–559.

Romano, A. N. (2007) 'A Changing Landscape: Implications of Pregnant Women's Internet Use for Childbirth Educators', *Journal of Perinatal Education*, vol. 16, no. 4, pp. 18–24.

Roncarolo, F. (2002) 'A Crisis in the Mirror: Old and New Elements in Italian Political Communication', in *Political Journalism: New Challenges, New Practices*, ed. R. Kuhn and E. Neveu. London: Routledge, pp. 69–91.

Rosanvallon, P. (2008) *Counter-Democracy: Politics in an Age of Distrust*. Cambridge: Cambridge University Press.

Rose, R. (2005) 'A Global Diffusion Model of E-Governance', *Journal of Public Policy*, vol. 25, pp. 5–27.

Rucht, D. (2004) 'The Quadruple "A": Media Strategies of Protest Movements since the 1960s', in *Cyberprotest: New Media, Citizens and Social Movements*, ed. Wim van de Donk, Brian Loader, Paul Nixon and Dieter Rucht. London: Routledge, pp. 29–56.

Ryan, C. (1991) *Prime Time Activism: Media Strategies for Grassroots Organizing*. Boston: South End Press.

Sales, R. (2007) *Understanding Immigration and Refugee Policy: Contradictions and Continuitie*s. Bristol: Policy Press.

Sampert, S. and Trimble, L. (2010) 'Appendix', in *Mediating Canadian Politics*, ed S. Sampert and L. Trimble. Toronto: Pearson Education, pp. 326–337.

Sartori, G. (1976) *Parties and Party Systems: A Framework for Analysis*. Cambridge: Cambridge University Press.

Satterlund, M. J. McCaul, K. D., and Sangren, A. K. (2003) 'Information Gathering Over Time by Breast Cancer Patients', *Journal of Medical Internet Research*, vol. 5, no. 3, p. e15.

Scheufele, D. A. and Nisbet, M. C. (2002) 'Being a Citizen Online: New Opportunities and Dead Ends', *Harvard International Journal of Press/Politics*, vol. 7, no. 3, pp. 55–75.

Schier, S. (2000) *By Invitation Only: The Rise of Exclusive Politics in the United States*. Pittsburgh, PA: University Pittsburgh Press.

Schneider, S. and Foot, K. (2002) 'Online Structure for Political Action: Exploring Presidential Campaign Web Sites From the 2000 American Election', *Javnost –The Public*, vol. 9, no. 2, pp. 43–60.

Schor, J. (1999, Summer) 'The New Politics of Consumption: Why Americans Want So Much More Than They Need', *Boston Review*. Available at http://bostonreview.net/BR24.3/schor.html (last accessed: 22 February 2010).

Schosberg, D., Zavestoski, S. andShulman, S. (2005) '"To Submit a Form or Not to Submit a Form, That Is the (Real) Question". Deliberation and Mass Participation in US Regulatory Rule-Making', paper presented at the Western Political Science Associaton Conference, 17–9 March, Oakland, CA.

Schroeder, A. (2000) *Presidential Debates: Forty Years of High Risk TV*. New York: Columbia University Press.

Schudson, M. (2003) *The Sociology of News*. New York: W. W. Norton and Company.

Schudson, M. (2007) 'Citizens, Consumers, and the Good Society', *Annals of the American Academy of Political and Social Science*, vol. 611, no. 1, pp. 236–249.

Schulman, S. W. (2004) 'The Internet Still Might (But Probably Won't) Change Everything', *I/S: A Journal of Law and Policy*, vol. 1, no. 1, pp. 111–145.

Schumpeter, J. (1942) *Capitalism, Socialism, and Democracy*. London: Allen and Unwin.

Scott, D. Travers (2007) 'Pundits in Muckrakers' Clothing: Political Blogs and the 2004 U. S. Presidential Election', in *Blogging, Citizenship and the Future of Media*, ed Mark Tremayne. New York: Routledge, pp. 39–58.

Senellart, M. (2008) 'Course Context', in *The Birth of BioPolitics: Michel Foucault Lectures at the Collège de France*, ed. M. Senellart. New York: Palgrave Macmillan, pp. 000–000.

Seymour-Ure, C. (1974) *The Political Impact of Mass Media*. London: Constable.

Shannon, R. (2010) 'The Most Popular Web Directories and Search Engines'. Available at www.yourhtmlsource.com/promotion/searchengines.html (accessed 10 May 2010).

Sharf, B. F. (1997) 'Communicating Breast Cancer on-Line: Support and Empowerment on the Internet', *Women and Health*, vol. 26, no. 1, pp. 65–84.

Siegler, M. G. (2008, 12 May) 'Twitter is First on the Scene for a Major Earthquake — But Who Cares About That, Is It Mainstream Yet?' *VentureBeat*,: http://venturebeat.com/2008/05/12/twitter-is-first-on-the-scene-for-a-major-earthquake-butwho-cares-about-that-is-it-mainstream-yet/ (accessed 25 May 2010).

Silverstone, R. (2007) *Media and Morality: On the Rise of the Mediapolis*. Cambridge: Polity Press.

Small, T. A. (2008) 'Blogging the Hill: Garth Turner and the Canadian Parliamentary Blogosphere', *Canadian Review of Political Science,* vol. 2, no. 3, pp. 103–124.

Small, T. A. (2010, Fall) 'Canadian Politics in 140 Characters: Party Politics in the Twitterverse', *Canadian Parliamentary Review*, pp. 49–45.

Smeeding, T. M., Wing, C. and Robson, K. (2009) 'Differences in Social Transfer Support and Poverty for Immigrant Families with Children: Lessons from the LIS', in *Immigration, Diversity, and Education*, ed. E. Grigorenko and R. Takanishi. London: Routledge, pp. 239–267.

Smeeding, T. M., Robson, K., Wing, C. and Gershuny, J. (2009) *Income Poverty and Income Support for Minority and Immigrant Children in Rich Countries*. Madison: Institute for Research on Poverty, University of Wisconsin-Madison. Available at www.irp.wisc.edu/publications/dps/pdfs/dp137109.pdf (accessed 2 January 2010).

Smith, A., Lehman Schlozman, K., Verba, S. and Brady, H. (2009) *The Internet and Civic Engagement*. Pew Internet and American Life Project. www.pewinternet.org/Reports/2009/15--The-Internet-and-Civic-Engagement.aspx (accessed 23 October 2011).

Smith, J. (1997) 'Characteristics of the Modern Transnational Social Movement Sector', in *Transnational Social Movements and Global Politics*, ed. J. Smith, C. Chatfield and R. Pagnucco. Syracuse, NY: Syracuse University Press, pp. 42–58.

Smith, J., Kearns, M. and Fine, A. (2005) 'Power to the Edges: Trends and Opportunities in Online Civic Engagement'. Available at http://evolvefoundation.org/files/Pushing_Power_to_the_Edges_05–06–05.pdf (accessed 30 August 2005).

Snow, D. A. and Benford, R. D. (1992) 'Master Frames and Cycles of Protest', in *Frontiers in Social Movement Theory*, ed. A. Morris and C. Mueller, New Haven, CT: Yale University Press,, pp. 133–155.

Snow, D., Rochford Jr., B., Worden, S. and Benford, R. (1986) 'Frame Alignment Processes, Micromobilization, and Movement Participation', *American Sociological Review*, vol. 51, pp. 464–481.

Soderlund, W. C. and Hildebrandt, K. (2005) *Canadian Newspaper Ownership in the Era of Convergence*. Edmonton: University of Alberta Press, 2005.

Soroka, S. N. (2002a) *Agenda-setting Dynamics in Canada*. Vancouver: UBC Press.

Soroka, S. N. (2002b) 'Issue Attributes and Agenda-Setting by Media, the Public, and Policymakers in Canada', *International Journal of Public Opinion Research*, vol. 14, no. 3, pp. 264–285.

Sotirovic, M. (2001) 'Media Use and Perceptions of Welfare', *Journal of Communication*, vol. 51, no. 4, p. 750.

Sparks, R., Young, M. L. and Darnell, S. (2006) 'Convergence, Corporate Restructuring, and Canadian Online News 2000–2003', *Canadian Journal of Communication*, vol. 31, no. 2, pp. 391–423.

Squire, P. (1988) 'Why the 1936 Literary Digest Poll Failed', *Public Opinion Quarterly*, vol. 52, no. 1, pp. 125–133.

Squires, J. (1998) 'In Different Voices: Deliberative Democracy and Aestheticist Politics', in *The Politics of Postmodernity*, ed. James Goog and Irving Velody. Cambridge; Cambridge University Press, pp. 126–146.

Statistics Canada (2010) 'Canadian Internet Use Survey'. Available at www.statcan.gc.ca/daily-quotidien/100510/dq100510a-eng.htm (accessed June 2010).

Stein, L. (2009) 'Social Movement Web Use in Theory and Practice: A Content Analysis of US Movement Websites', *New Media and Society*, vol. 11, no. 5, pp. 749–771.

Stevenson, A. (ed.) (2010) *Oxford Dictionary of English*. Oxford: Oxford University Press.

Stewart, K. (2005) 'Equality and Social Justice', in A Seldon (ed.), *The Blair Effect*. Cambridge: Cambridge University Press, pp. 306–336.

Stoker, G. (2006) *Why Politics Matters: Making Democracy Work*. Basingstoke: Palgrave Macmillan.

Strömbäck, J. (2008) 'Four Phases of Mediatization: An Analysis of the Mediatization of Politics', *Press/Politics*, vol. 13, no. 3, pp. 228–246.

Strömbäck, J. and Dimitrova, D. V. (2011) 'Mediatization and Media Interventionism: A Comparative Analysis fo Sweden and the United States', *Press/Politics*, vol. 16, no. 1, pp. 30–49.

Sullivan, D. (2006) *Neilsen Netratings Search Engine Ratings*. Available at http://search-enginewatch.com/2156451 (accessed 10 May 2010).

Sunstein, C. (2001) *Republic.com*. Princeton, NJ: Princeton University Press.

Sweetser, K. D. and Weaver Lariscy, R. A. (2008) 'Candidates Make Good Friends: An Analysis of Candidates' Use of Facebook', *International Journal of Strategic Communication*, vol. 2, no 3, pp. 175–198.

Tannock, S. (2009) 'Immigration, Education and the New Caste Society in Britain', *Critical Social Policy*, vol. 29, pp. 243–260.

Tarrow, S. (1998) *Power in Movement: Social Movements and Contentious Politics*. New York: Cambridge University Press.

Taylor, J. A. and Burt, E. (2001) 'Not-for-Profits in the Democratic Polity', *Communications of the ACM*, vol. 44, no. 1, pp. 58–62.

Taylor, M. (2010, 13 April) 'Ellie Gellard: Manifesto Poster Girl Who Posted Attack on Gordon Brown', *Guardian*. Available at www.guardian.co.uk/politics/2010/apr/13/ellie-gellard-manifesto-gordon-brown-bevaniteellie (accessed 19 October 2011).

Teorell, J., Torcal, M. and Montero, J. R. (2007) 'Political Participation: Mapping the Terrain', in *Citizenship and Involvement in European Democracies: A Comparative Analysis*, ed. J. van Deth, J. R. Montero and A. Westholm. London: Routledge, pp. 334–357.

Tewksbury, D. and Rittenberg, J. (2009) 'Online News Creation and Consumption: Implications for Modern Democracies', in *Routledge Handbook of Internet Politics*, ed. A Chadwick. New York: Routledge, pp. 186–200.

Tilly, C. (1978) *From Mobilization to Revolution*. London: Addison Wesley.

Tilly, C. (2004) *Social Movements, 1768–2004*. Boulder, CO: Paradigm.

Topf, R. (1995) 'Beyond Electoral Participation', in *Citizens and the State*, ed. H.-D. Klingemann, and D. Fuchs. Oxford: Oxford University Press, pp. 27–51.

Touraine, A. (2000) *Can We Live Together? Equality and Difference*, translated by D. Macey. Stanford, CA: Stanford University Press.

Toynbee, P. (2008, 7 October) 'In the Face of Apocalypse, Heed Not Horsemen's Advice: Brown Should Tread Wary of the City Voices in his Economic War Cabinet', *Guardian*, p. 31.

Trippi, J. (2004) *The Revolution Will Not Be Televised: Democracy, the Internet, and the Overthrow of Everything*. New York: Harper Collins.

Tsagarousianou, R., Tambini, D. and Bryon, C. (1998) *Cyberdemocracy: Technology, Cities and Civic Networks*. London: Routledge.

Tuchman, G. (1978) *Making News: A Study in the Construction of Reality*. New York: Free Press.

Twitspam (2009, 17 June) 'Fake Iran Election Tweeters'. Available at http://twitspam.org/?p=1403 (accessed 25 May 2010).

Twitter. (2009, 15 December) 'Top Twitter Trends of 2009', Twitter blog available at http://blog.twitter.com/2009/12/top-twitter-trends-of-2009.html (accessed 25 May 2010).

Twitter. (2010a, 22 February) 'Measuring Tweets', Twitter blog available at http://blog.twitter.com/2010/02/measuring-tweets.html (accessed 25 May 2010).

Twitter. (2010b, 23 March) *State of Twitter Spam.* Twitter blog available at http://blog.twitter.com/2010/03/state-of-twitter-spam.html (accessed 25 May 2010).

UNICEF (2007) *Child Poverty in Perspective: An Overview of Child Well-Being in Rich Countries.* Florence: UNICEF–Innocenti Research Centre. Available at www.unicef-irc.org/publications/pdf/rc7_eng.pdf

Vaccari, C. (2008) 'Research Note: Italian Parties' Web Sites in the 2006 Elections', *European Journal of Communication*, vol. 23, no. 1, pp. 69–77.

Vaccari, C. (2009) 'Web Challenges to Berlusconi: An Analysis of Oppositional Sites', in *Resisting the Tide: Cultures of Opposition under Berlusconi (2001–06)*, ed. D. Albertazzi, C. Brook, C. Ross and N. Rothenberg. New York: Continuum, pp. 135–147.

van Dijk, T. A. (1989) 'Mediating Racism: The Role of the Media in the Reproduction of Racism', in *Language, Power, and Ideology: Studies in Political Discourse*, ed. R. Wodak. Amsterdam: John Benjamins, pp. 199–226.

Van Gorp, B. (2007) 'The Constructionist Approach to Framing: Bringing Culture Back In', *Journal of Communication*, vol. 57, no. 1, pp. 60–78.

Van Kempen, H. (2007) 'Media–Party Parallelism and Its Effects: A Cross-National Comparative Study', *Political Communication*, vol. 24, no. 3, pp. 303–320.

van Selm, M., Jankowski, N. W. and Tsaliki, T. (2001) 'Political Parties Online: Digital Democracy as Reflected in Three Dutch Political Party Web Sites', *Communications: The European Journal of Communication Research*, vol. 27, no. 2, pp. 189–210.

van Zoonen, Lizbeth (2005) *Entertaining the Citizen: When Politics and Popular Culture Converge.* Lanham, MD: Rowman and Littlefield Publishers.

Vedres, B., Bruszt, L. and Stark, D. (2005) 'Shaping the Web of Civic Participation: Civil Society Web Sites in Eastern Europe', *Journal of Public Policy*, vol. 25, pp. 149–163.

Verba, S. (2003) 'Would the Dream of Political Equality Turn Out to Be a Nightmare?' *Perspectives on Politics*, vol. 1, no. 4, pp. 663–679.

Verba, S., Nie, N. H. and Kim, J.-O. (1971) *The Modes of Democratic Participation: A Cross-National Analysis*, Beverly Hills, CA: Sage.

Verba, S.; Schlozman, K. L. and Brady, H. E. (1995) *Voice and Inequality: Civic Voluntarism in American Politics.* Cambridge, MA: Harvard University Press.

Vromen, A. (forthcoming) 'Youth Participation From the Top-Down: The Perspectives of Government and Community Sector Decision-Makers in Australia', in *New Participatory Dimensions in Civil Society: Professionalization and Individualized Collective Action*, ed. J. van Deth and W. Maloney. London: Routledge.

Waddell, C. (2009, June) 'The Future for the Canadian Media', *Policy Options*, Montreal: Institute for Research on Public Policy. Available at www.irpp.org/po/archive/jun09/waddell.pdf (accessed 7 October 2009).

Walgrave, S., Bennett, W. L., Van Laer, J. and Breunig, C. (forthcoming) 'Network Bridging and Multiple Identities: Digital Media Use of Protest Participants', *Social Forces*.

Walker, A. and Walker, C. (eds) (1997) *Britain Divided: The Growth of Social Exclusion in the 1980s and 1990s.* London: CPAG.

Wall, M. (2005) 'Blogs of War: Weblogs as News', *Journalism: Theory, Practice and Criticism*, vol. 6, no. 2, pp. 153–172.

Ward, J. (2008) 'Youth, Citizenship and Online Political Communication', PhD thesis, Amsterdam School of Communications Research.

Ward, J. (2009) 'Social Academia: The Impact of Web 2.0 on Research Practices', *The Broker*, vol. 15, pp. 11–18.

Ward, J. (2010, 8 May) 'The Web Presence of Youth Organisations: Comparing Offline

Philosophy and Online Structure', presented at 'Youth, Media and Social Change', Northampton, UK.

Ward, S. and Vedel, T. (2006) 'Introduction: The Potential of the Internet Revisited', *Parliamentary Affairs*, vol. 59, no. 2, pp. 210–225.

Ward, S., Gibson, R. and Lusoli, W. (2003) 'Participation and Mobilisation Online: Hype, Hope and Reality', *Parliamentary Affairs*, vol. 56, no. 3, pp. 652–668.

Warkentin, C. (2001) *Reshaping World Politics: NGOs, the Internet and Global Civil Society*. Lanham, MD: Rowman and Littlefield.

Webb, J. (2007) 'Seduced or Sceptical Consumers? Organised Action and the Case of Fair Trade Coffee', *Sociological Research Online*, vol. 12, no. 3. Available at www.socresonline.org.uk/12/3/5.html (accessed 9 July 2009).

Weissman, A., Gotlieb, L., Ward, S., Greenblatt, E. and Casper, R. (2000) 'Use of Internet by Infertile Couples', *Fertility and Sterility*, vol. 73, no. 6, pp. 1179–1182.

Wellman, B. (2001) 'Physical Place and Cyberplace: The Rise of the Personalized Networking', *International Journal of Urban and Regional Research*, vol. 25, pp. 227–252.

Wellman, B. and Haythornthwaite, C. (eds) (2002) *The Internet in Everyday Life*. Oxford: Blackwell.

Wellman, B., Quan-Haase, A., Boase, J., Chen, W., Hampton, K., Diaz, I. and Miyata, K. (2003) 'The Social Affordances of the Internet for Networked Individualism', *Journal of Computer Mediated Communication*, vol. 8, no. 3. Available at http://jcmc.indiana.edu/vol8/issue3/wellman.html (accessed 10 September 2011).

Wells, C. (2010) 'Citizenship and Communication in Online Youth Civic Engagement Projects', *Information, Communication and Society*, vol. 13, no. 3, pp. 419–441.

White, R., and Wyn, J. (2008) *Youth and Society: Exploring the Dynamics of Youth Experience*, 2nd edn. Melbourne: Oxford University Press.

Wiegers, W. (2002) *The Framing of Poverty as 'Child Poverty' and its Implications for Women*. Ottawa: Status of Women Canada. Available at http://publications.gc.ca/site/eng/110948/publication.html

Wiegers, W. (2007) 'Child-Centred Advocacy and the Invisibility of Women', in *Reaction and Resistance: Feminism, Law, and Social Change*, ed. S. B. Boyd, D. E. Chunn, and H. Lessard. Vancouver: UBC Press, pp. 229–261.

Wikipedia (2009). '2009 G20 London Summit Protests'. Available at http://en.wikipedia.org/wiki/2009_G-20_London_summit_protests (accessed 26 July 2009).

Wilhelm, A. G. (2000) *Democracy in the Digital Age: Challenges to Political Life in Cyberspace*. New York: Routledge.

Winner, L. (1986) 'Do Artifacts Have Politics?' in *The Whale and the Reactor: A Search for Limits in an Age of High Technology*. Chicago, Chicago University Press, pp. 19–39.

Worcester, R. (1999, 31 December) '*The Sun* and Voodoo Polls', Ipsos Mori. Available at www.ipsos-mori.com/newsevents/ca/ca.aspx?oItemId=100 (accessed 30 September 2010).

Xenos, M. and Bennett, W. L. (2007a) 'The Disconnection in Online Politics: The Youth Political Web Sphere and US Election Sites, 2002–2004', *Information, Communication and Society*, vol. 10, no. 4, pp. 443–464.

Xenos, M. and Bennett, W. L. (2007b) 'Young Voters and the Web of Politics: The Promise and Problems of Youth-Oriented Political Content on the Web', in *Young Citizens in the Digital Age: Political Engagement, Young People and New Media*, ed. B. Loader. London: Routledge, pp. 48–67.

Xenos, M. and Foot, K. (2008) 'Not Your Father's Internet: The Generation Gap in Online Politics', in *Civic Life Online: Learning How Digital Media Can Engage Youth*, ed. W. L. Bennett. Cambridge, MA: MIT Press, pp. 51–70.

Yalnizyan, A. (2007, 1 March) *The Rich and the Rest of Us; The Changing Face of Canada's Growing Gap*. Ottawa: Canadian Centre for Policy Alternatives. Available at www.policyalternatives.ca/Reports/2007/03/ReportsStudies1565/index.cfm?pa=A2286B2A (accessed February 2008).

Yalnizyan, A. (2009, 29 April) *Exposed: Revealing Truths About Canada's Recession*. Ottawa: Canadian Centre for Policy Alternatives. Available at www. policyalternatives.ca/publications/reports/exposed-revealing-truths-about-canadas-recession

Yalnizyan, A. (2010, 17 August) *The Problem of Poverty Post-Recession*. Ottawa: Canadian Centre for Policy Alternatives.

YouGov (2010, 22 April) 'Instant Reaction to the TV Debates'. Available at http://today.yougov.co.uk/pdfarchives/instant-reaction-tv-debates (accessed 8 March 2011).

Young, I. M. (1996) 'Communication and the Other: Beyond Deliberative Democracy', in *Democracy and Difference*, ed. S. Benhabib. Princeton, NJ: Princeton University Press, pp. 120–135.

Young, I. M. (2000) *Inclusion and Democracy*. Oxford: Oxford University Press.

Youniss, J. and Yates, M. (1999) 'Introduction: International Perspectives on the Roots of Civic Identity', in *Roots of Civic Identity* ed M. Yates and J. Youniss. New York: Cambridge University Press, pp, 1–15.

Zamaria, C. and Fletcher, F. (2008) *Canada Online! The Internet, Media and Emerging Technologies: Uses, Attitudes, Trends and International Comparisons*. Toronto: Canadian Internet Project.

Zhang, W., Johnson, T. J., Seltzer, T. and Bichard, S. L. (2010) 'The Revolution Will Be Networked: The Influence of Social Networking Sites on Political Attitudes and Behavior', *Social Science Computer Review*, vol. 28, no. 1, pp. 75–92.

Zhao, D. and Rosson, M. B. (2009) 'How and Why People Twitter: The Role That Micro-Blogging Plays in Informal Communication at Work', in *Proceedings of the ACM 2009 International Conference on Supporting Group Work, May 10–13, 2009, Sanibel Island, Florida*, p. 243.

Zittel, T. (2003) 'Political Representation in the Networked Society: The Americanization of European Systems of Responsible Party Government', *Journal of Legislative Studies*, vol. 9, no. 3, pp. 1–22.

Index